Mapping Women,
Making Politics

Mapping Women, Making Politics

Feminist Perspectives on Political Geography

Edited by Lynn A. Staeheli • Eleonore Kofman • Linda J. Peake

ROUTLEDGE
NEW YORK AND LONDON

Published in 2004 by
Routledge
270 Madison Avenue
New York, NY 10016
www.routledge-ny.com

Published in Great Britain by
Routledge
2 Park Square
Milton Park, Abingdon
Oxon OX14 4RN U.K.
www.routledge.co.uk

10 9 8 7 6 5 4 3 2 1

Library of Congress Cataloging-in-Publication Data

Mapping women, making politics: feminist perspectives on political geography/edited by
Lynn A. Staeheli, Eleonore Kofman, Linda Peake.
    p. cm.
Includes bibliographical references and index.
ISBN 0-415-93448-6 (hb: alk. paper)—ISBN 0-415-93449-4 (pb: alk. paper)
1. Feminist political geography. 2. Sex role—Political aspects.
3. Feminist theory—Political aspects. I. Title: Feminism and political geography.
II. Staeheli, Lynn A. III. Kofman, Eleonore. IV. Peake, Linda, 1956-
JC321.M36 2004
320.1′2′082—dc22   2004005601

Contents

Preface   vii

1 Mapping Gender, Making Politics: Toward   1
  Feminist Political Geographies
  LYNN A. STAEHELI AND ELEONORE KOFMAN

2 Contextualizing Feminist Political Theory   15
  PATRICIA M. MARTIN

3 Mapping Feminisms and Difference   31
  RICHA NAGAR

4 From Dualisms to Multiplicities: 49
  Gendered Political Practices
  RUTH FINCHER

5 Placing Gendered Political Acts   71
  MEGHAN COPE

6 Doing Feminist Political Geographies   87
  JOANNE SHARP

7 Development, Postcolonialism, and Feminist   99
  Political Geography
  NINA LAURIE, WITH PAMELA CALLA

8 Critically Feminist Geopolitics   113
  MARY GILMARTIN AND ELEONORE KOFMAN

9 Gendered Globalization   127
  SUSAN M. ROBERTS

10 Territory, Territoriality, and Boundaries   141
  DORIS WASTL-WALTER AND LYNN A. STAEHELI

11 Embodied Nationalisms   153
  TAMAR MAYER

12 The (Geo)Politics of Gendered Mobility   169
  JENNIFER HYNDMAN

13 Crossing Borders: Gender and Migration   185
  PARVATI RAGHURAM

14 Social Movements, Protest, and Resistance   199
    JOAN FAIRHURST, MAANO RAMUTSINDELA,
    AND URMILLA BOB

15 A Gendered Politics of the Environment   209
    JOSEPA BRÚ BISTUER AND MERCÈ AGÜERA CABO

16 Making Feminist Sense of the State and Citizenship   227
    VERA CHOUINARD

17 Framing Feminist Claims for Urban Citizenship   245
    GERDA R. WEKERLE

18 Feminizing Electoral Geography   261
    ANNA J. SECOR

    References   273

    Contributors   305

    Index   309

Preface

This book emerged out of years of discussion among feminists who are interested in political geography. Many of us noted with excitement the research by feminists that cast politics and political geography in a new light. We were thrilled to read the research but were puzzled and somewhat troubled by the sense that feminist perspectives had not been recognized by many in the field. A series of panels at the annual meetings of the Association of American Geographers in Pittsburgh convinced us it was time to highlight feminism's contributions to the subdiscipline. *Mapping Women, Making Politics: Feminist Perspectives on Political Geography* is an attempt to recognize the breadth and vitality of feminist contributions in this field. We hope that this volume goes some way to demonstrate the ways in which fundamental concepts within political geography are enriched—and in many ways unsettled—by feminist perspectives.

We wish to thank several people who made this collection possible. First and foremost, of course, are those feminists who have brought their perspectives to bear on pressing political issues, demonstrating both the importance of gender in shaping political issues and ideas and the role of feminism in helping to make sense of them. We believe the authors in this volume have played an important role in highlighting those contributions. We also thank David McBride, acquisitions editor at Routledge, for his enthusiasm for the project and his patience as we confronted numerous delays. Finally, we thank Sugandha Brooks for her assistance in putting together the book, working her way through references, computer glitches, and the inevitable confusion of compiling so many chapters with editors and contributors from different places.

Lynn A. Staeheli, Boulder, Colorado
Eleonore Kofman, London
Linda Peake, Toronto

1

Mapping Gender, Making Politics: Toward Feminist Political Geographies

LYNN A. STAEHELI AND ELEONORE KOFMAN

Belonging and *inclusion* are contested terms. They also are terms that have particular resonance for political geographers at the beginning of the twenty-first century, because they speak to the processes of democratization and the incorporation of political subjects as citizens. *The End of History and the Last Man* (Fukuyama 1992) and *The Third Wave* (Huntington 1991) declared that democracy was on the verge of sweeping the globe with the promise of expanded procedures and institutions to ensure the rights of universal citizenship. In the context of proclamations about democratization, long-standing debates about political inclusion and belonging took on increased importance, because it seemed that beyond the establishment of formal institutions of democracy, marginalization and exclusion of particular ideas, people, and social groups continued. As became increasingly clear, the exclusion characterizing political processes also was indicative of processes of knowledge production, because the experiences and perspectives of marginalized groups seemed absent from the study of political processes and geographies.

It is in this context that we want to situate *Mapping Women, Making Politics: Feminist Perspectives on Political Geography.* We intend the book to be a step in demonstrating the ways in which feminist perspectives on politics and political geography contribute to a better, richer understanding of political processes, activities, and behaviors. But we also hope that the book will draw attention to the considerable work by feminists that has not been included in or incorporated into political geography's vision of itself. In so doing, we use this introductory chapter to provide a short overview of political geography, highlighting questions of how it is defined and bounded. The marginalization—and even exclusion—of gender and of feminist perspectives has yielded a field that is partial in the understandings and knowledges produced within it. We outline what a specifically feminist political geography could entail through a consideration of key concepts and issues. In so doing, we demonstrate the importance of situated knowledges that are derived from the lives and experiences of

1

women in different social and geographic locations. Through this discussion, we hope to provide a guide by which the rest of the chapters can be read.

Approaching Political Geography

The field of political geography is broad, covering myriad topics including nationalism, territory, elections, trade, state institutions, citizenship, resistance, social movements, and quotidian political practices and identities. Given its eclecticism, it is a difficult subfield to describe and to characterize. As we try to make sense of the field and to highlight the significance of gender in the making of political geographies, we choose to emphasize the different understandings of "the political" that underlie theory and research and what these mean for a feminist political geography.

Before proceeding, however, we should be clear what a feminist political geography would entail. In 1990 Kofman and Peake conceptualized politics as an activity relevant to all spheres of public and private life; it is manifested in activities of cooperation, negotiation, and struggle over the production and distribution of resources, and it involves the transformative capacity of social agents and institutions. This feminist perspective on the political involves a radical reworking of concepts that moves beyond the boundaries created by a topical focus on formal political spheres and spaces. In addition to an expansive approach to political issues, processes, and relationships, it includes normative visions of social change to combat exclusion, oppression, and marginalization. In so doing, feminists' concerns are with the formal institutions associated with conventional definitions of politics and also with the relations and practices in sites other than the state that construct, maintain, and sometimes challenge power.

Feminist political geographers have conceptualized the political in three overlapping approaches that involve the political as distribution, the political as antagonism, and the political as constitutive.[1] As we argue, gender relations are important in understanding distributional issues and antagonistic politics, but they have been underrepresented in political geography. The contributors in this book demonstrate that these issues of distribution and antagonism—which might be thought of as mapping gender—are central to the constitution—the making—of polities, political relationships, and political geographies.

A distributional approach to the political emphasizes the distribution of power, resources, and privilege in societies. In Lasswell's (1936) terms, distributional approaches emphasize who gets what and under which circumstances. Power is of central importance in creating and maintaining distributions, through the ability to control institutions, and in the ability to use the distribution of resources to achieve certain goals. Distributional approaches within political geography often have focused on spatial patterns of inequality as a way of demonstrating the exercise of power. Hartshorne identified the emphasis on areal distributions in the 1950s as the defining characteristic of political geography; it can be seen in the focus on boundaries, territorial identities, and the mapping of political outcomes that provides the backcloth of much research on geopolitics, nationalism, and the state.

Political geographers have gone beyond the study of patterns, however, to consider the antagonistic processes that give rise to distributional patterns. This perspective draws attention to the processes of interest formation, coalitions, and place making that shape political struggle. The empirical entrées to these processes by political geographers typically include elections, the passage and implementation of policy, state formation, international agreements, and wars, among other topics. The combined emphasis on distributions and antagonisms has been at the core of political geography from its inception. As with research in other disciplines, however, the significance of gender as an element of distribution or as a relationship at play in antagonism was largely absent in the early stages of political geography.

Yet at key moments, certain disruptions occurred within political geography that are significant to the development of the subdiscipline and that opened a space through which feminism could be incorporated through a focus on a wider range of experiences and through a focus on the constitutive. The constitutive implies an approach to the political as an ongoing process in which societies are made—are constituted—in and through struggle. This is understood to be a complex and multivalent struggle, involving actions and behaviors in both the formal spaces of the state and spaces of home, neighborhood, workplace, community, and media. These struggles have a strong normative element, as they revolve around the recognition of personhood and debates about what this means for the formation of just, democratic societies (Brown and Staeheli 2003).

The introduction of critical social theories (e.g., Reynolds and Knight 1989), postmodernist ideas (Dear 1988), and critical geopolitics (Dalby 1994; Ó Tuathail 1996b) into political geography was part of an increased attention to the constitutive. With this acceptance came a broader range of theoretical perspectives that were seen as relevant to politics, including theories of cultural and identity politics. The incorporation of these theories was part of a cultural turn in which feminists also participated (Sharp 2000c). In addition, these theories pointed to new sites or arenas of politics that moved outside the state and formal institutions, thereby changing the ways in which politics could be conceptualized and spatialized. Similarly, new social movements theory pointed to the ways that agents outside the state turned away from formal politics to eschew change in culture and society (Melucci 1989), thus promoting the democratization of civil society and an expansion of citizenship in substantive and formal senses.

It was in this context that feminist approaches to political geography gained currency in the 1980s and 1990s. Feminists highlighted the significance of gender and gender relationships in shaping the distributions and antagonisms that had been the focus of much political geography; in so doing, they made claims about the ways in which those distributions and antagonisms shaped polities and societies. But despite a growing body of research in the 1980s and 1990s, the integration and recognition of feminist perspectives have not yet been achieved. Dalby, for example, argued in 1994 that critical geopolitics tended to overlook gender issues and perspectives. This is somewhat disheartening, because critical geopolitics was one of the developments in the subdiscipline that would seem to be particularly receptive to feminism, given its theoretical and methodological orientations. As recently as 2001, Dowler and Sharp argued that critical geopolitics simply reproduced the masculinism of the subfield. And the absence of feminist perspectives and of gender extends beyond critical geopolitics. A review of political geography textbooks, progress reports, overviews, and programmatic statements suggests that political geography remains largely unaffected by developments in feminist geography (Staeheli 2001). Taylor's (2000a) assessment is acute: political geography has not accepted the challenges of feminism. As Dear (1999) noted, one would be hard pressed to know what political geographers think of feminism.

Toward a Feminist Political Geography

One reason that political geography has not met the challenge of feminism may lie in its masculinism. As applied to research and ways of understanding the world, masculinism is associated with the illusion of transparent space and an all-seeing vision, often described as the "view from nowhere" (Haraway 1988; Rose 1997). Such a vision allows practitioners to name, codify, and classify the world in ways that bring order to places. But it is more than this. The assumed transparency of space and its accompanying universalism typically is associated with practices that do not engage research subjects in the building of categories and the assignment of names; those categories and names appear pre-given and portable in that they can be carried from place to place so that research can be replicated in the building of theories that are spatially and temporally extensive. The field has thereby emphasized trends and changes at an aggregate level, rather than with respect to an individual or to a specific territory. Empirical research within political geography often is based on information from the latter, but that information is quickly abstracted to provide an argument at a higher level of generalization.

The implications of this approach to understanding the world and the goals of research have led to the privileging of Western theory with its emphasis on macro levels of theory and of empirical research and a concern for formal, institutional politics, particularly at the level of the state. The effect often has been to overlook the significance of gender and the ways in which power relationships structure what appears at the macro level and is represented in institutional politics. There is a tendency, for example, to focus on elite actors who either have institutional power through their roles within the state or are able to influence the state through nonstate institutions such as firms or nongovernmental organizations; the agents who wield such power are typically men. By contrast, feminists have redirected attention from elite agents to the structures and processes that create marginality and the ways in which these are necessary to the operations of political systems. In so doing, the focus shifts from the operations of elite agents to the construction of political subjects and the ability of diverse subjects to act.

Similarly, the tendency to analyze issues at a macro level makes it difficult to undertake a detailed consideration of the ways in which gender relations are implicated in the contexts of politics and in the ideas about households, families, and the body that are critical in the development of ideas about space and spatialized politics (Kofman forthcoming). In addition, the focus on formal institutions of the state has lent itself to analysis using secondary information, typically produced by the state. Yet those sources of information often are abstracted from the local and certainly from the household and body. And very often, researchers rely on aggregated statistics that are not amenable to gender-based analyses; such analyses are simply not the reason most of the information was collected. As such, a great deal of contemporary political geography describes a "world without people" or at least a world of abstract, disembodied political subjects. Feminist research, however, often combines quantitative and secondary sources of information with more qualitative and primary sources. The use of qualitative methods draws attention to the role of everyday lives. The triangulation of information and methods of analysis also makes it easier to see the ways in which gender and other dimensions of difference operate in political processes (see Sharp 2004 [this volume]).

Taken together, the ways in which knowledge is produced within political geography constitute a masculinist practice. It yields a kind of knowledge that is claimed to be universal (or at least all-encompassing) and impartial. Feminist political geographers, however, challenge the masculinism of political geography by reworking its basic concepts and the practices involved in knowledge creation. The reworking of concepts includes core ideas related to the constitution of the political, such as power, citizenship, and difference. In so doing, feminists and other critical social theorists[2] often invoke geographies or locations for politics that have not been the traditional focus of the subdiscipline. But it has not been enough to simply reconstruct political concepts and locations; feminist political geography has challenged the very processes of knowledge construction within the field. In particular, it has attempted to democratize knowledge production through recognition of the importance of situated knowledge and through critical engagement between scholarship and the world in which we live and work.

We introduce these issues, each of which is taken up more fully, but in diverse ways, in the chapters that follow. We do not attempt an exhaustive overview of the literature about these concepts, nor do we present a history of their development, as those would constitute a book in and of themselves. Rather, we introduce these concepts as they are developed and used in the subsequent chapters as a way of highlighting the ways in which we can move toward a political geography that better addresses the significance of gender and gender relationships in constituting the societies in which we live.

Reworking the Political

As we described previously, reworking the very concept of the political has been at the center of creating feminist political geographies. This has involved a conceptualization of the political that moves away from the masculinism of much of the field; it moves away from the macro level of analysis to consider the ways in which political relationships are shaped by—and resisted through—gender roles and relations in a variety of settings. The political is not just relevant to elections, the state, and international conflict writ large; it is seen in the ways in which women mobilize at the grass roots, in the ways an ethic of care is brought into political discourse, in the ways masculinity and femininity are invoked in ideas of nation and in international conflicts. What is important is that reworking the political involves a commitment to social change.

To say that the political involves a commitment to social change, however, is not to say that the vision of social change is shared among feminists (see Martin 2004 [this volume] and Nagar 2004 [this volume]). Although they share an abstract goal of change, there are lively, important, and often painful debates between feminists that revolve around issues of identity (e.g., racialized, sexual, religious), North-South differences, methodology, and strategy. These debates are also part of the reworking of the political, creating a sense of openness in terms of the issues, relationships, and perspectives that are brought to bear on the concept. There is no—and should be no—totalizing discourse of feminism. Rather, the political is a contested concept within feminism. The political is not tethered to particular sites or institutions as much as it is a struggle for inclusion in a wide range of settings, acts, perspectives, and embodied experience (see Cope 2004 [this volume]). But the political is not just about differences—either between people or between perspectives; it is also about the webs of power and social relationships that are the basis of connections. One of the goals of feminist political geography, then, is to disrupt the seemingly coherent—and perhaps closed—project of the subdiscipline. As demonstrated by the authors in this book, its definition of the political is one that implies a radical openness to new voices, perspectives, relationships, and strategies.

Power

Power often is conceptualized in terms of the capacity to control or shape an event, person, or process. Power has long been thought of as the ability to do certain things or of having control over events or people (e.g., Bachrach and Baratz 1970). Power, then, is associated with control, authority, or the ability to govern or rule. Power also has been thought of as an attribute or a possession associated with particular institutional roles or with types of individuals.

Social theorists (and feminists among them) have expanded on these conceptualizations of power in several ways. One way has been to situate power in networks or in webs of relationships. A second way has been to recognize the different sources of power, and, in particular, the sources of power that may be rooted in the private sphere. For example, feminist analyses of women's suffrage in the United States have shown the ways in which women mobilized moral authority (i.e., power) stemming from middle-class women's role in the home and nurturers to press their claims for more political power through voting (Ryan 1990). Power is thus conceptualized as being multifaceted, diffuse, and relational, even as it is understood that power is not equally distributed or always available in its different expressions. The emphasis is on power *relationships* rather than on the distribution or quality of power in and of itself. Hence, there is an explicit recognition that power does not only reside in formal institutions such as the state, however broadly the latter is defined. As a result, feminists have increasingly focused on the embodied nature of power.

Finally, feminists and critical theorists are interested in empowerment—or the struggle to reposition marginalized groups in the webs of power that organize life. This concern with empowerment and the resources and strategies that are used in those struggles are highlighted in several chapters of the book (see in this volume, for example, Nagar; Cope; Fairhurst, Ramutsindela, and Bob; Brú Bistuer and Agüera Cabo; and Wekerle).

Citizenship

Citizenship is a term that is bandied about in popular, political, and academic discourses. It is a complex, messy, and multifaceted concept that is widely contested. Authors in this book take citizenship to signify membership, standing, and inclusion in a political community, a definition that is only in part shaped by legal status. They have deconstructed citizenship to delink it from the nation-state and racist, heterosexual, and male-defined norms to a more diffuse notion of social and cultural citizenship based on affinities with immediate communities and public spaces. Ultimately the concept describes the construction and meaning of political subjectivities. Feminists have argued that women have to be recast as agents and have critiqued the ways in which the divide between the private and the public situates them differentially and partially as citizens (Lister 1997; Pateman 1989; also see Martin 2004 [this volume]). Tensions between the universal and the particular also play themselves out through inclusionary and exclusionary practices. The struggles over inclusion and over the constitution of the political subject are themselves at the heart of the political, for they entail normative visions of the communities in which we live and participate (Lister 1997; Mouffe 1992). These communities are not singular or necessarily located in one place. Many social movements have used discourses of citizenship to claim an expansion of rights. The struggles for inclusion are waged on many fronts—antiracist, anti-imperialist, antihomophobic, for example—with respect to many facets of identity and social life, and in many arenas beyond those bounded by the formal institutions of the state (see Chouinard 2004 [this volume] and Wekerle 2004 [this volume]). Although geographers have contributed to the engendering of citizenship, there needs to be more attention paid to spaces of citizenship in divided societies, in the South (McEwan 2000), and of migrant women (see Raghuram 2004 [this volume]), as well as linking citizenship to processes of international migration and its feminization.

Difference

To some people, attention to difference seems to define feminism. Titles such as *Justice and the Politics of Difference* (I. M. Young 1990), *Democracy and Difference* (Benhabib 1996), and *Cities of Difference* (Fincher and Jacobs 1998) tend to support that idea. And, indeed, difference is a central preoccupation of feminism. But what does it mean to be concerned with difference? As ever, there are many competing understandings of this term.

The emphasis on difference in feminism stems from a prior critique of the assumption of universalism and abstractness of many of the theories that emerged in modern social science in the West. The concept of "economic man" may be the most widely known (and pilloried) example. This "person" approached problems using only abstract reason; despite the name, the "man" has no gender nor class standing, race, family, or history—none of the defining features that many of us associate with personhood or the embeddedness that make us who we are and that shape our experiences, opportunities, and potential. In a similar fashion, the citizen who is the subject of liberal political theory is disembodied and unencumbered. Feminists—and others—have critiqued these constructions of the subject and have highlighted the positionality, identity, and structures of privilege and oppression that shape the experiences of individuals and social groups (see Nagar 2004 [this volume] and Chouinard 2004 [this volume]).

The question remains, however, of how we should conceptualize and talk about difference. The easiest and most intuitively obvious way may be to take a categorical approach and to define groups on the basis of characteristics such as gender, race, sexuality, ability, and so forth. Such an approach has several limitations, and feminist geographers such as Jacobs (2000) have argued that we should move away from them. These limitations include a recognition that we are not defined simply by the categories that may be used to describe us and by the ways in which the multiple dimensions of identity and difference interact. These interactions are further shaped by the specific constellations of power and political opportunities within places, places that are themselves differently positioned in transnational structures and processes (Secor 2002). Furthermore, categorical approaches have the unintended effect of reifying categories that are created through representational strategies and through the very structures of oppression that feminists seek to change.

Most of the authors in this volume accept those limitations but argue that categories do have real consequences that feminists can ill afford to ignore; the categories through which difference is expressed and experienced may be ideological constructions, but they have material effects. This is not to say that categories—or more important, the meanings attached to those categories— are fixed over time and space, for they clearly are fluid. Yet the ways in which those categories are understood and acted on are important in shaping the experience of difference. When these experiences involve oppression, differences need to be named and struggled against. The tension or difficulty is that the categories of difference may impede the identification of common goals, but ignoring those categories and the differences associated with them may lead to a tendency to unify and homogenize the experiences of people who are differently marginalized. There has, moreover, been increasing recognition of the need to focus on the ways in which difference is constructed and of the relationships out of which difference is carved. The recognition of difference is central to the political strategies of feminism, even as it leads to debates between feminists as to goals and tactics.

Geographies of the Political

As we intimated previously, there are geographies to the ways in which difference is structured and experienced and to the political struggles that address it. Geographers have long been concerned with these geographies of positionality. As a simple example, the way one moves through a place—and thereby comes to gain an understanding of that place—is shaped by gender, age, (dis-)ability, family status, sexuality, and race, to name just a few axes of difference. Those differences may affect the features people perceive as significant, such as uneven surfaces, nooks, and crannies, or people who look or seem similar to oneself. These differences also may condition feelings of safety and acceptance, the kinds of actions one might undertake, and even the ability to enter a place. These embodied experiences of place shape the political goals and strategies that are part of feminist politics. Although the range of geographies is much broader, there are two key elements of geographies of the political that have been of particular concern to feminists.

One element is the relationship between the public and private. Feminists have demonstrated the ways in which ideas about "formal" and "public" politics rely on gendered constructions of "informal" and "private" (see Brownill and Halford 1990). Although politics has primarily been associated with the public sphere—and accordingly with public spaces—feminists have shown how these public activities rely crucially on more private, informal spaces and spheres. But because women often have been associated with the private sphere, their political activities and values have been ignored or deemed irrelevant to the public world in which the abstract citizen debates ideas. Feminists have attempted to recover the private sphere as a space of politics through slogans such as "the personal is political," by demonstrating the fluidity of the private and public spheres, and by highlighting the ways in which power and experiences from one sphere infiltrate the other sphere, becoming resources that can be used in political struggle. One of the key contributions of feminist political geographers has been to explore the geographies of public and private that shape power relations, that give meaning to difference, and that condition the political (see Nagar 2004 [this volume]; Fincher 2004 [this volume]; and Cope 2004 [this volume]).

Scale

Feminists also have challenged the geographic construction of the political that locates politics within particular scales; together with other critical social theorists, they have attempted to rework concepts of scale to highlight its rela-tionality and to expand the range of scales that are considered. The attention to scale derived from a theoretical argument that the world is structured by the interaction of scalar processes. Early explications focused on three scales, the global, national, and local (Taylor 1982), but increasingly critiqued the emphasis by political geographers on the national and the state. This argument provided an opening for feminists in that it labeled the local as a constituent element of political geography. Although not all feminists worked on the local, many did (Women and Geography Study Group 1984; Bondi and Peake 1988). As a theo-retical framework, arguments about scale provided a hook to connect urban and place-specific studies to the traditional concerns of political geography located in the national state and in larger territorial entities.

Thus, the local is a key scale, but feminists go further and demonstrate the significance of the home and the body in the structuration of the political (Massey 1994; Nast 1998; Marston 2000). Both, for example, are sites of oppression and resistance. Bodies have been used to press political claims, such as in hunger strikes and in civil disobedience. They also are used to exert control, such as rape, whether in wartime or in domestic settings (see Nagar 2004 [this volume] and Mayer 2004 [this volume]). They are used as symbols of nationhood. And they can be sites of conflict that link scales in asylum and human rights claims (see Hyndman 2004 [this volume] and Raghuram 2004 [this volume]). This expanded understanding of scale is central to our attempts to understand political processes.

Masculinity, Femininity, and Political Subjectivity

Closely aligned with arguments about scale and the body are ideas related to masculinity and femininity in the construction of the political subject. Masculinity and femininity refer to the practices through which ideologies related to the characteristics of men, women, and gender are created and contested; they include, as well, the effects of these practices in the construc-tions of bodies, cultures, and normative expectations for men and women

(Laurie et al. 1999; Longhurst 2000; Berg and Longhurst 2003). As such, masculinity and femininity are intensely political and have implications for the conduct of politics and for the ways in which we understand political processes.

Feminist political geographers, for example, have demonstrated the ways in which colonialism rests on a feminized colonial subject that is dependent on a masculine imperial ruler, bringing order and rationality to an otherwise irrational native (see Gilmartin and Kofman 2004 [this volume]). The constructions of "developed" and "less developed" nations rely on similar ideas, justifying the imposition of order in the form of structural adjustment policies from institutions such as the International Monetary Fund (see Laurie with Calla 2004 [this volume] and Roberts 2004 [this volume]). Masculinity and femininity, then, are tightly bound up in the framing of political relationships and in the construction of political subjects, their power, and their capacities. These ideas are at the root of citizenship and the ways in which politics are constituted (see Martin 2004 [this volume]).

But masculinity and femininity are themselves produced in and through political struggle and, thus, are not pre-given. Feminist political geographers seek to understand hegemonic controls on the construction of femininity and masculinity, the norms and practices associated with them, the implications for the continuing salience of sexuality for the construction of political subjects, and the discursive positioning of countries in the socioeconomic hierarchy of nation-states.

Situated Knowledges

The recognition of difference, of the expanded geographies of the political, and of the role of masculinity and femininity has important implications for the ways in which feminists understand knowledge and knowledge claims. If social agents are differently situated with respect to power and to structures of power, then these positionings will lead to different experiences and understandings of the world. These understandings—this knowledge—is inevitably partial, as our ability to "see" or to gain perspective is conditioned by how we are positioned. Rather than rejecting partial knowledge as biased or incomplete, however, feminists argue that all knowledge is situated (Haraway 1988). Recognizing the situated nature of knowledge has profound implications for the ways we understand decision making, rationality, and the interpretation of the political.

Accordingly, the partiality of knowledge is reflected in the approaches to research and knowledge production used within feminist political geography (see Sharp 2004 [this volume]). Perhaps most important, feminist political geography is open to the bodily, lived experiences of place and space (see Hyndman 2004 [this volume]), the understanding of which has been important in the reworking of several theoretical concepts, such as development (see Laurie with Calla 2004 [this volume]), nation (see Mayer 2004 [this volume]), territoriality (see Wastl-Walter and Staeheli 2004 [[this volume]), the environment (see Brú Bistuer and Agüera Cabo 2004 [this volume]), glob-alization (see Roberts 2004 [this volume]), and indeed, the political. As the chapters that follow demonstrate, what may be taken for granted about the way the world works is challenged when one recognizes—and incorporates into one's thinking—the embodied and situated ways in which we learn about and make sense of the world.

Critical Engagements between Scholarship and Practice

Concern for the embodied, and therefore differential, experience of the world and care to ensure a wide range of perspectives are closely linked to another way in which feminists challenge knowledge production. As we have argued, feminism carries a normative goal of changing—if not completely breaking down—structures and practices that create marginality and oppression. As such, feminists need to link scholarship with critical engagements in the societies and "fields" in which they live and work (Hanson 1999; Nast 1994; Katz 1994; Kobayashi 1994). In so doing, feminist political geographers attempt to engage counterhegemonic practices in academic discourse, in the academy itself, and in the peoples of the world whom they encounter. In other words, they attempt to forge a praxis in which theory, research, and practice are linked.

As might be anticipated by the comments about situated knowledge and difference, one element of this praxis is an attempt to include a wider range of perspectives and embodied experiences in research and in politics. It also involves a willingness to allow the people we study, or with whom we study, to play a role in shaping research questions and concepts and to make the research useful to—and in some cases, empowering for—those communities and indi-viduals who participate in research projects. As Harding (1991) argued, this approach recognizes and builds on situated knowledges to forge research and political practices that are more rigorous and useful than the social science that ignores the partiality of all research.

Critical engagement, however, carries its own difficulties, as researchers try to negotiate competing claims and political strategies of participants in the research as well as the researchers' own positions in the communities they study, the communities in which they live, and the academic communities. This sense of "betweenness" (Katz 1994) is never fully resolved and is rarely described as a balance. As Kobayashi (1994) wrote, betweenness requires that we think not so much about including research subjects in "our" research but rather that we seek to understand how we can engage with subjects' projects (see also Peake and Trotz 1999; Nagar 2002). Feminist scholars keep this at-tempt at engagement in the forefront of their work.

Conclusion

At the outset of this introduction, we wrote that we intend this book to dem-onstrate the ways in which feminist perspectives can contribute to a richer, and more useful, understanding of political processes and spaces. We believe that the chapters in this book extend the gambit of political geography by using feminist perspectives to understand the ways in which gender interacts with other dimensions of difference to shape political processes and the politics of space. At the same time, the collection enriches feminist approaches to political geography by addressing the multiplicity of feminisms and feminist theory. Our hope is that this collection will help to highlight the contributions feminist political geography has made and will continue to make. In mapping gender, we hope to make politics in the subdiscipline as well as in the societies in which we live.

Notes

1. This framework draws on Michael Brown's conceptualization in his forthcoming book *Local Political Geographies.* See also Brown and Staeheli (2003).
2. We recognize that feminists are not alone in their critiques and attempts to rework these concepts. Throughout this section, we will emphasize the work of feminists but do not claim they are alone in their endeavors to create a more inclusive political geography.

2

Contextualizing Feminist Political Theory

PATRICIA M. MARTIN

The landscape of feminist theory has changed dramatically since second-wave feminism emerged in the West in the late 1960s. As Jaggar (1988) noted, this reflects the fact that as an articulated body of thought, feminism is still new and, therefore, rapidly evolving. It also relates to the fact that in general, feminist theory is grounded theory and has emerged in relation to the experiences of women in diverse and intersecting social locations. When Pateman (1989) critiqued, for example, classic liberal political theory, the critique was based on a close theoretical scrutiny of those ideas in relation to the *experiences* of women. Given the geopolitical sea changes throughout the world over the past decade, the grounding of women's experiences also has shifted—not only in a crude material sense but also in the thick layer of discourse that provides a continually shifting terrain for analytical and political purchase on the world. Of course, overstating the degree of change is also problematic; women's experiences continue to display both " 'endless variety' as well as 'monotonous similarity' " (Rubin 1975, quoted in Jaggar 1988, 139) across space and through time. In this sense women's experiences and feminist analyses can provide a needed pause for the headiness of the reorganization of space and the erasure of history related to the current round of postsocialist global capitalist restructuring. As Collins (1998) suggested, there can be dramatic shifts in borders, boundaries, and institutions that underpin political and social life, while at the same time inequalities based on class, race, and gender—among other socially constructed and politicized forms of difference—continue to be reproduced.

These tensions between continuity and change provide an implicit framework for this chapter. In the first part, I present certain key debates that have been central to feminist politics and feminist theory since the 1970s. These include analyses of the public-private divide, debates about difference, and feminist attempts to construct feminist political subjectivity, particularly through the lens of citizenship. In the second section of this chapter, I engage more directly with contemporary, highly spatialized feminist politics, particularly in relationship to the processes of globalization.

I make an argument in favor of grounded feminist political theory, and in so doing I also introduce certain feminist geographical analytics that may be of use for such contemporary groundings. Before moving to those two sections, however, I begin with a brief general discussion of feminism, power, and politics.

Feminist politics and feminist theory might be defined as analyses, experiments, and efforts to theorize and reimagine the nature of politics and power. One way in which feminist analyses can be distinguished is through distinct conceptions of power. For example, with the publication of *Sexual Politics* in 1969, Millet shifted the terrain of an understanding of power and politics for feminists. She defined politics as "power-structured relationships, arrangements whereby one group of people is controlled by another" (Millet 2000, 23). This definition arose in relationship to her exploration of the private realm of sexuality and the household as one key arena in which men established dominance over women. This perspective varied dramatically with the predominant understanding of the political at the time, which located politics and power in the public institutions of government and the actions of public figures in political parties, unions, and so on. More recently, some feminists have engaged with the insights provided by Foucault to rework understandings of power (e.g., Bordo 1989; Bartky 1997; Laurie et al. 1999). Rather than thinking of power in terms of one group having power over another, they argue that modern power is located in institutions that produce, discipline, and regulate individualized subjectivities, particularly at the level of the body (producing femininity, for example). By contrast, other feminists have engaged in a more positive sense of power, as reflected in the word *empowerment*. Townsend et al. (1999), for example, framed empowerment in three ways. "Power from within" emphasizes the search for an individual sense of agency; "power with" emphasizes a productive and collective sense of power, signaling the ability to do something in concert with others; and "power to" highlights the development and use of multiple skills and abilities.

Kofman and Peake (1990) advocated a slightly different understanding of power and politics that may help to incorporate these distinct understandings. Although they acknowledged that politics is shaped by power arrangements and ideologies that inform those arrangements, they suggested that politics lies in activity and the struggles, conflicts, and cooperation related to the uneven distribution of power and resources. Such a perspective emphasizes a sense of agency and the possibility for transforming power arrangements. Peake (1999a, 1999b) added to this an emphasis on locating politics within discursive practices that set relationships between people. Discursive practices link language with materiality and point to ways in which legitimacy and truths are produced in relationship to unequal distributions of power. Within such a setting, a feminist political agenda might be about the development of a "feminist imaginary" (Peake 1999a, 203). As politics has become increasingly spatialized, constructing a feminist geopolitical imagination also might be an important agenda. I return to this point at the end of the chapter. I now turn, however, to debates in feminist political theory that illuminate particular facets of power, subjectivity, and politics and that engage with a range of understandings of power and politics, as I introduced previously.

Feminists Critique Political Liberalism

Second-wave feminist politics often is associated with critiques of the ideals and practices of political liberalism, which had emphasized the inherent abstract universal freedom and equality of human beings as individuals. In practice these abstract values were not extended to all groups (Marston 1990) and often served, in fact, to mask inequalities among groups (J. Mitchell 1987). Feminist critiques of political liberalism marked an overall shift in the language that feminists used, moving from arguments for equality and inclusion within the polity to an emphasis on the existence of patriarchal oppression and women's liberation (Jaggar 1988). This shift indicated a change in how feminists interpreted and understood their exclusion. Rather than being a question of learned differences derived from education, or psychological and social conditioning, the source of women's oppression was understood in the dynamic and systemic terms of patriarchy and capitalism. As Jaggar (1988, 6) stated,

> Oppression is the imposition of constraints; it suggests that the problem is not the result of bad luck, ignorance, or prejudice but rather is caused by one group actively subordinating another group to its own interests: the oppressors and the oppressed. It is a world view, moreover, that strongly suggests that liberation is unlikely to be achieved by rational debate but instead must be the result of political struggle.

In a broad sense, second-wave feminism challenged the naturalized view that the state and the public sphere provided the arena of politics. Rather, politics existed wherever power was perceived to exist; thus, the horizon of the political has expanded rapidly (Squires 2000). Feminist political theory has been heterogeneous, nonetheless, and critiques have taken place along several axes, opening up and questioning naturalized assumptions about the nature of the political.

The Public and the Private

In the expanding horizon of the political, one fundamental social-spatial structural division that Western feminists saw as a source of structural oppression was that of the public and the private. Although numerous understandings of the public-private split circulate in classical and contemporary Western liberal political theory (e.g., state-civil society, society-individual, state-economy), they all tend to relegate, or confine, women to the familial private sphere (Benhabib 1998) and at the same time fail to acknowledge the centrality of the familial private sphere as a central organizing principle of social and political life

(Pateman 1989; Davidoff 1998). In a complex sense, the public-private split has operated as both an explanation for and an ideology of women's oppression (Davidoff 1998).

There are many political implications that result from this combined relegation and erasure of women's lives that continue to have discursive weight. First, the idealized universal citizen remains unmarked as a masculine (white, bourgeois, Western) subject of democracy (Fraser 1997). Despite liberalism's emphasis on the individual as exemplified in the notion of "citizen," Pateman (1989) demonstrated that male citizens hold a social and fraternal identification linked to national identity. This masculine social identity helps to explain why women are inevitably marked as "women" and not as "citizens" when gaining inclusion in the public political sphere. Second, the liberal democratic discourse of equality and justice does not extend into the private sphere of the household; the household persists as a realm of premodern patriarchal relationships. Although public space was a container for the universal, private space operated as a container for the particular (Pateman 1989). Because women's subjectivity is so centered in the private sphere of the household, the lack of equality or justice in the household fundamentally undercuts women's subjectivity as rights-bearing citizens. Pateman (1989) linked, for example, women's lack of rights to consent in private (vis-à-vis marriage and sex) to the inability to consent as citizens in public. A third implication that derives from the marginalization of the familial private sphere in political theory is that domestic work—the reproduction of the family and the household—is not viewed or valued in the same way as waged work (Davidoff 1998). This devaluation, in turn, creates an unequal access to resources—material as well as cultural—across gender.

Numerous critiques have been leveled at the feminist preoccupation with the public and the private. As women of color and working-class women have been quick to point out, such structural and institutional arrangements vary across other lines of difference. Hurtado (1989, cited in Mohanty 1991a) argued, for example, that the state has always intervened much more directly in the domestic lives of working-class women and women of color, as the politics of welfare, abortion, birth control, and sterilization demonstrate. Collins (1998) highlighted, moreover, the employment of black women as domestic workers in white households to demonstrate that the normative notions of the public and the private also were predicated on class-based and racialized social structures and not just on gender. Moreover, for social groups that suffer racialized oppression, bringing politics into the home conflicts with the importance of such private spaces for generating solidarity and opposition to racism. In addition, the public-private split also displays heterosexist normativity.

Fixing answers to the dilemmas posed by the public and private divisions that permeate modernity seems exceedingly difficult (Davidoff 1998). Having women or "women's interests" simply enter into the public sphere in a more visible manner does not necessarily ameliorate the situation. For example, in a process Kelly et al. (2001) referred to as "feminization," many women throughout the world have moved into the capitalist waged labor force. Although they may be the primary wage earners for the household, wage rates often are set with the assumption that such income is, in fact, supplementary. At home, furthermore, women still assume much of the responsibility for housework and, in addition, women often are looked to for community participation, resulting in the triple role or triple burden of work (Moser 1993). Thus, although women have moved into the public sphere, they often carry with them an identity read through the familial private sphere, and they move into the public under circumstances they do not necessarily control. In Latin America, Alvarez (1999) suggested that as democratizing states incorporate a more public set of policies aimed toward women's interests, they create technologies of control while at the same time co-opting and transforming feminist political interests.

Highlighting the political nature of the private destabilizes the lines between public and private, yet it remains unclear that dissolving such boundaries is either desirable or possible. Elshtain (1981, 1987), for example, argued in favor of redeeming the value of sexual difference, the family, and everyday life. She suggested, following the work of Carol Gilligan, that the distinct moral language developed in the private sphere should be protected and that "maternal thinking" could be introduced into the public, making the public more inclusionary (Elshtain 1981). More recent research also points to the importance of protecting the noncapitalist private sphere, in the face of new surveillance technologies and genetic engineering, for example (Staeheli and Mitchell 2004; Squires 1994). Collins (1998, 35) suggested, moreover, that the ubiquity of capitalist privitization in the United States reflects a new racialized politics of containment, in which public institutions and spaces such as schools and parks are both degraded and surveilled:

> This new politics of containment signals a distinct reversal—the public sphere becomes a curiously confined yet visible location that increases the value of private services and privacy itself. Public places become devalued spaces containing poor people, African-Americans, and anyone else who cannot afford to escape.

These examples are suggestive of the shifting nature of social reality; the command lines between public and private are continuously being redrawn but in ways that do not necessarily reflect a feminist kind of politics.

In trying to reformulate an understanding of the public sphere in a manner that may provide more space for feminist politics, many feminist political theorists have turned to the notion of a public sphere, as formulated by Jürgen Habermas, particularly in *The Structural Transformation of the Public Sphere* (1989) and *The Theory of Communicative Action* (1985) (e.g., Fraser 1997; Benhabib 1998; Landes 1998). In short, Habermas's theorization provides the possibility for a public political sphere outside the institutions of government where an active citizenry can offer critique and thus influence the formal politics. Both engagement and critique have characterized feminist readings of Habermas. As Landes (1998, 197) suggested,

> Habermas's construction of the public sphere had a singular advantage for feminists; it freed politics from the iron grasp of the state which, by virtue of the long denial of the franchise to women and their rare status as public officials, effectively defined the public in masculine terms. The concept of the public sphere was suffused with a spirit of openness that feminists found inviting.

Nevertheless, feminists also have argued that Habermas presented an idealized view of the public sphere shaped by exclusions based on class, race, and gender (Ryan 1998; Brooks-Higginbotham 1993). Fraser (1997) offered a reformulation of the public sphere in specifically feminist terms. The metaphorical model she suggested is that of multiple, overlapping public spheres and, hence, is more plural. For societies traversed by systemic inequalities, she provided the notion of "subaltern counter-publics" as vital spaces from which marginalized groups can formulate public critique and discourse (see also Alvarez et al. 1998). Benhabib (1998), on the other hand, focused on Habermas's discourse ethic in an autonomous democratic public sphere. Such an ethic emphasizes a notion of democracy built through public dialogue. Such dialogue is "radically proceduralist" and allows for the introduction of mutual respect, sharing of perspectives, and egalitarian reciprocity and enables "controversial general debates about the validity of [social and political] norms" (Benhabib 1998, 2). Such an ethic, furthermore, would provide a means for reevaluating private relationships and questioning as well as challenging the gendered moral codes that underpin the private, familial sphere.

Locating the Politics of Difference: Differing Registers of Debate

The emphasis on the public-private distinction helped to bring the issue of gender difference to the fore in second-wave feminist thinking. Traditionally, liberal feminists had argued for political inclusion by extending the logic of universal disembodied human equality to women (Jaggar 1988; Phillips 1992). Notwithstanding this, second-wave feminists were more decidedly split over the manner in which to achieve equality and what equality really meant (Fraser 1997). For some, the existence of gender difference was the outcome of patriarchy. Therefore dissolving difference and creating conditions in which men and women were similar and equal were the goals. This view was later challenged as it became increasingly clear that a goal of inclusion based on sameness and equality was in fact built on a masculinist vision of the world and, therefore, radically denied the experiences, perspectives, and ethics of women (Pateman 1989). In turn, some feminists argued for revaluing the perspectives, experiences, and distinct worldviews of women, in what Fraser (1997) referred to as "cultural feminism" and Dietz (1987) called "maternalist thinking." Examples include the work of Nancy Chodorow (1978), Carol Gilligan (1982), Jean Elshtain (1982), and Sara Ruddick (1980) (sources cited in Dietz 1987). Such debate also marked the initial success of constructing women as a visible site for political, academic, and activist work (S. Friedman 1998).

According to Fraser (1997; see also S. Friedman 1998), the equality-difference debate in Western feminism was never fully resolved and instead was partially displaced by two other registers of debate about difference. Both challenged the notion that women could, in a straightforward manner, be the authors of their own liberation. On one hand, antiessentialist perspectives toward gender informed by poststructuralist theory shifted the terms of the debate. Poststructuralism refers specifically to developments in linguistic theory that highlighted the inherent instability in the meaning of words and texts. One result of this was a fundamental critique of the possibility of an autonomous and knowing subject or position, such as a woman's standpoint. As Mouffe (1992, 316) wrote, "One common tenet of critics of essentialism has been the abandoning of the category of the subject as a rational transparent entity that could convey a homogeneous meaning on the total field of her conduct by being the source of her action." Ong (1994, 372–73) demonstrated the discursive effect of such a knowing subject, in relationship to women in development studies:

> Feminist voices in the social sciences unconsciously echo this masculinist will to power in relationship to non-Western societies. Thus, for feminists looking overseas, the non-feminist Other is not so much patriarchy as the non-Western woman ... when feminists look overseas, they frequently establish their authority on the backs of non-Western women, determining for them the meanings and goals of their lives. If, from the feminist perspective there can be no shared experience with persons who stand for the Other, the claim to a common kinship with non-Western women is at best, tenuous, at worst, non-existent.

The "subject," Mouffe explained, is the result of a series of linguistic significations that precede individuals; there is always a double movement toward fixity and transformation among such significations. Recognizing the inherent linguistic instability in the meaning of "man" and "woman" provides one way of moving beyond the binary opposition posed by the same-different debates. Poststructuralism suggested that the male-female dichotomy was a key example of the binary, logocentric linguistic divisions that inform modernist, Enlightenment thinking.[1] At the same time, poststructuralism called for the problematization, or a process of continual critique, such that feminism's "essentializing or totalizing gestures and its roots in Enlightenment humanism" (S. Friedman 1998, 209) also had to be brought into question. In this sense, fixing the subject of feminism, or a feminist political project, became inherently problematic. The work of Judith Butler (1990, 1995), who advocates delinking a definition of woman from feminism, has been particularly influential in this regard. She framed feminist theory in the following manner, instead:

> If feminism presupposes that "women" designates an undesignatable field of differences, one that cannot be totalized or summarized by a descriptive identity category, then the very term becomes a site of permanent openness and resignifiability. I would argue that the rifts among women over the content of the term ought to be safeguarded and prized, indeed, that this constant rifting ought to be affirmed as the ungrounded ground of feminist theory. To deconstruct feminism is not, then, to censure its usage, but, on the contrary, to release the term into a future of multiple significations, to emancipate it from the maternalist or racialist ontologies to which it has been restricted, and to give it play as a site where unanticipated meanings might come to bear. (Butler 1995, 50)

A second register of the debate about difference came from the perspectives of women of color and women from the South. They challenged the notion that gender was the primary axis of difference along which systemic patterns of oppression occurs. They argued that gender identities operate in complex relationship to other social identities such as race, ethnicity, class, nationality, First World–Third World, religion, sexuality, and so on. hooks (1984, 18) helps to explain the importance of this issue in this manner:

> Do women share a common vision of what equality means? Implicit in this simplistic definition of women's liberation is a dismissal of race and class as factors that, in conjunction with sexism determine the extent to which an individual will be discriminated against, exploited, or oppressed. Bourgeois white women interested in women's rights issues have been satisfied with simple definitions for obvious reasons. Rhetorically placing themselves in the same social category as oppressed women, they were not anxious to call attention to race and class privilege.

The struggle against such exclusion has developed a new set of political and analytical tools, as suggested by such terms as "contradictory subject position," "multiple oppressions," "multiple intersecting differences," and "intersectionality" (S. Friedman 1998; Fraser 1997). Valerie Smith (1990) demonstrated the importance of intersectionality to understand how race and gender work in complex relationship to one another. She did so by focusing on border cases such as politics and discourses around interracial rape. The dynamics are complex and demonstrate how gender codes are racialized, classed, and vice versa. She argued, for example, that in cases of interracial rape (understood as black men raping white women), white males mobilize against black males in a manner that claims white women's bodies as white male property. Furthermore, the politics around interracial rape demonstrate that certain female bodies are valued over other female bodies, based on the interlocking relationship of class and race. Contemporary discourses draw on long-standing racist and gendered cultural narratives—invoking, for example, the violence of lynching and myths of desire and sexuality. Kovacs (1996) offered a second example that demonstrates the importance of understanding the way in which socially constructed identities intersect in an architecture of power. She demonstrated the ambivalence present in the politics around women's suffrage in Hungary of the 1920s, a newly independent country with minority Jewish and German populations. Although there were apparent advances in women's rights (suffrage was achieved in 1920), anti-Semitic legislation was passed at the same time; as the women's movement continued through the 1920s, it increasingly allied itself with conservative national political groups (that also obviously discriminated against ethnic minority women). These complex workings of power demonstrate that social groups or social identities do not operate as discrete interest groups, as they often are portrayed in liberal democratic terms; this calls for a radical reworking of how justice is understood and administered (Young 1990).

There are some similarities and yet some tensions between poststructuralist understandings of feminism and postcolonial understandings of feminism. Both perspectives address questions of representation in trying to interpret who speaks for whom, and toward what end. One point of tension, however, circulates around identity as enacted through individuals versus social groups. With poststructuralism, one has the sense that the discussion focuses around the inherent instability of identities as they traverse individuals. In turn, this suggests an individual ability to play with identities—to assume, discard, or redefine them. Progressive politics, from a poststructural vantage point, calls for shifting patterns of signification, establishing new chains of linguistic equivalence (e.g., feminism-antiracism-environmentalism). Certain feminists of color and feminists from the South posit a social subject, on the other hand, understanding that diverse social groups intersect. There is a greater emphasis on social experience and communal solidarity, with a politics of coalition forming the basis of a political strategy. As Reagon (1983) suggested, however, coalition is built out of the political need for survival and not a celebration of difference. Both of these registers of the debate about difference demonstrate that feminist movements take place in a wider set of social relations and that there are broader implications than a deceptively simple focus on women implies.

Citizenship: Feminists Construct Political Ground

Collins (1998) cautioned against the degree of introspection and demobilization that an exclusive focus on identity and representation can bring. In a similar vein, Fraser (1997) argued that a "politics of recognition" has been overemphasized in comparison to a "politics of redistribution" such that in the postsocialist period, identity politics has displaced a concern for patterns of economic inequality (see also Phillips 1999). Indeed, within feminist political theory there appear to be sites of recovery from the fragmentation and introspection that debates about identity rendered. This is not to suggest that concerns for identity in feminist political projects have been abandoned; rather such positions signal the construction of broader sites of political engagement.

Within feminist political theory there has been a long-standing interest in participatory or radical democracy. In her critique of social contract theory, Pateman (1989) described the theoretical impoverishment of citizen political rights. Although classical political theory recognizes that humans have natural political rights, these are rights that are always given up to the state through the social contract. Pateman called instead for an understanding of democracy in which citizens can act politically in a manner whereby political rights can be reaffirmed, regained, or strengthened; in other words, she imagined a situation in which political liberties are positive and not just negative (Dietz 1987).

Reflecting this reimagining of a feminist politics, one site of feminist political recovery that incorporates difference has been through the construction of substantive tools for democracy, particularly around ideas of citizenship. To be sure, this literature has diverse roots growing out of the equality-difference debates (e.g., Lister 1997) and poststructuralist-inspired radical democratic politics (e.g., Mouffe 1992). Here I can provide only a range of examples. In articulating one perspective of a lesbian democratic politics, Phelan (1995) challenged the notion that there is a direct link between an identity (as a "lesbian" or a "farmer," for example) and a specific set of interests. Rather, she returned to the Latin roots of "interest" (*inter:* "among," "between"; *esse:* "to be") (Phelan 1995, 339) to suggest that "to have interests" does not necessarily mean material, consumer-like needs. Rather, having interests implies a sense of publicity, giving public recognition to and recognizing a multiplicity of public needs. Thus, having a set of interests provides a mediating space of dialogue between a lesbian community, for example, and the wider public. Phelan's overall argument resonates with Mouffe's (1992) call for a commitment toward a set of political ideals around citizenship rather than a specific identity. In this sense, citizenship is a self-conscious engagement in political community. Such a community does not represent a pre-given organic unity but is plural and subject to continuous redefinition as the tension between liberty and equality is constantly renegotiated. For Mouffe then, democracy remains an unrealizable goal.

Lister (1997) also offered a feminist reformulation of citizenship. She advocated a notion of citizenship that combines official political status, conferred through a set of rights, and practice, defined through a broad sense of participation. This combination draws attention to the political structures that reinforce or transform inequalities, as well as human agency. Lister also argued for a multi-scaled, internationalist sense of citizenship. In doing so, she raised questions about the changing geography of citizenship, an issue that feminist geographers also have addressed. For example, Susan Smith (1989) introduced the notion of citizenship as a way of politically negotiating the shift from a social welfare state toward a post-Fordist neoliberal state. Because spatial restructuring has been one characteristic of this shift, Smith argued that linking citizenship to "the locality" might provide a way to renegotiate equality, individual and social rights, and plural democracy (see also Staeheli and Clarke 1995). In turn, feminist geographers Marston and Staeheli (1994, 844) advocated a relational model of citizenship. They wrote,

> The interweaving of notions of rights, responsibilities, and struggles . . . implies that citizenship is defined by relationships between individuals, social groups, the state and civil society. . . . Struggles over citizenship, then, are struggles to transform the state, civil society, and the terrain of participation by changing the webs of power relations in which individuals and social groups are positioned.

This understanding of citizenship places political struggle and agency at the intersection of webs of power that may exist in relationship to a variety of locations and spatial processes. Such an understanding is very valuable today, given the increasing spatiality of politics, particularly with regard to the processes of globalization. I turn to this concern in the next section of this chapter.

The Spaces of Feminist Political Theory

Feminism and feminist politics have many histories and geographies. If feminism ever was a strictly Western-Northern project, it now emerges in complex, recombinant forms in places across the globe. For example, as Chun (1997) described, in China, ideas about women, gender, and politics have been shaped by the trajectory of twentieth-century Chinese history. She argued that the contemporary word for Chinese feminism, which she translated into English as "womenism," carries connotations shaped by a history of communist feminism, by a particular set of political relationships to the state, and by anticolonialism. This term is distinct, therefore, from an older term for feminism that gained currency at the turn of the century and that was linked more closely with Western feminism.[2] She also indicated that the contemporary womenist movement in China may be opening new, autonomous, public spaces. In such a context, she suggested provocatively that an emerging autonomous public sphere might have a feminist rather than a masculinist character. Similarly, Mushakoji (2001) described the complex contextual terrain for feminist politics in Japan. She argued that patriarchal codes contained in liberal democracy have been imported into Japan and overlap with other, similarly patriarchal, worldviews. The resulting overlap doubly obscures racialized and gendered discrimination. In this situation, a feminist politics may construct a new set of languages, strategies, and spaces that works against both heritages.

These histories and distinct contexts suggest an argument in favor of grounded feminist political theory (see also Hanson 1992; Staeheli and Martin 2000; Nagar et al. 2002). Such a position posits that there can be no truest representation or articulation of feminist political theory or the feminist subject, for truth implies a sense of disciplinarity and, ultimately, exclusion. As Mouffe (1992, 329) argued,

> We must be aware of the fact that . . . feminist goals can be constructed in many different ways, according to the multiplicity of discourses in which they can be framed: Marxist, liberal, conservative, radical-separatist, radical-democratic, and so on. There are, therefore, by necessity many feminisms and any attempt to find the "true" form of feminist politics should be abandoned.

In this light, feminist political theory is about constructing diverse tools and ideas that advance feminist movement. Collins (1998) had a similar perspective:

> No social theory is inherently dominant or oppositional—these categories gain meaning only in relationship to one another. The oppositional nature of any social theory lies not within the essence of its constructs, paradigms, or epistemology. Instead, the types of socially constructed relations it has with other social theories—themselves representing varying patterns of dominance and opposition to yet other discourses, all changing through time—frame its oppositional practice.

Thus, the point of feminist political theory is not to get the answer right in an abstract sense but rather to produce "representational experiments" (Massey 2001) or a combination of discourses, practices, and strategies that are relevant to and useful for feminist movements. As feminist political theory moves between ideas, experience, and politics, it should work against "seamlessly mapping" (Ramamurthy 2000, 243) one interpretation of a particular context-agent nexus onto another place. Rather, conversations can be held across those contexts. Such an argument does not imply localized relativism; it is also important to recognize there are long-standing, large-scale patterns and structures that operate in relationship to the nation-state and that cross borders. Mohanty (2002, 501) recently argued, while reflecting back on her pathbreaking article "Under Western Eyes,"[3] that "cross-cultural feminist work must be attentive to the micropolitics of context, subjectivity, and struggle, as well as to the macropolitics of global economic and political systems and processes."

The process of grounding feminist political theory is both complicated and enriched by the ongoing spatialization of feminist and critical theory. As many have noted, feminist theory and cultural studies more generally have become saturated with spatial metaphors (e.g., borders, mapping, position, traveling, transnationalism, diaspora, displacement) (Smith and Katz 1993; S. Friedman 1998). Such metaphors reflect a variety of processes. First, they reflect the desire for the construction of knowledge from social positions and social groups that have systematically been excluded (groups that literally have been displaced or that are on the margins of centers). Second, such spatial metaphors help to enact the feminist epistemologies articulated by Sandra Harding and Donna Haraway, which insist that knowledge is partial, situated, and marked by its origins (Rose 1997). In this perspective, political and knowledge claims should be located and contextualized. Third, the plethora of spatial metaphors reflects the hold globalization has claimed on popular and academic imaginations. Taken together, such processes have transformed our geographical imaginations in ways that can be vertiginous. Feminist political geographers can provide important interventions in order to understand the complex relationship between metaphor and materiality in the process of making worlds (see collection edited by Aiken et al. 1998).

To illustrate the role feminist political geographers can play, I now turn to certain analytics feminist geographers have provided for reading globalization and politics. In an era of globalization, the spatiality of politics has become more evident. Yet, as I suggested previously, such spatiality can have a metaphorical aspect as well as a material aspect. This terrain of metaphor and materiality can be exceedingly complex. As some have indicated, marginal locations do not always indicate processes of exclusion (Liu 1998; see also K. Mitchell 1997a for critical readings of hybridity and diaspora). This demonstrates the need to move between metaphor and materiality when locating gendered subjects and articulating feminist politics. Some of the concerns of feminist political geography provide important entries into such an agenda. They provide ways of beginning to unravel the transformed set of gendered social and political relationships shaped by the ongoing process of globalization.

I begin with Doreen Massey's now-classic notion of a "power-geometry" as a way of critically reading globalization and the spatialization of politics:

> Now, I want to make a simple point here, and that is about what one might call the *power-geometry* of it all; the power-geometry of time-space compression. For different social groups and different individuals are placed in very distinct ways in relation to those flows and interconnections. The point concerns not merely the issue of who moves and who doesn't, although that is one element of it; it is also about power in relation to the flows and the movement. Distinct social groups have distinct relationships to this anyway-differentiated mobility; some are more in charge than others; some initiate flows and movement, others don't; some are more on the receiving end of it than others; some are effectively imprisoned by it. (Massey 1993, 61)

Here, Massey suggested that complex geographies of power are constructed in relationship to the processes associated with globalization. A power-geometry implies that what is important is not just one's location within a set of spatial relationships but also one's ability to control or construct the sites, flows, scales, and spaces that comprise that geometry. Such geometries are political and related to economic, political, and cultural relations. They may refer to a politics of mobility, a politics of scale, or the process through which particular places are constructed. Such geometries shape and are shaped by multiple, differentiated, and unequal subjectivities. Feminist political geography can help uncover these geometries and thus provide a helpful analytic for feminist politics under conditions of globalization, as a way of critically reading metaphorical and material spaces to advance feminist movements.

More recent work by feminist geographers that resonates with Massey's notion of a power-geometry include Hyndman (2000) and Katz (2001), which I address in turn. Hyndman (2000) examined the distinct sites, flows, and bodies associated with refugees and humanitarian aid in the Horn of Africa, particularly in relationship to Somali peoples. In what might be considered a continually transforming power-geometry, she described how the political and geographic positions of Somalis have shifted from the colonial period onward. In relationship to a changing set of geopolitical circumstances, practices of Somali marginalization and containment have also continually shifted. These practices of containment are associated with distinct geographies, which range from colonial buffer zones, to the drawing of national boundaries, to the construction of refugee camps. Hyndman reformulated, furthermore, Massey's notion of a power-geometry, through the concept of a "geopolitics of mobility" (also see Hyndman 2004 [this volume]). In evaluating the circumstances of displaced Somalis, she illustrated that certain things flow more easily over borders than do others (humanitarian aid, for example, as opposed to refugees). In this sense, spatial processes, including mobility, serve as a conduit for constructing and reinscribing social, cultural, and political hierarchies at a variety of scales.

In another example, Katz (2001) introduced the notion of a "topography of globalization" to highlight how processes related to globalization restructure the landscape of places, including gendered social relationships within those places. To make this argument, she described three particular "traces of globalization" (Katz 2001, 1219) in a central Sudanese village she calls Howa. These traces include economic restructuring associated with development; a local "time-space" expansion, in which economic stresses have caused the geographic space and length of time dedicated to agricultural and economic activities to expand; and the effects of ongoing civil war linked to religious conflict, colonial legacies, and natural resources. Each of these traces can be linked, furthermore, to shifts and resistances around gendered roles and identities. In outlining this topography of globalization, Katz also presented the notion of a "countertopography" (Katz 2001, 1229). The global processes that shift the topography of particular places can be carefully traced to other locations in a manner that may produce the possibility of a grounded yet transnational feminist politics.

Conclusion

As I began to outline in this chapter, feminist politics emerge in multiple forms in many places throughout the world and partially disrupt linear accounts of feminist thought and practice. Moreover, longer-standing histories and geographies work in complex tension with a contemporary spatialization of politics, which often emphasizes crossing borders in new ways. Yet no spatial metaphor or abstract location provides the avenue for constructing contemporary feminist politics. Instead, contemporary feminist politics should work through the complex interweaving of spatial metaphors and materiality in a way that is attentive to distinct historical contexts and global processes, which together construct new webs of power. Such navigation also requires, nonetheless, historical anchors that would enable a means for reaching back toward and retaining a historical memory of the struggles of feminism, whatever their provenance.

Notes

1. Derrida (1978) provided the concept of logocentrism to describe binaries that structure Western thinking, such as West-East, North-South, male-female. A hierarchical order underpins such binaries, in which the first is seen as the original, in no need of explanation, whereas the second is understood as derivative of the first (Manzo 1991).
2. This older word is also the term used to describe contemporary non-Chinese feminism.
3. "Under Western Eyes" was first published in 1986.

3
Mapping Feminisms and Difference

RICHA NAGAR

"Difference," "intersectionality," and, more recently, "transnational feminist politics" have emerged as some of the most crucial and politically vexing themes in feminist theorizing over the past two decades (Grewal and Kaplan 1994; Crenshaw 1991; Rose 1993). How have these conversations shaped feminist engagements with difference in geography? In this chapter I elaborate on the ways in which feminist geographers have deployed concepts such as "situated difference," "grounded knowledges," and "spatialized politics" to produce rich analytical frameworks that explore the material and symbolic constructions of identity, power, and difference in space and place. At the same time, I argue that the grounds of these feminist interventions have remained predominantly northern (based in the United States, Canada, and United Kingdom, for example), with a result that some of the critical aspects that define the politics of difference in "other" worlds have found limited space in feminist geographies of difference. To ground this discussion, I focus the bulk of the chapter on a historically and geographically specific example: the debate over the institution of *mut'a* in Tanzania.

Locating Difference

"Politics of location"—a term first coined by Adrienne Rich in the early 1980s—is labeled by some "as a particularly North American feminist articulation of difference" that insists on interrogating and deconstructing the position, identity, and privilege of whiteness (Kaplan 1994, 139). This concept arose from more than a decade of struggles over definitions and meanings of feminism in a context marked by intense racism and homophobia in the U.S. women's movement and in academic feminist discourses. The painful splits created by these struggles forced the white feminist mainstream to turn its attention away from assertions of similarity and homogeneity to examinations of difference—"an uneven, divisive, and slow process of shifts" that remains incomplete in both theoretical and political terms (Kaplan 1994, 140).

In feminist theory, these processes translated into critiques of universalism and the unified subject, the destabilization of the category "woman," and the idea of situated and partial knowledges (Haraway 1988).[1] At the same time, Third World and U.S. multiracial feminists continued to shake the epistemological ground on which Eurocentric feminist critique was raised and to erase the silences about the gulfs that divide women on the basis of race, class, and national positioning in the global relations between "sovereign" nation-states (Mohanty et al. 1991; Mufti/Shohat 1997). In dismantling such universalizing and homogenizing categories as woman, nation, race, and class, these discussions mounted significant challenges to mainstream feminist articulations that posited intrinsically conflictual male-female relations and prioritized their operations in the realm of family and sexuality while rigidly conceptualizing the meanings of public-private (Eschle 2001, 125–26). They also underscored the significance of geographic territories and borders by focusing on the material and symbolic struggles of indigenous and diasporic populations whose marginalization and dispersal necessitate the critical scrutiny of insider-outsider categories and notions of belonging (Anzaldua 1990). At the same time, they recognized that "the highly hybrid nature of diverse colonial, neocolonial and postcolonial displacements and diasporas, must be historicized and contextualized, spoken about from, within, and in relation to specific locations" (Mufti/Shohat 1997, 6). Alive to the need for a true coalition politics, these scholars sought "to point the way toward oppositional practices and alternative epistemologies and institutional strategies necessary for a diversified feminist empowerment" (Mufti/Shohat 1997, 6).

Feminisms, Difference, and Geography

For feminist geographers, the developments of the 1980s translated into a commitment to understanding how empowerment, oppression, and exclusion operate through regimes of difference and the ways in which space and place are implicated and imbricated in the structural processes and everyday practices that (re)constitute both marginality and difference. They drew, for example, from I. M. Young (1990, 41–42), whose "plural explication of the concept of oppression" dismantled essentialist definitions of oppression and viewed oppression as a consequence of complexly structured regimes of difference that are systematically reproduced in major political, economic, and cultural institutions. I. M. Young (1990, 157) challenged the assimilationist ideal of justice that emphasized the need to transcend group difference, arguing instead for an "egalitarian politics of difference" that recognized difference as fluid and relational. These new understandings led feminist geographers to chart more nuanced, uneven geographies with a heightened sensitivity to the manner in which sociospatial specificities transform structures of power and privilege and to the ways that oppressed groups enact resistance, subversion, and change through the politics of place and identity (Fincher and Jacobs 1998; J. P. Jones, Nast, and Roberts 1997). Reconceptualizing the political in this manner entailed a deliberate collapsing of the traditional divide between "cultural" and "political economy" perspectives while also reinforcing the idea that justice must be built around both redistribution and recognition of difference (Fraser 1995).

The reconceptualization of difference in and across spaces, times, and scales was enhanced further by analyses that highlighted the significant conjunctures between women's roles, their life course, and the production of space (Katz and Monk 1993). These scholars underscored how—far from being structures set in place—international, state, and corporate policies and practices are actively deployed locally and regionally by historical agents in their everyday lives. It is through this interpenetration that structures and practices of the social relations of production and reproduction are maintained, subverted, and reconstituted. At different scales and in vastly different settings, redefined patterns of social relations may lead to and be sustained by new spatial forms; women's agency is critical in negotiating and altering these articulations within and against historically and geographically specific cultural constraints (Katz and Monk 1993, 276–77).

At the same time, reiterations of the trinity of class, gender, and race sparked criticisms in several quarters for their lack of engagement with questions of ableism and heterosexism (see, e.g., Valentine 1993; Chouinard and Grant 1995). Other scholars similarly raised concerns about analyses that treated religion, caste, and ethnicity as fixed—and often, exoticized—"cultural" markers, rather than as dynamic and politicized discursive practices existing in mutually constitutive relationships with gendered, class-based, and racialized subjectivities (Kong 2001; Nagar 1998). Although motivated by different kinds of political agendas and intellectual investments, these critiques can be viewed as part of a new wave of feminist geographical analysis that committed itself to more nuanced explorations of sexuality, space, and gendered mobility. Among the common, overarching themes that surface in this scholarship are embodied geographies, negotiated difference, and struggles over heteropatriachal norms (Dwyer 1999; Podmore 2001).

This body of work interrogates sociospatial practices and choices surrounding dress and veiling, for instance, and reveals how "different, spatially realized sets of hegemonic rules and norms" regarding women's bodies are "themselves produced by specific constellations of power" and result in different degrees of formality, enforcement, stability, and contestation (Secor 2002, 9). It also attends to the ways that specific nexus of racial and class-based oppressions reinforce group identity and the manner in which femininity becomes both a tool and a source of women's disempowerment in constructions of racial and cultural homogeneity at the margins (Mohammad 1999). Finally, these writings underscore the need to challenge easy assumptions regarding correlations between the (in)visibility of certain bodies in specific spaces and the articulation of gendered and sexualized subjectivities (Podmore 2001).

These contributions have undoubtedly enriched feminist geography and played a vital role in creating new theoretical and methodological spaces from which to reconceptualize and advance the politics and spaces of difference. At the same time, however, with a few noticeable exceptions (Silvey 2000a, 2000b; Oza 2001; Secor 2002), the bulk of this work hinges on experiential or theoretical frameworks that are firmly rooted in North American and European contexts. For example, the subject of Muslim women and veiling became an analytical focal point in geography as the question of Islam and femininity became contentious in the United States, Canada, United Kingdom, and Germany. But this interest in women's bodies and the politics and praxis of the *hijaab* (veil) did not spark a broader interest in exploring or theorizing the diverse articulations of politicized religion, heteronormativity, patriarchy, and privilege in locations outside North America and Europe. This limitation, I would argue, has undermined our ability as feminist geographers to develop sophisticated analytical tools that can engage with the nuances of "difference" in ways that are transnational in scope and in sociopolitical relevance. It has, furthermore, compromised our ability to make geography relevant to feminist conversations on critical topics such as women's participation in right wing political projects of Third World states, the struggles of poor and rural lesbians for identity and survival in the South, and the relationship between the reinvention of heteropatriarchy and gendered labor practices in the context of globalization (Basu 1995; Swarr and Nagar 2004; Afshar and Barrientos 1999; Afsaruddin 1999).

To illustrate and build on these points, I analyze in the rest of this chapter a religious controversy that took place in the city of Dar-es-Salaam in postcolonial Tanzania. By delving into the themes of difference, domination, resistance, and nested geographical scales in a contextually grounded manner, I show how insights from feminist geography, multiracial feminisms, and postcolonial theory can be integrated to extend ongoing discussions of difference, heterosexuality, and postcoloniality and to produce feminist analyses that are transnational in their aims and scope.

Grounding Difference: The Controversy over *Mut'a*

Mut'a, or temporary marriage, is a contract between a married or unmarried man and an unmarried, divorced, or widowed woman that is religiously sanctioned by Shia (Shi'ite) Islam. In the early 1990s *mut'a* became the focal point of an intense debate in Dar-es-Salaam among the Khoja Shia Ithnasheri Muslims, one of the most populous and prosperous South Asian (hereafter, Asian) minority groups in Tanzania. Although people participating in this controversy were Ithnasheri men and women from predominantly middle- and upper-class backgrounds, the debate involved complex differences and hierarchies based on gender, religion, race, and class that are deeply rooted in the sociopolitical realities of Tanzania.

Here I summarize this debate not to examine the institution of *mut'a* itself but to provide a glimpse of how processes at local, national, and transnational scales intersect to define the (hetero)sexist communal norms that regulate women's bodies in a particular context; the ways in which women confront, defend, or negotiate the terms of this regulation; and the implications of this regulation for women of different backgrounds in a place where gender hierarchies are enmeshed with religious, racial, and class-based distinctions.[2] In focusing on these issues, my purpose is neither to exoticize a Muslim community nor to play on the extremely problematic dominant images of women oppressed by Islam. My goal, rather, is to highlight how (re)construction of religious difference among the Ithnasheris has entailed a deployment of gendered, raced, and class-based inequalities.

Zinn and Dill (1996) observed that despite their efforts to contextualize gender in terms of races, classes, and cultures, mainstream feminist thinkers have frequently tended to reduce difference to mere pluralism. To counter this tendency, they argue for a multiracial feminism that considers race and class differences not as individual characteristics but as "primary organizing principles of a society which locates and positions groups within that society's opportunity structures" (Zinn and Dill 1996, 323). Attending to questions of power means understanding how differences and domination intersect; how those intersections are historically, socially, and structurally constituted; and how privilege and subordination are interrelated.

These interconnections between domination and difference, privilege, and marginalization must be grounded in the particular configurations of structural inequalities that exist in each specific historical and geographical context. Some axes of difference, for example, religion, sect, or caste, that serve as the chief organizing principles in one social setting might be immaterial, absent, or quite differently interwoven in another. The following discussion of *mut'a* reveals how religion, a category that is not always salient in many Western contexts, can profoundly reinforce and complicate racial and class-based distinctions and provide one of the main nodes around which heterosexual relations and everyday gender politics are played out. The regulated and mediated nature of sexual boundaries in a community, then, must be understood in relation to how that community negotiates its socioeconomic and spatial boundaries vis-à-vis other social groups in the specific context within which it is situated.

But the story of *mut'a* also demonstrates that focusing on the place-based context does not mean simply talking about the local. "The social relations which constitute a locality," noted Massey (1992, 7), "increasingly stretch beyond its borders; less and less of these relations are contained within the place itself." Like a locality, the gendered configurations of a community also are formed out of the simultaneous convergence and coexistence of a particular set of social interrelations at varying geographical scales, "from the intimacy of the household to the wide space of transglobal connections" (Massey 1992, 12). These intersections, frequently shaped by colonial pasts and neocolonial and imperialist presents, define the socially (and spatially) differentiated "geopolitics of cultural exchange" (Shohat 1996, 321).

Mut'a in Dar-es-Salaam

In Shia doctrine *mut'a* is sanctioned along with *nikah* or permanent marriage; the objective of *mut'a* is sexual enjoyment, whereas that of *nikah* is procreation. In a *mut'a* contract witnesses are not required, and the marriage need not be registered, but the duration of the marriage and the bride price must be specified. The period of *mut'a* can be as long or short as the partners wish. Despite the apparent resemblance between *mut'a* and prostitution, they are ideologically different on the grounds that children born of *mut'a* unions are considered legitimate and theoretically have equal status with siblings born of permanent marriages (Haeri 1989, 2).[3]

The popularization of *mut'a* among Asian Ithnasheri men in Dar-es-Salaam occurred as part of the religious revival and growing identification with Shi'ite Iran in the 1980s. Religious publications and preachers from overseas stressed its relevance to modern Shi'ite societies "as an Islamic substitute for the 'decadent' western style of 'free' [heterosexual] relations" (Haeri 1989, 8). In Dar-es-Salaam, where Muslims are predominantly Sunni, the diffusion of *mut'a* translated into a predominantly racialized and class-based practice in which racially mixed Sunni Muslim women from relatively poor backgrounds secretly opted for *mut'a* unions with wealthy Ithnasheri men in exchange for generous payments.[4] Many Ithnasheri women were enraged by the frequency of such unions and the prominence that *mut'a* acquired as a topic of discussion in religious gatherings. Despite its active promotion in public religious places, however, opposition to *mut'a* arose mainly in the form of women's passionate arguments inside their own homes.

Two central factors served to restrict the debate over *mut'a* to the domestic spaces. The first concerned the status of the Asian Ithnasheris as not only a relatively privileged racial minority but also a religious minority in predominantly Christian and Sunni Muslim Tanzania. Although Shi'ites and Sunnis share two primary sources of Islamic law (the Holy Qur'an and the Traditions of the Prophet Mohammad), the two sects have emerged with different, though overlapping, corpuses of authenticated traditions, the *hadiths*. Sunnis do not accept the *hadith* that allows *mut'a,* and they often consider it fornication (Haeri 1989, 4, 20, 30). Given this context, many Ithnasheri women feel somewhat defensive and reluctant to voice their views against *mut'a* in public, not wanting African or Arab Sunnis to condemn it as rationalization for prostitution.

Second, public debate on *mut'a* within the community was contained through a combination of social control and religious legitimation. A number of discursive and material processes at different geographic scales came together to define the structures that shaped the *mut'a* controversy and the discourses that swirled around it. These processes included the intersections of race and class divisions in Tanzania, the growth of Ithnasheri organizations transnationally, and the diffusion of specific gendered ideologies among the local Ithnasheris. To address these processes, I present in the remainder of this chapter two main sections, each highlighting how nested hierarchical scales (N. Smith 1992a) interacted to shape these multilayered politics of difference. In the first section I sketch Tanzania's political economy to identify processes that constituted the Ithnasheri community in relation to other Asian groups and the African majority. I discuss the ways that the material privileges of Tanzanian Asians vis-à-vis the African majority translated into gendered policing of (hetero)sexual, racial, and communal frontiers, and then I consider how gender politics among the Ithnasheris in the early 1990s were shaped by intersecting processes at all scales. In the second section I center on the debate over *mut'a* and how it enables us to consider, in rich and nuanced ways, the relationship between heterosexist policing of communal frontiers and the negotiated construction of racial, religious, and class differences.

Contextualizing *Mut'a*

Race and Class in Colonial and Postcolonial Tanzania

The Ithnasheris were among the earliest groups from northwestern India to settle in East Africa. Although the first settlers from the Indian subcontinent came long before European colonization, most Asians migrated to Tanganyika and Zanzibar during the British colonial period (1918–61). The British established a tripartite racial pyramid in Tanganyika in which Asians (who never formed more than 0.7 percent of the population) occupied the middle tier of the socioeconomic hierarchy, with a few Europeans (0.25 percent of the total) at the top and the vast majority of Africans (98 percent of the total) at the bottom.[5] This overlap between race and class hierarchies under the colonial system involved residential segregation as well as economic and social privileges for Asians, who dominated commerce, trade, transportation, civil services, and construction and who enjoyed considerably higher salaries and better educational and health facilities than Africans did.

After Tanganyika's independence (1961), this racialized hierarchy came under attack. The adoption of socialist policies in Tanzania between 1967 and 1976 resulted in the nationalization of many Asian-owned enterprises and buildings. Marketing cooperatives replaced the notorious presence of Asian middlemen in smaller towns of the countryside. As a result of these developments, 50,000 Asians, more than half of whom held British passports, emigrated to the United Kingdom and Canada during the 1970s.

But the socialist government could displace neither Tanzania nor Asians from their positions in neocolonial political economic structures. In the mid-1980s, the economic climate became overtly favorable for Asian businesses when Tanzania entered the trade liberalization period. But with the rise of multiparty politics in the 1990s, popular antagonism against the Asians resurfaced, along with a demand for the transfer of economic power to "indigenous" Tanzanians.

Although class differences within the Asian and African groups have never been insignificant, Asians (forming approximately 0.3 percent of Tanzania's population in 1991) still dominate the commercial sector and enjoy higher economic status than the vast majority of Africans. Within the Asian communities, discourses of Asians' cultural and moral superiority over Africans play a critical role in legitimizing Asian racism and economic status. Although Asian or African women appear only indirectly in most discussions of British imperialism and Asian capitalism, gender and sexuality have been pivotal in shaping the discourses that perpetuate existing racial hierarchies and prejudices.

The Policing and Crossing of Gendered Communal Frontiers

[Asians] accept it when men have affairs. But they think that . . . [for women] sex is just a duty to procreate. . . . A lot of Asian men here have . . . a "respectable" wife who is Asian—the visible wife. And then there is always an invisible [African] wife. . . . The Asian wife is not supposed to satisfy you in bed, so you go for the African woman. It is a myth here that they are all very good in bed. (Interview, Farida Jaffer, an Ithnasheri journalist, 26 January 1993)

The heteronormative gendered boundaries of Asian communities in Tanzania constitute an all-too-familiar racialized double standard. Asian women who are sexual with men outside their ethnic group (particularly Africans and Arabs) are marginalized and constructed as betrayers. By contrast, Asian men's communal affiliation is not threatened by sexual relations with women from outside. Asian men's right to seek heterosexual pleasure beyond the border is premised on the denial of sexual activity to Asian women outside marriage. This denial plays a crucial role in the maintenance of an ideology of community distinctness and racial, moral, and religious purity.

Asian communal discourses often construct the African, Arab, and *chautara* women as sexualized objects. In the context of coastal Tanzania, the term "Arab" connotes a racially mixed heritage and a Sunni Muslim religious affiliation. The terms *chautara*, "half caste," and "mixed blood," in contrast, are used interchangeably by Tanzanian Asians to refer to racially mixed people irrespective of religious background. Arab and *chautara* are seen as neither Asian nor African—they are between the two. African, Arab, and *chautara* women are all regarded by Asians as more promiscuous than Asian women, but the Arab or *chautara* woman is also constructed as more exotic and desirable than the African woman. Indeed, many Asian men believe that Arab and *chautara* women can provide them "with the best kind of sexual enjoyment you can ever get"—the kind of pleasure that an "Indian woman is simply incapable of giving you." Asian men frequently defend their sexual relationships with African, Arab, and racially mixed women on the grounds that they are the "normal and natural" result of an undeniable male need, a need that "respectable" Asian women often are unable to fulfill because they are "too conservative and sheltered" (interviews, D'Souza, 20 October 1992; Rathod, 23 January 1993). In contrast, the African man is denied access to the

Asian woman's body. Asians of all classes and communities generally perceive the African man as socially inferior, sexually "primitive," and "someone to be careful of" because he threatens the honor of "our women, . . . our family, and community" (interview, Othmans, 1 July 1991).

Thus, the colonial and neocolonial racial and class hierarchies can be fully understood only when we examine how racial and gendered politics operate in the context of everyday regulation of Asian communal boundaries. Although religious differences are critical in defining social lives of Asian people, it is the oppositional construction of Asian women as virtuous and of African and racially mixed women as promiscuous and sexually available that underpins the gendered policing of the communal frontiers.

Ithnasheri Communal Organizations and Gender Politics in Dar-es-Salaam

In 1991–93 the 40,000 Asians living in Dar-es-Salaam constituted 2.9 percent of the city's total population of 1.4 million. The Ithnasheri community (whose members grew from 1,700 in 1961 to approximately 7,500 in 1991) formed one of the three largest and most affluent Asian communities.[6] Although they were clustered together in one residential area, the communal affairs of all the Asian groups were mutually independent. In the Ithnasheri community, all the religious and social affairs were organized through a body called the Jamaat.

Three sets of processes at the local, national, and transnational scales enmeshed to configure Ithnasheri communal politics in Dar-es-Salaam: the socioeconomic changes taking place in postindependence Tanzania, the growth of global communal networks among the Ithnasheris, and the Iranian Revolution. These sociospatial processes intersected in complex ways to vastly increase the power of the Dar-es-Salaam Jamaat over the lives of local Ithnasheris and to invigorate the religious beliefs of the community, creating both an interest in *mut'a* among men and a feminist Islamic consciousness among women. These intersecting processes fed off each other to shape the social milieu in which the debate over *mut'a* took place.

Until the mid-1940s the Dar-es-Salaam Jamaat operated with little contact with other Jamaats. By the mid-1960s, however, this Jamaat became the main religious and social center of Ithnasheris in Tanzania and also the most influential Jamaat in Africa. Locally, its power was enhanced in the 1960s by the in-migration of more than 4,000 Ithnasheris from Zanzibar and the upcountry as well as through its acquisition of new trust properties. In the 1970s the secular government of Tanzania granted statutory authority to communal associations to manage the religious and social affairs of their communities, thereby creating a vast space for male Ithnasheri religious leaders to interpret, clarify, and formalize Islamic law in explicitly gendered terms. The Jamaat became the national representative of all Ithnasheris to the government and assumed the responsibilities for providing religious instruction, regulating marriages and divorces, and determining inheritance. It provided social services, including burial, education, housing, welfare, marriage reconciliation, and religious instruction. To counter African politicians' criticisms that Asian religious associations were racially exclusive, Ithnasheri leaders also began to proselytize Africans through the Bilal Muslim Mission.[7] However, they took pains to minimize intermingling between African Ithnasheri men and Asian Ithnasheri women.

In the 1970s the emigration of more than 1,500 Ithnasheri families from East Africa to the United Kingdom and Canada led to the formation of the World Federation of the Khoja Shia Ithnasheris. This expansion of transnational religious networks coincided with the rise of Ayatollah Khomeini in Iran, who came to be revered among the Ithnasheris as a selfless, devoted son of Islam who rekindled the religious fervor among the world's Muslims and restored their faith in the practicality and superiority of Islam. With this new consciousness, Dar-es-Salaam's male Ithnasheri leaders emphasized how Islam covered the personal, familial, social, and commercial aspects of people's lives and young men became very involved in the community's activities.

Among the women, the profound impact of the Iranian Revolution was visibly manifested in the adoption of *hijaab* (veil). Inspired by the religious revival, as well as by the swelling number of Ithnasheri women in Dar-es-Salaam, the Ladies Management Committee of the Jamaat started inviting influential female preachers from overseas to women's religious gatherings (*Majalises*), especially during Moharram, the month of mourning for the Shi'ites. And when Zakira Hamida Abbasi from India preached in the *Majalises* during the Moharram of 1982, more than six hundred women embraced the *hijaab* within a week. Although not all women chose the *hijaab*, it became the strongest symbol of Islamic and Shia identities for most Ithnasheri women.

This rise of religious consciousness among the local Ithnasheris was greatly aided by economic reforms and trade liberalization at the national level. After the government adopted free market policies in the mid-1980s, Ithnasheri men increasingly profited from export-import ventures, facilitated by strong business and religious connections with Ithnasheris in the West. As they prospered, they gave generous donations to the Jamaat, enabling the Jamaat to fund religious institutions, community publications, and influential religious preachers from abroad. At the same time, religious connections strengthened among Ithnasheri Jamaats internationally, spreading the ideas of the Iranian Revolution and the edicts (*fatwas*) of religious leaders from Iran and challenging Western notions about Islamic fundamentalism.[8] In Dar-es-Salaam these developments translated into an increasing social control by affluent businessmen over the lives of poor Ithnasheris, especially women. Poor women who did not want to wear the *hijaab* felt pressured to adopt it because they feared losing the financial and social support from the Jamaat.

In reinforcing the identities of women and men as Shi'ites and Muslims and in urging them to resist the pressures of Westernization, the Shia male leadership of both local and international organizations underscored the importance of *hijaab* and constructed women's "natural role" as keepers of home and family. But this increasing regulation of gendered bodies and sexualities during the 1980s was simultaneously marked by the emergence of a new feminist Islamic consciousness among women, which led upper-class women to demand greater participation in communal affairs and direct representation in the Jamaat. Although male leaders often ignored such demands, they failed to contain the growing discontent among some women who felt that it was "not only high time" but also "Islamic" that educated and intellectual women should have a central voice in the decision-making processes of the community (interviews, Abbas, 21 July 1993; Dewji, 7 February 1993). This emerging consciousness among women, however, was firmly rooted in their own class position and emphasized the need for a greater representation of women without addressing issues either of racial or of class inequalities among Ithnasheri women or the overarching structure of Ithnasheri communal organizations. This limited awareness of race and class differences played an important role in shaping the contours of the debate over *mut'a*, as I reveal in the subsequent section.

The Debate over *Mut'a*

Although religiously sanctioned among Shi'ites, the practice of *mut'a* was highly restricted and most Shi'ites were either vaguely informed or ambivalent about it before the Islamic Revolution. After 1979, however, Haeri (1989, 7) reported that the Islamic regime in Iran launched a campaign "to educate the public of the specifics of the institution, its divine roots, its contemporary relevance, emphasizing its positive effects for the individual and social moral health."

It is not surprising, then, that like the diffusion of the *hijaab*, the promotion of *mut'a* in Dar-es-Salaam's Ithnasheri community occurred at a time when the influence of Iranian religious leaders was at its peak. The fervor of religious revival combined with the social control of the Jamaat over women, especially the poor ones, in ways that made it impossible for most women to openly question *mut'a*. Jamila Jaffer noted,

> A lot of well-off Ithnasheri men are doing it and their homes have become battle-fields. But where can their wives go with their complaints? The religious leaders themselves say that it's okay to have two *mut'as* at the same time as you have a wife at home! (Interview, 31 July 1993)

Working-class women such as Jamila felt that they could not publicly oppose *mut'a* because of their dependence on important men in the Jamaat. A similar fear was echoed by Rukhsana Banu, who lived in the Jamaat-run house for destitute widows. Rukhsana (interview, 29 November 1992) felt that as someone who was "forced to live on Jamaat's charity," it was best for her to not voice her opinion about *mut'a*.

According to a local female preacher, the gendered logic underlying *mut'a* is that men are naturally polygamous and heterosexual. They like women naturally and instinctively and they cannot control their sexual urges. Women, in contrast, are seen as having self-control; if a woman cannot control her sexual desires, she is thought to be "suffering from a problem" (interview, Dewji, 7 February 1993). Another female religious scholar emphasized men's role as protectors of women. *Mut'a* is regarded as good for widowed and divorced women because temporary marriage can allow such women to gain a social position in a society that otherwise marginalizes them (interview, Abbas, 21 July 1993).

Upper- and middle-class women frequently accepted that logic and agreed that *mut'a* allowed men to take care of their sexual cravings without committing adultery. Waheeda Lalji, who comes from a renowned scholarly family, commented,

> These days only rich men are doing *mut'a* and they are expected to take care of their responsibilities for the *mut'ai* wife and children, but they don't. They are doing *mut'a* just for their own pleasure. But at least it is not adultery because it has been allowed in the *hadiths.* (Interview, 31 July 1993)

Thus, prominent upper-class women who were considered as female role models by the male leaders publicly supported *mut'a* because it was religiously prescribed. For example, Tahira Abbas, one of key women pushing for a greater representation of women in the Jamaat, said, "It is allowed in Islam, so we can't complain. . . . [Women] become very emotional and possessive when it comes to *mut'a*. They shouldn't." She also pointed out, "If a man's wife is disabled for some reason, he doesn't have to suffer because he can do *mut'a*" (interview, 21 July 1993). Thus, *mut'a* enables a man to protect his "permanent" wife and provide for her even if she is unable to give him the sexual pleasures that he requires. And not only that, he simultaneously does a favor to his temporary wife by giving her financial support, "security, and the bliss of marital life" (interview, Raza, 15 January 1993).

The only people who verbalized their disapproval were a few divorced women who did not depend on the Jamaat for their economic or social survival and who were already dismissed by the community leaders because of their defiant attitudes, including their failure to embrace the *hijaab*. These women were incensed by the suggestion that *mut'a* could grant them a social status that they would not otherwise have. For example, Nargis Alam, an upper-class woman who emigrated to London in the early 1970s, returned to Dar-es-Salaam as a divorcée in the 1990s to fight a property dispute with some powerful male relatives on behalf of her father. Alam defiantly opposed *mut'a*:

> The community leaders hate my guts. . . . Most Ithnasheris assume that because I don't have a man in my life, I have no social standing and I must be dying to do *mut'a* with some rich man. That's ridiculous. . . . We [divorced women] do not need men to give us any social status by making us sex objects. No, thank you. I already have a position in my society. (Interview, 31 July 1993)

Farida Jaffer, a divorced feminist journalist who distanced herself from the Ithnasheri community, also opposed *mut'a*. She saw *mut'a* as prostitution legitimated by religion and observed that all the religious scholars who promoted *mut'a* were men who had reinterpreted religion to serve their own interests (interview, 26 January 1993). Similarly, Nargis argued that Shia leaders could choose which *hadiths* they wanted to promote: "Why have they picked up a *hadith* like this one? Just because it serves men's interests and gives them a green signal to have as many sexual partners as they want?" (interview, 31 July 1993). Both Nargis and Farida held that the historically specific circumstances that led to the religious sanctioning of this custom were no longer relevant.

Although public discussions of *mut'a* in communal spaces were not feasible in the light of the strong support that it received from male leaders, the home front was a different matter and several women openly expressed their feelings about *mut'a* with their husbands. For example, two middle-class women, Shahnaz Dewji and Tabassum Sultana, believed that men could claim that they were performing *mut'a* in a lawful way only if they could fulfill all their responsibilities toward their wives and families. Sultana said,

> My husband was joking that now he can do *mut'a* because it is *halal* (lawful). I said, "Look, it is only *halal* if you can simultaneously provide for your permanent wife in every way—economically, sexually, emotionally—and for your children. If you can't do that [according to one of the *hadiths*], I don't have to respect you. So, go ahead and do *mut'a,* but don't expect me to stick around with you later, and cook for you, and share your bed, and agree with you that it is *halal.* The day you do *mut'a,* I am out of this house. (Interview, 19 July 1993)

In a similar vein, Shahnaz Dewji compared men's hunger for food with that for sex: "My husband comes home to me when he is hungry. If he gets his food at home, why should he look for food outside? If you get *halal* at home, why go to hotels and look for something which only satisfies you momentarily even if the preachers say that it is okay?" (interview, 7 February 1993). Secure and confident in their *hijaab* and in their knowledge of Islam, both Shahnaz and Tabassum comfortably confronted their husbands on the issue of *mut'a* in their own domestic space and made it clear that irrespective of what the religious leaders said, they were not going to accept such relationships in their own households.

Such discussions between wives and husbands became so commonplace in Ithnasheri homes by 1993 that even without a communal public forum, women continuously questioned the relevance of *mut'a* in their own families. No longer did they ask their leaders whether *mut'a* was really Islamic or valid or advantageous for women. Rather, through informal discussions with each other and with men in their households, they communicated to the leaders that their main concern was with the publicization of *mut'a* as permissible and desirable. In this highly gendered arena of struggle, all Ithnasheri women came together to resist popularization of *mut'a*. Even those upper-class women who accepted *mut'a* as Islamic did not think it was a good idea to promote *mut'a*, especially among the youngsters.

The tension between women and men on the matter of publicizing *mut'a* was made worse by overseas preachers who contributed to the breaking of the implicit social restrictions that were earlier placed on the practice of *mut'a*. Women normally expected a man to seek his wife's permission before performing a *mut'a*. In 1992–93, however, both male and female preachers invited by the Jamaat repeatedly stressed that a man did not need his wife's permission unless the wife laid down a condition at the time of the *nikah* that her husband must seek her approval before performing *mut'a*. The increasing promotion of *mut'a* in this way angered Ithnasheri wives:

> [My friend] Shirin never talked about *mut'a* but yesterday [she was upset because] the *Muliyani* [female preacher] from Pakistan gave the *fatwa* that men can have *mut'a* without the wife's permission. . . . She also said that a man can have a wife and two other women as *mut'ai* wives at the same time. It is now an open license to men. . . . The younger men are rejoicing that they can have so many women without getting married. (Interview, Alam, 26 July 1993)

One instance of the gendered struggle around *mut'a* was the debate surrounding the publication of a book on *mut'a* that Mukhtar Raza, a divorced Ithnasheri religious scholar, coauthored with two male friends. In this book the authors examined the Qur'an and the *hadith* "and argued that in Islam *mut'a* is still there. . . . And then we gave out the rules—how to go about it. . . . We [stated] it clearly that a married man can go and do it" (Interview, 15 January 1993). The publication of this book was disallowed by the community leaders because they feared that it would upset Ithnasheri wives and result in marital discord. Mukhtar Raza felt that the community's attitudes toward the book reflected an unfortunate gap between what was preached and what was practiced:

> People said, "Don't publish it. . . . If somebody doesn't know about [*mut'a*], then for him ignorance is bliss. But if he's [told] that he is allowed [to do *mut'a*], after all, he is a man—he might be tempted. If he performs *mut'a* and the wife comes to know, there'll be discord in the home and we will end up with more cases of divorce." . . . [Later] another *Aleem* [religious scholar] started a discussion [on *mut'a*] . . . and somebody ran up to him and said, "Look, you'd better stop because you are striking a hornet's nest." . . . So, such are the social attitudes towards *mut'a*. . . . It is something that people would not like to talk about in public, but practice is quite different. Quite a number of [men] perform *mut'a*. A few do it openly . . . others do it on the sly—the wife wouldn't know, but we [leaders] would know and we wouldn't want to go tell the wife. (Interview, 15 January 1993)

Ithnasheri men often defended the publicity about *mut'a* on the grounds that telling men that they could perform *mut'as* was better than telling them that they can have four wives at home (interview, Ali, 31 July 1993). However, women commonly expressed, "Even if *mut'a* is allowed, the community should not have made this fact so public. Now everybody wants to do it. It is better not to broadcast such things if you want families to stay happy." Women saw *mut'a* as granting men license to seek sexual pleasures as, when, and from whomever they liked. As a result of the vehement opposition by women, including some local female preachers, few men disclosed their *mut'a* relationships to their wives or immediate families. This concealment was facilitated by the fact that men primarily formed such relationships with young women outside the Ithnasheri community.

In the context of discussions surrounding *mut'a*, only one Ithnasheri woman observed how *mut'a* translated into a racialized sexual exploitation in a context marked by a deeply entrenched racial and class-based hierarchy:

> You won't find a woman of means going into *mut'a* with a man of means. So [there is a] class difference and again it is about women's oppression. That's why I feel that it . . . is just an attempt to give [prostitution] a face of respectability and I find it very phony. . . . [I]t does not fit with the principles of Islam. . . . The girls who are caught in this are poor [Arab and *chautara*] girls. It is done in secrecy. And it's very exploitative. (Interview, Jaffer, 22 October 1992)

This is where the position of Ithnasheris as an economically privileged racial and religious minority imparted *mut'a* in Dar-es-Salaam a very different social character from *mut'a* in a place like Iran where Shi'ites are a majority. In both Iran and Tanzania, the likelihood of young and unmarried Shia women entering into *mut'a* contracts is quite small because although a woman who has been in a *mut'a* contract can do *nikah* in theory, the popular culture in both places still demands that a woman be a virgin at the time of her permanent marriage. In Iran, Haeri (1989) found that the greatest frequency of temporary marriages was among young divorced or widowed women of lower socioeconomic class, who were often poorly educated and economically needy and who felt marginalized in their families and communities. But Haeri challenged the assumption that women's primary motivation to enter into temporary marriages was financial. Although the financial arrangement provided temporary assistance to women in difficult economic circumstances, money was not the main impetus for most of these women's contracts. "Confused by the rhetoric of the religious leaders as to the absence of fundamental differences" between *mut'a* and *nikah*, "many women contracted a temporary marriage in the hope of being integrated into another family group" and shedding their social marginality (Haeri 1989, 50). *Mut'a* also provided "young divorced and widowed women with an opportunity to sidestep the limitations of the formal structure, to negotiate on their own behalf, to choose their own marital partner(s), and to exert greater control in the outcome of their lives" (Haeri 1989, 149).

In Dar-es-Salaam, however, the majority of women who contracted *mut'a* were not Ithnasheris. There were also no reported instances of *mut'a* between Asian and African Ithnasheris; whereas *mut'a* unions between Asian Ithnasheri men and African Ithnasheri women would risk seriously jeopardizing the efforts of the Bilal Mission, any possibility of such a union between African Ithnasheri men and Asian Ithnasheri women was foreclosed by the social and spatial segregation of the Asian and African Ithnasheris and by the simultaneously racist, classist, and sexist processes of boundary maintenance I described earlier. Because of the ambivalence and stigma associated with *mut'a* within the Asian Ithnasheri community, most of the women who entered into *mut'a* contracts with Ithnasheri men were young Sunni Arabs, among whom *mut'a* is not religiously prescribed. In effect, then, *mut'a* did become "legalized prostitution" because the religious sanctioning of *mut'a* only benefited the Ithnasheri men, and the Sunni women who entered the contract were still seen as immoral and irreligious. But this unevenness of religious prescriptions was not seen by most Ithnasheris as exploitative or problematic because of the image of a promiscuous Arab woman. Mukhtar Raza (interview, 15 January 1993) voiced the predominant stereotypes about the sexual availability and promiscuity of Arab women when he commented, "[Arabs] are not particularly strict, and they are not particularly worried [whether it is religiously sanctioned]. They [are usually women] looking for financial support ... or adventure, or gratification."

Thus, the particular locations that Ithnasheri women and men occupied within prevailing social structures and processes tended to limit the scope of the *mut'a* debate in spatial and topical terms. Spatially, the debate was largely played out in the domestic realm, whereas topically it shifted from the religious sanction of *mut'a* to its appropriateness in individual households. However, even as they challenged and resisted the gendered religious ideology of *mut'a*, most Ithnasheri women continued to reproduce the racial and class-based ideologies that reinforced the already existing social hierarchies in Tanzania and discouraged solidarity across racial lines. The story of *mut'a* in Dar-es-Salaam not only uncovers how Ithnasheri men and women of various economic backgrounds and marital statuses differently perceived, benefited, and suffered from *mut'a*, but it also reveals the intricate ways in which religious, racial, and class distinctions were created and maintained by *mut'a*.

Approaching Sexuality, Difference, and Postcoloniality: Lessons from the *Mut'a* Debate

The controversy surrounding *mut'a* in Dar-es-Salaam can be apprehended only by locating Ithnasheri communal politics in relation to the position of Asians as an economically privileged racial minority with a particular historical experience in Tanzania. The previous discussion highlights how the gendered policing of communal frontiers and the negotiated construction of racial, religious, and class differences intersect with a dynamic sociopolitical context at scales ranging from the body to the international.

The increasing peripheralization of Ithnasheri women in their community was facilitated by several mutually reinforcing processes: the rise in the power and influence of the local Jamaat, the growing prosperity of Ithnasheris in Tanzania, and the emergence of their global communal networks. At the same time, these developments also created a space for women to register their resistance and defiance within the same religious framework that marginalized them. The popularization, opposition, and practice of *mut'a* in Dar-es-Salaam were intimately linked with these intricate, and often contradictory, processes, which were further complicated by the racial and class divisions existing in the Tanzanian society.

What is critical to recognize about the *mut'a* debate is the way that its examination exposes a set of broader struggles and processes underway in postcolonial societies. Writers such as Shohat (1996) and Frankenberg and Mani (1996) provided powerful critiques of the term "postcolonial," its ahistorical and universalizing deployments, and its potentially depoliticizing implications. Their interrogation raises some important challenges for feminists studying contemporary Third World societies, most central of which is to resist the connotation that colonialism is now a matter of the past. Such resistance, as Shohat (1996, 326) argued, implies a need to negotiate "the relationship of difference and sameness, rupture and continuity." This analysis of *mut'a* in Dar-es-Salaam illustrates how attention to processes at multiple geographical scales allows us to understand the nuanced ways in which neocolonial relations of power and political-economic structures of domination and subordination combine to shape gendered politics of inequalities, difference, and resistance in a community.

I have argued in this chapter that in order to create alternatives to problematic universalisms, we must emphasize historically and geographically grounded specificities that are at once discursively and materially produced and negotiated. This analysis of the *mut'a* debate shows that one way to approach this goal is to examine how processes at multiple scales intersect and interlock with multiple structures and discursive practices of difference in particular places. Although much feminist work in (and outside) geography is committed to producing such analyses, the theoretical frameworks that are deployed in these discussions often are based on narrowly defined understandings of heteropatriarchy, racial privilege, religiousness, and sexuality. Interrogating these theoretical priorities and allowing them to shift in response to the sociopolitical imperatives of locations that might seem quite marginal from the "core" must constitute the first step toward imagining and enacting more radical transnational feminist politics of difference.

Acknowledgments

The analysis of *mut'a* I presented here is extracted from a more detailed article, "Religion, Race and the Debate over *Mut'a*," which first appeared in *Feminist Studies* 26, no. 3 (2000): 661–90. All names of interviewees used in the main text of this chapter are pseudonyms. I wish to express my warmest gratitude and appreciation to Katie Kosseff for her assistance with library research, to Lynn Staeheli for her engagement, and to David Faust for his extremely helpful comments on several versions of this chapter.

Notes

1. Haraway (1988, 589) defined situated and partial knowledges as "politics and epistemologies of location, positioning, and situating where partiality and not universality is the condition of being heard to make rational knowledge claims on people's lives."
2. The debate discussed here was confined to the Asian Ithnasheri community in Dar-es-Salaam. The African Ithnasheris did not participate in it.
3. Although theoretically it seems possible for "temporary" spouses (through *mut'a*) to become "permanent" spouses through *nikah*, such a phenomenon is rare in Dar-es-Salaam.
4. In Tanzania, Sunnis include Africans, Arabs, and Asians, and the term "Arab" is often employed to refer to people of mixed racial background. African Muslims and Arabs are predominantly Sunni (*CIA World Factbook*, retrieved 2 July 1999, from http://www.odci.gov/cia/publications/factbook). The stigma associated with women who contracted *mut'a* and the intense racial segregation in Dar-es-Salaam made it extremely difficult for me to interview women about their personal *mut'a* relationships, especially if they were not Ithnasheris. However, in my interviews with Ithnasheris and other Asians, at least eight racially mixed (Arab) Sunni women from poor backgrounds were named, all of whom had contracted *mut'a* multiple times as a way of supporting themselves or the children that they had from these unions, or both.
5. In 1970, shortly before the massive exodus of Asians from Tanzania, the total Tanzanian population was roughly 11.6 million, of which approximately 75,000 were Asians, 30,000 were Arabs, and 17,000 were Europeans; the remaining majority were Africans (The United Republic of Tanzania, *Statistical Abstract 1970* [Dar-es-Salaam: Government Printer, 1972], 52). However, these racialized categories overlooked the tremendous ethnic and regional differences within these three groups, and they also made little room for racially mixed people who did not easily fit classification.
6. Tanzania's estimated Asian population in 1993 was approximately 70,000. Although the Ithnasheri, Bohora, and Hindu communities expanded in numbers and developed strong community organizations in the postindependence period, Dar-es-Salaam's other Asian groups, including the Sikhs, the Goans, and the (Asian) Sunnis, suffered from dwindling sizes and weakened communal bodies.
7. *The Standard* (Daily), 15 December 1964; *Tanganyika Standard* (Daily), 21 November 1964; interviews, Muhsin Alidina, 15 January 1993; Abdul Sheriff (in Zanzibar), 23 September 1992. Proselytizing was also encouraged by an Iranian religious leader who visited Dar-es-Salaam in the early sixties. By 1993 there were approximately 1,200 African converts in Dar-es-Salaam.
8. Khoja Shia Ithnasheri Jamaat, *Biennial Report* (1988–89): 22; *Federation Samachar* (September 1989), (January 1990), and (March 1992); *Shia International* (Summer 1992) and (Autumn 1992). The community publications include *Knowledge*, *Pillar*, Jamaat reports; the Federation's newsletter, *Federation Samachar*; and a new journal called *Shia International* (published in Canada).

4

From Dualisms to Multiplicities: Gendered Political Practices

RUTH FINCHER

Everyday places like the domestic home, the playground, and the community center exhibit power relations that are differentiated and fractured by relations of gender, ethnicity, age, ability, and class. They are no different in this from the famously "big-P" political sites of public space, the parliament, the city council, and the large unionized workplace. Knowledge building in feminist geography has sought to extend understanding of how gender relations can be profoundly political in all these many contexts, limiting the options of some and benefiting others. Gendered practices occurring in these everyday places also can be politicizing, in providing a cause or identity around which activism and the exercise of effective citizenship can occur.

Feminist geographers have sought to show that sites, scales, and spheres of activity cannot themselves be separated into political and nonpolitical categories. The local, the domestic, and the private cannot be deemed "apolitical" and the national or international, the public sphere, and the world of paid work "political." There also has been questioning of the epistemological tradition leading to such categorizations, of distinguishing things using binaries or dualisms. Pile (1994, 255) wrote well on this issue in *Antipode*:

> Dualisms—at particular times and in particular places—are intended to mark and help police supposedly fixed, natural divisions between the powerful and the disempowered (as in the masculine versus the feminine), and . . . if we accept these dualisms then we collude in the reproduction of the power-ridden values they help to sustain.

But the difficulty, even impossibility, of avoiding categories altogether is also noted—Pile cited Penrose's earlier comment: "To some feminists, categories are by their very nature antithetical to the diversity that feminism seeks to encourage. In general, though, we have recognized that in spite of their limitations, categories are essential to our communication of ideas, to our transfer of knowledge, and, in some instances, to our processes of (self)-definition" (Penrose 1992, 219). Kofman and Peake (1990, 321) shared this view, commenting, "Critiques of oppositional categories, which we may want to preserve, reconcile, dissolve or fragment, . . . are essential for a better understanding of gender differences . . . but it should not be forgotten that these dualities are political and ideological constructions."

As feminist geography has followed feminist writers from other disciplines, like Fraser (1989), into the rich field of analysis of language and discourse, so geography has gained from insights about how gendered groups can be advantaged or disadvantaged by their positioning in influential public statements and how activist groups can themselves use terminology persuasively and politically. These interests in epistemology and language are now ever present in feminist political geographies as they reconsider the seductive and simplifying dualisms of public and private, male-masculine and female-feminine, and production and reproduction, and the ways the use of these in geographic analyses may have hidden the power of gendered political practices in countless realities. The upshot of this interest has been a clear statement that not only are forms of knowledge-building based on dualisms inaccurate but they are also, themselves, political.

Going beyond dualisms requires recognition that concepts placed in binary relationship to each other are, in fact, often mutually constitutive in complex ways. They are multiplicities, not binaries. If, for example, we think of "the state" as a sphere of political practices, and of "the market" and "civil society" as spheres outside the state whose practices are not political, then this kind of dualistic bracketing (state versus nonstate spheres, political versus nonpolitical practices in these spheres) is open to criticism. For the spheres are inseparable, in any reality: the market and civil society involve actors and processes that help constitute the state; the procedures and actors of the state similarly influence the market and civil society. In analysis of gendered political practices in any sphere or site, one such sphere or site is often foregrounded. We may study the state, the market, or civil society. But these spheres are, in actuality, utterly connected to other spheres. If the state has long been the interest of political geography, then feminist political geography has sought to emphasize that sites identified as largely outside the state should be of interest to students of the political, as well, even as they will (to varying degrees, in varying contexts) be responsive to the state, a part of its relations and networks.

In this chapter, to make the point that all spheres have gendered politics, I foreground spheres we often identify as largely outside the state. I emphasize that these spheres have porous boundaries and are entwined with the state in the ways I have mentioned already (and often with each other). There are three sections to follow. First, I take time to discuss the fate of the familiar dualism of public-private, as an example of how feminist geography has sought to undermine the separation of public sphere or site from private sphere or site, showing how this clear conceptual distinction hides inseparable, political, gendered realities. Then, in a second section, I consider gendered practices and outcomes in the market sphere, in particular in labor markets (in communities or regions) and workplaces. Third, I show in an account of the civil society sphere of (largely unpaid) caring work, and activism associated with it, how these forms of activity contain gendered and political interactions.

In this task, as I seek to show that there are gendered political processes at work in a range of spheres of activity and sites, not just in those of "the state" pure and simple, I think it is important analytically to be able to signal that there are some gendered practices, in any sphere or site, that are not political. If every site can have political practices, then every site (even big-P political ones) can have practices that are not political or that are not "politicized" or, at least, can have political potential that has not been realized. In this I do not wish to be at odds with writers who argue that some events and contexts not usually regarded as political are indeed political—for example, Brownill and Halford (1990, 398) in their comment that "negotiation of gender relations in the household . . . should in our view be regarded as political." But it seems to me that the politicizing of a set of gendered relationships depends on (1) their context and (2) the power being exercised that has some consequences or outcomes that could be recognized as unequal or unjust (at least in analysis, if not in acknowledgment by the individuals exercising the power or being affected by it) (see Kofman and Peake 1990, 315). For example, in a workplace in which men and women were employed in equal numbers, the gendered nature of the employment profile could become politicized if all the men were in senior positions and were using their situation to limit the opportunities of the women; in another context in which senior men were using their positions to enhance the career opportunities of junior women, the same politicization would not be evident. It also might be claimed that political practices cannot be considered as activism unless there is collective action being taken, resisting some exercise of power in the distribution of resources, but that there can be political practices that do not give rise to activism. Feminist geographies have sometimes described practices that are not primarily political or, at least, not primarily identifiable as such (e.g., Dowling 1998; Hanson and Pratt 1995), even as they give rise to socially constructed identities of difference among people in communities or places that may later be used as the sources of political practice and activism. Dowling (1998), for example, documented the varied "cultures of mothering" in two Vancouver suburbs, noting the relationships practiced in these cultures between paid work and raising children, the interaction between the mothers and the children's schools, the participation of mothers on volunteer committees, and the role of religion in supporting the narratives developed about mothering. Interaction with neighbors did not occur across the religious lines identified—a matter Dowling does not portray as political but that could become so in a different context or analysis.

Public and Private: Moving from Binary to Mutual Constitution

The long-standing debate about the public and the private ushered into feminist political geography focuses on sites largely outside the state as sites of gendered political practice. Equally, this debate allowed us to understand that gendered political practices are centerpieces in the relations of political practice and activism that include the state apparatus and government policies. Chipping away at the public-private dualism, feminist geographers have, by now, thoroughly deconstructed and collapsed it.

There are some fine theoretical statements about the public-private dualism. Kofman and Peake (1990) described its roots in particular writings of political philosophy that relegated women's lives and actions to the private sphere and men's to the public. They found themselves agreeing with the claim that public and private spheres and sites should be regarded as a continuum: "We should not think in terms of a gender-structured duality, in which qualities and processes are relegated to one or other sphere, but rather of a continuum" (1990, 321). In this reading, there are still distinct spheres of action corresponding to the duality, but any process or reality can fit into one or the other end of the continuum, more or less. More recent writing has complicated the use of the dichotomy further or specified its usefulness and relevance more clearly. Staeheli (1996) emphasized the importance of separating the content of political action from the actual spheres in which it occurs. That is, private political concerns are not always expressed in political practices within the private sphere or within private spaces, and public ones are not always expressed in public spheres or public sites. It is common to have airings of concerns often thought of as private (having to do with caring in the domestic home—for example, for the elderly or for children) in the public arenas of the state or of activism in the street. Brown (1997, 122) spoke of the "blurred boundaries" between public and private spaces and of the "fluidity of public-private divides" as he described the private friendships initiated by a public organization in the provision of services to people with AIDS in Vancouver and the use of public venues for the private interactions of friendship.

The discussion is productively extended by Anderson and Jacobs's (1999) feminist revisiting of the Sydney Green Bans movement of the 1970s, a well-known activist moment in Australian urban history in which a coalition of unionists and residents from working-class and middle-class suburbs saved parts of inner Sydney from demolition by a state government in league with major developers. Anderson and Jacobs made some further claims, reminding us of the many geographic accounts to demonstrate that the "the boundaries of the two spheres are permeable and that the 'private' and the 'public' are not *pure* spaces" (p. 1022), and taking up in particular Staeheli's (1996) ideas that the spaces used in politics are constructed according to ideas of publicity and privacy that are utterly porous, with the public able to be private and vice versa, depending on the context. First, they argued that there are many diverse publics and many diverse privates, which may be unevenly embedded spatially. These are contested, often discursively, in practices in a range of spaces and at various scales. Following Fraser, they see the multiple ways that publics and privates are constituted as a matter we should be examining; the varied processes of their constitution make it quite clear that these are neither stable categories of meaning for our lives nor the basis of an irrefutable conceptual framework. Second, they use Fraser's idea of the "counterpublic" to interpret the Green Bans activism, drawing on an understanding of contests as discursive spaces in which circulate diverse interpretations of events. Different social groups formulate and present discursively their analyses of their positions and needs, countering these to the positions offered by other groups. Counterpublics are these discursively constituted social groups, confronting more commonly recognized publics like big firms, government departments, or instrumentalities like the police. Accordingly, rather than there being a clearly defined public sphere argued about by a group of people (the women residents) who are outside it occupying a separate private sphere, Anderson and Jacobs painted the activism of residents against government as one counterpublic (the women and their allies) engaging in a discursive contest with another more certified or legitimized public (the state government and its allies). Third, and following from their complex rendering of the idea of the public, they argued the case for paying greater attention to our understanding of privacy. For there is need, say Anderson and Jacobs (1999, 1022), to continue the feminist project of uncoupling "privacy from its conventionally understood placement with home space." Quoting Squires (1994), they laid out a series of concepts of privacy that set it apart from occurrences in domestic spaces or by virtue of home ownership—it can also mean being alone, making up one's own mind, or keeping one's own counsel, in whatever context these occur. (In my work with Ruth Panelli [Fincher and Panelli 2001], our finding also has been that the private can be associated with the local—though there are publics in the local, too, and the local should not be seen to have an invariant spatial definition in all cases.) In their subsequent depiction of the Green Bans activism, in the light of their theoretical discussion, Anderson and Jacobs were able to demonstrate that the middle-class women fighting for or caring for the retention of urban parkland should be viewed as engaged in the production of a strategic counterpublic rather than seen as "community mothers" as the existing literature has tended to depict them. Furthermore, for the working-class women, fighting the replacement of their homes with high-rise public housing, their privacy was opposed to the "caring" agenda of a major public institution (the housing authority). Caring is not only in the sphere of the private and in the domesticity of the family and the home.

If we extend spatially this thinking about the public and the private, publicity and privacy, and oppositional counterpublics, we can consider the possibility that processes of immigration and transnationalism, resting as they do on home and away, and on the national domestic and international distant, forge political geographies—interestingly gendered—at a larger scale than is usually considered. Yeoh and Willis (1999) provided an interesting example. Exploring Singapore's regionalization policy—its attempts to encourage its nationals to establish economic interests overseas—as a way to extend the economic reach of the nation, they demonstrate how national encouragement of diaspora, in fact, rests on a gendered discourse offering particular subject positions to Singaporean men and women.

> While men are associated with mobility and agility to grapple with newly fluid and somewhat erratic forms of transnational capital, women are often positioned in official state discourse as stabilising forces of the "home"—the cultural carriers of "Asian values," the antidote to westoxification and the preservers and reproducers of the family, the next generation, and ultimately, the nation, in an increasingly fluid and uncertain world. (Yeoh and Willis 1999, 359)

Within families, the suggestions of this governmental discourse have been widely followed; Yeoh and Willis noted from their interviews the many cases in which the male of a family is posted overseas but the female stays behind with their children, withdrawing from the paid labor force in order to look after the home and household. Even when wives go overseas with husbands, the study revealed that the "responsibility of navigating between home and diaspora" continues to fall on women (Yeoh and Willis 1999, 363). The public policy underpinning Singapore's economic regionalization is quite dependent on the gendered politics of male executives' private households.

At quite another scale, a focus on the sexualized body is taken in some feminist geographies of the politics of domestic violence. This issue may be examined within the family and the home but also at the scale of whole communities or groups in some circumstances. Here, the private is extended beyond the body to the family and community—but the community belongs, as well, to the public sphere and is firmly linked to the state. Or, more appropriately viewed, counterpublics bridging public and private are forming as unlikely alliances to tackle the question of reducing domestic violence. Thus, in Australia at present, violence against women's bodies is a target in policies aimed at improving the lives of Aboriginal women. A recent report detailed the extensive geography of community-led campaigns to reduce this violence, with travel to remote communities and regional towns, use of Aboriginal dance troupes to communicate ideas, and development of wide-ranging consultation strategies. At the same time, there is a political claim by an established and respected Aboriginal community worker quoted in this report that it is important also to situate this violence as part of the politics of an identified private realm, so that actual perpetrators, in actual homes, can be held responsible. What is going on is "domestic violence," meaning that it is the violence of one partner to another, one body to another body, rather than being a broader issue of "family violence" that might be attributed to a whole national community or unreachable public. This woman who is an "indigenous training and development consultant" in the program, said, "If we can't say the words, then we can't do anything about it," and then,

If the definition is wide and so broad that it's almost like anybody doing violence to anybody else in the community, I think it takes away from what we know domestic violence is. The victims and survivors know that it's a partner, it's somebody who supposedly loves somebody else who beats them regularly, puts them down and then sometimes murders them. So I think that we have to be clear, we have to name the issues as they are, to keep them where they are. (Australian Domestic and Family Violence Clearinghouse 2001, 14)

In this example, the argument is being made that protest against the violence will be aided if that violence is named as an objectionable private political practice or a practice of power in private, even if this alliance for intervention against it, this counterpublic, spans scales beyond any usual definition of the private and draws on the public power of the state.

In feminist geographic studies of domestic violence in other contexts, activist intervention by an alliance of community women and families within the public sphere of the capitalist state appears less ideal. Cribb and Barnett (1999) viewed the extended families of women living traditional lives in Western Samoan villages as insurance against any domestic violence those women might encounter when they move in with their new husbands. As the women relocate into settings defined by the cash economy, either in Samoan towns or in New Zealand, they are more likely to suffer domestic violence because they are distant from the shelter of their extended families. They are, furthermore, in situations where the churches or the police, institutions to which they might turn for assistance, perpetuate a masculinist stereotype of male-controlled family life. In quite another setting, Elman (2001) found that the Swedish state, though it seeks to make reforms in the interests of battered women, has not succeeded in changing certain practices of its social workers that have failed to support the women adequately. In both cases, then, aspects of the formation of counterpublics against domestic violence are criticized for failing to stem that violence.

In each of these public-private sites I have named, and the activist counterpublics that ally aspects of the public and the private within them—those associated with immigration and transnational processes at the national and international scale, and those associated with the private and public expressions of domestic violence at the scale of one body against another—the state is implicated in various, often layered, ways. Immigration is a government program, whose purpose varies according to the definitions of nation building being pursued by the country in question. In the fight against domestic violence, a struggle that has a politics of its own to set alongside the politics of the violence itself, governmental programs and resources are often relied on, and arms of the state in the form of the police and the courts are weapons to be deployed. (This is quite apart from the long-term politics of state-led oppression, which forms the context of the particular indigenous domestic violence discussed in the Australian example above.)

A good number of research articles concentrating on domestic violence expose the ethnicized contexts of the violence. In Australia domestic violence is often raised in the context of indigenous or immigrant communities. In the paper mentioned previously about Western Samoan women, Cribb and Barnett (1999, 52) are of the view that a focus on the cross-cultural dynamics of domestic violence is important because it allows "an interpretation of domestic violence as a culturally varying dimension of patriarchal social control," most marked when women experience circumstances of rapid change, like migration, or shifts from communal village settings to those of capitalist social relations. Violence against women, argued Susan Ruddick (1996) in her analysis of the shooting of a woman at Toronto's Just Desserts restaurant in the early 1990s, receives greatest public attention, especially in the media, when it can be racialized. In her analysis, attempts in the media to racialize the shooting into a gendered "black threat to the white community" trope allowed a covertly racialized discussion about immigration to occur. Ruddick noted a jumping of scales occurring in the public discourse associated with this violent incident, with the public space of the restaurant, scene of the shooting, becoming aligned with the public space of the nation, the scene of immigration policy.

Foregrounding the "Market Sphere"—Gendered Political Interactions in Workplaces and Labor Markets

Consider now one set of sites in which gendered political practices of various kinds occur—the private sector workplaces and labor markets of the world of paid work, which, oddly enough, we often think of as part of the public sphere. Though these may be considered, foregrounded, as sites separable from the state, in fact of course there are workplaces within the institutions of the state, and of course government policies and regulations influence the social and political relations of workplaces.

Jobs in Workplaces

Workplaces, the localized sites of enactment of paid employment, are sites of gendered political practice. In workplaces, the establishment of lived workplace norms of behavior that distinguish the lives of women and men in paid employment and their likely career success must occur within the regulatory structures of government that address equal opportunity. Nevertheless, this clearly does not occur evenly or equally across employment sectors or in different types of jobs in workplaces.

McDowell's (1997) account of the finance sector of the City of London is a fine feminist geography of a particular kind of workplace and the jobs contained therein. The context of her study is the old British firms of merchant banking and their masculinist ways of being. There, people's bodies at work are precisely gendered and sexualized; this is associated with the expectations of career success held by those in control. There is a profound politics at work in this set of workplaces. The statement "brains aren't enough" (1997, 145) introduces McDowell's description of the ways women dress for acceptance in these workplaces, attempting to blend with their male colleagues' work attire, in a context in which their clothing and makeup are commented on by coworkers and are significant signals of competence to clients. McDowell stated,

> The ability to construct a distinctive bodily image and gendered identity is an integral part of selling financial advice, making money and attaining power . . . corporeality—in the threefold sense of anatomical sex, gender identity and gender performance—is a crucial part of selling a service. (1997, 207)

Some glimmers of possibilities for change are appearing:

> There are several gender performances that are acceptable and appropriate fictions in the particular circumstances of the different arenas of merchant banking, with the important proviso that they are within an exclusively heterosexual scenario. . . . In these circumstances the characteristics associated with femininity, conventionally of women, may become a positive advantage. The establishment of masculine corporeality, the disruption of conventional dichotomised gender divisions and the acceptance, albeit limited, of "complex and generative subject positions," . . . for men and women, seem to contain a liberatory promise. These changes may open a potential space for the development of a variety of coalitional strategies in the workplace, that neither fix the binary gender divide in place nor rely on a singular notion of equal opportunities or social justice. (McDowell 1997, 207)

McDowell's work follows in the footsteps of a remarkable book by the feminist sociologist Pringle (1988) on secretaries, which presents the specific, sexualized, and political construction of secretarial work and secretaries as the product of power relations in the workforce. The preface to Pringle's book remains an important statement of her theorizing of the political processes that make jobs and their working occupants, in particular contexts:

> Feminists still tend to treat sexuality and work as entirely separate areas of analysis. The main meeting ground so far has been in accounts of "sexual harassment." There is a vast gulf between feminist debates on psychoanalysis, discourse theory, cultural production and semiotics, and the frameworks of political economy and industrial sociology within which most studies of work are situated. . . . This book is an attempt to bridge the gap by locating "work" in the context of debates concerning culture, sexuality and subjectivity. . . . The focus here is on the relationship between secretaries as an identifiable social group and the discursive construction of secretaries as a category; on the relationship between power structures and the day-to-day negotiation and production of power; on the connections between domination, sexuality and pleasure. (Pringle 1988, ix–x)

A sexualized politics infuses the workplace cultures described by other authors, too, underpinned by a gendered division of labor that presumes the relevance of family circumstances as judgments are made about distributing the rewards of those workplaces. Yeoh and Willis (1999) demonstrated how "a particular gender order continues to dictate the diasporic workplace" (p. 365). Their study of Singaporean expatriates working in corporate workplaces in large Chinese cities found the expatriates to be married and single men, in the main, with a few women, almost all single. The study described the logics of the personnel managers of these firms, who do not regard expatriate Singaporean women, especially married ones, as likely candidates for these career-advancing foreign postings, and the logic of married Singaporean women with children, who can see no way that such postings would be possible. In addition, they argued that there is another dimension of strong sexual politics at play here:

> The presence of Singapore women-as-wives [although not in the workplace] is represented as necessary to prevent husbands from being ensnared by predatory Chinese girls, hence preserving the integrity of the family and ultimately safe-guarding the nation-in-diaspora. As men's proclivity to stray is seen as a "natural" fact of masculinity when surrounded by the temptations of the other's promiscu-ity, wives are essential to strengthen their husbands' moral armour to ward off danger and navigate successfully in diasporic space. (Yeoh and Willis 1999, 367)

Back to Australia and a study of human resource management in four organizations in which women made up a large proportion of the lower-level workforce. Wallace (2001) found that particular discursive practices assigned subject positions to women workers that made "common sense" of decisions to limit the training opportunities offered to those women. In one typical example, a football club that also served as an entertainment venue where gambling occurred, workplace training options were made up of

> informal on-the-job training ("sitting next to Nellie"), more structured on-the-job training, the Access program and . . . [other formal, external] programs. Those who received structured in-house or external training were those who were managers or supervisors, all permanent members of staff and thus male. Management discourses positioned women as unreliable, as they may either have left to have children, currently had family responsibilities, or were physi-cally unable to deal with security issues and relegated them to certain serving roles, for which they did not need training. In management's view they already possessed the "natural" domestic qualities or experience from domestic or paid work. The women in the organization, because of their casual status and the roles in which they were enclosed, received on-the-job training of the "sitting next to Nellie" variety and developmental training was not available to them. (Wallace 2001, 442)

Though Wallace noted that her results were the product of their context in a conservative town in rural New South Wales, her article does not report the ways in which that rural context helped to construct the situations described. In contrast, Cope (1996) made a feature of situating the power and political relations of workplaces in their precise place and spatial context. Examining the ways in which the identities of participants in workplace-based strikes and protests were shaped by the social relations of those places, or in fact disrupted the expectations about behaviors in those places, Cope considered the political actions of individuals in certain subject positions in the town of Lawrence, Massachusetts, in the 1920s and 1930s. Women or men of particular ethnic or religious affiliations, working in particular jobs or sections of the town's textiles mills with certain teams of people, and people also of particular age groups and family arrangements participated differently in political acts in the workplace and suffered a range of consequences if discovered by management to be undertaking those political acts. Neighborhood connections influenced the forms of political participation in the workplace undertaken by individuals, as well as family affiliations. Cope's theoretical endeavor is highly sophisticated—to view power, and the political, as a set of relations in which

> an individual can hold multiple power positions simultaneously and in the same space, even if they place the person in a contradictory situation of power (e.g., male and working class). By allowing this multiplicity into the analysis, and by adopting a strategy that purposely looks for overlaps, contradictions, and complexity in power relations, this paper has shown that multiple positions of power, diversity of experience, and the power of self-determination create conceptual openings for power in places and among people that may have been thought of as powerless. (Cope 1996, 201)

With this feminist view of the multiplicity of power relations and their sources in contexts and places, Cope joins feminist geographers Nagar (1998) and Gibson-Graham (1996) as an accomplished theorist of the complex identity forming that occurs in workplaces and the way it is sourced in myriad situations outside those workplaces as well as within them.

Labor Markets

If the modes of employment in workplaces are the product of gendered and sexualized processes, then so too is the operation of labor markets—those networks in which people's labor is advanced and procured, and people obtain work of certain kinds by searching for and finding that work in particular ways. Feminist geographers have revealed a politics in the operations of labor markets that (unsurprisingly, and utterly like what happens in actual workplaces) turns on the reality, and the expectations of employers, that women have familial obligations that limit the ways they can participate in labor market networks. Labor market segmentation results—the situation in which women are found disproportionately working in certain sorts of industries, firms, and jobs. If we were persisting with the private-public dualism, this would be interpreted as the private sphere of the family and the domestic home limiting women's participation in the public sphere of paid work. In an interpretation stressing the mutual constitution of home and work, we recognize how the possibilities of participation in labor markets are complexly related to a range of institutions and discourses in place and to the identities that form in response to the subject positions offered in those institutions and discourses.

Taking up the matter of employers' gendered expectations of suitable workers, and how this influences who is sought and hired in the labor market, we have the evidence that has been with us for some years that employers see women as the bearers of family responsibilities that constrain their labor market prospects. Across the labor market the same processes occur, as was observed in the research on firms and workplaces by Yeoh and Willis (1999), demonstrating that Singaporean women are rarely offered foreign postings in the way men are, and in the research of Wallace (2001), showing that women in some Australian enterprises are not viewed as eligible for the same training opportunities that men are. In the network of recruiting and hiring processes that constitute the labor market, Nelson's (1986) work in the 1980s made it clear that large firms seek back office workers in the U.S. suburbs among educated women trapped there by the family obligations they accept for bringing up their children in a certain fashion. Jamieson and Webber (1991) found that Australian employers designed certain jobs to be part-time, and with limited prospects for career advancement, in order to take advantage of the suburban mothers they could recruit on this basis relatively cheaply. This flags a situation in which part-time work is the norm for women with young children, and this norm allows it to seem acceptable that child care services should remain limited in scope and expensive. It also, at least in Australia, underpins a situation in which any growth in jobs of the past two decades has been primarily a growth in part-time jobs, taken up disproportionately by women. The point is that labor markets, in the jobs offered and the candidates their discourses present as eligible for those jobs, rest on comfortable and taken-for-granted views among the designers of jobs (employers) that women's familial obligations and feminine characteristics render them suitable primarily for certain forms of employment. This certainty is aided by other institutional structures (of the state, churches, schools, and so on) and by the demand for such jobs by women who logically interpret these jobs as their best prospects, given their desires to fulfill familial as well as workplace obligations.

Hanson and Pratt (1995) presented a profoundly geographical analysis of employers' strategies in designing the labor market of Worcester, Massachusetts, to take advantage of the gendered (and other, including spatial) characteristics of the available pool of labor.

> We are particularly attentive to how employers' sensitivity to the availability of particular types of labour influences their locational decisions, creating distinctive

labour markets and literally mapping labour market segmentation into place. Their hiring practices then reinforce the localization of distinctive labour markets, as well as gender- and class-based occupational segregation. At an even finer spatial scale, spatial segregation within establishments mirrors and reproduces occupational segregation. (Hanson and Pratt 1995, 158)

Quite apart from expectations by the organizers of workplace opportunities about the way that domestic life constrains people's workplace eligibility in particular places, there are other pathways through which aspects of domestic life influence labor market outcomes. One pathway of interest to feminist geographers has been that of recruitment of women to lower-paid work. It has been found that women recruit their relatives and their friends from their neighborhoods to join them in lower-paid work. In consequence, studies have found that employers in manufacturing factory jobs, but not only in these, have sometimes been able to rely on their female and male workers (through those workers' familial obligations and networks) to recruit effectively for the firms' workforces. Not only is hiring by word of mouth inexpensive for employers but it also delivers a stream of workers with a good work ethic and facilitates easy on-the-job training (Hanson and Pratt 1995, 171). It is a system that entrenches gender and ethnic segmentation, however, and can exclude those outside the favored groups from opportunities for employment or advancement. In this sense, such recruiting methods, designing labor markets in particular ways, are political acts even if they are not so labeled by employers or indeed by employees. Accordingly, Webber and Weller (2001, 144), in a recent Australian study of changes in the textiles, clothing, and footwear industries, criticized the Australian government and the owners of firms for failing to "allocate resources to reproduce a supply of labor for the clothing industry." Quoting another commentator that the clothing industry has been a "notorious plunderer of labor markets," Webber and Weller (2001, 144) noted how employers relied on a stream of married immigrant women taking up work in the industries' factories and also on word-of-mouth recruitment of these women. This not only excluded those from beyond the particular ethnic and neighborhood groups in question from participation in this labor force, as was noted in the case of Worcester, but it also rendered the Australian textile, clothing, and footwear industries vulnerable to labor shortages when immigration of a particular group of nationals declined and was replaced in the migration stream by another national or ethnic group that was not readily reached by word of mouth.

Geraldine Pratt has continued her work in the feminist geography of labor market segmentation, publishing recently on the ways that subject positions are developed for and by Filipina child carers in Vancouver in the situated practices of child care work. Charting the ways in which these workers' identities are understood, in interviews about them conducted with immigration agents, employers of the women, and the women themselves, Pratt exposed the limited possibilities available to Filipina women working as child carers in Vancouver by virtue of their positioning within Canadian immigration and employment law, within the home of the nuclear (usually) Canadian families within which they work, and within the Canadian Filipino community where they are sometimes seen to be sexual predators (Pratt 1999). In this work, Pratt demonstrated the ways in which discourses marginalize people, showing that the subject positions created have political effects in the material realities they help to create and naturalize.

In recent research, as well, Jess Walsh has indicated how the difficulties of unionizing Baltimore's workforce of female service workers (janitors, hotels' domestic maids, etc.) have to do with their part-time contract positions in the labor market and also with the location of their work in places all over the city. They are not workers located for the duration of their working days in one spot; rather, they move to different jobs on different sites, rarely laboring alongside a regular team of fellow workers. Word-of-mouth union recruiting is difficult to rely on in this spatially fragmented situation. It has parallels, in this, with the poorly paid workforce of home-based carers in that city (and in others), situated at a distance from other workers in their industry and isolated from the forms of communication that have traditionally facilitated union membership (Walsh 2002).

Why are the inequities of women's lives in jobs, workplaces, and labor markets and the differences of their positions there the product of political practices? What gendered political practices are steering the situations described in these economic geographies? The literature described in this section signals that in the discursive positioning of groups according to their gender, as well as the actual distribution of opportunities to women and men in workplaces and labor markets, marginalization occurs for some and advantaging occurs for others. The processes that give rise to such outcomes for people, processes that I analyze here for the particular significance they accord to gender and sexuality in place or space, are political because they have these uneven outcomes. The particular contribution of much feminist writing on these subjects is its scrutiny of the taken for granted, its exposure of political positioning and biases located in our everyday activities, and of the long-term and often wide-ranging consequences of these positionings and biases—for people, industries, and cities.

"Civil Society"—Gendered Politics in the Worlds of Caring and Community Activism

Placing to the fore the spheres of caring and community activism that support and help to define the nature of our civil society, we see clearly that binary thinking in the identification of gendered political practices is conceding ground to feminist understandings that those practices are multiply constituted. Three decades ago, we distinguished women's work in the paid and unpaid spheres—in the workplace, for the paid side of the equation, as against the home and the community, for the unpaid part. Claims were made about the value of the unpaid work, the necessity of it, and how it was unrecognized, taken for granted, and principally done by women. This was the primary gendered political practice, for feminist geographers, associated with civil society and women's contribution to it.

If I look at my own work in the 1980s and early 1990s, it adhered closely to this conceptual binary in documenting and decrying the gendered politics of women's work. It started from the proposition that women were entering the paid labor force in growing numbers and that this was revealing the special difficulties of their material lives as people additionally responsible for caring for their families in the home (Fincher 1991). My own particular interest was in showing how the local state in different places, through its community service policies, seemed to cement reliance on women continuing to undertake these caring tasks. Women would work for their children and elderly dependants, unpaid, accepting this as the price of their kinship obligations. Though policies and practices of the local state were contested in different ways in different places, this expectation of the state (reflecting societal expectations, of course) was never overridden, nor, even in circumstances in which the expenditure of governments on social services provision was declining, was reliance on the unpaid and volunteer work of women in civil society acknowledged (Fincher 1996a).

The work of other scholars was devoted to documenting the daily lives of women in these circumstances—how they coped, what strategies they used to manage the range and number of their tasks, how they ended up taking part-time jobs in order to fit in their family responsibilities, and so on (e.g., Vanden Heuvel 1993). Feminist social scientists all sought to debunk the familiar dualism of home and workplace as spheres separating men and women, unpaid and paid work, and less and more valued activity. Within the sphere of economic public policy, Waring (1990) was particularly significant for her strong voice revealing and resisting the way that governments' national accounts present women's unpaid work as "counting nothing."

Still operating largely within this dualistic frame, women's collective activism in support of those for whom they care—their children, families, suburbs, and home spaces—has been of long-standing interest to feminist political analysts of the private sphere and the ways it links to public spheres, often of the state. Radcliffe (1993) provided a well-known example of the development and use of a politically effective image of womanhood and motherhood by activists engaged in collective protest in a repressive, Latin American, political context. Feminist environmentalists have noted the ways that women's caring for home and kin often has extended to caring for the physical environment and to activism to heal it and to stop continued environmental degradation (Seager 1993).

The emphasis on the state in the activist literature of feminist political geographers, reflecting the frequent reality of the direct engagement of feminist activists with the state, has perhaps served usefully to complicate analyses that had relied on postulating a simple binary relationship between women's unpaid caring and paid working roles. The state is often the target of feminist activism seeking greater support for women's lives through the provision of services. But the state is more than this, for it is as well a source of allies for activists, a source of counterpublic alliances in feminist political campaigning. The state also has been conceptualized in sophisticated ways by a host of progressive social scientists, feminists among them, as a terrain of conflict. So the presence of the state as a key focus for activism about women's caring work and also as a source of community services to be criticized, lobbied, or worked with has been one influence on analysts that has complicated their frames of reference, rendering the binary conceptualization of women's lives clearly too simple.

Although women's activism is frequently against the state, seeking both to criticize the actions of government and to draw more resources from it, it also is often activism against the ways women's lives are understood in families and communities, even in industries and workplaces. So when success occurs for activists, when they achieve their apparent goal of gaining a shift in government stance or gaining extra resources for their cause, there often is also a shift achieved in the discursive positioning, or recognition, of women and their caring work in other environs. In this sense, community organizing can achieve more than it sets out to do; it can be simultaneously successful within state and nonstate sites.

Ruth Panelli's project on women's organizing in rural Australia in the 1980s and 1990s illustrates both the way the conceptualization of women's activism has moved away from a binary analysis and the way this work has demonstrated the importance of discursive recasting of the significance of women's contributions. Her work documents the Australian Women in Agriculture movement (Fincher and Panelli 2001; Liepins 1998). This was a network of organizations of women farmers located throughout Australia but concentrated particularly in Victoria, which sought to increase the recognition accorded to women in agricultural occupations. It set out to publicize the inappropriate ways women were characterized in rural industries, even by their husbands in some cases and certainly by the rural media. Much attention was paid to building up a set of stories of the ways in which farming was gendered in Australia, with particular exclusionary consequences for women. Gaining publicity was the reason for collecting the stories, as well as developing solidarity among the women, who were sometimes spatially quite isolated. In this sense, the rural women's activism was at once directed at the state, and within a network dominated by the state, but also pitched at a range of nonstate sites—agricultural domestic places (farms and homes), small-town communities in which the women lived their nonfarm lives, the agricultural extension programs in which they participated, and the agricultural industry boards on which they were not often members. In the range of organizations to which women living farming lives were linked, it was clear that a binary split of their lives into two parts, in which family concerns were separated from another set identified as paid workforce lives, was inappropriate. (Maybe lives lived on family farms, where the workplace and the homeplace are so close spatially, makes this multiple integration of the spheres of activity especially clear.)

But the state, one set of organizations "outside" the private sphere (in binary thinking), is not the only source of activist endeavor. Panelli's work also hints at the family as a site at which some programs of women's activism are directed. Her example of husbands whistling at their wives, as they do at their sheep dogs, is not an image suggesting gender equality within the rural household. Whatmore's (1991) earlier British work was clear in its charting of gender-based inequities in British farming households, as well. In any examination of community organizing associated with women's caring roles and commitments, the basic unit of communities and neighborhoods, the family, needs critical scrutiny as both a public and private site.

Anderson and Jacobs (1999) remarked on the decoupling of the private from its association with the family in its domestic home space. They described how feminist writing on domestic violence has been effective "by insisting that people (usually women and children) have privacy claims that may need protection against the family unit" (p. 1023). As was the case with the Australian Women in Agriculture movement, which had to find ways to organize their activism spatially over the considerable distances of Australian farming settlements, so too the spatial scale is vast over which the movement to counter domestic violence within Australian indigenous communities is conducted (Australian Domestic and Family Violence Clearinghouse 2001). Funded by governments, but in partnerships with communities, tertiary educational institutions, and Aboriginal women, and with publicity generated by conference participation domestically and internationally, this activist intervention demonstrates how sophisticated women's activism has become, how capable it is of countering the tyranny of distance with national approaches that remain driven by local communities, and how the state is drawn on for resources, even as the sites of real action are outside its formal boundaries (though never, of course, beyond its reach). These complex counterpublics forged in women's activism illustrate the multiply constituted spheres of women's activities and the inadequacy of separating their lives into binary boxes.

It follows from this observation that we can reveal many aspects of women's lives by focusing on the domestic caring work in which they engage, without just focusing on this work as the binary opposite of women's paid work. Though analysts properly criticize the definition of women's activism and political practice as primarily related to their domestic caring roles, and therefore as very particular forms of the private, there remain important issues of contestation to do with expectations of women's parenting and caring roles. Often these are the subjects of heated exchange in the media, a site of publicity where opinions are formed (quite apart from representations in fictional television shows and popular music). In Australia the feminist, community-based activism of the 1970s that led to the availability of child care services for many Australian children with employed parents, at least in major urban areas, coupled with the presence of femocrats in the apparatus of the Australian state, led to child care policies serving parents and women of particular characteristics. To this day there is heated discussion of the adequacy of government provisions for children's services and for women at home with children. The way this issue is considered in government policies and women's activism, in countries around the world, is described and compared in Fincher (1996b).

As we have seen already, it has become an important contribution of feminist geographers to show how public and majority discourses justify and produce taken-for-granted roles for people. Women's caring, especially with regard to their kinship obligations, is one topic of discourses shaping a range of settings that situate women firmly within the family. We noted Yeoh and Willis's (1999) finding that part of the meaning of Singaporean women's caring for their husbands when those husbands are posted to employment away from home is to "save" those men from the sexual predations of other women. This meaning is found in national discourses that define a benefit for the country and its economic growth in the caring actions of these wives. Nagar (1998) commented in a different context, though one also about migration, on discourses sustaining community boundaries among South Asians in Tanzania through the twentieth century. These discourses, to do with religion, race, and caste, have long directed the sexual behavior of women and men, with the women required to guard their own and their community's "purity," whereas the men have been able to justify sexual relationships with African women in certain circumstances. Far from viewing this as a circumstance able to be treated conceptually as a set of dualisms distinguishing men and women, South Asians and Africans, Hindus and Muslims, Nagar made the following statement about the real complexities of the situation she so deftly described:

> In simple terms, a social boundary can be described as a dynamic and fluid line of demarcation that defines the "in group" and "out group" in a given context. . . . Because each of us simultaneously belongs to multiple social collectivities, the boundaries which circumscribe our social lives are constructed through power relations along a number of different axes, for example, gender, race, class and caste. . . . These multiple boundaries permeate, overlap, and cross-cut each other in complex ways and are frequently characterised by shifting

rules of inclusion and exclusion. As a result, far from being separate, race, gender, class and caste constructs become inextricably intertwined. . . . Thus, relationality is an important characteristic of articulated categories and of the social boundaries that sustain them; each category and boundary is positioned, and therefore gains meaning, in relation to other categories and boundaries. (Nagar 1998, 123)

In such an analysis, there is no way to separate caring activities into an intellectual box called the private sphere, thinking of them as associated only with the unpaid and bounded goings-on of the household. The communal discourses sustaining such social boundaries, Nagar said, justify the practices and narratives of "purity, pollution, honor, and values" (1998, 123). Women's sexuality and marital practices have been regulated according to these discourses. Even in the latest period of the twentieth century (from the early 1960s) studied by Nagar, discourses of sexual purity have remained important in the South Asian patriarchy of Tanzania

as relationships between Asian women and African men became more threatening than ever to Asian men. As in the earlier periods of Asian migration, it was not men's but women's sexual purity that marked the purity and honor of race, religion and caste, and this ideology of communal purity and honor was played out on the bodies of Asian women of all classes through strict control over their sexualities. . . . At the same time, these very discursive norms and ideologies gave married and unmarried Asian men the freedom to have relationships with women from other races, religions and castes. (1998, 133)

Clearly, in Nagar's analysis the influential communal discourses disciplining certain women more strictly than certain men are unable to be contained in a view of the private sphere. For they reach across the religious and communal organizations of the society as well as into people's homes and domestic family lives. Analytical severings of public actions from nondomestic spaces, and of private actions from domestic spaces, have been basic steps in revealing how political acts and activist practices can occur in association with caring tasks in previously unanticipated settings and contexts. Another example of this is McDowell's evidence that the attributes of femininity (of caring and gentling) were starting to be valued in some contexts in the workplaces of British merchant banking—though it must be said that caring behaviors in this setting were very unexpected there and certainly not ubiquitous.

How then can we see the gendered practices of civil society, examples of which I have presented in discussions of women's caring and community activism, as political? It is, in fact, fairly clear I think. In the case of activism, alliances are bringing claims and demands to the institutions of the state, seeking recognition and support for caring and nurturing activities usually associated with women's unpaid work. Those caring and nurturing activities can be sited in the home or in different organizations of locality, neighborhood, or community; the recognitions or shifts in discourse required also can be in workplaces and in a range of quite public organizations. These places of recognition of women's work and of caring activities are poorly described as the private sphere and inadequately understood in relation only to some discrete public realm. In the case of the caring work itself, and the ways it is maintained as restrictive women's work by prevalent ideologies in communities and nations, then this is an allocation of roles and opportunities to some gender groups that is not the same for others, and so it may be seen as inequitable and as a situation awaiting political challenge.

Conclusion

In foregrounding the spheres of the workforce and of caring and community activism, I have endeavored to show two things. First, these spheres, that are not contained by the state although they are related to it, have active gendered politics and political practices embedded within them. Second, their gendered character and politics are conceptualized now in feminist geography as the product of multiple intersections rather than binary oppositions.

The demonstration by feminist geographers of the multiply constituted processes that produce gendered identities, gendered expectations, and gendered discourses also has revealed the surprising ways and contexts in which gendered political actions can occur. A real advantage of the move beyond dualisms in feminist thinking about political practices is that it encourages us to see the potential for effective political actions to take unexpected forms. Cope (1996), Gibson-Graham (1996), and McDowell (1997) in their different analyses revealed for us new political actions and strategies associated with the complexly determined gender identities of certain contexts, contexts in which such actions might not have been suspected if binaries rather than multiplicities had been these authors' way of theorizing political possibility. There are different ways of being political, then, that a focus on multiplicities rather than on binaries allows us to see. In the spheres of the marketplace and of civil society, it is possible to identify gendered political actions in the entrenchment of advantage and disadvantage in jobs and labor markets and in the influential discourses that naturalize certain gendered realities and therefore deny opportunities to some rather than others. It also is possible to observe political alliances and groupings, even the formation of counterpublics of strange bedfellows in some circumstances, that shape new activist identities and have successes in confrontational encounters.

All this takes me back to a question posed earlier in the chapter about whether some actions must be understood as apolitical, if the term *political* is to have any analytical purchase. What a dualistic question this is—asking for a clear-cut response as to whether some act or practice falls within the category political (even with a small "p") or outside it. If we think with multiplicities rather than binaries, the only possible response to this question is that a political practice can be formed in the most surprising circumstances, that a subversive response can come from an act that one would not "normally" or "naturally" think of as subversive. Feminist political geography now demands close under-standing of the context in question before the act can be interpreted, where that context is understood through the intersecting lines of difference and identity that define it. As Nagar (1998, 123) so eloquently reminded us, recogni-tion is required of the many social collectivities to which each of us belongs and therefore of the set of categories and boundaries against and within which we live. Only through this understanding can the connected social relations that render some act or practice political be known.

Acknowledgment

I am grateful to Natalie Jamieson for her expert research assistance.

5
Placing Gendered Political Acts

MEGHAN COPE

Storytelling, street theater, and beer brewing do not commonly spring to mind when we think of "politics," but, in certain circumstances, these could indeed be considered political acts. There are many ways through which gender politics take place, ranging from voting and holding office to individual and collective acts of resistance, including activities such as those mentioned. Part of the purpose of this chapter is to continue the feminist project of expanding what counts as politics, while recognizing that there is a risk of marginalizing women's political action if we label it "alternative" or "informal" or as located in the "private" sphere.

Feminists (including feminist political geographers) have been instrumental in breaking down dichotomies between formal and informal politics and the public-private divide (Brownill and Halford 1990; Staeheli 1996). They argue, for example, that conceptualizing women's activism of various forms as informal and as located in the private sphere, or as occurring mainly in private spaces, serves to further marginalize women's political acts. However, we also know that women around the world tend to be excluded, in different ways and to different degrees, from the institutionalized operations of the state and economy that typically constitute the public sphere and formal politics (see Fincher 2004 [this volume]). How, then, can we develop a conceptual framework that examines diverse political acts performed by women that does not rigidify these processes of marginalization, while still acknowledging the real-life limitations on women's access to economic, political, and social institutions? Drawing from work in feminist geography, I suggest three strategies for creating a framework to understand gender-significant political acts from a geographical standpoint. First, I look at ways in which women have actively created new or different spaces for political action, which can enable them to engage directly with mechanisms of oppression and provide a base from which to directly intersect the state. Second, I consider ways in which women have used the socially embedded codes of specific places to highlight their grievances and strengthen their political efforts. Third, I examine how some women's politics have "jumped scale" (Smith 1993), that is, how political actions that draw on everyday life and local resistance can have impacts that jump to broader levels (e.g., national, global). Rather than engaging in extensive theorizing around these issues, however, I draw from the actions of women to demonstrate the multiplicity, diversity, and complexity of political acts. These three themes are woven through the chapter and exemplified by accounts of women's diverse political actions in varied geographical contexts. By taking the empirical examples of women's activism as the primary lens here, I hope to recognize the continued processes of exclusion and oppression women encounter without further marginalizing their actions by seeing them solely through Western and Northern theoretical concepts.

Although there are certainly significant examples of women who have successfully operated within formal political structures and have made important gains, many women around the world have been excluded from the formal sites of public politics and therefore have typically been left off the official record of political engagement. As has often been the case with social movements and struggles for inclusion, women have been creative in their efforts to gain rights and resources and to have their claims heard. This creativity, borne of necessity from living under the many diverse forms of gender oppression across the globe, has enabled women to push open the concept of what counts as political by looking at a wide range of actions and activities as well as the varied places and spaces where these actions are performed.

The Diversity of Women's Politics

Where Does Politics Happen?

Women do take part in the formal political systems of their governments, though rates of participation and voting vary enormously between regions. Scandinavian countries typically have the highest levels of women holding formal elected office, followed by other Western European countries, the former socialist countries, the United States and Canada, and then developing nations (Gal and Kligman 2000). Since 1980 there has been a noted gender gap in U.S. voting patterns, whereby women tend to favor more liberal candidates and different types of referendum issues than men (Shelley et al. 1996), suggesting that women's formal political sensibilities are independent of men's. Women's involvement in formal politics of countries around the world varies tremendously in both quantity (proportion of women voting, numbers holding office) and quality (e.g., in Nigeria wives of high-level officials are appointed into leadership positions but are not typically elected [Abdullah 1995]). The years in which women's suffrage was approved is another phenomenon with great geographical variation. New Zealand was first to approve women's suffrage in 1893; Canada, the United States, and most of Europe followed in the early decades of the twentieth century; most African nations granted women's right to vote with independence after World War II, as did India, Japan, and Latin America; and there remain several holdouts such as the Persian Gulf states of Oman, Qatar, and Kuwait where women cannot vote (Pleck 2002).

Participation in formal politics is considered to be central to involvement in the public sphere, that is, the abstract arena of governance, legislation, and rights. This participation is seen as central to the exercise of citizenship, particularly in the global North, where the meaning of citizenship is rooted in Western Liberal theory as involving both political and economic rights. However, feminist scholars have demonstrated repeatedly that merely having the formal right to vote or hold office does not guarantee women (among other social groups) the de facto status of true citizens, because women usually encounter many barriers to full engagement in politics, such as discriminatory barriers, social limitations, and economic constraints (Shklar 1991; Staeheli and Cope 1994). These barriers are also compounded by forms of discrimination such as racism, class or caste exclusion, and religious bias. Overall, then, the access of women around the world to formal political systems is often constrained and, even when access is guaranteed, there are often other biases that, for example, limit the ability of women in political office to pass laws that address gender issues. Despite these hurdles, of course, there have been positive results coming from the tireless efforts of women—voters, activists, and officials—to create better situations and greater equity. These efforts include the United States' Title IX, which legislates equal funding for boys' and girls' education (Title IX Educational Amendments of 1972), and the United Nations' Convention on the Elimination of All Forms of Discrimination against Women, which attempts to eliminate "any distinction, exclusion or restriction made on the basis of sex which has the effect or purpose of impairing or nullifying the recognition, enjoyment or exercise by women, irrespective of their marital status, on a basis of equality of men and women, of human rights and fundamental freedoms in the political, economic, social, cultural, civil or any other field" (United Nations Division for the Advancement of Women 2002).

Because women often are constrained from participating fully in formal political structures (voting, holding office) and are often limited in their access to public spaces, it is important to acknowledge many different actions that are constituted as political and the diverse locational contexts in which they occur. Staeheli (1996) suggested that by conceptually separating the content of political actions from the spaces in which they are performed, the meaning of *efficacy* is not necessarily connected to success in the public sphere. For example, if a certain action is effective in reaching its goal and the goal is to change behavior in private space (for instance, publicly shaming men into ceasing domestic violence—see Nagar 2000), then engagement with the formal state is not necessarily important. A public action can have private implications, and a private action can have public implications. Staeheli's separation of the content and the space of actions enables a better understanding of many forms of women's activism without peripheralizing gender politics. I draw on and extend this insight in the next section to examine ways in which not just the content and the space of political acts matter but also who does them and why.

Understanding Political Actions: What, Who, Where, Why?

To understand a given political event or action, I break its characteristics down into several key factors by answering four questions: *what* was the act, *who* performed it, *where* did it happen, and *why* was it done (what were the motivations or goals of the act). I discuss each of these issues in turn, drawing from real examples of gender politics from around the world.

First, the range of what can be considered a political act is very broad. From telling stories to carrying signs, from purposely slowing down on the job to going on strike, from street theater to letter writing, from nonviolent sit-ins to suicide bombs, the scope of possible actions is limited only by the strategies and motivation of the actors. The social construction of gender, however, influences the ways that political acts are performed and how their meanings are interpreted. For example, in places (especially the global South) where women have little access to resources but are charged with maintaining families— such as in Nigeria where many women remain in rural areas to subsistence farm while men go to cities to earn cash (Abdullah 1995)—access to economic opportunities may be the subject around which women become politicized, and the political actions women take will reflect this. Alternatively, in contexts in which broader struggles for national recognition and religious and human rights are primary, such as for Palestinian and Israeli women activists, political acts will be gendered in a different way.

In some cases, gender roles are used to shape the political nature of an event. For example, in the 1990s women in Mexico City set up collective kitchens to distribute breakfasts to schoolchildren and, because of the publicity and praise this effort received, they realized the value of their daily domestic work, which typically had been unappreciated and unaccounted for by their families and broader society. The women were able to turn this realization into a rallying call for other women to organize around issues of household work and domestic violence (Cubitt and Greenslade 1997). This is one example of how women's activism creates spaces for politics in ways that challenge typical public-private dichotomies: these women literally constructed public kitchens, which raised awareness of several issues that were socially coded as private and— by disrupting the divide between these—the women were able to mobilize and make some changes.

A second key factor in evaluating political acts is who performs them. Because of social codes and cultural norms—such as gender relations and roles—certain acts may be more or less politically charged depending on who does them. In some cases, superficially nonpolitical actions in certain places at certain times may be considered acts of protest or resistance against oppression. This was the case in South Africa in the 1980s, when local black women continued their tradition of brewing beer in their homes despite a new law prohibiting such activity. Under apartheid, women's brewing had been outlawed and beer was restricted to municipal beer halls, to which only men had access, as a way of controlling the social spaces of black South Africans (Kuumba 2001). By engaging in the traditional activity of brewery, women were using a gendered practice to resist the oppressive regime under which they lived.

The ways gender is constructed in different places affects the forms, meanings, and impact of women's political acts. Even when women's political actions are oriented toward an issue—for example, Palestinian statehood—that is not read as primarily a gender issue, social constructions and meanings of gender still matter. For example, the phenomenon in 2002 of female Palestinian suicide bombers attacking Israeli sites produced new levels of shock and dismay precisely because of the gender of the bombers. This is why *who* performs an act is so important, and gender is one of several significant social locations or identities that matter a great deal for political actions (see next section).

Because all members of a society have certain identities thrust upon them by the mainstream (a political process in itself), acts of resistance or calls for an expansion of rights are inherently influenced by these identities. Gender identity can be used politically in many ways: as a common ground for mobilizing, as a way to highlight unjust legislation (as in the beer example), and even as a way to mitigate repercussions, as when women go to the front lines of demonstrations and strikes in the (often mistaken) expectation that they are less likely to be beaten by police. Gender matters for political acts not merely because of the identities of who is doing the action but also because of the larger social context of gender that perpetuates norms, expectations, and power relations.

A third key factor to look at is *where* politics happen. The context—both physical and social—in which a political act takes place is highly significant. Bringing actions to the streets or to other public or semipublic spaces (such as cafés, marketplaces, and community centers) where social, political, economic, or environmental practices may be questioned or resisted is a common strategy—after all, the goal of much political action is to raise awareness, to change social or cultural practices, to challenge existing policies, or to protest rights violations. Public spaces of all types have socially embedded meanings and are imbued with cultural codes of behavior that can enable political action or squelch it. In many countries of the global North, for example, public political action (with appropriate state sanctions, like permits) is protected as part of the ideal of the classical agora of public political expression. However, in these settings the state also has an interest in limiting the use of public space for politics for various reasons (often framed as public safety issues). The line between a street demonstration and a riot is often too thin for the comfort of police and politicians and, therefore, demonstrations may be constrained. There are many examples of the ways that public space is regulated and political expression contained, as highlighted by the work of geographers such as Neil Smith (1993, 1999), Don Mitchell (1997), and Maureen Hays-Mitchell (1995).

Gendered political actions that take place in public spaces are shaped by these same processes and, because of social perceptions of women as belonging in private spaces in many areas of the world, women's mere presence in public spaces—particularly in groups—can be politically effective. For example, several feminist scholars of Latin America have written about Las Madres (the Mothers) of La Plaza de Mayo in Argentina (Radcliffe and Westwood 1993; Jelin 1997). These older women drew on their individualized grief from the disappearance (and certain deaths) of their adult children by the hand of the government, and they gathered in the city's central plaza in protest of state violence. The Madres dressed in mourning and carried photographs of their lost loved ones. As their daily numbers increased, the women found support among others who had experienced these losses, and they became a visible, public condemnation of the policies of the ruling leaders. The Madres used their identities as older, bereaved, Catholic mothers to carve a safe political space out of public places within an oppressive regime (though there have been arrests and violence too), thus enabling the beginnings of public awareness and resistance. This one example demonstrates all three themes I suggested in the introduction. The Madres constructed a space for politics that had not previously existed, they used social and cultural meanings embedded in a particular place (the plaza, as a site of oppressive state power, was turned into a site of resistance against that oppression), and—because of media publicity around their actions—the Madres' protests drew international attention and increased pressure was brought by human rights groups, thereby enabling them to jump scale from an individual tragedy to a global awareness of abuses.

The use of spaces toward the private end of the spectrum also has been very important for gender politics, individual resistance, group organizing, and other actions such as letter writing or production of political materials. Often, nascent collective politics that take place in private serve as precursors for later public actions and as initial mobilizations for broader movements. For example, in the 1990s women in Kenya gathered in their homes to organize work parties and collective economic enterprises; by doing so, they used locations that are socially coded as "women's space" to create new economic opportunities for themselves within a context of few available options (Oduol and Kabira 1995).

On one hand, the kitchen may be a domain for women that is safe from the prying or censuring eyes of the public (and there are many anecdotes of kitchen table politics, whether around gender issues, civil rights, or economic ventures), but on the other hand, home spaces are often the most dangerous locations for women. All over the world, most episodes of domestic violence against women occur at home. For example, as Nagar (2000) pointed out, many dowry deaths (the murder of a new wife or daughter-in-law because of dissatisfaction with the dowry she brought to the family) in India are due to burns sustained in the kitchen, precisely because burns are easy to dismiss as "accidents." Nagar's account of women's grassroots activism in northern India against the mainstream's tacit sanctioning of dowry deaths demonstrates the use of particular places for political purposes. The primary tactic of these organizations is to facilitate public dialogue about women's murders in two types of locations: the villages where the murders took place (that is, the husbands' villages) and in the victims' home villages. The women's organizations travel from place to place to stage open-air plays and storytelling for entire village populations on the themes of violence against women and dowry deaths. The plays and stories generate discussions among the audience and (it is hoped) raise awareness of the value of women in society, of the collusion of police and family members to cover up women's murders, and of the social practices that generate the conditions that allow violence against women. The location of these plays was crucial to their success as a political strategy: they had to be staged in areas that were shaded from the hot sun, in a space that was socially accessible to all castes and cultural groups of the village, and they had to be public so that the organizers were able to begin "removing public silence" around dowry deaths (Nagar 2000, 349). Although the grassroots groups certainly hoped that the weak existing law against dowry deaths would be strengthened and enforced, their primary goal in staging public plays and storytelling was to change private behavior at a very local and everyday level. Just as Brownill and Halford (1990) found among women activists in London, England, in the 1980s who challenged assumptions about informal and formal politics, these Northern Indian women complicate the traditional interpretations of public and private spheres and formal and informal politics.

The location of political acts also matters because even everyday actions can be political if they are conducted "out of place," a strategy that can offer an effective means of protest (D. Mitchell 1995; Cresswell 1996). For example, in the United States, women who resist attempts to prevent them from breast-feeding their babies in public have been instrumental in facilitating legislation that protects women's rights to be present in public while nursing their babies. Although in no state has it been illegal to breast-feed in public, individual women often have been harassed and asked to move elsewhere, even when they are discreet, on the basis of laws against public nudity or indecent exposure. In several documented cases, nursing mothers were asked to leave museums, malls, restaurants, department stores, and other public or semipublic places (and in one case a woman was even asked to go somewhere other than her car in a parking lot), which brought protests from mothers' groups, including public "nurse-ins" (Baldwin and Friedman 1994). These strategies proved effective in several states in generating "right to breast-feed" legislation. Through this example we can see that the definition of public, the social construction of gender, and the cultural meanings of women's bodies are intertwined and together have important influences over the ways that women live their everyday lives, right down to how they nourish their infants.

In another example of performing actions out of place as a form of resistance or protest, Cresswell (1996) examined "transgression" (purposely crossing social or spatial boundaries) through the instance of a group of women at Greenham Common (United Kingdom) in the 1980s. The women camped out for months at a time, hung flowers and ribbons on fences, and heckled workers to protest the presence of U.S. nuclear warheads at the facility. Cresswell suggested that by reconstructing everyday life in the tents outside the military base, through the performance of cooking, child care, bathing, laundry, and other "domestic" chores, the protestors brought attention to the threat of destruction of everyday life by nuclear war. However, the protestors also rejected traditional gender identities by leaving their homes for long periods (often permanently), in some cases maintaining lesbian relationships, actively contesting standards of feminine beauty and behavior, and rejecting notions of women as passive, cooperative, or quiet. By simultaneously using and rejecting mainstream gender identities and creating private habitations in a public space, the women transgressed both social and spatial expectations, raising the shock value of their protest and potentially increasing its impacts. This serves as an excellent example of both the active construction of different spaces for politics through creative and multidimensional strategies and the use of a particular place with its embedded meanings (military defense, power, potential mass destruction, war, the placement of U.S. warheads on British land) to resist national policy and raise awareness. And the Greenham Common women also were able to jump scale by performing private, everyday, and local activities on an internationally sensitive site, garnering both media and state attention.

Finally, when considering a political event, it is helpful to have some indication of the motives or goals of the action and the individual or group performing it, that is, the *why*. Listing all of the reasons for political action is impossible, but some common causes of mobilization can be exemplified here, many of which have special resonance for women. Goals of political actions are typically to raise awareness, to challenge social practices or government policies, to educate people about certain issues, to support specific objectives or individuals, to increase access to rights and resources, or to further a broader cause. It is important to remember that political actions can span the spectrum of right to left, conservative to liberal, including gender politics. That is, political uses of gender identities can be explicitly geared toward breaking down gender oppression (as in the examples in this chapter) or they can be geared toward maintaining or even reverting to traditional roles of women, as in the fundamentalist Christian Coalition of the United States and fundamentalist Muslim organizations around the world.

Therefore, many aspects of political actions must be accounted for as we attempt to understand them, put them in context, and consider the gendered nature of diverse political events. In this section I demonstrated that not only do we need to pay attention to the what, who, where, and why of political acts, but we also need to understand the ways in which gender is constructed in different places because the meanings of gender saturate the meaning of politics. To consider the many ways that women's political actions are framed on the basis of gender identity in particular, in the next section I turn to the issue of identity politics, again using empirical examples to explore central questions.

Identity Politics

We each carry multiple identities, some of which are ascribed to us through broad social and cultural processes in combination with (or sometimes in contrast to) our own awareness and politicization (such as gender and race), and others of which we may choose (such as parent, activist, or teacher). Insofar as individuals hold identities that are subject to discrimination or oppression, identity can be a valuable component of ourselves that may be politicized and used to establish common ground with others. In both the first and second waves of feminism (late nineteenth and early twentieth century and the 1970s onward, respectively), the first step was to raise consciousness among women about the ways that gender oppression affected them. Other identity-based social movements, such as the civil rights movement in the United States and the lesbian, gay, and transgendered movements, also have worked on the issue of consciousness raising, although the impacts of racism and heterosexism have probably been more immediately apparent to member individuals.

It is important to recall that gender is one of many identities held by people, one that may or may not be the most important mode of oppression for them. Therefore, in looking at gender and political acts, we must attempt to consider the multiple identities of participants and think about how multiple forms of oppression complicate our analyses of gender. For example, black women in the United States have been marginalized in both the feminist movement and the civil rights movement; race issues have not been a central concern to white feminists (though some progress has been made in recent years, thanks to active and vocal black feminists), and gender has not been a central concern of civil rights organizations to the extent that women were rarely able to become leaders. These dual exclusions have greatly affected black women's activism in the United States and have contributed economically and socially to their further oppression (Collins 1990).

However, it is not always a straightforward process to identify which aspects of identity are important and meaningful for a given movement, event, or group. A sense of commonality between individuals might be formed around a particular experience (e.g., the Madres' losses) or a less-visible set of relations than gender (such as sexuality or membership in a particular ethnic group). Therefore, while we (as scholars, outsiders) attempt to understand people's multiple positions and identities—and how these affect their politics—it is impossible to achieve full representations of these intersections. For this reason, I concentrate here primarily on gender identity, and I attempt to acknowledge other forms of collective positionality case by case through the examples presented.

How Are Groups Mobilized through Gender Identity?

Motivations for political actions tend to pivot around at least one, but usually several, of the following issues: civil rights and social justice, human rights, religion and culture, nationalism, war and peace, state violence, gaining access to resources (economic or other), employment and work, domestic violence, and other issues such as education and literacy, health and health care, food, housing, population and reproduction, and AIDS. For some of these issues, the gender connection is clear—domestic violence and reproductive rights, for example. For others, the connection is less direct but is still significant.

Establishing access to resources for the maintenance of daily survival is often central to women's activism. For example, Kumar (1995) recounted women's protests against inflationary pressures in the Maharashtra region of India in the 1970s:

> Conditions of drought and famine in the rural areas of Maharashtra in the early 1970s led to a sharp rise in prices in the urban areas. . . . The [United Women's Anti Price Rise Front] rapidly became a mass women's movement for consumer protection and its members demanded that the government fix prices and distribute essential commodities. So many housewives were involved that a new form of protest was invented: at appointed times housebound women would express their support for demonstrators by beating thalis (metal plates) with lathis (rolling pins). The demonstrations themselves were huge, comprising between ten and twenty thousand women. Commonly, demonstrators would protest rising prices and hoarding by going to the offices of government officials, members of Parliament, and merchants, surrounding them, and offering them bangles [bracelets] as a token of their emasculation. (Kumar 1995, 62)

This brief account raises many questions about the politics of gender identities and the ways that gender influences politics. Note that women, as those primarily responsible for the provision and preparation of food, were the instigators of and main participants in this movement. Note too that "housebound women" (the author does not explain this) who were constrained to act from within their home spaces supported the public demonstrators by using kitchen implements (gendered tools) to create a noisy solidarity. And notice that the method of shaming public officials and merchants was to give them symbols of femininity. What does that say about the status of women? Did the women have a sense of irony in offering bangles to powerful men to emasculate them (i.e., make them more feminine), or was it a baser gendered insult? The passage by Kumar does not illuminate on these points, but we can consider different interpretations.

To return to the three themes outlined in the introduction, first, the creative uses of space and gendered cultural artifacts (rolling pins, bracelets—in other food riots, pots and pans have been used in similar ways) enabled women to construct new spaces for political activism. Second, by hounding public officials outside their offices, the women used their occupation of places coded with public power and the presence of feminine, everyday objects to suggest that the officials really did not have much power if they could not even help put food on the people's tables. That is, the officials might have had power in the institutions of the state, but they clearly were ineffectual in real, everyday matters such as adequate sustenance. Third, this protest demonstrates the possibilities of jumping the scale of protest from the individual and household to the city, the region, and the nation. In more recent cases of drought and famine, we have seen the tangible links between these environmental and social disasters and political unrest, one notable recent example being the rise of the Taliban in Afghanistan in the 1990s in a context of dire environmental conditions, a political vacuum, and international ignorance. The global and local impacts of this cannot be underestimated.

In another example of how groups may be mobilized through gender identities, consider the context of Latin America, where struggles surrounding issues of human rights and state violence have (re)shaped women's lives in recent decades as serial military dictatorships and other strict (including Marxist) regimes have dominated formal political, economic, and social structures. In some contexts these struggles have facilitated the formation of active women's movements, whereas in other contexts they have left gender considerations aside as meaningful issues for mobilization. For instance, in Chile during the 1970s and 1980s regime of Augusto Pinochet, "The women's movement grew and flourished in the context of a struggle against the dictatorship" (Frohmann and Valdés 1995, 278). Conversely, within the leftist Sandanista government of Nicaragua, women's traditional roles as deeply subordinate, combined with overwhelming work and household responsibilities, greatly limited the extent of women's political involvement of all types: "Gender subordination persisted in every space and at every level. Women were confined by a complex conjuncture of material and cultural difficulties, ranging from the social system itself, to the perceptions and adaptability of women themselves" (Fernandez Poncela 1997, 45). So different sets of conditions and constraints result in varying opportunity scopes for gender politics. As Kuumba remarked in her work on gender and social movements, "Mobilization [in social movements] is dependent on a delicate balance between the existence of objective conditions that stimulate the emergence of protest movements and, on a more individual level, the subjective awareness and interpretation of these conditions" (Kuumba 2001, 5). This is why consideration of context—the physical and social settings in which activism and mobilization occur—and identity—the social, political, and economic positions of individuals and groups—are crucial for understanding political actions.

In What Ways Does Gender Identity Matter for Political Actions?

Gender identity can be a mobilizing force for political action in several ways. First, women's objective conditions (as Kuumba called them) or situations of everyday life may spur them to action. At a local level, social and cultural constraints, such as limited spatial mobility, can confine women to place-bound straits. Limited education opportunities around the world keep many women illiterate, which in turn affects employment prospects and engagement in other economic activities. Religious practices and values—especially of the fundamentalist varieties—can severely circumscribe women's activities and behavior. Low wages and exploitative work conditions, such as those of the Export Processing Zones and *Maquiladoras* of the world (Wright 1997), perpetuate poverty, generate countless health concerns, and contribute to gender discrimination in employment. Situations such as these can bring and have brought women together to organize, protest, and sometimes change their situations. Additional concerns, such as for children's issues, housing, food security, environmental hazards, and domestic violence, have also served as sparks for women's political involvement in ways that are inherently connected to their gender identities and their geographical contexts.

Second, gender identity can spur women to political action with regard to state policies, rights, and citizenship issues. For example, South African women formed the Women's National Coalition (WNC) in 1992 to ensure that gender equity issues were explicitly addressed in the country's transition from apartheid. Rights were especially important here: "The WNC found that women were particularly concerned with the customary laws that defined women as perpetual minors and limited their ability to inherit property, enter into contracts, or seek divorce. . . . By colonial and traditional law, African women were forbidden in many instances from political, land ownership, and child custody rights" (Kuumba 2001, 129). In the United States and Western Europe, welfare rights also have been recent areas of gendered mobilization, particularly as "Third Way" governments actively dismantle social supports that overwhelmingly benefited women and their families in real economic terms (Cope and Gilbert 2001). Indeed, Mink (1998) argued that the United States's 1996 Welfare Reform Act withdraws rights from poor women. In reference to the act's requirement that individual states actively encourage marriage, discourage the births of additional children, and enforce work requirements, Mink argued, "Rights trampled by the welfare law include fundamental constitutional rights to make one's own decisions about marriage, about family life, and about pro-creation. Also endangered is poor mothers' vocational freedom, that is, their Thirteenth Amendment freedom from coerced labor" (Mink 1998, 6). These examples suggest that the political framing of an oppressed gender identity for women based on social and cultural traditions must constantly be resisted in order to prevent the loss of existing rights and to expand the scope of women's citizenship around the globe.

However, it is perhaps instructive to again consider the nature of everyday life for women in different contexts to understand why issues of rights and citizenship are not always mobilizing forces for women. Amina Mama, of the University of Capetown, South Africa, pointed out that the Western concept of citizenship has little meaning for women in volatile African states with little or no democracy, who live in households where gender roles are such that they must serve their husbands' meals to them on bended knee (Mama 2002). Mama's juxtaposition of the condition of African governments (many of which are military dictatorships) and women's extreme subjugation in the home remind us that an awareness of context and the meanings of gender in diverse global settings necessitate that we constantly challenge assumptions, such as the Western and Northern belief that citizenship rights are and should be a primary goal of women's activism around the world.

Third, gender identity matters for political actions because there is some level of affective concern for each other among women. The early second-wave feminist claims to global sisterhood may indeed have overstated the significance and extent of gender identity, but we can see evidence of political coalitions being generated by a sense of commonality between women, often across space, class, race, and other boundaries. One example is the Clean Clothes Campaign, which has an international secretariat in Amsterdam and member organizations in ten countries of Western Europe. The goals of this organization are "to improve working conditions in the garment industry worldwide. The campaigns are coalitions of consumer organizations, trade unions, researchers, solidarity groups, world shops, and other organizations. . . . The Clean Clothes Campaigns cooperate with organizations all over the world, especially self-organized groups of garment workers in factories of all sizes, homeworkers, and migrant workers without valid working papers" (Clean Clothes Campaign 2001, 3). For example, consider the report on one campaign in which the Clean Clothes Campaign was active in protecting union leaders and members in a Nicaragua blue jeans factory:

> In April and May 2000, the factory's management fired 700 workers who were affiliated with a union that was working to get an 8 cent wage increase. The factory, owned by the Taiwanese business consortium Nien Hsing, employs 1,800 workers who produce 25,000 pairs of jeans each day. These workers, mostly young single moms, make on average 20 cents per pair of jeans they sew. The jeans are sold in Kohl's department stores in the United States for $30. Since the workers were fired, activists, including the [Clean Clothes Campaign], took up the case. Most of the solidarity action took place in the US, where more than

400 actions were held at Kohl's stores, and about 4,000 letters were written to Kohl's, Nien Hsing, and officials in Nicaragua. Importantly, Taiwanese activists also took up the issue of the right to organize at Chentex. The Chentex workers also had the support of the Lesotho Clothing and Allied Workers Union (LECAWU), which is trying to organize workers at a Nien Hsing facility in Lesotho, where union rights are regularly repressed. . . . On Wednesday, April 4th, 2001, the Managua Court of Appeals, in a 2 to 1 decision, ruled in favor of Chentex union leaders in their third and final legal appeal to be reinstated to their jobs. (Clean Clothes Campaign 2001, 5)

This account suggests multiple layers of international support among women (both the membership of Clean Clothes Campaign and most garment workers in the world are overwhelmingly women) that crosses ethnic and racial, class, and geographical boundaries. Particularly interesting is the involvement of garment workers in Lesotho in the struggle of Nicaraguan workers employed by the same Taiwanese multinational corporation, in combination with protests and letter writing in the United States. As capitalist production has become increasingly globalized and geographically dispersed, the political opposition to the exploitation of women workers has also, by necessity, become more globally organized. Consider all the instances of scale jumping in this example. Significantly, organizations—like the Clean Clothes Campaign—that mobilize around issues of wage work are increasingly having not to merely react but to engage proactively with workers' groups, local and national governments, and corporations in new ways, to incorporate diverse social constructions of gender, and to use multiple political strategies ranging from traditional letter writing and law suits to new tactics such as employing the Internet for information dissemination.

Gender identity matters for politics in so many ways that it is sometimes difficult to organize them in any meaningful way. In this section I focused on three dimensions—common objective circumstances of women's lives, rights work, and affective solidarity—to instantiate some of this diversity. I have not touched on ways that gender identities matter for the ways that men engage in politics, for example, though this could certainly form an important discussion point. Women around the world tend to have few protected rights (to mobility, self-expression, independent economic standing, choice in marriage and reproduction, employment, child custody, political participation, recourse for grievances) and poor access to resources (land and property, capital, education, health care, housing, and even food), due at least in part to gender biases but certainly also due to other forms of discrimination, widespread shortages or hardships, corrupt governments, the vicious effects of international policies such as structural adjustment programs for debtor nations, and the effects of globalization on economic and political instability and environmental degradation. Thus, for large numbers of women who are involved in political acts of various kinds, the goal or motivation is not singularly arranged around gender issues but rather must target multiple inequities (class, ethnic group, religion, etc.) that reside in multiple and interlocking systems of oppression.

Conclusion

I began this chapter with a discussion of three concepts that are important for political geographic analysis: the construction of spaces for politics, the strategic use of social and cultural meanings embedded in particular places to highlight political concerns, and the notion of scale, particularly the ways in which political activism can transcend multiple levels to become significant in different sites and arenas. The choice of these three concepts was informed by a feminist approach to the task of analyzing political acts and emerged from concrete examples of women's politics from around the world. That is, because feminists have explicitly tried to expand the boundaries of what counts as politics, particularly paying attention to issues and events outside the formal or public realm (which itself is problematic), the three concepts examined here were ones that could readily be interpreted across the public-private and formal-informal divides, thereby aiding in the project of complicating and dismantling these overly rigid dichotomies.

Although women continue to experience extreme gender-based discrimination, the range of strategies and spaces they use to resist and organize politically can inform us about not only the issues that matter to women but also the social, cultural, and economic contexts in which they are operating. However, taking a geographical approach to understanding specific political acts does not merely result in a cataloguing of these varied strategies but, rather, enables a more comprehensive understanding of the intersection of space, place, and society. The construction of alternate political spaces, the use of culturally meaningful places, and the connections forged between local and global arenas of action may not be the initial goals of women's political acts, but they are concepts that we can use to understand these acts without necessarily imposing rigid theoretical frameworks on them.

The focus on women's political activism also does not mean that women are necessarily engaging in feminist efforts or even that gender oppression is particularly important to them as individuals. In many instances, women organize, resist, protest, or mobilize around issues of daily survival or basic human rights. We as outside observers may identify ways in which gender as a set of power relations or cultural norms influences or is affected by their actions, but we cannot necessarily assume that our readings are correct or meaningful. As Hussaina Abdullah wrote of the Nigerian women's movement, "Very few women leaders accept that the movement is feminist in orientation. Those objecting to the feminist label view it as Western terminology that should not be employed in Africa ... the concept of feminism should thus be contextualized within each society where it applies. Yet, in a certain sense, the Nigerian women's movement can be considered feminist in orientation because it is *attempting to transform gender relations in society*" (emphasis added; Abdullah 1995, 212). Therefore, the analysis of women's political acts must attempt an uneasy balance between, on one hand, questioning our own definitions of feminism and our readings of women's political acts, and, on the other hand, simultaneously recognizing the tremendous struggles women around the world engage in to make better lives. One solution to this dilemma, as Abdullah suggested, is to attempt to understand the context of the political acts, both in terms of an accounting of social, economic, and political settings and in terms of the construction and meanings of identities and oppressions.

Acknowledgment

I would like to acknowledge the wonderful intellectual support and cozy office provided by the Five College Women's Studies Research Center in South Hadley, MA, during my research associateship in 2001–2002, which greatly aided the writing of this chapter. Particular thanks to Amrita Basu, Katalin Fabian, Alev Cinar, and Kate Kruckemeyer for their critiques, conversation, and friendship.

6
Doing Feminist Political Geographies

JOANNE SHARP

Given the diversity of feminist and political geographies, it is of no surprise that there is a wide variety of methods adopted by feminist political geographers. This diversity is particularly significant if we take account of those feminist geographers who do not consider themselves to be political geographers but who nevertheless do work that interrogates the political processes and structures through which societies and other social groupings are reproduced.

Political geographers have considered how political geographies should be researched. In the past, introductory texts tended to devote a separate chapter to research methods. One example is Prescott's 1972 book *Political Geography*. Although Prescott regarded the methods of political geography to be very similar to those adopted by geographers more generally, the question of objectivity was of primary significance in this subdiscipline:

> The point which is uniformly stressed by political geographers is the need for an objective viewpoint in research programmes. This is not meant to suggest that objectivity is more important in political geography, but just that it is harder to achieve. It is difficult to think of anyone becoming emotionally involved about moraines, or port forelands, but many people would immediately take a mental position if the political geography of Israeli-occupied Arab lands or of Bantustan Homelands in South Africa was discussed. (Prescott 1972, 27)

Prescott went on to admit that true objectivity was impossible but then detailed the ways in which political geographers could "maintain the highest level of objectivity possible" by ensuring an unpartisan approach that would be achieved primarily by avoiding areas about which the researcher had deep political commitment (Prescott 1972, 27–28). His methods involved the collection and measurement of "geographical facts," their description, and their analysis. Interviews also were promoted with significant decision makers such as politicians. Prescott (1972, 35) explained that the aim of any piece of political geography research should be "total explanation," although he acknowledged that in certain situations, this will be impossible for some: "the student will have to settle for a partial explanation."

Clearly, political geography has moved on from Prescott's vision, but, whereas recent feminist geography has spent a great deal of time considering questions of methods (e.g., the special issues of *Professional Geographer* 1994, 1995; Moss 2002) on the whole, political geography has not. Indeed, unlike many earlier political geography texts, more recent introductions (e.g., Painter 1995; Agnew 2002) do not consider *how* political geographies are researched. It could be argued that whereas political geographers see themselves as adopting methods generally suited to geographical research, feminist perspectives necessitate the adoption of particular values and, therefore, methods that go beyond mainstream political geography.

Broadly put, feminist methodology not only is about the design of research, modes of data collection, analyses, and dissemination of results but also involves the less often considered "relationships among people involved in the research process, the actual conduct of the research, and process through which the research comes to be undertaken and completed" (Moss 2002, 12). But, as Moss (2002, 12) continued, making "a method 'feminist' implies politicizing a methodology *through* feminism." Thus, in addition to the methodological questions considered by political geographers more generally, feminist political geographers frequently have a commitment to inclusion and self-reflexivity that may or may not be the concern of political geography. This means that although there are traditions in political geography that are consistent with feminist methods, there are some that are less compatible.

In this chapter I discuss the range of methods adopted by feminist political geographers by considering three of the most important methodological issues concerning feminist political geography.

Quantification

Like all subjects in geography, political geography was influenced by the discipline's quantitative revolution, wherein the role of science—in a particularly positivistic guise—was held up as the most appropriate approach. With the rise of new quantitative and scientific techniques from the 1950s and 1960s onward, political geography was seen by some as a "moribund backwater," to use Brian Berry's oft-quoted phrase from the late 1960s, in the otherwise forward-looking discipline. As a result, a number of political geographers embraced the quantitative revolution in geography with enthusiasm. Quantification offered, for example, political geographers the ability to correlate socioeconomic data with voting patterns, the spatial characteristics of "successful" states, or, more recently, the multiple layers of political data on a Geographical Information System (GIS). Dramatic claims have been made for such methods by some of their practitioners (e.g., Openshaw 1996), implying that statistical or cartographic descriptions of large data sets provide an accurate representation of political processes and phenomena. Readers of quantitative research are even presented with a statement of confidence in the results with certain statistical models.

Although this is a statistical measure, it is, in practice, often granted further weight, leading to a reinforced sense of certainty.

This approach was further encouraged by the development and proliferation of computing power that allowed the expansion of data sets with easier and more rapid analysis. The development of the quantitative revolution in geography, and later new GIS technologies, has facilitated the manipulation of large data sets from which to extrapolate laws and predictions. Some researchers have been criticized for manipulating data just because it is there rather than adopting a GIS approach when it offers a potential solution to a pressing problem (Taylor 1993b). Furthermore, the majority of these large data sets are state or industry driven, and there have been critiques of the dependency on industry and the military in GIS research (N. Smith 1992b; J. Pickles 1995). This has raised important ethical questions regarding for whom it is that political geographers do their work. Some expressions of quantitative geographers also have troubled feminists. Terminology such as "data capture," "harvesting," and "gathering" appears to give little care to the nature of the materials being researched. Furthermore, military metaphors are not infrequent in the paraphernalia surrounding GIS systems, the intellectual genealogy of which does, after all, link it to military hardware. Thus, GIS systems are sold as "strategic business weapons," offering consumers a "secret weapon" within which they can "zero in" and "hit targets" (see Roberts and Schein 1995).

Of course, there is now ample evidence for the fallacy of the researcher's ability to create objective results through the adoption of quantitative approaches. Numerous critical examinations of quantification have highlighted the biases inherent within statistics and models. Even the most basic use of quantitative techniques requires categorization, and this requires stable and bounded entities. Although this is true of all forms of analysis, quantitative techniques require a greater stability of meaning than do qualitative ones. This means freezing often fluid or changeable processes into a fixed and identifiable entity. Furthermore, statistical tests often depend on preexisting categories that might be based on the experience of men (Kwan 2002c, 162). Using cartographic representations and statistical techniques has led to the establishment of correlations but not necessarily the theorization of relationships. For example, Siegfried's (in)famous geography of voting in Ardèche, France, placed maps of various physical and social distributions together to demonstrate relationships: "He could identify those aspects of the social and economic milieux most likely to underlie the voting decisions, and was then able to trace those aspects back to the physical environment" (Taylor and Johnston 1979, 27). Those who followed Siegfried produced many other correlations; sometimes they produced results that defied reasoned explanation (see the discussion in Glassner 1993, 184). The existence of a spatial or statistical relationship between two data sets does not necessarily mean that there is a relationship between them in practice or theory. Moreover, it does not indicate the direction of causality. This exposes a problem with the quantitative turn in political geography: however technically sophisticated the methods seemed, these approaches tended to be treated as though they were conceptually and theoretically empty without sufficient reflection on assumptions or context. Methods based on analysis of the shape of states, for instance, were carried out in isolation of contextual information involving history, economics, and military conflict (Glassner 1993, 67–69).

Such critiques have not meant that feminist geographers have abandoned quantitative research. Many have argued for the importance of maintaining a view of the quantitative, particularly if this is part of a mixed methodology wherein qualitative analysis can provide the context for the numerical analysis. There is a continued recognition of the importance—often the strategic importance—of numbers and attempts to theorize at the larger scale. Kwan (2002c) highlighted the importance of adopting mixed methods: qualitative approaches ensure the inclusion of the voice of those being researched in addition to making sure that the issues under discussion really are the key concerns, whereas quantification can provide the context and some kinds of evidence that can be used by feminist research to make a difference in the real world. Feminists committed to producing work that is relevant to community activism have also sometimes chosen to adopt quantification as a strategy to ensure that the importance of issues is recognized by decision makers.

Some feminist geographers argue for the importance of adopting "critical quantitative methods that are consistent with feminist epistemologies and politics" (e.g., Kwan 2002c, 163), which would mean, for example, using quantitative methods to make the spatial dimensions of women's inequality apparent (Mattingly and Falconer-Al-Hindi 1995, 429). Many recognize that counting and descriptive statistics can be very important in establishing the need for further, more detailed, and perhaps more interpretative research. Lawson (1995, 452) insisted that there are particular questions that are best answered with quantitative techniques, arguing that it is not the use of quantification per se that is the problem; the problem is when it is used in a decontextualized and totalizing way. She further said that one result of feminist critiques of science "has been the understanding that with *any technique* whatsoever, we have to take seriously the ways that we as researchers mark the knowledge that we produce" and that all methods are partial (Lawson 1995, 452). Feminist use of quantification, then, tends to be highly conscious of the embeddedness of data rather than considering numbers in abstract spaces (see Moss 1995). Many now combine qualitative and quantitative research tools. As I addressed earlier, feminist geographers are revisiting GIS technologies. The new possibilities offered by recent digital techniques mean that narrowly numerical GIS data can now be linked to other forms of data such as personal narratives, transcripts, and alternatives to the traditional "god's eye" visualization of most GIS interfaces (Kwan 2002b). For example, Kwan (2002a, 652) argued that these developments mean that using GIS techniques no longer "necessarily preclude the use of contextual qualitative information of subjects or locales." In her research, she combined GIS visualization with interviewing and personal narratives to understand the racialized spatial practices that lead to a "closed spatiality" of the particular group of women she interviewed (Kwan 2002a).

Radical Geographies

Although quantification was one response to the dominance of descriptive political geography and geopolitics, which had dominated the field until the 1960s, it was not the only one. The general discomfort that was felt in geography toward quantitative methods also had an impact on political geography. The 1970s witnessed the rise of radical political geography based on Marxist political economy approaches (e.g., Harvey 1973). Advocacy geography emerged from this to consider urban conflicts, unequal distribution of resources, and issues of social welfare. As well as critiquing overdependence on statistics and numerical calculations, these moves broadened the range of issues from understandings of economic and political processes to include issues such as quality of life. These moves valorized the experiences of those living the lives being studied in ways that data manipulation could not, so methods followed that necessitated experiencing the places being studied and talking to the people who were influenced by the processes in question. For some advocacy geographers, however, the involvement of the communities involved in defining key criteria has not meant the disregard of the importance of including quantitative materials to demonstrate the significance of an issue; these quantitative methods have been used alongside qualitative methodologies (e.g., Rowe and Wolch 1990).

Many Western feminist geographers in the 1970s and 1980s began their careers as radical geographers, drawing on Marxist and other radical approaches in their attempts to expose and challenge the dominant structures operating in society. The shift by some to consider patriarchal structures also was based on a radical commitment to social change, such that they included the experiences and voices of those silenced by dominant forms of representation. Feminist methodology has tended to draw in the views and concerns of women, stressing the importance of listening to the voices of others so that research is a collaborative process rather than the product of an expert analysis or reading of the world (see Moss 2002). The inclusion of the voices of those who have experiences of different situations and those who have different and marginalized viewpoints is central to much feminist methodology, particularly that influenced by ideas of "standpoint epistemology" or "situated knowledge" (see Haraway 1988). Feminist researchers have been determined to respect their research participants' views, to include their voices and concerns in an attempt to empower them and validate the experiences of women and other marginalized groups (Mattingly and Falconer-Al-Hindi 1995; Reger 2001). This means that, on the whole, feminist approaches require the adoption of more interpretative methods. Despite adopting a range of methodological and conceptual approaches, in general, feminist political geography has maintained a radical tradition in its attempt to include the voices of those being studied as knowing subjects rather than as objects of research.

Other strands of political geography have been more clearly focused on qualitative techniques such as interviews and textual analysis. Many feminist political geographers feel happier following these methods than those based more exclusively around quantification. For example, in making sense of state nationalism, Walter (1995) and Johnson (1995) interpreted the meaning of the landscape, place, and statues, and F. Smith (2000) used media sources and participant observation in understanding local politics. Here, rather than being distanced researchers, feminist political geographers are involved in a double hermeneutic. This means that in addition to having their own professional interpretations, they have to take seriously the interpretations that people give the world around them, as it is this, rather than any sense of "correct" interpretations, that guides their actions. Others have celebrated the "partial explanation" that Prescott (1972) lamented as the only way of pressing for a feminist objectivity, an attempt at faithful representation but from a grounded, and acknowledged, position. For instance, Nagar (1997) foregrounded her own personal narrative to provide a context for her interactions with her research participants, their reaction to her, and her own understanding of the situation.

Belief in the necessary value of feminist analysis has sometimes led to an imposition of feminist theory onto the world, hence ignoring the voices of those who have been analyzed. Third World feminists have been particularly concerned about Western feminist analyses privileging theoretical and political concerns over the conditions of people's lives and struggles in the Majority World. This raises important questions about how to represent others and about the responsibilities that come with any form of representation (Staeheli and Nagar 2002). Thus, the notion of committed research and the ideas of what research participants can expect to take away from the research process are things that both feminist political geography and radical political geography share. Feminists have variously argued in their discussions of methods that researchers must be willing to give up the privileges and authority traditionally associated with the academic, to learn to listen, to be aware of their positionality, and, perhaps most important, to involve others in research design, implementation, and writing up (McDowell 1992b; Gibson-Graham 1994).

Arenas of Politics

The methods applied to different research projects also depend on the scale at which work is done and on which scale(s) researchers perceived that the political process or phenomenon happens. Clearly, research that attempts to understand global, regional, or national processes tends to apply more extensive methods than those projects that study local politics. The first expression of political geography as a formal academic subject was dominated by questions of the global.

For many, the "founding father" of political geography was Halford Mackinder. Like many who followed him, Mackinder was interested in explaining political geography at a global scale. Writing at the turn of the twentieth century, Mackinder perceived the world to be closing with the end of the colonial period. As, from a European perspective, there seemed to be no territory left to be claimed, he perceived the role of geopolitics to be the examination of the political tensions that would play out in this closed system (Agnew 1998). Geopoliticians have since tended to see the world as a complete system within which all international political activity can be explained through various spatial laws; certain laws of geography such as distance, proximity, and location are understood to influence the development of political situations. Mackinder presented his "Heartland Thesis," which insisted on the importance of the Asian Heartland, as the unfolding history of great powers. He believed that controlling the territory of the heartland provided a more or less impenetrable position and could thus lead to world domination. Unless checked by power in the "outer rim" of territory proximate to the heartland, the occupying power could quite easily come to control Europe and then the rest of the world. Mackinder's methods—and those of many who followed him—were based on deductive reasoning based on a study of history on a grand scale.

More recent political geographers have continued to base research around the global map. In the cold war period, geopolitics led to theories such as the domino theory and to conceptualizations of the spread of communism as being like a disease. On the basis of cartographic "evidence," political geographers argued that proximity would lead to revolution. The idea of toppling dominoes charting the path of Soviet takeover until the final domino—the United States of America—came crashing down had no basis in any theory of how states change or revolutions occur but, instead, was based on a cartography of peril defined as a juxtaposition to communist-dominated territory.

Conventional geopolitical ways of understanding the world have been described in terms of a theatrical viewpoint (Ó Tuathail 1996a) with the unfolding of events following grand spatial scripts. It is, moreover, an elite approach, with the political geographer as geopolitician being able to understand everything through reference to his or her study of history. Current events could be interpreted by a trained observer through reference to past events, often from an understanding of the great battles of Greek antiquity (Agnew 1998, 5). This totalizing narrative does not require a methodology that incorporates the interpretations of those acting, for any alternative explanation could only offer an account distorted by its ignorance of the lessons of history.

Geopolitics is not the only significant movement in political geography that has privileged the global. World Systems Theory had a great influence on political geography, especially in the 1980s (Taylor 1993b). This Marxist-based approach states that analysis must be based on the global scale, as it is impossible to isolate individual national or regional modes of production. Research, therefore, has to be at a grand scale in order to understand this single, integrated society. Other traditions, including those based on (neo)realism and theories of globalization, similarly focus on the global scale (although these have faced challenges [Keohane 1986; Appadurai 1990]).

Clearly, this approach focused attention on the formal arenas of politics and the official actions of members of state, of the military, and of commerce. Thus, a realm of the political has become established in which the majority of political geography study has concentrated. Although not wanting to draw all efforts away from the global, feminist political geographers have pointed out that such global visions and grand theorizing tend to miss out on the politics of the every day. The effect of the cultural turn on political geography has generated a turn toward nontraditional geographical knowledges and a concern with the every day as a valid space of political analysis. This has facilitated the opening up of spaces within the discipline of political geography to examine relationships previously taken for granted. Increasing numbers of political geographers and others working in related fields have taken seriously the role of the mundane in the construction of political activities. Anderson (1991), Billig (1995), and Chatterjee (1993) have turned from the formal sphere of politics to consider the role of everyday, mundane, often private, practices in the construction of political identities.

These new conceptualizations of political geography have led to the adoption of new methodologies. Most significant in recent years has been increasing interest in the ways in which political identities are constructed by recourse to various metaphors or metonyms through discourse analysis. For example, some works have decoded the texts of political elites for the references to cultural values they make in their creation of the world. Dalby (1990) examined the imagined geographies produced by the U.S. Committee on the Present Danger, and Ó Tuathail and Agnew (1992) decoded the geopolitical concepts persisting in international relations texts. More recent work in critical geopolitics has further expanded understandings of political texts. Analyses of media, for instance, have revealed the ways in which the political world is explained to different groups on a daily basis (Dalby 1996; Power 2001). In some cases, political geographers also have examined the textual methods by which people are drawn in as subjects of particular representations of the world, whether as social groups, such as audiences of popular media (Sharp 2000a), or as individuals, such as the "Oklahoma Bomber" (Sparke 1998). These works take their methodology from literary and postcolonial theory in order to make sense of the words and images commonly used to explain the world to audiences and readers. Each looks for the words and phrases associated with particular political phenomena and processes, looks for the content of what is said and what is missing from discussion, and looks for the construction of various geographical imaginations invoked in different political situations. Others have looked to the gendered language characteristic of much political discourse in order to understand the subjectivities this offers men and women in political communities (Dalby 1994; Sharp 1996; Walter 1995).

Yet others have examined constructions of political identity through involvement in political movements (see Routledge 1997; Dowler 1998; Agnew 2002), cultural preservation movements (Hague 2002; Till 1999), and performances of self (Bell and Valentine 1995b), among other things, to acknowledge that political identities and actions are not only constructed through some formal political sphere. The spaces of home, leisure, and privacy are equally important. Participatory techniques also have been adopted in work with communities excluded from politics. Such methods involve the use of prompted discussions rather than interviews in an attempt to generate a more natural form of communication or have used props in communities where people are not as happy with verbal representation (see, for instance, Parr 2001).

Of course, the idea that politics takes place in everyday spaces, and not only in the formal sphere of politics, is not a new line of research for feminist geography. From the maxim "the personal is political," feminists have shown how the most private and intimate spaces of life are infused with power and are caught up in various relationships of domination and resistance. Feminists have illustrated the importance of the everyday in the mundane creation of political identities and political activity, and they have illustrated the importance of power relations that work through domestic spheres. If an aim of feminist methodologies is "to validate women's and other marginalized groups' experiences" as Reger (2001, 605) suggested, then there is no possibility of distance. Instead, there are attempts to deal with emotions, beliefs, and other day-to-day feelings (Reger 2001). This has meant a methodological turn away from some of the formal arenas of politics to considering the role of behavior and representations of spaces of home, culture, and privacy supposedly outside the political. Others have challenged the division of space into political and apolitical spheres, instead examining the complex interdependency of both (Secor 2002; Staeheli and Lawson 1994).

This shift in the place of political geographies also signalled a necessary shift in methods. Such research cannot be distanced and objective but instead aims to understand and interpret the rich detail of everyday life. There is a tendency for studies to be intensive rather than extensive, and, as a result, most have been localized. Much work is linked with small-scale politics, for instance, the establishment of lesbian communities (Rothenberg 1995), the everyday political interventions of Republican women in Northern Ireland (Dowler 1998), or the charting of the geographies of women's fear in the city (Pain 1991; Valentine 1989). A number of political geographers have looked to the daily practices that make up political activities and behaviors. Ó Tuathail (1996b) offered Maggie O'Kane's impassioned reports of the war in Bosnia as a situated, moral, and subjective alternative to the distanced all-seeing eye of the traditional geopolitician. Her reports emphasized the agency and acts of people and the materiality of violence. She discussed not only the imagined geographies and representations through which the region gains its political identity and through which conflict has been configured but also the actions of people—heroic acts and violent repression—the impacts of which are not only words or discourses but also pain, sorrow, and death. Dowler (1998) also uncovered alternative forms of resistance and conflict enacted by women in the Irish Republican Army, although not recognized as a legitimate form of political action in the nationalist struggle. For example, although not actually jailed themselves, some interviewees explained that their long years visiting their husbands and then their sons in prison and coping alone with raising a family might as well have been a prison sentence for women like themselves who could never escape these responsibilities (Dowler 1998, 165). Her methods had to suit the informality of the situations in which she met these women, and they involved participation in the daily routines of her interviewees, socializing with them, as well as intense ethical issues regarding her own presentation of self (Dowler 2001).

As qualitative methods such as ethnography tend to be carried out in localized situations, they can be critiqued for ignoring regional and globalizing forces that operate on many different scales, such as "the body, home, communities, nations" and "international political economies" (Staeheli and Lawson 1994, 98). Although feminist methods often are adopted at the local scale (Moss 2002, 10), they are not necessarily constrained by scale. Massey (1991) illustrated clearly the complexity of the local, the necessarily global nature of any place. Others have examined the gendered dimensions of national identities through analysis of national rhetoric (Sharp 1996), public statuary (Johnson 1995), and cultural societies (Hague 2002). Those who have focused on the politics of employment and the workplace are required to consider not only the politics in the workplace but also its interconnections with processes at regional, national, and global scales (Hughes 2000).

The story of international politics has traditionally been one of the spectacular confrontation of mighty states led by powerful statesmen, of the speeches and heroic acts of the elite, and of the specialist knowledge of "intellectuals of statecraft." Enloe (1989) refused to accept this story as the extent of the workings of international relations and instead focused on those elements that the traditional story excludes and silences: the role of international labor migration, the availability of cheap female labor for transnational corporation investment, the availability of sex workers for the tourist industry in southeast Asia, and so on. Enloe's is a very different account of international politics than the conventional story and illustrates well the different types of knowledges of the world that exist. Her story may lack the excitement, confidence, and apparent power of the more usual one, and yet the knowledges of which she wrote are equally important. For her, the international is linked intimately to everyday events of gender relations as well as to the grand narratives of international trade, diplomacy, and war. Her account links together the personal and the political, not simply a micropolitics of the body or a local politics of struggle but a politics of international linkages and exploitations. She highlights the flows of migrants, representations of other places in geographical imaginations, constructions of "women and children" to be protected by the state, new social movements, and ecological resistances (see also Seager 1993). These powers are not formally channelled through the politics of statecraft, which means that they are not part of the political sphere. Nevertheless, they do create political geographies. Furthermore, the practices of geopolitics could not operate in the same way without them. These practices are not marginal to state geopolitics but are intimately entwined with them. For example, Orientalism (Said 1978), one of the first great textual geopolitics, required images of sexually submissive women and emasculated men, and the cold war simultaneously domesticated and contained both the communists and female sexuality and identity. It is imperative, then, that feminist methodologies include attention toward all aspects of political identity and activity. It is important to understand the nature of both the flows of people around the world and the representations that they carry with them. If not, as Enloe (1989, 1) suggested, "if we employ only the conventional, ungendered compass to chart international politics, we are likely to end up mapping a landscape peopled only by men, mostly elite men." The methods we adopt, in other words, will allow some voices to be heard but may silence others.

The significance paid by feminist researchers to the voices of others and the political project of facilitating the empowerment of others through the research process wherever possible mean that it is difficult to undertake work that is not grounded in participatory research. Fieldwork does have uncomfortable associations with the masculinist exploits of empire (see the exchange between Stoddart [1991] and Domosh [1991b], and Rose [1993] who has critiqued geographical writings on the field as being part of a particularly masculinist endeavor). However, many feminist geographers have a commitment to fieldwork for the possibility it offers for the inclusion of other voices into various parts of the research process and for the genuine collaboration that this type of work can facilitate (see *Professional Geographer* special issue 1994; Sparke 1996a).

This does not mean a naive return to the field, as the discussion in "Women in the Field" in the *Professional Geographer* in 1994 demonstrates. A number of contributors fear the dangers of "exoticizing" the other, of choosing a difference to study for its difference rather than any particular commitment to the group in question. For example, Katz (1994, 68) used a comparative approach, not only to foreground her relationship to those involved in the research but also to allow the research to reflect on larger-scale processes:

> By displacing the field and addressing the issue in rural Sudan and East Harlem, New York—settings that on the surface appear to have little in common—I am able to tell a story not of marginalization alone where "those poor people" might be the key narrative theme, but of the systemic predations of global economic restructuring.

Hence, Katz and others have recognized their ambivalent position within the research process: they are not part of the communities being researched but they are not entirely separate—each of us is always already in the field. Katz does accept the possibility, though, that there are times when the most appropriate method might be one of silence, acknowledging that "ethnographic work can (inadvertently) expose sensitive practices of subaltern people to those who (might) use this knowledge to oppress them" (Katz 1994, 71; see also Stacey 1988). Others have examined their positionality and the role that this has in research (e.g., Sparke 1996a). There are, then, important ethical issues linked to the adoption even of sensitive ethnographic methods. However, these ethics are very much context dependent. Moss (2002, 11) suggested that interviewing elite women "perhaps could and should be approached differently than interviewing women marginalized by the same economic processes that made the first woman a member of an elite." In elite situations—in which power relations do not straightforwardly privilege the researcher—many researchers are willing to hide their true identities and beliefs in an attempt to uncover practices of exclusion (but see Mullings [1999] on the complexity of this performance).

Conclusion

Feminists have been active in bringing to the foreground the silenced politics of the self, the body, the private sphere, nature, work practices, and so on. The inaccessibility of these to traditional methods of political geography, which locate politics solely in the formal arena of the state, has helped to reinforce a political map that has left women out. And yet institutions of statehood and processes of nation building are of great significance in contemporary society. It is important not to lose track of this in the context of the cultural turn, which, at times, can appear to recognize every act as political. There is a danger that the dissolving of all boundaries of "the political" will mean that anything could be studied as political geography.

Feminist political geography must not lose sight of the formal political sphere, because the processes that dominate formal politics do need constant examination and questioning from a position that is aware of the gendered consequences of decision making. It is important to make methodolgical interventions here. Feminist political geographers also will have to continue to engage with quantitative methods, even if this is a strategic adoption, to ensure their voices are heard in these debates. However, feminist political geographers need to use a wide range of methods in order to also get at the less formal spaces where hidden and marginalized, but no less important, political identities and processes are formed and reformed.

7

Development, Postcolonialism, and Feminist Political Geography

NINA LAURIE, WITH PAMELA CALLA

Feminism's commitment to interdisciplinarity and internationalism has made it central to encounters between development and postcolonial studies in recent years. In geography, feminist research on development emerged as a key agenda in the late 1980s, following the publication of the first book on gender and development by Momsen and Townsend (1987). Since then, gender and development has remained a strong area of research, influencing work in all areas of geography, including feminist geography. Postcolonial studies have yet to become integrated in the discipline to the same extent.

Feminist commitment to interdisciplinary and international work is in part epistemological; at the heart of feminist scholarship is a questioning of the power hierarchies of knowledge formation and taken-for-granted categories. In this chapter we argue that the political priority for feminist geography is to embrace a postcolonial agenda wholeheartedly. This agenda means fostering research that tackles the unequal power relations of North-South interactions (including knowledge production) and examines their gendered and exclusionary dimensions. In this chapter we argue that the greater integration of critical work on gender, development geography, and international relations into mainstream geography will help advance these goals.

The chapter outlines the theoretical debates in three literatures pertinent to feminist political geography. It highlights feminist critiques of development (especially neoliberal agendas), examines postcolonial research that emphasizes the authority of subaltern voices, and explores moves to sexualize politics and geopolitics. In each section we further examine the theoretical debates by using examples to illustrate points of tension and emerging themes of research.

We begin the chapter by defining postcolonialism and highlighting how the colonial origins of Western social science continue to influence academic research, particularly in the area of development studies. We examine new approaches that attempt to move beyond the colonial gaze, highlighting the example of the Guyanese women's organization Red Thread (see Peake and Trotz 1999), which attempts to deal with culture, ethnicity, and development in new ways. Second, we examine the gendering of development. We consider the importance of gender and development work in understanding globalization and the global economy and discuss how race and gender have usually been conceptualized separately in this literature, illustrating our argument with reference to the compartmentalization of gender and ethnic studies in the Andes. We finish this section by examining new work that integrates race and gender into analyses of masculinities. Finally, we examine the politics and geopolitics of development from a gender perspective. Discussing how masculinist narratives have focused attention on formal institutions, we indicate how social movement approaches have attempted to redress this balance by examining women's activities in informal politics. We argue, however, that an overemphasis on social movements has produced a limited set of political subjectivities (actor identities). We indicate how attempts to sexualize geopolitics represent a new opportunity to move away from social-movement-led analyses. Our conclusion returns to questions concerning crossing borders and the politics of North-South and "Core-Periphery" (Potter 2001) representations in geography, arguing for greater attention to be given to the work of development geographers in the discipline as a whole.

Defining Postcolonialism

Postcolonialism has emerged as an important concept that focuses attention on how colonialism has influenced the ways we see the world and the actors in it, as well as our abilities to imagine possibilities for change. Although emerging from historical, literary, and cultural studies problematizing the construction of Western knowledge (Kothari 2001), postcolonialism's concern with both colonial discourse (narratives and representations) and neocolonial processes (unequal power relations) clearly highlights the politics of development across space and place. Consequently, authors such as Slater (2000) have argued that postcolonialism challenges Northern geographers to move on from Eurocentric visions to ask questions such as who is heard speaking about political geography, those from the North or the South? "Moving on," however, is not easy for disciplines like geography that became institutionalized through the colonial project and remain imbued with colonial histories (Driver 2001), imaginaries, and methodologies (Nagar 2002). Major challenges must, therefore, be addressed in order for feminist political geography to fully embrace a postcolonial agenda.

The first challenge is the need to overturn hierarchies of representation by recognizing and disavowing colonial histories and the power relations and spaces through which colonial practices continue to reproduce themselves over time. This requires new ways of dealing with the political economy of knowledge production. Focusing attention on questions of discourse, representation, and authenticity highlights the importance of the position from which people speak and emphasizes the need to decenter analysis (hooks 1984). Postcolonial studies in geography have emphasized that it is not enough merely to decenter and deprivilege the hegemonic white-male, Anglo gaze but also to question which people and which understandings of development and development priorities are promoted. Rivera and Barragán (1997) discussed the influence of postcolonial Indian subaltern studies in countries of the South and pointed out that it is paradoxical that a debate started in the South arrives in places like Bolivia mediated by the academic filter of the North where the postcolonial turn has become popular. As Jacobs (1996) argued for aboriginal politics in Australia, such ironies point to the persistence of the unequal global relations of knowledge production and underline the need to respect subaltern knowledge and voices.

The second challenge is to move beyond fixed, dichotomous understandings of change that emphasize a shift from traditional to modern societies. New approaches toward framing development issues and constructing theory in ways that do not prioritize the experiences of the North are needed. For some authors, constructing alternative paradigms involves developing new frameworks without making reference to colonized ways of seeing the world and being able to think beyond visions of change colonized by a language of economic progress and modernization (Escobar 1995). For such postdevelopment thinkers, the professionalization of the global and local development industry has colonized the possibilities of thinking about change in a powerful way. Development has been reified to such an extent that it becomes difficult to think outside its categories. However, postcolonialism has produced a whole wave of writing that contests universalist assumptions about development and instead conceptualizes it "as a historically singular experience, the creation of a domain of thought and action" (Escobar 1995). Postcolonialism has inspired the search for new approaches that are able to conceptualize coexisting and multiple modernities, spaces, and traditions and that have policy implications as well as conceptual reach.

Next we explore one such example of postcolonial conceptualizations of development. We chose this example because it illustrates feminist political geography's commitment to retheorizing development while actively seeking to identify innovative forms of political change in relation to gender issues.

Rethinking and Redefining Development: Red Thread Women's Development Program in Guyana

Postcolonial realities often circumscribe attempts from the South to develop imaginaries that challenge mainstream Northern-led development and its practices. Peake and Trotz (1999) emphasized the frustrations faced by Red Thread, a Guyanese women's organization that attempts to develop a holistic vision and practice of development. Although focusing initially on income-generating activities, the remit of Red Thread is now much broader and has long-term goals of bringing together differently radicalized and classed women in order to learn from their differences and similarities. Tackling the racism inherent in a society that differentiates the femininities of Afro-Guyanese and Indo-Guyanese women along racist lines, Red Thread seeks to strengthen women's identities and solidarities as part of a development agenda. They organize sessions that promote mutual understanding and break down boundaries between women, discussing taboo issues such as racism, sexuality, and domestic violence while also promoting group skills. According to Peake and Trotz (1999), multilateral donors promoting good governance agendas see Red Thread as a successful organization. Yet Red Thread insists on the need for independence and core funding for their activities and infrastructure rather than relying on what is often offered by multilaterals—support from outside expert consultants advising on institutional strengthening. The agendas of multilateral organizations drives development by prioritizing short-term projects and failing to see the need to support locally embedded grassroots organizations between projects in order for them to achieve self-defined long-term goals. For Red Thread, interventions by multilateral agencies represent a reversal of development goals; short-term gain is prioritized over Red Thread's own emphasis on longer-term social, cultural, and economic change. In the words of Peake and Trotz (1999, 189), "So long as Western knowledge or 'expertise' defines what is known as 'development,' the global (mal)distribution of power continues to sustain images of South groups as 'receivers' and Northern organizations as 'transmitters' of culture."

The example of Red Thread illustrates how women's organizations in the South actively resist the colonizing power of Northern understandings of development. By doing so, they promote postcolonial conceptualizations of change, which do not prioritize economic modernization over social goals. Not all gender and development approaches, however, share a postcolonial agenda. Women's organizations and networks have a long-standing engagement with the development industry, and gender mainstreaming is now well established in development. In the following section we examine some of the achievements and pitfalls of gender and development approaches.

Gendering Development

The flourishing of gender and development perspectives from the 1980s onward involved a number of approaches that focused on work, divisions of labor, and the household (Kothari 2001). The most well-known of these are Women in Development, Women and Development, and Gender and Development (Rathgeber 1990). Critiques of neoliberal development, emerging largely from Marxist feminist work on the global economy, have been important to these gender and development analyses. For example, they have shown how, during the privatization of social services and the rollback of the state under neoliberalism, the most vulnerable people (women and children) bear the greatest burden of structural adjustment.

The benefits of new employment opportunities under neoliberalism also have been questioned. Although new jobs for women as low-wage workers continue to emerge across the world, notions of appropriate gendered behavior and femininities, such as stereotypes of women as docile and obedient, control most new neoliberal work environments. Feminist geographers have shown how the relationship between global restructuring and increases in female labor rest on the intimate link between formal and informal work and the blurring of work and domestic space through homeworking, outworking, and subcontracting practices (Women and Geography Study Group 1997; Radcliffe 1999; Laurie et al. 1999). Consequently, the extent to which power relations and gender identities change as a result of female employment remains a key area of gender and development research. Although divergent representations of Third World workers in the gender and development literature exist, Southern scholars have been particularly critical of representations that focus on Third World women as victims of the development process (see Lim 1990). Such criticisms reflect wider postcolonial concerns about the Westerncentric gaze in gender and development research and the promotion of homogenous cartographies of the category "Third World woman" (Mohanty 1991b). Such critiques suggest that research has questioned the authority of modernization narratives in development but has often generalized about what work means to different people in different contexts. International, interdisciplinary, feminist research has failed to disaggregate the category "Third World women workers" by not engaging with complex constructions of multiple gender identities in the South.

In the next example we discuss how, in part, these shortcomings reflect the fact that gender and ethnicity have largely been conceptualized separately in development studies; for example, identities have been discussed in terms of gender or ethnicity but not both. This separation has facilitated the use of homogenizing categories and taken attention away from efforts to conceptualize race and gender as intersecting influences on identity formation.

Development, Ethnicity, and Gender in the Andes

In the Andean context, gender and ethnicity remain constructed as antagonistic conceptual and empirical camps. Some authors argue that this antagonism goes against the democratization processes that both positions claim to uphold. Barrig (1999) pointed out that in Peru both camps have created ways to impede integration and dialogue. Much like Paulson and Calla (2000) stated for the Bolivian case, Barrig identified these impediments as coming from contrasting philosophical and methodological stances that put urban and Westernizing feminist stances in opposition to those holding purist and absolutistic visions of the Andean past along with essentialized notions of gender and ethnic identity.

Paulson and Calla (2000) were specific about the theoretical premises, methodological procedures, and political effects of both positions. They distinguished two antagonistic ways in which Andean reality is approached: "classical" gender analysis (in keeping with the gender and development movement mentioned previously) and the "Andeanist" exploration of gender (following more anthropological, ethnographic approaches toward culture and ethnicity). The former approach argues that ethnicity has been associated with tradition that needs to be overcome through education and the improvement of life conditions. It is this kind of modernization that Andean culturalists oppose and makes them reject classical gender analysis. They argue that gender constitutes an imperialistic stance that divides communities and erodes what is left of Andean culture. Andeanists such as Apffel-Marglin (1998), moreover, reject the discourse and practice of development and see the category of gender as an imposition by Western development planners. Thus, Andeanists tend to claim that gender and development perspectives homogenize relationships and identities that they consider to be unique, harmonic, and complementary. They argue that feminist approaches tend to deny local specificities because of their reliance on universal concepts, quantitative categories, and Western logic. On the other hand, gender analyses question the androcentric nature of Andeanist analyses that makes the feminine marginal and invisible, and they also are concerned about Andeanists' rejection of historical concerns related to gendered identities and power relations (Paulson and Calla 2000).

This antagonism has had limiting effects at a policy-making level and has prevented agencies (governmental and nongovernmental) from achieving integration in their analysis and coordination in their activities. Paulson and Calla's (2000) analysis also pointed to the failure of both approaches to engage with masculinities.

The lack of attention given to masculinities has been widely held as one of the failings of gender and development approaches. Gender mainstreaming often has ignored gender relations and men and, instead, has focused on adding women into development processes. Next we argue that the examination of masculinities allows the postcolonial gaze to fall on the construction of unequal power relations at a range of scales. In particular, we discuss how recent work in international relations usefully highlights new research questions and subjects.

Masculinities and Masculinist Agendas

Altman (2001, 130) claimed that male narratives in international relations and development studies "are centred in a vast array of micro practices and cultural forms enacted, constituted and legitimised by men and/or in male gendered terms." Moreover, these narratives have taken the state as the main subject, thereby excluding other actors and subjects. Notwithstanding these masculinist traditions, new research is beginning to address the influence of development processes on masculinities and gender dimensions of divisions of work, identities, and household power relations (see C. Jackson 2000). Analyses reveal, for example, the importance in some cases of "heroic" masculinities in shaping resistance struggles at a national level and also point to the continuities and discontinuities in development discourses about men and work, which rest on colonial representations of rural men as lazy (Whitehead 2000). Along these lines, some authors have started to examine the effects of structural adjustment in relation to changing work situations, masculine identities, and authority. For example, Calla and Rojas

(1998) explored the ways in which structural adjustment during the 1980s affected the mining sector in Bolivia. Because of mining shutdowns, women had to incorporate themselves into the informal labor market in large numbers and men had to dedicate their time to small (informal) economic activities. Men could no longer produce, provide, and protect as they used to, much in the same way that the state could no longer fulfill a similar paternal role under neoliberal adjustment. This situation triggered a crisis in which the family became the last bastion of authority, and many men ended up imposing violent authoritarian control over the household.

New research on embodiment and globalization by international political economy scholars highlights another possible avenue for work on masculinities and development by examining the connections between macroeconomic processes and changing masculine identities. Hooper's (2000) discourse analysis of job adverts for top executives in the *Economist* (a leading current-affairs magazine with worldwide circulation), for example, shows how globalization becomes embodied in particular masculine subjectivities (masculine actor identities).[1] For Hooper, globalization subjectivities combine all that is successful in business terms about Anglo-American hegemonic masculinity (a veneer of social informality, teamwork, and flexibility while pursuing competitiveness) with an attention to specificity, local culture, team learning, and knowledge sharing, which Hooper identified as characterizing Asian (Japanese) business masculinities. Hooper's argument is that the way we experience globalization in any place reflects current social epistemologies, entailing specific and competing notions of masculinity, femininity, and gender relations. Speaking of the modern capitalist era and globalization, she suggested,

> The discourse of globalization itself becomes one site . . . [for] gendered interpretative struggles as the meaning of globalisation is contested. In the process, different "elements" or ingredients of masculinity and femininity are co-opted in new or old configurations to serve particular interests, and particular gendered (and other) identities are consolidated and legitimated or downgraded and devalued. This involves power struggles between men and women, but also between different groups of men as they jostle for position and control; articulating and re-articulating the relationship between masculinity and power as they go. (Hooper 2000, 60)

As international development agencies seek to secure "adjustment with a human face," these neoliberal discourses of globalization are contested in the development arena. In the poststructural adjustment era of harsh economic reforms, negative growth, and social collapse, the promotion by donors of "socially inclusive" and "proindigenous" neoliberalism is indicative of the relationship between globalization and competing gendered subjectivities, as we illustrate in the next example.

As part of proindigenous development in Latin America, new university professionalization courses are becoming increasingly common for development planners focused on indigenous issues (Laurie et al. 2003). Replete with an international range of methodologies, conceptual frameworks, and comparative case studies, and familiar with the most up-to-date development-speak, courses train the next generation of development managers and experts. The ways in which masculine subjectivities are constructed in these spaces produces competition and conflict and triggers processes of masculinization, feminization, and indianization in day-to-day interactions.

In a diploma course in a Bolivian university on indigenous rights, students discussed national gender regimes in a course on interculturality and gender (Calla 2000). Class work concentrated on discussing Gill's (2000) careful explanation of the ways in which hegemonic and subordinated masculinities are forged in larger national institutions, such as the military, in which compulsory military service for young men shapes experiences of nationhood, ethnicity, and gender. The feminization of the Indian and the indianization of the feminine also were explained to show the similar ways in which Indians and women were historically disqualified, humiliated, and excluded from being citizens of nation-states. The men in this course self-identified as Aymara and Quechua, the two major indigenous languages of Bolivia associated with the largest ethnic groups. The male students started to narrate their experience in relation to their own subordinated and feminized masculinities. One of them explained that because he had finished high school, he was called *la señorita* (young woman) while in military service and so was publicly dressed with a *pollera*, a homespun skirt associated with indigenous women's dress. This occurred especially when he, and others like him, got into fights with *mestizo* (mixed race) men in order to defend those considered "more Indian," for example, more Quechua monolingual. An Aymara man explained that the use of the *pollera* as a symbol of public humiliation also was common in the day-to-day life of peasant union activity, whereby those considered traitors to the community and the union were publicly dressed as women (for a further discussion, see Calla 2000, 2001).

This example illustrates how recent research is beginning to theorize race and gender in conjunction with each other. It avoids homogenizing categories and instead provides new insights into the complex construction of multifarious identities. Such theorizations have implications for understanding the processes through which development imaginaries become hegemonic. On one hand, the students on these courses represent another face of Hooper's successfully globalized masculine subjectivity. Their training will enable them to become transnational indigenous development professionals (Laurie et al. 2003). They will become important development brokers, mediating between indigenous organizations and international donors in global forums. On the other hand, the way in which this specific globalized (indigenous) masculine subjectivity is being forged draws on racist and sexist practices and highlights the contradictory nature of the processes involved in the gendered representations that link global and local development practices.

In the following section we take up the issue of gender identities in development in more depth through a discussion of how current research on the relationship between culture, sexuality, and development opens up potentially fruitful trajectories for gender analyses.

Politics and Development—Hybridity, Social Movements, and Sex

Constructions of nationhood frequently rest on representations of women as bearers of culture and tradition, with femininity playing an important role in the maintenance of ideals of nationhood and cultural belonging (Yuval-Davis 1997). Although work in political geography has examined the role of gender iconography in nation building, with a few notable exceptions (see Radcliffe and Westwood 1996; Peake and Trotz 1999), little geographical research has examined gendered nation building or the gendered implications of nationalist discourse in countries of the South. Rather, research has tended to focus on democratization processes and social movements more generally.

Increasingly interdisciplinary in nature, the social movements literature has become extremely diverse in recent years. Gender analyses have been important in this literature in a number of ways. First, an extensive literature exists on women's social movements, focusing particularly on women's active role in democratization movements and women's collective economic survival strategies in the face of structural adjustment measures across the world. This literature is especially rich on Latin American movements (see Laurie et al. 1999; Laurie in press, for summaries). The main thrust of this research has been to question the extent to which women's involvement in grassroots informal politics fundamentally challenges gender relations in the household and beyond. Second, as debates over the significance of social movements and the extent to which they represent "a new way of doing politics" began to dominate political theory, women's participation was highlighted as one of the key markers distinguishing new social movements from previous, largely class-based alliances (Escobar and Alvarez 1992).

The social movements literature has refocused attention on human agency (and specifically gendered agency) and away from the state and formal institutions as the only important development arenas. Much of this literature builds on earlier reconceptualizations of resistance such as Scott's (1985) identification of everyday forms of struggle, whereas more recently the focus on the cultural politics of identity (Alvarez et al. 1998) has been influenced by postcolonial writing on representation and has increasingly highlighted the relationship between hybridity and sociocultural political change (Canclini 1992). The scale of analysis also has changed from an initial focus on the urban and national to the transnational. Social movements are now understood as being embedded within transnational networks that shape the politics of identity and are, in turn, influenced by the "scaling up" of grassroots activism and identity making (R. Cohen and Rai 2000; Castells 1997). The increasing attention given to the transnational aspects of social movements has renewed an interest in women's political networking (see Moghadam 2000) and the politics of feminist collaborations across the North and South (Staeheli and Nagar 2002), prompting examinations of the gendered representations inherent in transnational circuits (Laurie 1999; Radcliffe et al. 2004).

Although conceptually and empirically rich, the dominance of a social movements focus in geography, political science, and related disciplines has arguably narrowed the analysis of gender and politics. There is a tendency for analysis of empowerment and social movements to create iconoclastic identities for women. The celebration of women's emblematic political roles as *supermadres* (super mothers), for example, produces overly triumphant caricatures of women's political experience and promotes uncomplicated understandings of change. Such representations are as homogenizing as the victim-led descriptions of Third World women discussed previously. An overemphasis on processes of hybridity and identity formation can obscure very real material lacks and differences; *supermadres* can only fulfill *supermadre* expectations if they have the resources (material, emotional, psychological) and the socioeconomic, political conditions to do so. Seeing gender and politics largely through the social movement gaze narrows the impact of feminist studies on wider political theory and processes. When gender analyses become a separate chapter on social movements, feminist critique does not reach a wider audience, and agendas such as feminist analyses of the state, nation building, and international relations remain underexamined.

In contrast to the social movement emphasis in much feminist political analysis, research on sexuality often focuses on wider political arenas. Although this work engages with social movements, it avoids being reduced to such a framework and therefore resists the temptation to produce homogenous categorizations. In the following section we illustrate some of the emerging research on sexuality and politics, charting the overlaps between sexuality, international relations, and postcolonialism.

Sexualizing Globalization and Development

Enloe's (1989) pioneering work on the relationship between the sex trade and overseas military bases revolutionized the study of politics and international relations. Subsequently, sex trafficking, the international brides industry, sex tourism, and the use of rape as a weapon of war have all become legitimate foci of geopolitical analysis. As a result, poststructuralist feminist concerns with the body have been brought into contemporary political theory (see Youngs 2000b). Despite this work, the failure of international relations and development studies to address issues of sexuality seriously and systematically is increasingly being recognized (Chua et al. 2000; Kaur Puar 2002; Altman 2001). Although there is a well-established and growing literature on sexual geographies (Bell and Valentine 1995a; Nast 2002), little of this work has found its way into the international agenda of the discipline. Kaur Puar (2002) argued,

Studies of globalisation range from presenting the "global" as an overarching, homogenizing force, in opposition to a pure, resistant "local," to theorizing local-global exchange, hybridisation, and multidirectional flows. Sexuality as related to tourism, migration, identity formation and economic labour flows, though it is intrinsic to analyses of globalisation, often remains unaddressed in these accounts. (Kaur Puar 2002, 2)

One of the few notable exceptions is Peake and Trotz's (1999) examination of gender, ethnicity, and place through a case study of Guyana with sexuality as a key axis of analysis. Their book carefully unpacks the relationship between colonized gender relations and identities, globalization and global restructuring through different waves of economic adjustment and associated shifts in highly gendered industries. Central to their analysis is an intertwined focus on sexuality, race, and gender. They discuss the important role of Red Thread as a development actor in Guyana, yet they avoid the traps of a social movements approach. Instead of seeing Red Thread purely as a grassroots political movement, they emphasize the organization's insistence on imagining a wide-ranging development agenda while remaining outside the national political forum. While emphasizing the cultural politics of Red Thread, its members, and the women's communities with whom it works, Peake and Trotz do not shy away from naming and examining discriminatory practices and ideologies such as racism and homophobia. Their conceptualization of culture and cultural politics allows them to interrogate the ways in which the social epistemology of Guyana is structured by discriminatory constructions of sexuality rather than to render certain practices and ideas "untouchable" as eroticized local culture and cultural practice. The "within and without the project" positionality of Red Thread activists and their focus on recognizing cultural barriers to development avoid the temptation to create *supermadre* icons of the movement, the activists, and the women with whom they work. Such a focus on cultural politics, however, also means that understandings of barriers are not framed by modernization's discourses of change. Rather, the reclaiming, reinvention, and reworking of culture become central to defining development goals under a postcolonial agenda.

The coalescence of postcolonial and development studies agendas around reflexive cultural forms of analysis is producing a new interest in understanding the relationship between Third World sexualities and development. Chua et al. (2000) argued for a new interdisciplinary paradigm "women, culture, and development" to replace earlier approaches driven by economistic understandings of development that exclude consideration of sexualities. Women, culture, and development agendas call for a multiethnic and multiracial feminist approach together with an explicit engagement with materialist definitions of culture that emphasize the link between women's visibility, production, and reproduction in everyday life. They explore Third World sexualities in a number of ways. First, through an analysis of the historical reproduction of notions and practices of sexuality, they highlight the ways in which Western understandings of sexuality—heterosexual monogamy—have become hegemonic. They show how sex and sexuality are used to reproduce power, authority, and dominance while legitimating Western rule in colonial and postindependence contexts. Second, Third World sex work is analyzed as a form of production without prioritizing economic analyses that focus on the economic constraints for sex workers, their families, and their communities. Rather, the authors' understanding of the intertwined relationship between production, reproduction, and agency emphasizes the complicated aspects of the everyday and institutional lives of sex workers. Their analysis focuses on

> the conjunctural and contradictory elements of their [sex workers'] identities, practices, experiences, structure of feelings, signification and representation at both local and global levels. . . . This shift in emphasis moves the focus from the economic to one that captures the totality of women sex-workers' experiences and cultures without side-stepping the material and ideological. (Chua et al. 2000, 833)

Third, they examine agency through the sexuality and experience of Third World lesbians. They dispute claims that lesbian interests are marginal to development debates. They question the "West" and the "Rest" dichotomy that frames lesbian desire as a Western import into the Third World and that silences its voice in nationalist or revolutionary movements. They emphasize that lesbian experience and culture is historically and generationally contingent and expressed in diverse ways in different places. Yet they argue that all women's identities and sexualities (lesbian identified or not) are lived through the shared social changes associated with development, independence, and postcolonialism. They therefore identify and legitimate a platform for dialogue and contestation and argue that the agency lesbian women assert in development not only focuses on social experience but also foregrounds the importance of sexual desire, pleasure, and emotion.

Although we would argue against the need for yet another acronym to frame understandings of the relationship between gender and development, the emphasis that Chua et al. (2000) and Peake and Trotz (1999) placed on sexuality and their call to reexamine conceptualizations of culture in relation to development is very important. Such a position establishes a new agenda for studies of development, postcolonialism, and political theory. It also begins to suggest a framework with which these concepts and practices can be understood through gendered and sexualized bodies, institutions, and places inscribed with social and economic meaning, scaled in different ways.

Conclusion

In this chapter we argued that feminist agendas have long since engaged with development studies and, more recently, postcolonialism, enriching multidisciplinary work as well as political geography. These agendas have highlighted invisible, marginalized issues and redefined what are considered legitimate topics of political study. Although the relationship between development and postcolonialism has never been easy, feminist work has continued to struggle with and insist on the need for interdisciplinary and international ways of interpreting the world and formulating theory. Although current feminist geography is characterized by a commitment to reflexivity, we argue that reflexivity is often more evident in development geography and is certainly more evident than in what Potter (2001) termed "core geography." In core geography—that is, geography produced in the North that either focuses on advanced capitalist societies or prioritizes the interpretation of global processes from this perspective—assumptions about the researcher being like those he or she interviews often means that reflexivity and positionality remain underexamined.

Although Kothari (2001) suggested that we have yet to see what nonmasculinist, noncolonialist development studies might look like, we argue that glimpses of these characteristics are evident in feminist geography. For Peake and Trotz, this geography starts with the feminist postcolonial researcher herself:

> Engaging in the reclamation of self and historical agency, i.e., becoming self-conscious about the specificity of our own positions by creating alternative interpretations of colonial histories and geographies, and replacing an (inadequate) sense of personal culpability with that of a social and historic responsibility for whiteness (i.e. white not only as skin colour but as ideological norm), feminist research can work towards being free of imperial inscription. (Peake and Trotz 1999, 33)

Working toward being free of inscription necessitates particular working practices as the participant-researcher relationship becomes blurred. There are many examples of innovative working relationships between Southern and Northern scholars and between nongovernment organizations and feminist academics more widely. For example, Red Thread's collaborations mirror the myriad forms of collaborative working relationships that feminists and other radical geographers prioritize. Whether these working practices involve a commitment to bilingual writing projects (Townsend et al. 1999; Zapata et al. 2002) or long-term engagement in a single community and its everyday life (see Bassett 2002), the call to become involved remains strong.

The mushrooming of collaborative feminist scholarship in recent years, however, brings with it an absorption problem; it is simply not possible to know about and read everything. In writing this chapter, Nina Laurie commented to a colleague that the book by Peake and Trotz (1999) is one of the few books she knows by geographers that explore the relationship between development, globalization, sexuality, race, and femininities. "It wouldn't occur to me to read a book on Guyana," came the reply. Although the limits of our reading have to be drawn somewhere, this exchange supports Potter's (2001) claim that too often these borders are drawn in a way that excludes research by development geographers. He suggested there is a general failure to see development geography as contributing theoretically to "core" research:

Those who work outside the Euro-North American orbit are excluded, or at best marginalized, from the specialisms which see themselves making up the *core* of the discipline of *Geography*. Quite simply they are regarded as "ists" of the Latin American, Caribbean, African or Asian variety. If they endeavour to be comprehensive in their consideration of other regions of the globe, then they may qualify as the ultimate "ists": as full-blown "developmentalists." (Potter 2001, 423)

In looking for ways to combat the exclusionary way that theory is developed in geography, Potter suggested that the relatively new focus on globalization as a theme could provide an opportunity for "fertile grounds for sub-disciplinary interaction" (Potter 2001, 424). However, when the "who is speaking about what" issue is examined, development scholars from the South and North might prefer the term "colonization" to "interaction" to refer to the way in which theory is formulated in geography. Currently, geographers from other subdisciplines, following the "cultural turn," dominate studies on globalization, and development geography, with its emphasis on the politics of knowledge production, is in danger of becoming marginalized. Only when, as a matter of course, social science research draws on theoretical insights and empirical examples from work on development to understand and critique processes like globalization will the postcolonial agenda become fully established. At this point development studies and political geography will reach the "stage of full maturity."

Acknowledgments

We would like to thank Uma Kothari, Diane Richardson, Fiona Smith, and the editors for advice in writing this chapter. Thanks also to the DFID/British Council Higher Education link on gender and development for supporting collaboration between Newcastle and San Simón Universities.

Note

1. The term *subjectivities* refers to specific actor identities and emphasizes political agency. Analytically, gendered subjectivities make reference to identity categories (masculinities and femininities) rather than to individual men and women.

8

Critically Feminist Geopolitics

MARY GILMARTIN AND ELEONORE KOFMAN

Geopolitics, which can be defined as practices and representations of territorial strategies, emerged forcefully in the second half of the nineteenth century under the German geographer Frederich Ratzel (1844–1904) and the British geographer and politician Halford Mackinder (1860–1941). Its rise reflected heightened competition between dominant powers for economic supremacy and territorial containment and possession. This was the period of "Geography Militant" (Driver 2001), resulting "in a more practical exploration and conquest of territories, exotic species and resources" (Godlewska and Smith 1994, 1). Thus, the emergence of geopolitics as the object of academic and policy studies was closely connected with competition and struggle for a planetary space.

In this chapter we first trace the birth of geopolitics in an era when the world was virtually totally explored and occupied by Western powers. The end of the nineteenth century was seen to entail an end to a period of expanding geographical knowledge and territorial occupation, four centuries after Columbus's "discovery" of the Americas. It was a time of disquiet with the economic, social, political, and geographical transformation of the world (Heffernan 2000) and heightened competition, particularly between rival European states. Furthermore, Britain's undisputed hegemony in the middle of the nineteenth century was being challenged by the rising industrial power of Germany and the United States. Geopolitical knowledge and practices were also keenly appreciated and drawn on in the formation of the nation-state, also at its height from the second half of the nineteenth century, and then given impetus by the disintegration of empires after the First World War and later by the processes of decolonization after the Second World War (Hooson 1994). Thus, we examine the significance of geopolitics as a form of thought and practice in the acquisition and peopling of imperial settlements and knowledge of the world. We also examine the exclusion of women from active participation in this pursuit, as well as the relevance of gender issues for imperialism and geopolitics. Women's exclusion and later sequestration within a textual and metaphorical landscape continue today, as we show in the second section.

Development of Geopolitical Thought and Practices

Throughout the mapping of the world and the colonization and incorporation of new territories by European states, geographers had been involved in a variety of activities, such as performing cartography, making war and peace, and classifying different relationships between people and their environments (Livingstone 1992). The intellectual and practical knowledge necessary for their pursuits was increasingly valued toward the end of the nineteenth century. The discipline of geography also benefited from interstate rivalry, attempts to incorporate populations into the nation-state and a more extensive stage of imperialism, especially after 1870. Both the winners and the vanquished in wars sought to promote geography, as is evidenced in the expansion of geographical education in schools and universities in France and Germany in the late nineteenth century (Hudson 1977). In particular, geopoliticians sought to understand the world as an integrated whole and to offer explanatory geographical theories that would underpin practical politics (Heffernan 2000).

The role of imperialism in the development of geography and the engagement of geographers in imperial projects varied between states (M. Bell et al. 1995). Concerns with nation-state formation vied with the desire and need for imperial expansion, as in the case of France (Heffernan 1994), where imperial ambitions were highly contested among the political elite. Among academic geographers, as opposed to those individuals in geographical societies interested in the commercial value of colonialism, it was concern with the French nation and its identity that shaped French geography (Claval 1994). France's more restricted global expansiveness and vision of the world did not yield a major geopolitical thinker, unlike Mackinder in Britain or Ratzel in Germany. Although the growth of geography as an academic discipline in Britain initially benefited less from the push to expand the reaches of the state, as in France and Germany, it could be said that imperialism influenced geographical education even more in Britain, as demonstrated by the interest Mackinder displayed in geographical education at all levels (Mayhew 2000). Such intimate connections between imperialism and geography should not surprise us, given that Britain had constructed the first global empire (Fawcett 1933) on which the sun never set. "The turn of the century debate among colonial geographers over whether the colonial world should be seen as a space to be categorized and analysed or as a space to be remade for the benefit of the imperial economy had repeated manifestations among social scientists" (Stoler and Cooper 1997, 14).

Yet at the same time, radical geographies written by the anarchist geographers Kropotkin (Breitbart 1981) and Reclus (Dunbar 1981) critiqued the bases of dominant geographies and sought to understand geographical processes throughout the globe. Their conception of what constituted relevant influences in the relationship between societies and environments was broad and in tune with contemporary environmental sensibilities and use of resources. For example,

Reclus (1830–1905), a well-known and widely published French geographer of his time, argued that the shrinkage of the world was not in itself to be applauded, for it might mean a greater proportion of the world was becoming a victim of capitalist exploitation. It was becoming meaningless, he argued, to speak of the history of a single country, for Europeanization was eroding boundaries and creating an interdependent world. Reclus wrote,

> In spite of his aversion to foreigners, in spite of the tariff which protects him against outside business, and in spite of the cannon facing the two sides of the tabooed line, he eats bread from India, drinks coffee which is harvested by the Negroes or the Malaysians, dresses himself in materials made from American fibre . . . the very shrinkage of the earth, brought about by the progress of science and by increased facilities of communication, has the effect of enlarging men's minds and broadening every question. (cited in Fleming 1979, 241–42)

Although Reclus criticized the inequities of colonial expansion and the destruction of traditional societies and the environment, his attitude to colonialism could be ambiguous and contradictory, especially in relation to the distinction he drew between the populating colonialism of settlement (e.g., Algeria), as opposed to exploitative colonialism (e.g., India) (Giblin 1987). He was not at all ambiguous about the effects of patriarchy, however, which for him had developed as a result of man exerting force over woman and claiming her as private property. He believed that race was intimately connected with gender; as he stated, rarely does one encounter a racist who is not also a sexist, or vice versa. As with all social phenomena, the nature of racism and sexism varied between different contexts.

The relationship between gender and imperialism has been explored by a variety of different commentators. P. Williams and Chrisman (1994, 193–95) suggested that imperial discourse is gendered in a variety of ways. They highlighted, in particular, the ways white femininity was marked as the heart of Western civilization and also the ways women's interests became subordinated to those of the masculinized nation. For McClintock (1995, 23), imperialism worked through a metaphysics of gender violence, in which "the world is feminized and spatially spread for male exploration, then reassembled and deployed in the interests of massive imperial power." Working within this broader context, geopolitics was hegemonically masculine (Connell 1990)—that is, strong masculinity presented itself as the dominant form, dependent on subordinate female identities, though this was usually not explicitly enunciated. Geopolitics itself created an abstract landscape without figures or people (Kofman 1996), even as diverse imperialisms constructed gendered and racialized projects and unsettled settler societies (Stasilius and Yuval-Davis 1995). Furthermore, geographical and geopolitical projects were pursued without women, who were officially excluded from organized and funded explorations and from the new institutional bodies that proliferated at that time (Domosh 1991a, 1991b). Alexander Humboldt failed in 1821 to open the Société de Géographie in Paris (the first geographical society in the world) to women. Thus, women were not allowed to partake in early national and international societies, except as accompanying spouses. Women did, however, set up their own organizations, such as the Washington-based Society of Women Geographers in 1925, to enable them to undertake fieldwork and present their results (Rossler 1996). Women geographers also began to attend the International Geographical Congresses in the early twentieth century.

Materially and symbolically, how then did women actually participate in imperialism, despite their subordinate roles and exclusion from its most visible exploits?[1] From amid the catalog of "daring exploits" there emerged a symbolic empire that depended heavily on feminized imagery, offering important meanings to women who wished to share in the self-congratulatory adventure. In the early twentieth century, many leading imperialists turned their attention from the excitement of conquest to long-term issues of building a sustainable, civilizing empire dependent on female as well as male virtues. Imperial societies were founded, some of them admitting women, while others established separate groups for women (e.g., British Empire League [1894], the League of the Empire [1901], and the Overseas Club [1910]). Women's imperialist associations were also set up with the objectives of guiding emigration, supporting women settlers, and building churches and performing missionary work abroad. The beginning of the twentieth century was a time when female citizenship was debated, educational levels and career opportunities for middle- and upper-class women widened, and these women became more involved in voluntary work. Most of the upper- and middle-class women who predominated in these associations held conventional views on gender differences, although a large number were in favor of female suffrage (Bush 2000; K. Pickles 2002). Of course, women participated in all the key aspects of settlement as workers (domestics, nurses, educators), wives, and mothers, even if their role was not valued or was relegated to the back stage, as has traditionally been the case in narratives of international politics (Enloe 1989). The role of women in imperialist projects has been uncovered to some degree, but it remains largely unmarked in the descriptions of geopolitics after the First World War.

Geopoliticians played a prominent role in peacemaking following the First World War, and geopolitical thinking in the interwar period supported state expansionism and imperial rivalry. During this period, geographers such as Demangeon (1923), a French geographer, and Fawcett (1933) contributed to the analysis of the British Empire. As Fawcett noted, the British Empire was of a kind never known before and now constituted a world state (a thesis advanced recently by Hardt and Negri 2000). The American Empire, heralding a century of American global domination from the end of the nineteenth century, did not depend on territorial occupation and instead represented a solution to the economic geographic limits of European colonialism (N. Smith 2003, 24). Its global influence was championed by Isaiah Bowman (1878–1948), who acted as the presidential geographer for Woodrow Wilson and Franklin Roosevelt, at two key moments of global reordering after the world wars (N. Smith 2003).

However, the status of geopolitics was tarnished by its association with the spatial politics of Nazi Germany. Karl Haushofer (1869–1946), a prominent geopolitician in Nazi Germany, used Ratzel's concept of *Lebensraum*—the idea of the state as an organism that needed to expand in order to survive—to argue against the territorial constraints imposed on Germany by the Treaty of Versailles (Natter 2003). When allied with the racial rhetoric of the Nazis, *Lebensraum* underpinned and provided justification for German eastward expansion, in the process taking over territory necessary for Germany and the Aryan race to survive and prosper (Livingstone 1992; Ó Tuathail 1998a). The associations with Nazi policies meant a period of relative silence and invisibility for geopolitics after the war, however. Gray and Sloan (1999, 5) pointed out that in the period between the 1940s and 1975, no book title in English included the word *geopolitics*. Nevertheless, the strategic premises of geopolitics remained forceful, particularly in the form of Mackinder's heartland theory and the domino theory of communist expansion.[2]

A reawakening of formal interest in geopolitics began in the 1970s, when U.S. foreign and security policy advisors rehabilitated the concept (Dodds and Atkinson 2000, xiv; Gray and Sloan 1999, 1). Contemporaneously, academic geographers became interested in both the contested history of geography and geopolitics and in the relationship between geography and war. In France, Lacoste (1976/1985) challenged what he saw as the apolitical and descriptive practices of establishment geography. He issued a call to rethink the nature of geography in a book titled *La géographie, ça sert, d'abord à faire la guerre*, which demonstrated the role that geography and geographic data and representations had served in previous epochs to wage war. In the same year, Lacoste and a number of collaborators launched the journal *Hérodote* (Hepple 2000). In this journal, they sought to demonstrate that geography and geopolitical thinking could be practiced by a wide range of actors—not merely state agents—at a wide range of scales. Lacoste (1987) and Giblin (1987) were particularly influenced by Reclus, not only by his understanding of geography as strategic and political but also by the complexity of his thinking on social and political processes. As a consequence of their concerns, *Hérodote* published articles on postcolonial wars and revolutionary movements and on the problems of development and underdevelopment, interviews with thinkers such as Foucault, and reviews of books by Virilio and Bourdieu. In 1982 the journal adopted the subtitle *Geography and Geopolitics* to signify its shift in orientation away from more theoretical concerns about geography as a discipline and toward more place-based geography. There has never been any discussion of gender issues in the journal.

Anglo-American geopoliticians were slower to engage with the contested history of the discipline than their French counterparts were, though their critiques were no less trenchant. Hudson (1977), based at the University of the West Indies, argued that geography was promoted at the end of the nineteenth century to serve the interests of imperialism, through processes such as territorial acquisition, economic exploitation, militarism, and the practice of race and class domination. Geography prospered, he commented, because it was useful to the practice of empire. This early engagement with geography's imperial past was not immediately accepted. Hudson's provocative article was sidelined within mainstream Anglo-American geography, though others outside the geography project noted and commented on the connection (see Said 1978, in particular). By the 1980s, however, Anglo-American geopolitics began to critically engage with issues of power and hegemony and was strongly influenced by Wallerstein's world systems (Wallerstein 1974). Taylor's (1979) renewed political geography, based on a center-periphery geography of the world systems model, considered the different geopolitical codes adopted by states and the role of geopolitics in its historical conceptualizations. Traditional geopolitics, too, has become significant (Parker 1998; O'Sullivan 1986). The end of the cold war, increased regional conflicts, and accrued uncertainty have led to a further revival in the deployment and heightened popular interest in traditional geopolitics of regional and global strategic thinking, as evidenced by the growing number of books and journals. The Italian journal *Limes* and the Anglo journal *Geopolitics,* for example, were established in the 1990s.

Critical geopolitics developed out of an interest in globalization and hegemonic strategies, with the ground partly prepared by a world systems approach, but it also was influenced by poststructuralism and cultural analysis. This was paralleled by early work in the revival of interest in geographical enquiry in the 1990s among Anglo scholars who took colonialism as an object of study. Livingstone's (1992) *The Geographical Tradition* and edited volumes such as *Geography and Empire* (Godlewska and Smith 1994) and *Geography and National Identity* (Hooson 1994) demonstrated the intricacy of the relationship between the disciplining of space and the disciplining of geography. Later work heralded a change in focus. Drawing on Said's perceptive work on orientalism, geopoliticians became interested in the discursive construction of the "other." Early examples of this type of work included Dalby (1988) on the Soviet Union as "other" and Ó Tuathail and Agnew (1992) on the "other" in American foreign policy. A strong emphasis on discourse and textual analysis, drawing on the work of theorists such as Michel Foucault and Jacques Derrida, has since come to characterize the Anglo-American school of critical geopolitics.

When Gearóid Ó Tuathail's (1996b) text *Critical Geopolitics* was published in 1996, it served both to consolidate recent work that viewed geopolitics from a critical perspective and to point to future directions for geopolitical inquiry. Ó Tuathail argued that geopolitics is a discursive event; by this, he means that geopolitics, rather than being fixed and stable, is, in fact, mutable and contingent. The purpose of critical geopolitics is to "problematize how global space is incessantly reimagined and rewritten by centers of power and authority" (1996b, 249). According to Ó Tuathail, we need to understand geopolitics contextually— to interrogate the strategic thinking that underpins and motivates geopolitical thought and action at particular points in time. He was particularly interested in demonstrating the complicity of geopolitics in warfare. His chapter on Halford Mackinder, for example, characterized Mackinder's geography as a means of inciting and justifying imperialism. However, Ó Tuathail also was interested in the ways in which we can reimagine geopolitics. He closed with the assertion that "critical geopolitics is one of the many cultures of resistance to Geography as imperial truth, state capitalized knowledge, and military weapon" and argued that we need to "decolonize our inherited geographical knowledge" (1996b, 256) so that we open up the possibility of imagining the world in other ways.

The Silences of Geopolitics

The complicity of geography and geopolitics in the practice of empire was highlighted, as we have noted, by geographers such as Reclus and Kropotkin, but their critiques and alternative visions of geography were sidelined. Instead, geopolitics came to be dominated by state-centered, geopolitical strategists. It took many decades before the history of geopolitics and geography was opened up for a critical examination. Despite contemporary attention to the historical relationship between geopolitics, empire, and imperialism, the current practices of geopolitics are still marked by silences. We wish to highlight three such areas. The first area is the relationship between geopolitics and new forms of colonialism and imperialism, the second area is the continuing categorization of geopolitics as the practices of elites, and the third area is the gendered nature of geopolitics.

New Imperialisms and the Persistence of Difference

The concept of neocolonialism has come to mean the ways in which a former colony remains tied to a former or a new colonial power. Increasingly, these ties are less about the relationship between one state and another but rather are concerned with the relationship between elite institutions and individuals. There are obvious examples of neocolonialism at work in the importance of Western-based institutions such as the World Bank and the International Monetary Fund. Another, more subtle, example is the influence of the so-called Chicago Boys, a group of economists trained at the University of Chicago who were responsible for the introduction of neoliberal economic policies in countries such as Chile and Argentina, policies that were later applied more widely to restructuring programs.

Dependency theorists regularly used neocolonialism as a way of explaining geographical variations in wealth and power; in this way, neocolonialism has negative connotations, marking the continuation of the unequal spatial and social relations that prospered under conditions of imperialism and colonialism. Recently, though, neocolonialism has been replaced by globalization (see chapter by Roberts 2004 [this volume]) as a framework for understanding the inequalities that persist and the changes that have taken place in our modern world. The study of globalization has come to dominate political geography more broadly (Flint 2002), and neocolonialism is relegated to a stop on the path to postcolonialism (see chapter by Laurie with Calla 2004 [this volume]).

One problem with an emphasis on globalization is highlighted by the recent work of McClintock, who argued that "revamped economic imperialism has ensured that America and the former European colonial powers have become richer, while, with a tiny scattering of exceptions, their ex-colonies have become poorer" (1995, 300). McClintock described this as "imperialism-without-colonies" (Hardt and Negri 2000; McClintock 1995, 296) in that economic colonialism continues to enrich developed countries without requiring political conquest; discourses of globalization mask those trends. Her remarks were echoed by Hardt and Negri, who wrote, in *Empire,* "The geographical and racial lines of oppression and exploitation that were established during the era of colonialism and imperialism have in many respects not declined but instead increased exponentially" (2000, 43). These geographical borders have been drawn in a variety of ways: between colonizers and colonized; between the first, second, and third worlds during the cold war; and between the developed and the developing worlds as the cold war ended. Now, the divide is between the West and the non-West, and between the "civilized" and the less so. Racial borders had their most explicit spatial articulation in apartheid South Africa, where whites, blacks, coloreds, and Indians were socially and residentially segregated (Christopher 1994). Spatial divisions continue to be articulated through the migration policies of richer countries: in Fortress Europe, in Australian detention centers, and in U.S. immigration offices. The importance of these insights is that imperialism persists, both in terms of the spatial and social differentiation that developed under conditions of formal imperialism and in terms of continuing spatial practices that intensify these differences.

Geopolitics, however, often is blind to these differences and to the ways in which they represent a continuation of imperial practices. Traditional geopolitics retains an obsession with maintaining, strengthening, and enforcing borders, particularly from the perspective of more powerful states. The aftermath of September 11 has intensified this tendency; Neil Smith (2001) described this as "the nationalization of response." Some geographers have been quick to follow the patterns set out by the national elites. The recent collaboration between the Association of American Geographers and the National Science Foundation in the United States, in the wake of September 11, titled *The Geographical Dimensions of Terrorism: Action Items and Research Priorities,* suggests that "homeland security" should be based on a national geospatial infrastructure (Association of American Geographers 2002). The focus of this document is on redefining "the national" and on making new sense of "the international" from the perspective of the powerful homeland. It continues imperial practices that seek to privilege and protect centers of power through the construction of difference—in this case, the homeland as a sacred space and the profanity of international terrorism. Although critical geopolitics has drawn attention to the discursive construction of historical imperialism, it is less quick to show the ways in which geopolitics continues to bear the scars of its imperial past in the continued construction of hierarchies of difference. Those differences have been thrown into sharp relief in the aftermath of September 11 and the war in Iraq, as the alliance built around the United States battles for undisputed geopolitical and geoeconomic control.

The Emphasis on Elites

Peter Taylor (2000a, 375) commented that geopolitics, in common with other social sciences, has developed through what he called "embedded statism." By this, he means that practitioners of geopolitics have taken for granted the idea that the state is the essential scale at which analysis should take place. Traditionally, geopoliticial activists and academics have been concerned with wars, boundaries, and strategies for increasing state power and extending state influence and reach. Geopolitics, including its critical versions, focuses on global visions and has been most concerned with the viewpoints, attitudes, and actions of elites. Elites, after all, define state strategy.

However, we need to ask a very basic question of what it is about geopolitics that reserves it for elites. As we saw, geopolitics emerged at the height of imperialism at a time of conflict over global space and, hence, the need for an encompassing vision that could relate different parts (e.g., regions, types of spaces) to the totality. Charnay (1994, 297) defined geopolitics as globalizing and anthropomorphic; it considers as a whole everything in its presence. It is relational and situational in that it considers the respective interactions of each of its parts. Although we usually consider the state and its elites as deploying this form of rationality and strategic thinking, it is actually deployed at a global scale by multinationals and social movements (environmental, antiliberal globalization, antiwar). As we argue in the next section, we should think about democratizing geopolitics beyond the personnel of statecraft, which often is located within the most repressive echelons of the state (Kofman 1996). It is worth noting that the geopolitics revived by *Hérodote* emanated from an interest in the geopolitical thinking (tactical and strategic) deployed by anticolonial and resistance movements such as the Vietcong in Vietnam, the National Liberation Front (FLN) in Algeria, and the Sandanistas in Nicaragua (Girot and Kofman 1987; Lacoste 1984). Highlighting oppositional geopolitics allows for conflicting geopolitical visions and practices beyond the narrow circle of elites.

There have been some attempts to challenge the convention of analyzing geopolitics through state elites. The first approach was highlighted by Ó Tuathail's call to decolonize our geographical knowledge, which has been given expression in the concept of "antigeopolitics." Ó Tuathail demonstrated antigeopolitics at work in his study of journalist Maggie O'Kane. He described her impassioned reports from Bosnia in 1992 and 1993 in terms of an anti-geopolitical eye. By this, he means a way of seeing "that disturbs and disrupts the hegemonic foreign policy gaze" (Ó Tuathail 1996a, 173). Ó Tuathail quoted extensively from O'Kane's work and showed the ways in which her words challenge elite attempts to distance the West from events in Bosnia. Routledge (1998, 245) constructed a more wide-ranging antigeopolitics based on "an ethical, political and cultural force within civil society" that challenges the material and representational geopolitics practiced by those in power. The second approach highlights the importance of popular geopolitics and seeks to identify the geopolitical moments in a variety of representations: film, cartoons, and *Reader's Digest* (Sharp 2000a, 2000c). More recently, Thrift (2000) suggested that we focus on the "little things." As we shall see, this attempt also can be a crucial element in the gendering of geopolitics.

The Gendering of Geopolitics

Gray and Sloan (1999, 1) wrote that "the popularity of geopolitical theory from 1945 to the present has been rather like the length of hemline on a woman's skirt: it has fallen and risen with the vagaries of fashion." They were trying to make a serious point—that geopolitical theory is dynamic—but they did so using an analogy that is at best anachronistic, and at worst offensive. Their remark is telling, though. Despite the advances that have been made in feminism, and in feminist geography, geopolitics remains oppressively gendered. Strategic thinking, it appears, remains the preserve of the (male) political elite, and there is little room for women within that process.

The nongendering of geopolitics is not confined to traditional practitioners of the discipline. Critical geopolitics, though seeking to incorporate gender, has been roundly criticized by feminists for reproducing masculinist practices (Sharp 2000c, 363), for gendered representations leading to the creation of landscapes without figures (Kofman 1996), and for concentrating on elites and the global scale. In an introductory essay to a special issue of *Space and Polity*, Dowler and Sharp (2001) highlighted the lack of interaction between political and feminist geographers, despite an obvious overlap in terms of commitment to activism. They criticized much of the writing in critical geopolitics, arguing that it is reduced to "a genealogy of heroic men" (2001, 167): both elite practitioners and critical geopoliticians. Thrift (2000, 383) made a complementary point when he bemoaned the lack of attention to the body within critical geopolitics.

As a consequence, Thrift claimed, critical geopolitics has had difficulty in writing about certain aspects of gender.

In many ways, these contemporary feminist analyses of traditional and critical geopolitics draw on feminist analyses of the practices of imperialism. Feminist approaches to the study of imperialism highlighted the ways in which women often were excluded from the practice of imperialism and the ways in which women's participation in the practice of imperialism was marginalized, sidelined, and silenced. They drew links between the violence of imperialism and the violence of patriarchy. They pointed out the ways in which imperialism was discursively constructed as a masculinist endeavor that occurred in public spaces. Through the masculinized languages and practices of imperialism, the narrators of empire consigned women to a symbolic role. These practices are replicated in the work of both traditional and critical geopoliticians, who continue to be bound by masculinist modes of analysis and representation that create binary oppositions between elite and popular, between state and local, and between powerful and powerless, and by those who continue to use language that is marked by its apparent objectivity but that masks fundamentally gendered ideas and concepts.

Feminist geographers have attempted to come to terms with the gendered nature of representation and analysis within geopolitics and have argued that we need to advance beyond deconstruction and envisage new constructions. Hyndman (2001), in a lecture to the Canadian Association of Geographers, suggested three ways in which a feminist geopolitical approach could be constructed to create a more embodied way of seeing and providing security for people—that is, human security—rather than its traditional preoccupations with state security. She argued for shifting scales of analysis rather than an obsession with the nation-state and the global economy; for transposing feminist analyses of the public-private divide to a transnational scale; and for using mobility as an analytic of power and accountability. These themes were echoed in the special edition of *Space and Polity*. Dowler and Sharp (2001, 171), for example, suggested it will be necessary "to link international representation to the geographies of everyday life." The essays in their edited collection attempt to develop this link. For example, Secor (2001) wrote about "counter-geopolitics," which she described as an "alternative spatialization" of lived politics. In this, she tried to make sense of the ways in which women participate—formally and informally—in Islamist politics in Istanbul. Fiona Smith (2000) wrote about the gendered experiences of postunification Germany and used these experiences to suggest ways of "refiguring" geopolitics through a focus on "human security" and everyday life.

The work of Christine Sylvester also provides an alternative way of thinking about the gendering of geopolitics. Sylvester argued that women are "nonrecognized resources" for states, particularly in times of conflict and struggle. She illustrated this assertion with examples of the ways in which women carry out necessary—yet unrecognized—work. Two of these examples include the "comfort" that women living around overseas military bases provide to troops and the use of rural black women by the apartheid state as a social security service for migrant laborers. Sylvester (1992, 169–71) suggested that we need to identify "theory-subverting activities that are not supposed to have significance," and she built on this in recent work on the Kennedy administration, in which she argued that women—the "handmaids" of politics—have, in fact, had access to power and decision making that has not been acknowledged by official historians (Sylvester 1998). Thrift (2000), drawing on the work of Sylvester and Enloe, argued that women are crucial to the practice of geopolitics but that their work and importance are hidden as a result of their textual invisibility. The story of geopolitics is told in a wide range of documents—policy and strategy papers, letters between high-ranking officials, words protected by the Official Secrets Act in the United Kingdom—that together represent the bureaucratic strategies of the elite. Women's work is crucial to this construction of the geopolitical archive; in their clerical, administrative, and support roles, women "do" geopolitics. It is important that we acknowledge women's centrality to the day-to-day practice of geopolitics, not just in the documents that tell the stories of geopolitics, but also through their everyday lives that embrace the global (Kofman 2003).

Conclusion

Historically, geopolitics interpreted and provided strategic scenarios for imperial rivalries in an increasingly international world. Although the imperial project has come under feminist scrutiny and critique showing that settler societies were unsettled by gender relations in their attempt to impose white hegemony and incorporate diverse and subordinate groups, geopolitics has scarcely been subjected to similar critiques. Only the anarchist geographers, whose thinking was so ahead of their time, considered the play of gender relations, patriarchal systems, and racism in the geographies of societies and states.

Feminist political geographers have thus proposed moving between scales and between the private and the public spheres by embodying and grounding geopolitics, and doing so in locations outside the West and the centers of cultural and political power. However universalizing its ambitions are, geopolitics always come from somewhere; it is situated and seeks to reorder spatial and other relationships. Yet as we have argued, geopolitics, including many though by no means all of its critical variants (for exceptions see Dalby 1998; Routledge 1998, 2003), is not confined to elites or states. A feminist geopolitics involves an openness to conflicting geopolitical visions, strategies, and practices that encompass resistance and opposition that can take myriad forms and places and that some have called antigeopolitics. Obviously, differences in the power and positionings of individual and collective agents are reflected in their ability to influence geopolitical outcomes, but those devising antidominant geopolitical practices also engage in geopolitics. In short, going beyond the deconstruction of traditional geopolitics calls for its democratization, which would bring it out of the closet of elite institutions and enable one to recognize the profoundly gendered, racialized, and, not least, classed dimension of dominant geopolitical practices and strategies. And as feminist political geographers have argued, critical geopolitics must simultaneously deconstruct existing conceptions and practices and construct alternatives based on embodied and grounded subjects and social and political movements operating in multiple locations. These alternative approaches, however, should not be at the expense of the global dimension such that feminist geopolitical analyses and gender relations are relegated to the lower scales of the body, the everyday and the local (see Roberts 2004 [this volume]). Feminist geopolitics should seek to connect practices and strategies across the scales through which territorial power is formed and enacted.

Notes

1. In an all-too-brief chapter linking imperialism and geopolitics, we are unable to examine the multiple gendered "historical geographies of the colonised world" (Yeoh 2000). Many Anglo feminist geographers of postcolonialism tend to trace diffusion from the West and the experience of Western female explorers and travellers that, though welcome, "barely connects with the practical predicaments of formerly colonized people and places" (Clayton 2002). We want to draw attention to a wide-ranging review (Gautier 2003) of the gendered impact and responses to slavery; the domestication of women during the second period of industrial imperialism in the second half of the nineteenth century; the invention of traditional rights, educational programmes, and transversalities (religion, harems); and the erosion of female political influence.

2. Mackinder's heartland theory suggests that global dominance emanates from geopolitical control over Eurasia, a vast swath of territory he referred to as the heartland or the pivot area. This form of geopolitical thinking was central to cold war ideologies and practices. The domino theory was prevalent in geopolitical thinking during the cold war, and it conceptualized states as falling dominoes in a game between the two superpowers: the United States and the USSR.

9
Gendered Globalization

SUSAN M. ROBERTS

What does gender have to do with globalization? And, what does globalization have to do with gender? Increasingly, feminist scholars and activists are producing powerful and cogent relational analyses of gender dynamics and global processes and are emphatically answering such questions. Their answers include an exciting and varied body of theoretical and empirical work and all sorts of other imaginative political practices. Even so, at times it seems that feminists are bravely swimming against a powerful tide of purported authority on the global that happily dismisses gender. What is it about the global that seems, for many people—political geographers included—to preclude gender? Major recent analyses of globalization, from both left and right, have risen to best-seller status without any serious treatment of gender. For example, neither *New York Times* columnist Thomas Friedman's (1999) very popular *The Lexus and the Olive Tree* nor the heavyweight Marxian *Empire* by Hardt and Negri (2000) has even one single entry in its index under "feminism" or "feminist," "gender," or "woman" or "women." Absence from indexes is an imperfect indicator of absence from a text, but in these cases it is, at the very least, symbolic of a major reluctance to explicitly or critically address how globalization and gender may be related—despite ample opportunity in the two books' (very different) analytical structures for such an engagement.

Gender, Scale, and Binaries

In general, the ignorance of gender by most popular globalization analysts is just one expression of a wider skepticism about how gender might relate to the global. I argue that this situation has several roots. First, in dominant (Western) cognitive schemes, the global is one-half of a well-known commonsense binary: global-local. This binary stands in associative relation with a whole host of other binaries that relate in similar ways to the dominant (heteronormative, Western) gender binary: masculine-feminine. As such, the global-local binary and its relatives work espistemologically to relegate or contain gender. Furthermore, the relegation or containment of gender is achieved largely through implied understandings or refusals around the feminine and, specifically, the category "woman." Gender—and women—get written out, either explicitly or by association, of the global as a social reality and out of analytic attempts to understand it. In a very important article, Freeman (2001) identified at least six interrelated

Table 9.1. Associated Binaries

Global	Local
Economy/market	Culture/nonmarket
Theory	Ethnography
Production	Consumption
Formal sector	Informal sector
Public	Private[a]
Macro	Micro
Modernity	Tradition[b]
Reason/logic	Affect/emotion/belief[c,d]
Cause	Effect
Agent/action	Victim/passive[b,e]
History	Everyday life
Space	Place[f,g]
Abstract	Grounded[f,h]
Universal	Particular[i]

Note. Sources of inspiration for this table are various but include, for prompting relating to specific binaries, the following: Freeman (2001); [a]Youngs (2000); [b]Mohanty (1991); [c]Nussbaum (1995), Lutz (1995); [d]Alcoff (1995); [e]Gibson-Graham (1996); [f]Massey (2002); [g]Agnew (1989); [h]Nagar et al. (2002); [i]Prugl (1999, 149). These authors vary in their stances regarding these binaries and might not agree with the argument I am making concerning them.

binaries that work as oppositions or dichotomies to structure this exclusion. These binaries are listed as the first six binaries in Table 9.1. Beneath them are some additional dichotomous binaries that I believe may be usefully put into relation with those Freeman identified.

Of course, what is meant and understood by the terms "local" and "global," as well as what is experienced as "global" and "local," varies (Grewal and Kaplan 1994, 11), and the argument I am making is derived from my own understandings of dominant approaches to the global, the global economy, and globalization in the English-language popular and scholarly media, in which I have noticed these binaries at work. These "most obvious oppositions" (C. Kaplan 1994, 138) cannot necessarily substitute one for another, but exist in slippery yet close association with each other (and more) in discourses surrounding globalization and the global economy. Such slipperiness in combination with the sheer socially congealed power of some of these binaries means that the "equation between the local and the feminine gets reinscribed" over and over again, bringing along with it the corollary equation of the global with the masculine—even in the most critical of analyses (Freeman 2001, 1012). The equation, or even just association, of the global with the masculine takes various forms, as has been noted by many feminists. Chang and Ling, for example, noted how certain "techno-muscular" masculinities are associated with the successful in the global economy (Chang and Ling 2000; Ling 2000, 250). Benería critically examined the archetype of "Davos Man"—a "global and more contemporary version of economic man" (Benería 1999, 68)—and I have shown how a more "sensitive" cosmopolitan masculine subject is a project of much business school global management training (Roberts 2003). Gibson-Graham (1996) brilliantly critiqued political economy treatments of globalization, likening the way in which men become capitalism and women become capitalism's "other," in narratives of globalization. So, as Freeman (2001, 1008) pointed out, "Two interconnected patterns have emerged: the erasure of gender as integral to social and economic dimensions of globalization when framed at the macro, or 'grand theory,' level and an implicit masculinization of those macrostructural models." Nagar et al. (2002) documented the many ways in which even critical analyses of globalization can end up reproducing masculinist and exclusionary understandings.

So global-local is mapped onto masculine-feminine in pervasive and sometime contradictory ways, and the way in which the global (and the global economy and globalization in particular) is treated as separate from gender dynamics has much to do with its (usually implicit) coding as masculine. However, a second and related point is that some places are more associated with the space of the global than are others. Said differently, there is, underlying the more abstracted global-local and space-place binaries, a definite historical geographic and distinctly colonialist spatialization. The qualities associated with the global are more easily mapped onto the West than the "rest." By virtue of the colonialist cognitive habit of ascribing characteristics to great swaths of global space and all those who inhabit those spaces, the global south and the global north stand in quite different relation to these binaries. Critical scholars of imperialism, colonialism, and development have pointed out how the global south was, and still is, often described and treated in ways that imply its feminization, pathologization, and infantilization (Fabian 1983; Gupta and Ferguson 1992; Visvanathan 1988). These attributes are territorialized and, in the process, differences within each global zone thus designated are denied in favor of emphasizing differences between global zones (Ling 2000; Spivak 1996; Roberts et al. 2003). As Staeheli (2001, 185) noted, feminist political geographers are well positioned to question any straightforward "alignment between identity and place" of this sort.

Third, and relatedly, another root of the dismissal of gender from the global has to do with the ways that scalar relations are either explicitly or implicitly conceptualized. This is a point that Massey (1991, 2002), for one, has been making for more than fifteen years now and that Freeman (2001) also insists on—albeit somewhat differently. When the global is opposed to the local and each is seen as its "other," any opportunity to think about scale as a continuum is lost. More seriously, though, even a continuum understanding of global-local lets each stand as poles—apart and potentially essentialized or naturalized. Moreover, the local is seen as always and only "contained within the global" (Freeman 2001, 1012), which allows the slippage into equating the local with the derivative effects of social processes and the global with causality and agency. Thus, global processes (or globalization) can have local effects or can play out in places, but it is the global that is the scale that matters. Even those who seek to valorize and champion the significance of place or the local in an era of globalization can end up depicting the local as the playing field on which the global does its stuff: "Every global process is carried out only in and through specific and concrete places" (Kayatekin and Ruccio 1998, 90).

To treat scale as socially constructed, a point that is more or less accepted in critical human geography, at least (Marston 2000), permits a more complex relational understanding of categories such as the global or local. The local and the global can be seen as making sense only in terms of each other (as well as other scales) and one or the other is not prior or overarching. Furthermore, as Massey insisted, such an understanding permits the local and global to be seen as co-constitutive. For Massey, both the global and the local are historico-material but contingent effects of the intersections of multiple and asymmetrical social relations. Such relations (or "paths," "connections," and "inter-relations" [Massey 2002, 24]) make the global and the local just names we give to different aspects of these intersecting relations. Many feminists argue strongly for local or place-based analyses of globalization, typically pointing out the body, the home, and public spaces as appropriate places to analyze gender and globalization in relation (e.g., Harcourt and Escobar 2002, 10). Such local, grounded analyses, would, they claim, counter the more global or space-based perspectives, which are able to ignore gender or be only masculinist (Nagar et al. 2002; Harcourt and Escobar 2002; see also Hyndman 2004 [this volume]). However, I agree with Massey, who pointed out that she is worried about the "tendency to equate the terms local: grounded: everyday: meaningful" (2002, 24). In Massey's work the global is as grounded and is as meaningful as the local is. Unlearning, or relearning, scale in such a way is a major and difficult socioepistemological task. Graham (2002, 19) remarked,

> No matter how often we attempt to set localities on a path of freedom, they will tend to be re-inscribed within the global/local binary, and deprived of power and agency in that move. Creative revisionings are not enough to circumvent this drama of recursion. Globalization discourse has produced all of us as local subjects who are subordinated to, and contained within, a "global capitalist economy." Ultimately, then, the problem of locality is a problem of the subject, and the ethical challenge to a politics of place is one of re-subjectification—how to produce ourselves and others as local agents who are economically creative and viable, who are subjects rather than objects of development (however we may want to define that term).

In addition, if we can attempt to relearn (rebecome?) ourselves—which is what Graham thinks is involved in conceiving of the local differently—we also can attempt to rethink the global. Instead of it remaining abstract, universal, and the domain of globe-stomping capital and capitalists, it may be seen as constituted in a multiplicity of asymmetrically and contradictorily related locales and locals. Thus Massey (2002, 24) said that we ought not to completely take our eyes and minds off what we knew as the global, for "in an age of globalization we need to also be able to 'ground' our international connections, to recognize responsibility at a distance, to appreciate that 'the closest in' maybe should not always be the first priority." (See also Larner 1993, 97.)

The drastic and politically open reconceptualization envisaged by Graham and Massey is not merely a mind game. It will involve, and indeed is involving, real and varied social and political struggles. In the academic subdiscipline to which this volume seeks to contribute—the little world of political geography—we have our own subdisciplinary sociology that has served to perpetuate a mainstream conceptualization of globalization and other things global, notably geopolitics, that has almost totally ignored gender (Kofman 1996; Nagar et al. 2002). However, it should be clear that this has not happened only because of the dynamics at work in political geography, or geography for that matter. The containment of gender at the local has been a widespread and pervasive phenomenon.

Finally, the historical geography of feminism plays some role in the way gender and the global has not been widely taken up in analyses of the contemporary world. Because of the tendency to treat scale (the global-local) as a binary, and to see the global as the realm of the universal and abstract, many feminists who appreciate the forceful critiques of abstraction and universalism—critiques that have linked them with masculinist rationalities—have steered clear of the global, effectively ceding it as a domain of analysis. In addition, few feminists wish to repeat the unsubtle mistakes of a colonialist Western feminism that presumed "sisterhood is global" while downplaying thorny issues of differences between women. As Grewal and Kaplan (1994, 17) noted, "Conventionally, 'global feminism' has stood for a kind of Western cultural imperialism." However, while we should not forget the history of feminisms, I agree with Grewal and Kaplan's argument for a feminism that "address[es] the concerns of women around the world in the historicized particularity of their relationship to multiple patriarchies as well as to international economic hegemonies" (1994, 17; see also Prugl 1999, 149–51). My direction in this chapter accords with such feminists' insistence on the importance of analyses that see social relations, in all their unevenness and in all the ways they work through differentiation and categorization, as integral to the global, to globalization, and to the global economy (see Staeheli 2001, 186).

Gender and the Global Economy

I hope it is clear that I am not proposing to somehow correct for the masculinist bias heretofore displayed in understandings of the global by instead concentrating on the right-hand side of the binaries listed in Table 9.1. As I argued previously, a focus on the local can unwittingly leave the structuring binaries intact.

Conversely, if scale—and specifically the global—is seen in a more contingent, social, and radically open way, then there is room to identify gender at work in all relations, institutions, spaces, and places, be they ordinarily designated global, local, or something else. We can thus come to see the interrelations of gender at work as much in the policies and practices of, say, the International Monetary Fund (IMF) as we can recognize them at work in a person's home. This moves beyond adding and specifying women in the right-hand side of the binary logics I identified previously. Moreover, in such an understanding all locales and all women are not assumed, unless proved otherwise, to be victims of globalization or simply as experiencing the effects of globalization as if it were raining down on them. This is not to deny that many locales and most women are indeed negatively affected in some ways by processes commonly identified as part of globalization. What it emphasizes instead is an openness to see how gender works in the construction and projection of such processes and how gender (along with race, age, and other key axes of social differentiation) mediates how people experience the global and their own subjectivities (see also Elson 1998; Bergeron 2001).

The Global Economy

Many have pointed out that there is no such thing (in naturalistic or essentialist ontological terms) as *the,* or even *an,* economy. What we think of as the economy is a socially and historically created and demarcated bundle of social relations. Or, as analysts who draw on the language and concepts of Actor Network Theory might put it, the global economy is a relational effect—it is the apparent crystal-lization of multiple material relations and social enactments (e.g., Law and Hetherington 2001). Benería (1999) showed how the global economy has been socially made (and is sustained as a purportedly coherent entity) through a lot of labor—entailing cultural as well as more obviously economic work. Benería argued that—just as Polanyi (1944) showed how the national economy, or na-tional market society, was socially created through identifiable moments, such as the establishment of key laws by the modern territorial nation-state—we can see how the global economy has been made and is presently sustained.

Much work has demonstrated that, like the national economy, the global economy did not just somehow come about naturally as some inevitable stage of history (or its end) or of capitalism. Although there are tendencies in the global economy that work to limit the potential power of states, the contemporary global economy is, contradictorily, a child of the modern territorial state.[1] Specifically, it was largely shaped by key Organization for Economic Cooperation and Development states and the interests of social groups associated with different types of capital expressed within them (see, for example, Webber 1998). Helleiner (1994), for instance, conclusively showed how the global financial system—supposedly the most freewheeling and quintessential globalized market—was the creation of key states' actions. The architecture of the old regulatory regime known as the Bretton Woods system (1944–1973, roughly) was systematically dismantled. In its place has arisen a less regulated, more dynamic plethora of financial markets and products. These comprise the multiplying international financial circuits we live with today. The contemporary international financial system is only one part of the global economy. The gendered geographies of the extraction and exchange of minerals and commodities should not be forgotten. More visible might be the constantly restructuring gendered geographies of production. The adding of value (or the extraction of surplus value) in production and the ways new spaces and populations have been incorporated into the circuits of production and trade have garnered considerable critical attention, including that from feminists (e.g., Pearson 1998; Prugl 1999; Runyan 1996; Marchand 1996). The associated travels of millions of transnational migrants, men and women looking for work, are another salient feature of the global economy, a feature that has also received some attention (e.g., contributions in Kofman et al. 2000). In this chapter I instead focus on the financial system, in part because it has been relatively less well studied by feminists (see previous arguments about why this is so) and in part because it is crucial to the way globalization works, hand in hand with neoliberalism as a program or ideology to create and congeal inequalities and sociospatial asymmetries.

Global Finance

The staggering growth of financial markets, so that now the value of trade in financial "products" outweighs the value of trade in goods, has not always been the most visible of changes in the global economy—compared, say, to the drastic changes in the physical and social landscape wrought by the setting up of export processing zones—but it is a key change that is complexly related to the more tangible trends in the global economy. To give a sense of just how fast and big the international financial markets have grown, I quote from a recent survey by Eatwell and Taylor (2000, 3–4), who delineate the growth in the markets trading in foreign exchange:

> In 1973 daily foreign exchange trading around the world varied between $10 billion and $20 billion per day. The ratio of foreign exchange trading to world trade did not exceed 2/1. By 1980 . . . foreign exchange trading had reached a daily average of $80 billion, and the ratio of foreign exchange trading to world trade was about 10/1. By 1992 daily trading averaged $880 billion, a ratio to world trade of 50/1. In 1995 the amount was $1260 billion, a ratio to world trade of nearly 70/1, equal to the entire world's official gold and foreign exchange reserves.

It should be pointed out that world merchandise trade did not shrink in volume or value during this period; in fact, during the 1970s and 1980s it grew at an average annual rate of more than 40 percent. It is just that the foreign exchange markets grew much, much faster (Dicken 1998, 25). In addition to the speculative and very short-term foreign exchange market, international markets for bonds, stocks and shares, futures, and repackaged debt of all sorts have been established, have grown, and have gotten more complex over the past few decades. These financial markets appear to thrive on risk and volatility and have been associated with a series of spatialized crises, from the so-called Third World debt crisis of 1982 onward to the Mexican crisis of 1994 and the Asian financial crisis of 1997, events that have had severe and persistent effects.

The rise of international finance has had a differentiated global historical geography, of course. The deregulation of internal national markets, and also somewhat of their borders, was central to these efforts in the global north during the Thatcher-Reagan years, for example. Meanwhile, in the highly asymmetrical geography of deregulation and liberalization, countries of the global south were more or less forced or cajoled into extreme deregulation and liberalization. Such pressures were brought to bear by international institutions (most significantly the IMF) and found their most obvious expression in so-called structural adjustment programs (Floro 1995; Aslanbeigui et al. 1994; Singh and Zammit 2000). Indeed, the so-called Third World debt crisis and the pursuant structural adjustment programs gave the IMF a greater role than it had had before in the regulation of the world economy (Stiglitz 2002). Together with the Bank for International Settlements (Roberts 1995), the IMF is a major regulatory authority with purview over global financial markets. In addition to the IMF and the Bank for International Settlements, key formal institutions would include the World Bank as well as the World Trade Organization, which superceded the General Agreement on Tariffs and Trade in 1995. These are the major formal institutions that seek (contradictorily) to regulate and promote the global economy. They operate in conjunction with other less formal, but still powerful groups, such as the World Economic Forum, whose meetings in Davos are often cited as a significant forum for powerful global elites. These international institutions are related to states but are not states themselves.

We now live (in different ways in different places, and in different ways in every place) in or with a world economy that is bigger, faster, and more integrated than it was even ten years ago. It is an economic spatialization that does not have an exact formal political correlate, in the way that it used to be considered that the national economy and the modern state mapped onto one another congruently. In general, there has been a shift from states-based multilateral regulation of global economic dynamics (such as in the General Agreement on Tariffs and Trade) to a more international institution-coordinated and law-based regime of regulation and surveillance. This change in the regulation of the global economy is associated with the rise of international law and the increasing pervasiveness and effectiveness of rights discourse. Human rights, and hegemonic understandings of what they are, have been encoded in a series of multinational conventions and have become a major structuring global discourse (Dezalay and Garth 2002). Furthermore, the whole emerging regime of international law and of rights discourse has been encoded in ways that are neither wholly positive nor unambiguous in their relation to any kind of feminism (Charlesworth 1996; Romany 2000; Buss and Herman 2003).

The Global Economy as a Patchwork of Neoliberalizing Spaces[2]

Globalization is not just a series of material shifts in trade, finance, production, reproduction, migration, and regulation dynamics (to name but a few). It is riddled with interests and agendas, and it can be thought of as a project or program—albeit a contradictory and never completed one (McMichael 2000). Neoliberalism is a shorthand term used to identify the bundle of discourses and social practices that in large part animate the dynamics of the contemporary global economy. It stresses, first, the opening of markets through the dismantling of legal barriers to trade (e.g., tariffs, quotas), practices pushed by the World Trade Organization for example. Second, neoliberalism promotes the extension of markets (marketization) through the privatization of previously socially or communally held assets (such as land, water, electricity) and the commodification of previously un- or less-commodified things and practices (such as genetic materials or knowledges—what neoliberalism understands to be "intellectual property"). These projects of neoliberalism are justified on the basis that they are "good" and will ensure "progress" for participants.

Thus, neoliberalism is, like development or colonialism or imperialism, an ideological and programmatic exercise, which entails as a core element the job of "object constitution" (Runyan 1999; drawing on Spivak 1996). Neoliberalism has several key objects, such as the crucial "market." To a large degree neoliberalism's "success depends on promoting new ways of representing the world, new discourses, new subjectivities that establish the legitimacy of the market economy, the disciplinary state, and enterprise culture" (Jessop 2002, 467). Social categories such as women also can be understood as being objects (and, in a limited way, subjects) that neoliberalism seeks to frame or constitute in certain ways. Women are objects of neoliberalism in at least four ways. First, and somewhat contradictorily, they are not actually constituted as a group but rather seen simply as individual market actors, a characterization that in neoliberalism is linked clearly to liberal political identities (Tickner 1992, 71–78). As such, according to neoliberalism, women, like any other actors, are freer subjects when able to make more or less rational decisions in unregulated markets when they are, in Milton Friedman's words, "free to choose" (Freidman and Friedman 1980). Second, women (especially, but not exclusively, in the so-called developing world) are human capital. As units of human capital they can be developed (through education, training, health care, and so on) so that they may more productively participate in (formal) labor markets. Third, as political subjects, women in neoliberalism are seen as having rights, human rights, although human rights and women's rights do not coexist without contradiction and conflict (Charlesworth 1996; Romany 2000). Fourth, they are also, in latter-day versions of neoliberalism, seen as important components of "social capital" as

members and organizers of formalized civil society, specifically, of nongovernmental organizations (NGOs) (Lang 2000).

In neoliberalism the state is deliberately shrunken, leaving factions of capital
to grab what were previously socially held assets (like water in many places) and
at the same time devolving many social services (such as health) to a burgeon-
ing NGO sector. Indeed, the growth of NGOs of all sorts, but especially of formal neocorporate NGOs, has been a major feature of neoliberalism and has
presented feminists with particular opportunities and dilemmas (Eade and
Ligteringen 2001; Mawdsley et al. 2002). Problematically, the growing prevalence of NGOs and their increasing incorporation into (or co-option by) the
major neoliberal institutions such as the World Bank have occurred hand in
hand with the social turn in neoliberalism and the emphasis on social capital
(Bergeron 2003; Tinker 1999). That is, women as a social category have been
mainstreamed in these institutions, at the same time that NGOs have been
promoted as appropriate organizational forms for the enactment of social
agendas. This has led to the proliferation of women's NGOs or woman-
identified NGOs, and the Beijing Conference and linked NGO Forum of 1995
highlighted just such organizations assembling under the imprimatur of the
United Nations. The conference and forum, although they were heterogeneous
events, showcased for critics what was becoming of feminism under neoliberalism's global governance regime with its emphasis on NGOs as vectors of social development and inclusion (Bergereon 2003; Lang 2000; Runyan 1999).

Although I am claiming that neoliberalism is quite powerful, I do not wish
to create an analysis that reifies neoliberalism. Certainly, like any other project,
it is always contingent, and it requires a great deal of work (economic, political,
social, cultural) to sustain it. As Milanovic (2003) pointed out, there is tremendous
ingenuity and a lot of sheer hard work entailed in keeping the neoliberal story
at all plausible. The contemporary shifts in the nature of neoliberalism underscore
this point rather well.

Post-Washington Consensus on Neoliberalism

Although some protagonists in the debates would not care to admit it, it appears
there has been some change in the way neoliberalism is currently formulated.
What used to be identified as the Washington Consensus (Manzo 1999) seems
to have been modified in ways that change the processes of gendered object
constitution it entails. Based in large part on dominant thinking in (U.S.)
economics, neoliberalism has taken from so-called New Growth Theory discipline lessons about market imperfections and how these are handled by market
participants and thus by markets themselves. In part, the new economics is a
neo-Keynesian approach, at least as exemplified by the work of Joseph Stiglitz.
For geographers and feminists, Stiglitz's (2002) analysis seems to be better than
much neoliberal economics because it retains an insistence on difference—
social and spatial. That is to say, Stiglitz's analyses run counter to earlier, cruder

Washington Consensus neoliberalism with its insistence on a one-size-fits-all approach to development, in which each economy is treated as if it were more or less the same as every other economy. This approach was exemplified in structural adjustment programs and then taken to a higher order in the behavior of the IMF in post-1997 Southeast Asia, where symptoms and cures were more or less read off economic theory as rendered in neoliberal dogma. No account was taken of the particular and quite different circumstances of, for example, the crisis in Malaysia and Indonesia (Stiglitz 2002).

In general, the attention by Stiglitz and other economists to social, political, and historical attributes (even if they are rendered as factors) may be seen as hopeful. When such emphases are found at work in institutions such as the World Bank, though, it is clear that they very quickly get folded into habitually neoliberal framings (see Surin 2003; Bergeron 2003). Fine (2002) went further and argued that claims of a consolidating Post-Washington Consensus in economics are (through attention to social issues, for example) facilitating an even more virulent colonizing attack on other social sciences by economics that threatens to foreclose on critical analysis (Fine 2002, 2059). This could be interpreted as a parallel argument to that made by Peck and Tickell (2002), wherein they identified the present as an era of expansive "roll-out" neoliberalism.

Neoliberalized Gender and Gendered Neoliberalism

All in all, and as many critics have noted, neoliberalism and deregulated global financial flows are not somehow gender neutral—in either the discursive or the more obviously material practices with which they are associated. In particular, feminists have noted that at the very heart (in the form of the constitutive outside) of neoliberalism is the nonmarket. The outside in neoliberalism is that which is not the market. In roll-out neoliberalism the tendency might be to colonize such realms as just more imperfect markets. However, in neoliberalism as it is enacted in states' and transnational institutions' policies and regulatory practices, such activities as the work of informal economies, shadow economies, unpaid labor, subsistence work, barter, social reproduction, and care get treated as nonmarketized. Recalling Table 9.1 makes clear that such a demarcation is associated with gendered assumptions about what counts as the economy. Furthermore, such a realm can hardly be banished from sight. Even though unrecognized by neoliberalism, the so-called nonmarket realm is deeply imbricated in the ongoing practices of neoliberalism. For example, as many critics have insisted, women, whether neatly organized into formal NGOs or taking care of ensuring the survival of families and households, are relied on as the social safety net in neoliberalism. This is a particularly noticeable situation in times of recession and crisis—times that are recurrent (and, one could say, permanent in most parts of the world) in a volatile world economy. As a United Nations Report explained,

> Characterized by unregulated financial flows, the international economic environment tends to reduce, on the one hand, economic stability, and on the other,

the ability of countries to deploy counter-cyclical policies to fight recessions. Such trends tend to affect women disproportionately because recessions hit them harder, for two reasons. First, in the formal sector women tend to lose their jobs faster than men and usually have lower unemployment and social security benefits. Second, compared to men they assume greater responsibilities in cushioning their families from the negative effects of recession. They work harder at home, spend more time shopping for bargains, and provide more work as caregivers. (United Nations 1999, 46)

All these effects are made more severe by the fact that women do not typically have the same potential cushion provided by assets (such as land) that men often have (see, e.g., Deere and Leon 2003). The so-called Third World debt crisis, structural adjustment programs, and the various financial crises that have occurred in different regions have all been shown to be far from gender neutral (Aslanbeigui et al. 1994; Aslanbeigui and Summerfield 2000; Marchand and Runyan 2000). In every case, women (and children) have largely been unacknowledged but have nonetheless been relied on to be the providers of last resort. As such, they have been the safety net for the neoliberalizing global economy. And, even when there is not a situation designated as a crisis, women are among those who are caught in the pincers of neoliberalism in its business-as-usual mode.

Conclusions

The sorts of tracings of the gendering of the global economy that the foregoing discussion of neoliberalism points toward can be attempted for other more or less taken-for-granted aspects of the contemporary global economy. As I argued at the beginning of this chapter, such a critical, analytical, and feminist understanding of global processes is for the most part missing from political geography. Scholars in other fields such as international relations, international political economy, development studies, and even economics have contributed mightily to feminist analytics of the global, and I cited many of them in this chapter. It is true that there are wonderful analyses of the global economy that are critical and feminist and that are especially alert to the gendered political-geographic dynamics at work, and I also cited these here. However, there is so much scope for many more such contributions.

Diverse feminist scholarship joins with various feminist social activisms in different places to chart and change the way neoliberalism is reworking interrelations between places and their inhabitants in deeply gendered ways. Indeed, feminists are among the growing number of people and groups across the globe who recognize the spatial and social asymmetries inherent in the global economy, including in the international financial markets, and are organizing around these issues. Third World debt is still a focus of much heterogeneous activism. The IMF and the World Bank have become targets of antiglobalization groups as well as more specifically targeted actions seeking the institutions' reform or abolition. The linked issue of World Bank bonds has also been receiving attention as groups seek to raise awareness of this financial market and to encourage divestment movements. Even the often-ignored international tax system, with its growing injustices and inequalities, has begun to stir organizations. For example, in 1998 ATTAC (Action pour une Taxe Tobin d'aide aux Citoyens or, as it has been translated by English-speaking members, the Association for the Taxation of Financial Transactions for the Aid of Citizens) was formed in Paris. ATTAC was initially one of a number of groups seeking to push the Tobin Tax (see also War on Want). The Tobin Tax (proposed by Nobel laureate economist James Tobin) is a small (0.5 percent or 1 percent) tax on transactions in the foreign exchange market. This is the huge speculative market that I detailed earlier in this chapter. However, like other groups such as the Global Tax Justice Network, ATTAC now has a broad platform, adopted in 1998, that starts with the following statement:

> Financial globalisation increases economic insecurity and social inequality. It bypasses and devalues people's choices, democratic institutions, and sovereign nations responsible for the common good. In their place it puts a logic that is purely speculative and only expresses the interests of multinational corporations and financial markets. (ATTAC 2003)

Characterizing the international tax regime as a "machine of inequality, between North and South as well as inside the developing countries themselves" (ATTAC 2003), ATTAC seeks to mobilize support for campaigns and actions designed to alter substantially the way the globalizing financial system works. In addition to promoting the idea of the Tobin Tax on currency speculation, ATTAC also campaigns against offshore financial centers, against the privatization of state pension funds, for the cancellation of Third World debt, and for the reform or abolition of the World Trade Organization. These are steps toward, in ATTAC's words, the "recapture [of] the democratic space that has been lost to the financial world" (ATTAC 2003).

Although ATTAC is not an explicitly feminist organization,[3] it and other groups are increasingly making strong arguments for major reforms in the international financial arena, based on the goal of social justice. Such arguments and, increasingly, direct actions may seem far removed from feminist concerns with the gendered inequalities that are part and parcel of globalization. However, to echo an earlier call, "Finance is a feminist issue!"—as I hope this chapter has shown. Changes in the patterns of finance and the associated geographies through which they work are gendered and are promising avenues for feminist theorizing, analysis, and action—challenging the heart of globalizing neoliberalism. Neoliberalized finance is also a political issue and a geographical issue. I have not claimed in this chapter that finance is the most significant feminist issue arising from the contemporary neoliberal global economy, certainly, but it is an arena in which we may find the quotidian global and the quotidian local in relation in ways that shape the asymmetries of social relations and, as such, is a potential arena of (feminist geographic) theory and politics.

Notes

1. It may seem odd that in the discussion of global-local so far, the state has been barely mentioned. States certainly are a (or *the*) focus of political geography, and states are key institutional sites that at once differentially structure the global and the local. Yet, with Youngs (2000a) we should refuse, in a more relational scalar epistemology (what she calls a new "spatial ontology," actually), to accept the state as the only, or even natural, space of politics. Nor should we accept it as unitary or as somehow apart from social struggles.
2. This phrase is borrowed from Peck and Tickell (2002).
3. There is a significant feminist component in many ATTAC groups. See, for example, ATTAC Austria's Web site for details of a group called feministAttac (ATTAC Austria 2003).

10
Territory, Territoriality, and Boundaries

DORIS WASTL-WALTER AND LYNN A. STAEHELI

The concepts of territory, territoriality, and boundaries have long been featured in political geography, highlighting as they do the geographical expression of social power (Sack 1986; Hassner 1997; Paasi 2003); in fact, Cox (2003) went so far as to argue that the study of territory and territoriality is the primary contribution that political geography makes to the discipline of geography. In this chapter we wish to begin our discussion of territory, territoriality, and boundaries with a brief reprise of the ways in which the concepts have been used in much of political geography. We argue that in many studies territory is operationalized as the area governed by the state, and boundaries delimit those areas. We argue further that studies of territoriality and of boundaries have often been centered on big issues of sovereignty and security in ways that seem to make gender irrelevant to the concepts. Following feminist arguments, however, we demonstrate the ways in which territory and boundaries are inextricably linked with ideas and practices associated with difference (see Nagar 2004 [this volume] and Martin 2004 [this volume]). As expressions of social power, territory and boundaries are ways of enforcing ideas about who and what belongs in particular places and the kinds of activities and practices that belong to a place or are seen as being appropriate (Cresswell 1996); as such, questions of identity and difference are critical to the ways in which territory and boundaries are constructed. Without denying the important role of the state in structuring and enforcing ideas about territory and boundaries, we also argue that the state is not the sole institution through which social power is given geographic expression (see Fincher 2004 [this volume] and Cope 2004 [this volume]). As such, we broaden the discussion of territory and boundaries to include other sites and scales in which territorial expressions of inclusion and exclusion are formed.

Territory, Territoriality, and Boundaries: How Are They Gendered?

As with many ideas in political geography, the concepts of territory, territoriality, and boundaries draw from a range of influences, not all of which are obviously political or gendered. For example, some ways of thinking about territory can be traced to human ecology, which emphasizes biological and genetic influences on human behavior. These approaches argue that humans have an innate need to control territory; therefore, all territorial behavior is inherently natural (Tuan 1974; Storey 2001). The implication of this approach is that territorial behaviors are "normal" and are not subject to either feminist or political analysis. By contrast, borders and boundaries are clearly sociopolitical constructions and have been recognized as such, given that borders are used to delimit state territory. Many authors also have argued that border regions are bound up in the creation and representation of cultural landscapes (e.g., see contributions in Rokkan and Unwin 1983; Rumley and Minghi 1991; Pavlakovich et al. 2004; see also Paasi 1996). Prescott (1987), for example, suggested that researchers need to consider four concerns that highlight both the social construction of borders and their implications for the societies and spaces on either side of the border. These concerns include (1) the boundary as an element of the cultural landscape, (2) the effects of the boundary on economic activities, (3) the impact of the border on the attitudes of people living within the border region, and (4) the effects of borders on state policy. But much of this work is criticized as being overly descriptive. To this critique we add that there has been relatively little attention to gender in studies that analyze the construction of boundaries or the creation and representation of border landscapes (although we note this is beginning to change—see contributions in Pavlakovich et al. 2004 as an example). In this section of the chapter, we argue for an approach to territory, boundaries, and other allied concepts that highlights their political, social, and cultural character; we argue that these concepts reflect processes that are political and gendered in important ways.

But what does it mean to say that territory is a social-political-cultural construction? We argue that territory and the bounding of territory reflect power relationships in that they are "produced under particular conditions and are designed to serve specific ends" (Storey 2001, 15). This way of understanding territory is useful not only for political entities such as states but also for economic entities such as multinational firms. Territory, though, also has a cultural component, which links identity and sense of place (e.g., contributions in Rokkan and Unwin 1983; Meinhof 2002). Sometimes the cultural sense of territory is expressed as a feeling of belonging as a result of positive experiences, but there may also be a feeling of nonbelonging that may arise from negative associations and practices of exclusion. All of these are gendered. To understand how, we must do some basic definitional work for several interrelated concepts.

Territory is an area claimed by a single person or a group of people; it therefore is a concept that operates at a variety of scales, from the personal space of an individual to the space controlled by a street gang to the space claimed by a transnational corporation. The spaces are usually marked by *boundaries*,[1] which may be visible or symbolic and which may be more and less impervious to other claims on the same space. Functionally, the idea of territory works to provide a space for social action of various sorts and for various social actors. In providing such a space, territory is constructed through acts of inclusion and exclusion. *Territoriality* refers to the strategies by which control is asserted over territory (Sack 1986; Cox 2003; Paasi 2003). These strategies may rely on several "technologies," such as legal structures ensuring property ownership, social norms and sanctions that mark people and acts as being "in place" and "out of place," and state-sponsored violence to enforce borders and sovereignty. Critically, territoriality relies on notions of identity and difference—of belonging to a territory or of being different from those who do belong. Thus, territoriality is a cultural strategy as much as it is a spatial strategy; as Crang (1998, 61) argued, "We use a spatial shorthand to sum up characteristics of other groups." But territories are not fixed; rather, they are "made, given meanings, and destroyed in social and individual action. Hence, they are typically contested and actively negotiated" (Paasi 2003, 110).

These broad definitions of territory, territoriality, and boundaries are clearly applicable to a variety of spatial expressions of control, but in practice, the nation-state often has been at the center of studies of territory within political geography. In state-centered analyses, processes of identity construction in the nation are highlighted; major concerns have to do with issues of sovereignty and security and the construction of borders (Taylor and Flint 2000; Paasi 2003). These issues—largely falling under the rubric of geopolitics—have been central obsessions since the early twentieth century and the work of Friedrich Ratzel (see Gilmartin and Kofman 2004 [this volume]). Territory was seen as crucial both for a site in which the nation was rooted and for the security of the state. Thus, political geography often focused on the exercise of power and even violence to guarantee the integrity of the country as delimited by its borders. Power was also in evidence in state action to secure land, especially arable land for agriculture, because this was important to feed the population. Although the study of these issues was often an academic pursuit, many political geographers served their governments with such arguments during the two world wars of the twentieth century. Especially in Germany, political geographers like Karl Haushofer provided arguments for Nazi policy and their territorial claims, so that after World War II, political geography and geopolitics fell into disrepute. Over the years, other geographic technologies have been used to protect state territory, such as geographical information systems and digital terrain mapping. Geographic strategies are employed to secure the boundaries of the nation with fortified borders and walls that protect countries from "floods" of immigrants and from other "invaders." Furthermore, new geopolitical imaginations divide the world into territories that are "free" and "not free," positing the Clash of Civilizations (Huntington 1993; Freedom House 1999) between the "functioning core" of developed countries against a "nonintegrating gap" of less developed countries (Barnett 2003; see also Bell and Staeheli 2001 and Roberts et al. 2003 for critiques).

Although political geographers have studied territoriality and the state extensively, it often has been done in a way that seems to write gender out of the script; certainly it has been the case that recent political geography textbooks typically do not mention women or gender in their discussions of territoriality (but see Domosh and Seager 2001 and McDowell 1999 for feminist textbooks that do address gender in these contexts). Feminist geographers are interested in issues of territory and territoriality because they relate to the question of power and the way it is used by different groups; they often are critical of the ways in which power is exercised over territory in the attempt to control people. Rose (1993), for example, argued that territory is a kind of property won, often through violence and conquest in which women's bodies have been central sites of battle (see also Mayer 2004 [this volume]). Many feminists, then, have been concerned to demonstrate through their research the ways in which gender relations have been used in the territorial strategies of state agents and in the struggles to maintain state security.

Several studies, for example, demonstrate the ways in which ideas of homeland—or more precisely, motherland—are written into nationalist discourses of territory and territoriality (Enloe 1993; contributions in Mayer 2000b; Sharp 2000b) and several authors have discussed the fundamental masculinity of territorial projects (Sparke 1996b; Longhurst 2000; Morin and Berg 2001). But women are not merely symbols used to encourage brave young men to fight; they may be active participants in struggles, as well, and a large body of scholarship has demonstrated their roles (see, for example, Enloe 1983; Dowler 1998; Woodward 2004). These studies document both the ways in which war and territorial struggles rely on gender ideologies and the ways in which those roles and ideologies are changed through war. But as Dowler (2002) demonstrated, the ideology of masculinity on the front line and in other territorial devices remains strong.

Territories are defended, however, by means other than the military; here, the conceptualization of the role of boundaries becomes important. Boundaries no longer are understood as fixed lines but rather are conceptualized as "structures that are produced, reproduced and contested in and between territorially bounded groups of people" (Paasi 1996, 300f). As such, boundaries are social constructions; the ways in which they are constructed, performed, and perceived depends on the cultural, religious, social, and economic contexts in which they are located. They are symbolic lines of division and separation, enforcing ideas of difference, but this also means they are contact zones of different social and cultural groups. In this sense, boundaries are constantly negotiated and redefined, as are the social categories in which people are placed.

Perhaps the clearest expression of the negotiation of boundaries can be seen in border crossings. Hyndman (2000) demonstrated the ways in which boundaries are differently negotiated by refugee women and men and by the gendered subjects who establish the rules by which refugees cross borders and settle in refugee camps. Other authors also have examined the gendering of the border crossings for migrants, as demonstrated by Ragurham (2004 [this volume]).

In Ragurham's work, there is an implicit argument about boundaries as a gendered performance. For example, Biemann (1999) discussed the sexualization of the Ciudad Juarez region on the U.S.-Mexico border and reflected on gendered divisions of labor, prostitution, the entertainment industry, and sexual violence on the border. Women reproduce different forms of knowledge and power through their daily activities and behaviors; this holds whether they are Mexican or American, whether they are young or old, whether they speak English or not. But, of course, they do not do so from equal positions, so their performances are different. The boundary, as an institution, shapes their lives. But Biemann made the important argument that it is not the line or the wall that does this but, rather, the institutionalization of power that accompanies the border. It is the bureaucracy, it is the border patrol, it is the public discourse and understanding of life on the border that keeps apart and constructs differences between two peoples. Berndt (2001) also discussed the performative aspects of the border. He argued that women experience the continuous shift between different spaces and orders as they crisscross political boundaries and the social and economic barriers that accompany borders. Through these acts they engage in a continuous struggle over power and the redrawing of boundaries.

As the previous comment suggests, boundaries are not simply lines of demarcation and exclusion; they are also the subject of struggle and of negotiation in ways that pose challenges for the powers that maintain borders (Berndt 2001; Sisson Runyan 2003). For example, Kofler (2004; Janschitz and Kofler 2004) demonstrated the ways in which women in border regions have resisted state power along borders through artistic installations. She described an installation along the U.S.-Mexico border that cut a hole in the wall through which messages are passed; this symbolic breach of the border is intended to highlight both the porosity of borders and, at the same time, the ways in which the border makes communication and the interactions of daily life difficult, if not impossible. In Frankfurt (Oder) along the German-Polish border, similar sorts of art installations challenge the legitimacy of the states' attempts to control interactions and the flows of daily life.

These authors demonstrated the ways in which territory, territoriality, and boundaries are gendered in their representations and ideologies and in the actions of gendered subjects. As such, these are important contributions. But feminists (and other critical social theorists) do more than challenge the presumed gender neutrality of territory; they also challenge the common association between nation-state and territory that is so common in political geography. Reflecting on recent changes associated with globalization and theoretical arguments from social theory, feminists have tried to dislodge the concept of territory from the nation-state and have shown how territorial processes and boundary negotiations operate at other scales. In so doing, they move away from the state-centrism that has characterized so much of political geography and geopolitics (Youngs 1999).

Deterritorialization, Reterritorialization, and the Permeability of Boundaries

Much has been made in recent years about the ways in which globalization has changed the world. Chief among the (often overblown) claims has been the ways in which flows—informational, financial, cultural, and so forth—have changed the role of the nation-state in structuring territories and territoriality (e.g., J. Anderson 1996; Castells 1996; Ó Tuathail 1998b; Waters 2001; see also contributions in O'Loughlin et al. 2004 for a range of perspectives). In a nutshell, the argument often is made that the nation-state has a reduced ability to control what happens within its territories. Global geopolitics, new social movements, ecological threats, and terrorism cannot be fixed—in either the sense of being located or addressed—within the bounds of single territorial states; they are deterritorialized. Empirical research attempts to trace the changing relationships between global processes and flows, the nation-state, and localities, often concluding that deterritorialization leads to reterritorialization in which there are changed relationships between scales, processes, and institutions (see Swyngedouw 1997; Ó Tuathail 1998b; contributions in Cox 1997).

These arguments have been very important in that they imply a reworking of the concepts of territory and boundaries. Significantly, some of the ways in which they have been reworked are consistent with feminist arguments. For example, Paasi (1999) argued that there are three ways of thinking about boundaries in the context of globalization that have implications for the ways in which we should think about territory and territorialization. These ways include (1) boundaries as knowledge, narratives, and institutions; (2) boundaries as producing narratives of identity, inclusion, and exclusion; and (3) boundaries as they embody norms and values, which are also part of identity (see also Kofman 2003). Thinking about boundaries in this way means that we need to conceptualize territories as overlapping and boundaries as porous rather than as rigidly defined and completely exclusive. Furthermore, this conceptualization involves a wide range of institutions and processes in defining and bounding territory that goes beyond the nation-state. And territorial control is uneven. Thus,

> boundaries—as lines of inclusion and exclusion between social groups, between "us" and "them"—do not locate only on border areas but also are "spread"—often unevenly—all over the state territory. Boundaries penetrate the society in numerous practices and discourses through which the territory exists and achieves institutionalized meanings. Hence, it is political, economic, cultural, governmental and other practices, and the associated meanings, that make a territory and concomitantly territorialize everyday life. (Paasi 2003, 113)

This way of understanding territory and boundaries—which is not specifically feminist—provides a framework for analyzing the ways in which processes of de- and reterritorialization are gendered. For example, Yeoh and Willis (1999) examined the Singaporean state's "Go Regional!" policy. At some level, this policy can be seen as an attempt by the state to use offshore production to extend territorial influence in an economic sense beyond the limits of the legal, internationally recognized borders of Singapore. One way this was accomplished was by sending managers (usually men) and their families to oversee production. In the new contexts in which these families lived, women were affected by multiple processes of territorial control, including those of the Singaporean state, the societies to which they moved, and their families, as well as their own actions to achieve some territorial control. The result is a messy and complicated pattern of territoriality in which the nation-state was but one agent among many. Other studies of diasporas document the same layering and mixing of territoriality as gendered subjects negotiate the multiple territories and boundaries that shape their daily lives (for review see G. Pratt and Yeoh 2003). Some authors have demonstrated the ways in which processes associated with deterritorialization provide resources for feminist action; they argue, for example, that the development of international human rights regimes and institutions (e.g., Nolin Hanlon and Shankar 2000; see also Mayer 2004 [this volume]) and transnational social movements (see Wekerle 2004 [this volume] and Fairhurst et al. 2004 [this volume]) make it possible for women to press new claims that may not be recognized or be capable of being mobilized within their home territories without pressure from political agents from other places (see also Warkentin 2001).

New Territories and Territorialities

As we noted previously, most of the literature on deterritorialization does not suggest that political relations have dissolved into a space of flows; rather, it argues that political relations often are reconstituted in spaces and territories that link scales, including the locality. This is the premise underlying "glocalization," for example (Swyngedouw 1997; see Amin and Thrift 2002 for a similar argument). Feminists have extended this argument, demonstrating the ways in which forces associated with globalization are part of a broader process in which territories and territoriality are reconfigured at other scales, even beyond the locality.

The reconfiguration of territory and struggles to control territory at the urban level have been important to many geographers, even though they have not necessarily been the focus of political geography and geopolitics. Ley and Cybriwsky (1974), for example, examined the ways in which street gangs in Philadelphia marked territory with graffiti in order to set boundaries and claim control within the territory. More recently, several authors have documented the rise of gated communities, which effectively mark territory as the private domain of residents and bar undesirables from entering (e.g., McKenzie 1994; Graham and Marvin 2001); the phenomenon of establishing territorial control through privatization of formerly public spaces is witnessed in many cities around the world (Caledeira 1999; Graham and Marvin 2001; Capron 2002). Other research has demonstrated the ways in which women, children, and racialized groups are constrained in their use of space—in other words, the ways in which their territories are limited—by fear of violence (e.g., Valentine 1990; Pain 2000, 2002). Although there are many other examples that could be invoked, we wish to highlight the ability of nonstate powers to create and enforce territorial boundaries. In these and many other ways, lines of inclusion and exclusion are redrawn (Cresswell 1996). As Marston (2000) argued, we need an expanded conceptualization of scale that is capable of addressing the locality, the neighborhood, the home, and the body. We also need an expanded conceptualization of territory and boundaries capable of understanding territoriality at these scales and in these sites. This is an enormous task, and we do not pretend we can accomplish it in the remainder of this chapter. What we do attempt, instead, is to think about territory from the perspective of public and private spaces and from the body.

Territoriality in Public and Private Spaces

There is a lively debate within feminism about the utility of the division between public and private (see chapters by Fincher 2004 [this volume], Martin 2004 [this volume], and Cope 2004 [this volume]). Despite these theoretical debates, political agents continue to rely on distinctions between public and private spaces, and the distinctions between public and private are incorporated into strategies of territoriality (Staeheli 1996; Staeheli and Mitchell 2004).

Private space is premised on the ability to exclude, typically through the invocation of property rights. As a strategy of territoriality, the institution of private property has been a long-standing resource (Sack 1986; Mitchell 2003). It is also a strategy that clearly relies on identity and difference; in most liberal democracies, people can legally be excluded from private spaces on these grounds (Cresswell 1996). But although people can be excluded from private spaces on the basis of difference, it should not be implied that people belong equally to a private space, as the legal institutionalization of property does not obviate social relationships, such as patriarchy, that structure the relations of ruling within private spaces (D. Smith 1990); agents remain differentially able to dominate and to exert some measure of territorial control within private spaces. This is perhaps most clearly seen within the private spaces of the home, in which women often are in a subordinate position.

By contrast, public space embodies an ideal of access to all members of the public or polity, and the control of territory becomes less obvious—and in theoretical terms become irrelevant. Yet feminist scholars have demonstrated the ways in which public spaces are still marked by exclusion through the definition of who belongs to the public. Identity and difference shape access to public spaces and the ability to cross (sometimes metaphorical) boundaries (see Ruddick 1996; Bondi and Domosh 1998; Cooper et al. 2000; Podmore 2001; Secor 2002).

The territoriality of public and private is perhaps seen most clearly when boundaries between them are transgressed or challenged; significantly, however, transgressions not only are made by marginalized groups but also can be effected by more powerful agents. For example, the privatization of space can be seen as an act of transgression, but one that has longer lasting effects than mere trespass or other temporary occupations of space; the development of gated communities can be interpreted as a redrawing of territorial boundaries. Other examples include changing the social relations of public and private spaces, often making the boundaries between public and private more permeable. Permeability in this sense is not inherently good or bad but represents a strategy for different kinds of control. For example, the boundary between public and private spaces has been made more permeable through domestic violence laws that assign a public interest in what goes on within houses and families. Without denying the importance of addressing violence, some authors—feminists among them—worry that this incursion of the state into the family provides an opportunity for further intrusions, some of which may not be welcomed (e.g., Squires 1994; J. Cohen 1995; Elshtain 1995). And it is not just the state that transgresses those boundaries. The increasing frequency of working from home may be accompanied by corporate intrusions on family life and, in some cases, monitoring of personal computer usage. Increasingly, the home becomes a territory over which employers have some degree of direct control (see Staeheli and Mitchell 2004).

Territorial strategies, however, also offer the opportunities to recreate spaces for more radical, progressive, and feminist purposes. The designation of a territory as private does not mean that all of the actions within that territory have private purposes. Women's organizations often have used the private spaces of the home to launch projects that are intended to challenge patriarchal and state control of other spaces (Staeheli 1996; Naples 1998a; Fincher and Panelli 2001). Sometimes spaces that are exclusionary can be spaces of safety in which women can create the kind of subaltern counterpublic envisioned by Fraser (1990; see also Iveson 2003). And because territories are never fully and exclusively public or private—because of the porosity of boundaries and overlapping territorialities—spaces can take on a liminal quality in which political actors attempt to create new kinds of spaces—some with feminist potential (Brown 1997; Staeheli 2003). For example, the community gardens in low-income neighborhoods of New York City have been spaces in which community members attempted to seize control over a small plot of land. The gardens were typically established on abandoned property owned by the city. Neighbors—often led by women—essentially squatted the properties, cleaned them up, planted gardens, and used the plots as places for neighborhood mobilization and empowerment. These gardens have been the focus of several lawsuits, as various participants argue over the public nature of the gardens and the role that private property rights should play in creating spaces for the public (Staeheli et al. 2002). In this case, as in others, territory and boundaries were fully incorporated into political and legal strategies to claim a right to space for marginalized groups.

Territoriality, Boundaries, and Bodies

It is safe to say that most political geographers do not consider the body as territorialized. Indeed, Sack (1986, 33) argued, "Territoriality helps make relationships *impersonal*" and presumably creates disembodied subjects moving through space. By contrast, most feminists understand territory as personal and relational, starting from the body, through which we experience, perform, and interpret territoriality.

Yet the inattention to the body in studies of territory is somewhat curious. Valentine (2001, 15) argued that the body "is the primary location where our personal identities are constituted and social knowledges and meanings are inscribed." The body is thus an important bearer of symbolic value and is subject to norms, institutional regimes, and power relations. All of these are expressed and implemented in territorial rules, as described by Paasi (1996) and as mentioned earlier in this chapter. But it is through the materiality of our bodies that we experience the outside world and that the outside world perceives us. As Laws (1997, 49) put it, "Our bodies make a difference to our experience of places: whether we are young or old, able-bodied or disabled, Black or White in appearance does, at least partly, determine collective responses to our bodies." Indeed, one could reasonably argue that our bodies are what shape our access to the spaces of public and private and our experiences in those places.

Since the 1990s, there has been a profusion of work in geography on bodies in space. This research explores the ways in which different bodies, such as those of pregnant women (Longhurst 1996), lesbians, gay men and bisexuals (D. Bell and Valentine 1995a; Podmore 2001), Gypsies (Sibley 1995), the sick (Moss and Dyck 1996), the disabled (Chouinard 1999; R. Butler and Parr 1999), and those with mental illnesses (Parr 1997; Davidson 2000) are marginalized and excluded from a range of spatial contexts. The spaces of exclusion and inclusion—the territories—are constructed by formal and informal social boundaries.

Bodies, then, negotiate boundaries in multiple ways, a notion that challenges our mode of spatiality. Boundaries are constituted through personal contacts, social networks, knowledge of territories, and identification (Jukarainen 1999). And because our bodies carry multiple identities, the negotiations of boundaries and territories also are multiple (Christiansen and Joenniemi 1999). The spaces thus created—border regions—are fuzzy zones of interchange, dependency, and complexity. In many cases, these spaces are open and not codified and are flexible and dynamic with regard to definition, extension, and inclusion and exclusion of people. They are highly complex and dynamic spatial constructions, continuously experienced, constructed, and reconstructed by different actors and different bodies (Christiansen 1998; Wastl-Walter and Kofler 1999).

Conclusions

Feminists have made important contributions to the study of territory, territoriality, and boundaries. These contributions often challenge the understandings of territoriality common within political geography, although as we have argued, the contributions often represent extensions of the logic and reasoning that underlie much of the theoretical work on territory. In this brief chapter, we have only begun to indicate the feminist contributions to a richer, more sophisticated understanding of the topic. Of particular importance in this work, however, has been the goal of demonstrating the ways in which territoriality and boundaries—as sociopolitical constructions—rely on gendered relationships of power that operate in a variety of sites and scales. Women are not passive agents in the construction of territory and boundaries. As we hope to have demonstrated, gendered subjects continually negotiate—and sometimes challenge—the processes of boundary construction that shape our lives.

Acknowledgments

We benefited greatly from discussions with Luiza Bialasiewicz, Andrea Kofler, and Eleonore Kofman in writing this chapter.

Note

1. Quite frequently, political geographers use the term "borders," particularly when talking about the delimitation of the territory of the nation-state. We use the term "boundaries," however, to highlight our intention of moving beyond state borders and to think about the concept more broadly.

11
Embodied Nationalisms

TAMAR MAYER

The wealth of recent scholarship on nation and nationalism has coincided with, and perhaps followed, changes in the geopolitical map. With the end of the cold war and the dismantling of the globe's bipolar state, ethnonational and ethnoreligious conflicts have increased in magnitude and frequency around the world. Thus, although we might have expected that nationalism would eventually yield to a more global perspective, nationalist sentiment in fact remains high, bringing about violent national struggles for political recognition, autonomy, and independence. Scholars from the social sciences and the humanities have made immense contributions to the literature on nation and nationalism over the past two decades. These mainstream students of nationalism have illuminated the ethnic origins of nations, their ideological makeup, and their psychological, economic, and cultural components, as well as the attempts of various nations at state building. Feminist scholars, especially since the 1990s, have begun to fill the first gap by demonstrating that the nation cannot be discussed in gender-neutral terms. They have shown that employing *gender* and *sexuality* as specific categories of analysis enables us to understand more clearly not only how the nation is constructed but also the importance of *power* to this construction. In a sense they have taken the study of the nation to a different scale—one that focuses on the inseparability of the subjects of the nation from the nation itself—and they have demonstrated that manhood and womanhood are entangled in national (and nationalist) ideologies.

The question for feminist political geographers is "What can *we* offer to this subject?" I attempt to answer this question, arguing that political geographers, and more specifically feminist political geographers, can make major contributions to the study of nationalism by introducing the important concepts of scale and space. I first briefly review and critique the general literature on nationalism, political geographers' reading of nation and nationalism, and feminist analyses of the nation. I then give a general overview of the contributions that feminist political geography can make to a more nuanced analysis. Finally, using the example of rape as a war tactic in Bosnia-Herzegovina in the early 1990s, I examine the spatiality of both the nation and gender relationship in the context of war, the ultimate test of nationalism, and I analyze the relationships among nation, gender, boundaries, and scale from a feminist perspective. By probing the connection between nation and gender and by focusing on the spatiality of power, I hope to show that traditionally understood geographical scale is both limited and limiting.

Nation and Nationalism

Nation and *state* often are used interchangeably, and *nationalism* often is mistakenly equated with *patriotism* (Breuilly 1996). It is particularly important to keep the distinction between nation and state in mind, especially when we try to understand issues of national strife and "ethnic cleansing" and how gender figures in these processes. The state is a sovereign political entity with clearly marked boundaries and with tangible characteristics; it is defined and sanctioned by the international community—that is, it has internationally recognized boundaries and is often a member of a superstructure such as the United Nations. The nation is always in the process of becoming; it is self-defined, often evoked, and sometimes imagined (Anderson 1991). The nation often is referred to as a group of people who share similar characteristics, both objective and subjective, who believe in their common origin and the uniqueness of their history, and who hope for a shared destiny (A. Smith 1986). Members of the nation often share language, religion, customs, and symbols. Territory is perhaps the most important ingredient or focal point of the nation; it may call up the most extreme of emotions, so that members of the nation often are willing to die for their homeland.

Members of the nation share an ideology, which serves as an emotional glue. It is always connected to the process by which the nation was or is "othered," especially if the nation occupies a minority status or if it is threatened from outside. But when there is no threat from outside or when the threat is not imminent, the nation keeps its ideology alive through regular and sometimes repetitive exercises of solidarity, which become accepted by members of the nation as natural and ordinary (Billig 1995). Through religious, political, and cultural ceremonies, through education and the use of the media, the nation remains real in the minds of its members who, in return, become loyal to the nation. This act of loyalty is nationalism—an identity and a worldview that precede the individual.

The Study of Nationalism

Social scientists have produced the major part of the extraordinarily rich literature on nationalism. Their inquiries can be divided into three areas: the ethnic origins of the nation, the social and cultural roots of nationalism, and the nation as an imagined community. Scholars from the humanities also have contributed to our understanding of this phenomenon and have advanced our inquiry in profound ways, developing and refining the tools we use to analyze the nation as a social and cultural construction. By focusing on the cultural dimensions of nationalism, scholars such as Chatterjee (1993), Bhabha (1990), and Mosse (1985) argued that the nation can be viewed as a narrative with a specific language, cultural representation, and symbolism.

Many scholars of nationalism also have focused on the relationship between colonialism and the development of nationalism. Showing that the national identity of colonized groups often develops in response to the colonial system's inherently unequal power relationship, scholars like Chatterjee (1993), Fanon (1967), and Memmi (1965) demonstrated that colonialism's us-them structure gives rise to anticolonial movements. The us-them dichotomy is so profound for all nations that unless a nation fully occupies its homeland and there is a complete fit between the nation and its state, the nation will experience tensions, discrimination, and, at times, attacks. Such a complete fit is not possible, because there are more than three thousand nations and only about two hundred states (Connor 2001, 56).

What is important to this discussion is not necessarily the fact that the nation is unique but, rather, that the construction of the nation as unique can lead scholars (as well as members of the nation itself) to treat the nation as homogeneous and united. Not only are members of the nation positioned differently vis-à-vis economic resources and political power, but they may also be members of different ethnic and language groups, and these groups may be either favored over or disadvantaged by other national groups. But the inequality within the nation goes even further. Feminist scholars have shown that the nation is also the arena where gender inequalities are played out and that it is almost always a sexist project. Enloe (1989, 2000), Radcliffe and Westwood (1996), McClintock (1995), Yuval-Davis (1997), and others showed that national ideology often is used to favor one gender; in the national project women occupy a secondary position, and nationalism becomes the language through which gender and sexuality (specifically women and homosexuals) are controlled and repressed (Mayer 2000b). They further showed that because the national project is where masculine prowess is expressed and because women and men occupy different spaces within the nation, their national identity is constructed in different ways.

Geographers and the Study of the Nation

The importance of territory to geographical inquiry has not always been recognized by political geographers, and as important as it has been in most national struggles around the globe, they have not focused on it sufficiently when investigating the nation and national identity (C. Williams and Kofman 1989; Agnew 1987; C. Williams 1986). Knight (1982) was perhaps the first to call attention to the connection between territory and identity, whereas Garcia-Ramon and Nogué-Font (1994) illustrated the importance of geography as a discipline to the academic study of the nation in their work on Catalan nationalism.

Two important volumes, Herb and Kaplan (1999) and Hooson (1994), have contributed to the literature on the nation and furthered our understanding of the relationship between people and territory. All contributors seem to favor the nation-state over other scales. Even though the core of political geography has always been the nexus of nation, state, and boundaries, most political geographers have favored the state (the nation-state), its territoriality, and the way power is achieved as the focus of their inquiry (Sack 1986). So committed has political geography been to that scale that even examinations of culture and nationhood have been executed at the level of the state. If we continue to study the nation solely within the framework of the state, we are bound to miss the dynamics of nation building, the cultural and psychological aspects of nationalism, and the nation's intimate relationship to gender. Indeed, because most mainstream political geographers who study nationalism have been interested in understanding the state-building aspects of the nation and its bounded territory, they have overlooked issues of gender and have treated the nation as gender neutral. It has been left to feminist scholars (among them geographers) to expand the discussion of the nation to include issues of gender and power.

Critical Understanding of the Nation: Feminist Contributions

Prior to the 1990s most feminist scholars were not interested in the nation, perhaps because many of them came to feminism from a "hegemonic national and Western positioning" (Yuval-Davis 2001, 121) and have therefore been unable to be critical of the project in which they themselves participate. Thus, much of their writing remained Eurocentric. But once Third World scholars (Kandiyoti 1991b; Mohanty 1991; Jayawardena 1986) unveiled the struggles of Third World women and pointed to the centrality of women in anticolonial nationalist struggles, the door opened and Western scholars began to focus on issues relating to women and nationalism around the globe. At the same time, as theories of deconstruction and poststructuralism gained ascendance in the academy, much of the work in which feminist scholars engaged deconstructed power relations in many different settings, including in the context of the nation. Thus, as feminist literature about the nation explored the intimate relationships among nation, gender, and sexuality, it revealed that men and women do not participate in the national project in the same way (Enloe 1989; Yuval-Davis 1997; McClintock 1995)[1] and that the project itself is sexist. By recognizing gender, nation, and sexuality to be socially constructed categories, feminist scholars have been able to expose the ways in which power is manipulated to advance the national project to the detriment of women and homosexuals (Mayer 2000b).

Much of the literature on gender and the nation has focused on the centrality of women to the national project, primarily as its biological and cultural reproducers and as the producers and maintainers of ethnic and national boundaries (Bracewell 1996; Karakasidou 1996; Yuval-Davis and Anthias 1989). One of the most important aspects of the relationship between women and the nation is the fact that control of women's reproduction carries with it control of women's bodies and of women's behavior, for women's bodies (along with territory) are where the nation constructs its identity. Because women's bodies are so entangled with the nation's identity and "maternalized bodies become the site of *viewing* the nation" (Eisenstein 2000, 42), they become the battleground not only between men and women but also between men of one nation and the men of another. Women who defy the hegemonic ideology are outside the group; they are "them" in the us-them construction of the nation; they are the enemy, and in this sense, they mark the boundaries of the nation.

Focusing on women's lives, feminist literature about nationalism has concentrated on women's active participation in national struggles (Ranchod-Nilsson and Téreault 2000; Mayer 1994; Jayawardena 1986). It has shown that although women have certainly been victims of nationalism, they also have been active in the liberation struggle and, in many cases, have contributed to its success. Indeed, women always have been involved in progressive and reformist movements as well as in racist and reactionist politics (Blee 1998; Kofman 1997). They have been at the forefront of many of the successful protest movements (see Fairhurst et al. 2004 [this volume]), and because of their active role, women have gained a political voice and learned new skills that empower and politicize them even further. Women's activism and agency, especially for women on the left, can become complicated, even challenged, by the activists' dual and triple roles (as protestors and mothers or partners of participants in the very activities against which they protest). Thus, women's activism cannot be separated from gender identity.

Contributions of Feminist Political Geographers

Feminist political geographers have studied different aspects of national identity and nationalism, though not necessarily initially through gendered lenses (Johnston et al. 1988; Penrose 1990, 1994). By the mid-1990s they turned their attention to gendered iconography represented in landscapes, monuments, and symbols (Johnson 1995; Kofman 1993; Nash 1993). They also examined the nature of gendered hierarchies embodied in metaphors of the family, in which its different members know their appropriate places. Men protect and defend the nation; women provide safe and comfortable havens and, as they have noted, reproduce the citizens of the nation (Kofman 1997).

Feminist geographers are in a unique position to synthesize political geography and feminism in order to challenge the nature of constructed behaviors. Some feminists have begun the reconsideration and reconceptualization of geographical concepts such as space, place (local and global), sites of resistance, transgression of boundaries, and the public-private division of space (Duncan 1996; Jackson and Penrose 1993). They locate gender and sexuality, and more specifically the body, in places and spaces of social relations where interactions occur and power is employed and where both places and the body are further constructed (Nast 1998; Nast and Pile 1998; Sharp 1996). As feminist geographers examine the fluid interactions between gender and territory—as women's bodies are appropriated by (men of) the nation and are considered their or its territory, and as women's behavior marks the nation's boundary—they realize that each interaction further challenges the hierarchical nature of scale and produces new contexts. Thus, feminist geographers can rethink the dynamics between nationalism, gender, and power. By working within this framework of constant construction of place, boundaries, body, and power, and by challenging current notions of geographical and hierarchical scale, feminist political geography can best improve the understanding of the dynamic relationship between gender and nation. To provide an example of feminist political geography in action, I turn to the phenomenon of warfare rape in Bosnia-Herzegovina in the 1990s.

Rape as a Weapon against Women and the Nation

Rape, as a violent crime directed against women, is "a sexual manifestation of aggression" (Seifert 1994, 55) carried out by men as a way to control, terrorize, and dehumanize women. Its impact is so severe that the fear of rape alone has had a serious effect on the way most women live their lives. Even though rape occurs the world over,[2] it often is perceived as a unique event: a crime against a specific woman committed by a specific man. Because rape is frequently rationalized and explained as a social, physical, or psychological pathology of the perpetrator, the near-universal context of male domination and abuse of power remains secondary to individual cases. Unsafe homes, streets, and neighborhoods, which are indicative of power inequality—rooted in the heteronormative patriarchy— make up the landscapes of fear within which women move daily.

Rape, which poses an intense threat during politically peaceful times, becomes even more terrifying when it is used to advance military goals during times of war. Even though rape has been part of warfare since the early days of history (Brownmiller 1975) and has been accepted as war's collateral damage, perpetrators (at least until the late 1990s) have not been made accountable for their acts. Indeed, the magnitude of the phenomenon was seldom recorded. We know that in the twentieth century alone, war rapes have occurred throughout the globe as a way for both nations and states to fight each other. Despite the frequency of these acts and the staggering number of women involved, we know about them almost exclusively through victims' stories and victimizers' boasting; they have not been considered a separate war crime that historians record and analyze.

In the early 1990s, however, and only after the media began to report the widespread rapes in Rwanda and the former Yugoslavia (which took place during roughly the same time), the West started to respond to the trauma of rape during wartime (Swiss 1993). It became apparent that these wars—especially the war in Bosnia-Herzegovina—were unlike most other wars, for they targeted civilian populations explicitly. Civilians were no longer the innocent bystanders, the collateral damage; they were now the target. For this reason, as Kaldor (1999) argued, the war in the former Yugoslavia is the paradigm for a new warfare.

In Bosnia-Herzegovina the rape of Muslim women by Serb men, of Croat women by both Croats and Serbs, or of Serb women by Muslims was systematic and aimed at degrading and defeating women, men, and their nation.[3] These rapes were carried out as a means of "ethnic genocide" (B. Allen 1996). There are no exact figures, but estimates suggest tens of thousands of women, ranging in age from six to seventy, were raped during the war (Nikolič-Ristanovič 1999; Niarchos 1995; Stiglmayer 1994a; Swiss 1993). Thousands of hours of firsthand accounts, which were assembled soon after the war, chronicled the horrors of these women and provided the basis for establishing the first international war crime tribunal after Nuremberg. These accounts serve as data that can be used by feminist political geographers to analyze the geography of this war and to scrutinize the manipulation of gender in the name of the nation and nationalism.

The Geography of Assault

Firsthand victims' accounts suggest a specific spatiality and temporality of war rapes in Bosnia-Herzegovina. The pattern that the Serbs used to maximize their attack on the Bosnian nation consisted of five stages. First, before the fighting even began, individuals or small groups broke into houses and terrorized the inhabitants, stole their property, and raped the women. Second, as towns and villages were captured, women were raped either in empty houses or in public. Third, after a town or village was cleared and the men were either executed or sent to detention camps, the women were sent to separate camps where soldiers, camp guards, paramilitaries, and others were allowed to enter, pick out women, take them away, rape them, and then either kill them or return them to the camp. Fourth, women were sent to special rape camps where rapes occurred several times a day. In the fifth stage, women were forced into brothels to sexually entertain soldiers (Niarchos 1995, 655–57). This pattern underscores what many feminists have already established: that women's bodies are indeed a significant battlefield.

But if we add geographical concepts to this understanding, we can provide a far richer picture of the tactic and the connection between nation and gender. By moving from the private sphere to the public sphere, from home to rape camps, Serb soldiers increased the number of their victims. It is clear that the Serbs used scale as a tool of conquest; by moving up the scale—from private space to public space, from home to special camps—they were able to pursue their goals of ethnic cleansing more efficiently. Moreover, because power tends to increase with geographical scale, it enabled them to exercise ever more power as they moved to a bigger stage for rape.

It also is clear that the Serbs coordinated their sexual assaults with the advancement of their army. They raped in individual houses *before* the fighting broke out, they moved to raping in houses whose inhabitants had fled *as* the invasion of the village was underway, and they sent women to special detention and rape camps *after* the towns had fallen into their hands. Each stage was made possible by territorial conquest, and each combination of rape and conquest at one scale was the precursor for the next, more large-scale attack, each providing (with the increase in scale) a better stage for the theater of war and the performance of rape. Each was necessary for the completion of the goal of ethnic cleansing, because with each stage the number of performers and victims increased, involving more and more people in the national fight and drafting the body (of both men and women) into the national struggle. In this war, then, territorial and sexual aggressions were inseparable, serving the goals of the perpetrators more effectively. Although in conventional warfare the landscape may change hands but may also eventually return to its prewar state, rape victims and the victimized nation never will: the legacy of terror, the wide-ranging suffering, and the effect of genocidal rapes on the purity of the nation have a deep and permanent impact.

The Victim: It Is about Scale After All

Understanding that the rapes in Bosnia-Herzegovina intensified as Serbs moved from the private sphere to the public sphere, from the home to the camp, must not obscure the important fact that in all scales the woman was always the victim. Many of these women were raped so many times, by so many different men, and in so many different settings, that although hierarchical scale may help us make sense of the extent of these war rapes and see the relationship between ideology and war strategy, it cannot really describe and explain the magnitude of each woman's own horrors, nor can it describe the places where the contest took place. Hierarchical scale cannot explain and describe the pattern of rapes from the perspective of the victim. The best way to visualize them is to think about war rapes as a series of concentric rings, similar to those radiating from the epicenter of an earthquake.

The ripple effect of each woman's horrors is felt by her entire family, her children, or her siblings who may have watched the rape; her husband; her parents; the community; and even the nation at large. She experienced a horrendous physical and emotional terror, pain, and loss of dignity. The dignity and honor of her family and community are seriously compromised, as well. She is (at) the center of the disaster and (at) the eye of the storm, and her pain and that of tens of thousands of other women radiate outward in such a way that the impact on the nation as whole is compounded.

Even though laws of nature tell us that tremors decay with distance from the epicenter, this was not really the case in these systematic genocidal rapes. As the geographical location of the rapes changed and the epicenter moved geographically with the progression of the war (from home, to village, to the camp, and from one region to another) the entire nation was affected by the tremors. Although the *location* of the rapes can be identified in geographical terms, the *site* of the rapes was always the woman's body. Because the map of the nation is dotted densely by sites and locations of rape, not sparing even the most distant regions, the ripple effects of all the epicenters overlap and collide to create a greater tragedy for the nation as a whole.

Victims' pain radiates not only horizontally but vertically as well, for the trauma will be felt for generations to come. Many of the raped women were impregnated by their captors and were not released until it was too late to have an abortion; these women bore children who are no longer ethnically pure, because they are neither purely Serb nor purely Croat.[4] These children and their offspring will be a permanent reminder to the national community of this dark chapter in its history.

Boundaries

The battlefield in Bosnia was fluid and the defensibility of the boundaries was, to some extent, a matter of negotiation, especially because women's bodies were among the sites of the war. In many of the accounts, women recounted that wherever the place of the rape—whether in their own home, their village, or the rape camps and brothels—many of the rapists in uniform were men whom they knew quite well. They hoped that past social interactions could save them; they pleaded with the perpetrators as a way to protect themselves, their daughters, their mothers, their husbands, and their sons. But for most of the men in uniform, the face-to-face interaction was a way to assert their manhood and their Serb nationhood. Although the women thought that they could protect themselves through negotiations, in most cases previous interactions offered no protection.

In a few cases, however, the rape was averted precisely because of a face-to-face interaction with the perpetrator. Sometimes when a woman victim pleaded with a single perpetrator (although usually rape was a gang activity), he cast aside his formal role as soldier-rapist, as part of the war machine. This can be seen in the case of Sadeta, who after repeated rapes was ordered into a room to be raped again, this time by the unit's commander, and was spared when she positioned him outside the context of his military role. She recalled,

> When he saw that I was not feeling anything—I was just lying there staring at a point in space—I looked into his eyes and asked him if he had a wife. He said no. I asked him if he had a sister. He said yes. Then I asked, "How do you think your sister would feel if someone did with her what you're doing with me?" He jumped up and ordered me to get dressed and leave. As I was leaving I said, "If you're thinking of sending someone else to take me someplace again, I'd rather you just kill me here and now." He said I didn't need to be afraid, that no one would come get me anymore, and after that no one else did come. (Stiglmayer 1994b, 95)

Even though all Sadeta could think about was how she could survive the horror, her actions, in a small way, enabled her to renegotiate the boundaries of the nation as well as her own. In this case, with this specific perpetrator, she defended the boundary of the nation successfully and the enemy did not cross it.

The task of renegotiating and redrawing the nation's boundaries was accomplished in other ways, as well. By attempting to control their bodies from inside, and by trying to defend themselves from the rapes, women defined and defended the boundary of the nation. Dr. Jusuf Pasalic (pseudonym), a physician, who treated fellow prisoners in Trnopoljem internment camp, reported, "At first women and girls were beaten black and blue, especially in the lower body region. Later on we didn't find that kind of injury on them anymore. The first ones probably told the others the best way to survive. A nineteen-year-old girl told me that she closed up tight inside," (Stiglmayer 1994b, 91); this was a strategy women used to try to keep from getting pregnant.

But where exactly does the border lie—at the body's edge or inside the body? Is the boundary a tangible line drawn on the ground, or is it an imagined one? When a woman "closes up tight inside," her vagina and uterus are the boundary: if she could only close up, if she could only retreat inwardly to a defensible core, if she could only ensure that she did not get pregnant, then she would hold her line successfully, saving herself and the nation's honor.

Scale, War, and Masculinity

When we try to understand the spatiality of this war, we can see that the three (geographical) scales where the war was fought—home, village, and camp—do not fully capture the magnitude of the war. Because women's bodies were intimately and violently involved, it can be said that the Bosnian war was fought also (or perhaps primarily) at the corporal and intracorporal scales. And if this was the case for the victims, it was certainly also the case for the victimizers, who used their own bodies to advance the war. The victimizer's penis was the weapon in the service of his nation, and with it he emasculated—feminized—the enemy nation by raping its women. The body, then, was at the center of the war, regardless of geography and regardless of gender.

> Why did these men rape? Why did they employ this tactic? He rapes because he wants to engage in violence. He rapes because he wants to demonstrate his power. He rapes because he is the victor. He rapes because the woman is the enemy's woman, and he wants to humiliate and annihilate the enemy. He rapes because the woman is herself the enemy whom he wishes to humiliate and annihilate. He rapes because he despises women. He rapes to prove his virility. He rapes because the acquisition of female body means a piece of territory conquered. He rapes to take out on someone else the humiliation he has suffered in the war. He rapes to work off his fears. He rapes because it's really only some "fun" with the guys. He rapes because war, a man's business, has awakened his aggressiveness, and he directs it at those who play a subordinate role in the world of war. (Stiglmayer 1994b, 84)

The rapes appear to have been one big party for these men, who often laughed as they terrorized and humiliated the women: "They came and went, they drank and smoked marijuana. They laughed and had fun. . . . They said they were going to show us what real Serbian men were like" (Mirsada's testimony in Stiglmayer 1994b, 109).

Victims' accounts of their experiences have revealed the cruelty with which Serb soldiers carried out their missions. Serb propaganda was intended to make them so enraged that they would use the utmost cruelty and violence against the Muslims. As part of the brainwashing, they were told that Muslim men, many of whom they considered friends, "had lists with names of Serbian children who were going to be butchered" (Stiglmayer 1994b, 89). These soldiers, who were far from home, were angry and scared, and they could not verify the truth of such information. As a result, when they approached a Muslim village, they unleashed their fear and anger in a show of power. Furthermore, as a way to entice soldiers into the most violent behavior, their commanders also promised them the homes of their Muslim victims and the possibility of keeping their gold, jewelry, and money. They obeyed orders from their immediate commanders, and sometimes from headquarters in Sarajevo or Banja Luka, to rape (Stiglmayer 1994a, 147–61), but even if the orders were not always explicit, soldiers seemed to sense that it was the right thing to do. As one admitted rapist told Stiglmayer (1994b, 90), "The people in authority all knew what was happening. I had the feeling that the more it happened, the more there was rape and murder, the better they [the commanders] liked it. They liked it because of 'ethnic cleansing.'"

But not all soldiers engaged willingly, at least not initially: "Some of them enjoyed doing it [rape], and others were forced to do it. I know a few guys who used to work with me they were forced to do it. . . . The local Serbs, they went easier, they weren't so extreme. But as soon as the foreigners came, whether, they were Arkan people or Seselj people, then they had pressure on them" (Kadira's testimony in Stiglmayer 1994b, 120). What happened to those soldiers who did not want to participate? Such men were a liability to the nation, and because Serbian masculinity was reconstructed during the war, a refusal resulted in vicious ridiculing and harassment that forced them into participation, even if reluctantly. One way of making them "men" and ensuring that they would participate in the rapes was to send some of them to the front lines, where the fighting was fierce and the likelihood of returning home alive was not great (see transcripts of interview with Borislav Herak, a Serb soldier, in Stiglmayer 1994b, 148). To ensure their own survival, they learned to terrorize others and, in the process, they constructed their own masculinity and participated in nation building.

The asymmetry in power among the men also had a geographical dimension. It appears from several of the testimonies that Serbs who came from farther away were more vicious than the local men. The geographical asymmetry followed power asymmetry between men who were eager and willing to rape and those who were not. Thus, not only women but also men who refused to follow orders were feminized and victimized by Serb men who saw themselves as heroes fighting for their nation.

The International Face of the Local War—Jumping Scales

Although the war in Bosnia-Herzegovina was fought within the boundaries of the former Yugoslavia, it is a mistake to consider it solely as a local war. International women's organizations were instrumental in bringing world attention to the war and to the crimes against women, and eventually they aided victims in preparing their legal fight against Serb soldiers and leaders. In other words, although the war was fought at the home and in the village and the perpetrators were often from the same village or region, once the involvement of international women's organizations moved the fight beyond the political boundaries of the former Yugoslavia, the war became a global concern.

Women in Black, an international women's peace movement,[5] held weekly silent vigils around the world (particularly in Italy, London, and Spain) to protest the atrocities committed by the Serbian regime. Particularly important was the work of Women in Black in European and North American cities, for it called attention to the plight of women in Bosnia, a cause that most international organizations did not address. Moreover, through the support of these European vigils, Croat and Serb women were encouraged to protest against their own regime. Despite their ethnic differences, Croat and Serb women joined Women in Black, demonstrated in Republic Square in Belgrade, and condemned publicly the barbarity of the gender-specific tortures (Cockburn 1998, 171). Although these women protestors were not necessarily victims themselves, they were the extension of the victims who were pleading for help.

The work of Women in Black on behalf of Bosnian women and the work of Serb and Croat women (as members of Women in Black) on behalf of their sisters illustrate the fluidity of geographical scale. It is not possible to conceive of these protest activities as occurring at one scale or another; rather, they occurred at all scales at once, and protestors moved regularly between scales. Furthermore, the joint work of Serb and Croat women on behalf of Muslim women constructed a space that other members of the Serb and Croat nations (in particular the men) did not experience. Although the men were fighting the war, the women broke out of their expected national roles and joined other women whom their own national ideologies constructed as enemies. Women's activism transcends local tensions and establishes additional and more fluid geographical scales, moving from one context to another, negotiating and interacting in each of these settings.

A further example of the continuity of scales can be seen in another aspect of the work of international women's organizations in exposing the atrocities done to women during this war: aiding the victims in their legal efforts. Several international organizations collected firsthand accounts, and as Enloe (2000, 135) noted, "a combination of energetic journalism and organized pressure brought to bear by women in antiwar groups and human rights groups . . . eventually initiated serious methodical international agency investigation of the scope of rape and its purposes in the Bosnian war." Initially women victims were afraid to talk about their experiences. They often were ashamed of what had happened to them; they thought that their experience was isolated because they were unaware that their rapes were part of a larger war tactic. With the help of the international community, especially women's organizations that focus on violence against women, they learned that they were not alone. By listening to these victims in refugee camps, by taking seriously their accounts, and by recording each story, these international organizations enabled the victims to be heard. They exposed at the international scale the crimes that took place at the smallest of scales, the corporal and intracorporal scales.

Finally, the work of these organizations has challenged hierarchical geographical scale in yet another way. By providing Muslim women with a space in which to talk about their past, by giving them the tools to learn how to deal with that past, and by aiding in the early stages of the healing process, members of human rights groups helped construct additional geographical scales for the women victims as well as for themselves. These scales were further extended and challenged when victims were interviewed in the mid-1990s in preparation for the trial of the six Serb soldiers who were ultimately indicted for war crimes, when they testified in court, and when groups of them crowded the halls of the international court in The Hague. For the first time, in 1996 rape in war became a crime against humanity, representing a dissolution of the public/private divide. This combination of the public and private can contribute to new way of thinking about geopolitics (Hyndman 2001; see Gilmartin and Kofman 2004 [this volume]).

Conclusion

Nationalism is still among the most important of the sociopolitical forces that shape human history, and it continues to capture the attention of researchers and laypeople alike. Social scientists have done much to explain how the nation was borne and how it functions. Feminist scholars introduced gender to the study of nationalism and the complex ways in which it is constructed and expressed. The conclusions reached by scholars in these disciplines become more nuanced when they bring into the analysis some of the issues on which political geographers focus—boundaries, territory, scale, and power. The work of the feminist political geographer is to synthesize and build on all of these approaches, introducing the important concepts of scale and space and analyzing the relationship of gender and power in the context of boundaries and geographical scale.

The nation is always in the process of becoming: it is constantly being formed and is forever changing. This change is the result of a continuous contest between those who have and those who do not have access to power. Power, then, defines the real and imagined boundaries of the nation: it defines the relationship between men and women of the nation, between classes and ethnic groups within the nation, and between one nation and another. An examination of the war in Bosnia-Herzegovina from the perspective of feminist political geography reveals that the outcome was defined by the power of Serbs and Croats over Muslims, of Serbs over Croats, and of men over women. Women were made an extension of the landscape, and the war was fought on (and in) their bodies. Ultimately, they were seen as a territory—in this case, the Serbs' occupied territory.

When we study the war rapes in Bosnia-Herzegovina, concepts such as territory, boundaries, and scale, which are central in the study of nationalism, become more complex. They are no longer distinct and fixed in space; rather, they are fluid and determined by context. This war has shown us that the distinction between public and private spheres is irrelevant when national interests can so easily penetrate even the most sacred of private spaces. Sex acts, which normally take place in the privacy of one's home, occurred regularly in the public sphere, and the merging of private into public provided an arena for the construction of masculinity. Later, women victims were encouraged to relay their most private experiences to outsiders who made their private experiences part of the public record.

We also have seen that boundaries are fluid and that they may mean different things to different people. The example of Bosnia shows that the real boundary of the nation and its homeland is no longer a line drawn on a map or on the ground. Rather than being physically articulated, a national boundary can be imagined in men's minds or drawn within women's bodies. The exact location and extent of the boundary can sometimes be negotiated and thus defined differently, depending on national ideology and even national allegiance. The women who "closed up" and protected their most inner space redefined what personal and national boundaries are all about.

The use of war rapes as a deliberate tactic in the Bosnian war also has provided a useful case study in the importance of scale. We can no longer conceive of scale as fixed, as "a natural metric by which to order the world for the purpose of analysis" (Herod 1997, 146). As this example shows, scale is materially constituted and changes with context. Although the attacks on the Muslims appeared at the outset to have taken place at the three distinct scales of home, village, and camp, we have seen that in reality the picture was far less neat. Because the military campaign was accompanied by an offensive against the mind and body of the nation—and the sites of these attacks were women's bodies—the nested hierarchies of geographical scales are of little use to our analysis. Rather, an evaluation of the dynamics of this war has shown that geographical scales are regularly constructed as a result of interactions between social actors. The attacks on women's bodies meant that the war was fought at scales smaller than the home—at the corporal and intracorporal levels.

The body as a site of attack has not been considered by most mainstream political geographers a valid tool for understanding political phenomena. But by examining the dynamics of the war at the scale of the body and its specific organs, we can comprehend fully the ways in which Serbs engaged in national genocide, drafting the bodies of both victims and perpetrators for the national goal. Of course, the war was not always fought at the corporal level, and women moved from one scale to another. Because geographical scales are so fluid, it is not always clear where one scale ends and another one begins, as the interactions between victims and the international community further illustrate. Demonstrations around the world brought the pain of the victims to the international level, and the interactions among demonstrators internationally and among victims and human rights organizations have shown that all of these actors (regardless of their positionality) moved between scales regularly and in an unmarked way.

The war in Bosnia-Herzegovina was a war between nations about control of the homeland. The best way to control their homeland, the Serbs believed, was to rid it of the Muslims in any way possible. Thus, the many Serbs who willingly engaged in raping Muslim women justified their acts in national terms. We may wonder, however, about the future of a nation constructed on a foundation of rape and ethnic genocide. At the same time, of course, we may wonder about the impact of these rapes on the victims, their families, and their nation, both now and in the future. Is it possible for national pride to be reconstructed or for a vibrant nationalism to develop after such large-scale terror was carried out methodically against women?

Notes

1. Most of these authors discuss women's participation in the state project; they do not make the distinction between nation and state that I outlined in the early part of this chapter.
2. On the basis of ethnographic accounts, Seifert (1994, 56) suggested that rape is more prominent in some societies than in others. "Societies with high incidents of rape," she argued, "are those in which (a) male power has become unstable, (b) women have a subordinate status and low esteem, and (c) rigid definitions of 'masculine' and 'feminine' prevail."
3. The political goals of Bosnian Serbs and Bosnian Croats were to create ethnically homogenous territories, but because there were very few areas where the Bosnian Serbs, for example, were numerically dominant, the only way for them to achieve dominance was through ethnic cleansing (Kaldor 1999). In Croat towns the goal was the same, and there, too, ethnic cleansing was used to achieve ethnic dominance. In other words, it was not only Muslims who were the victims of ethnic cleansing or Serbs the only perpetrators; rather, ethnic cleansing was performed by Serbs, Croats, and Muslims [who were] all perpetrators and victims (Mrvič-Peterovič 2000). Their positionality was geographically defined, for they were perpetrators in the areas under their control. Having said this, it is important to underscore that in absolute numbers more Muslims were targeted for ethnic cleansing and, thus, were victimized more often than the other national groups.
4. It is important to remember that intermarriage had been practiced in the former Yugoslavia, and for years the purity of each nation was indeed challenged by such practices. But until 1991, when the war broke out, it did not appear to be an issue with either nation.
5. Women in Black is a forum through which women can mobilize and demonstrate against war and violence. The demonstrators are always women who dress in black; they hold weekly silent vigils in protest against war, war rapes, and human rights violations. This movement began in Israel in 1988 to protest against Israel's occupation of the West Bank and the Gaza Strip and spread to Italy, London, Spain, and Belgrade.

12
The (Geo)Politics of Mobility

JENNIFER HYNDMAN

Mobility is an outcome of various economic, geopolitical, gendered, and racialized relations and is constitutive of people's locations as social and political subjects. Yet human mobility and displacement have been relatively overlooked within the discipline despite being core geographical concepts. Moreover, they comprise a rich site from which to explore the intersection of feminist and political geography. In this chapter, after a brief introduction to the politics of mobility, I discuss the idea of a feminist geopolitics, an analytic that challenges taken-for-granted categories of "the political" and reconstructs new ways of thinking about mobility and access in relation to security. Reconceptualizing politics through a feminist approach raises pressing questions about the scale at which geographical analysis should occur, the primary unit(s) of analysis, and whose security is at stake. Hence, in this chapter I employ disparate strands of feminist and political geography to explore the politics of people's mobility, their displacement, and their containment.

Mobility, Displacement, and Containment

Mobility includes all types of territorial movements, including but not limited to migration. For the purposes of this chapter, I couch mobility within a more tacit economy of power, one driven by norms and expectations about the places particular people should move through or occupy (Cresswell 1996). Mobility is not simply an expression of individual agency or choice. When people are forced from their homes and physically dislocated or they experience the colonizing imposition of a foreign culture (Bammer 1994), one might speak of displacement. When kept in place, conditions of containment may apply. Often displacement and containment are linked. In this chapter I give emphasis to both mobility and displacement and to the power relations that shape and are shaped by such geographies.

Feminist geographers employ mobility as an analytic barometer of gender, class, and other sociopolitical relations.

> Mobility is greatest at the extreme ends of the socioeconomic spectrum. The mobility of the destitute is a hardship-induced rootlessness: the homeless, refugees, people on the margins of job markets, and people pushed into migration out of

need or crisis are all clustered at this end of the mobility curve. At the opposite end of the spectrum are the highflyers (literally and metaphorically). (Domosh and Seager 2001, 110)

One can speak, therefore, of "a political economy of mobility," whereby access to economic resources at macroeconomic and microeconomic scales shapes one's opportunities to move. Mobility and its connotation of agency, however, have significant limitations. In a scenario in which access to food and water become so scarce that people can no longer survive where they are, one can speak about *displacement* from one's home, a term that invokes political and environmental context to movement. One's location "at home" shapes and is shaped by the organization of political, economic, and social relations. As Pierre Bourdieu noted, it is through "the dialectical relationship between the body and a structured organization of space and time that common practices and representations are determined" (cited in Cresswell 1996, 9). Bourdieu's focus on the body in relation to institutionalized constellations of space and time points to the importance of examining power relations at multiple scales, an argument to which I will return.

Talk of mobility tends to focus on the agency (or lack of agency) that particular social or political groups of people have in relation to movement, migration, and access. Such an emphasis is important, but by itself it risks overstating the ways in which people are in charge of their movement, migration, or, in some cases, fixity. Massey (1993) raised the notion of a "politics of mobility and access," arguing that different groups of people have distinct relationships to mobility: "Some are more in charge of it than others; some initiate flows and movement, others don't; some are more on the receiving end of it than others; some are effectively imprisoned by it" (p. 61). Massey raised two important points: first, the production of space and one's mobility in it are not simply acts of individual choice; second, in a related vein, mobility is inherently political. Just as Scott (1992, 26) noted, "It is not individuals who have experience, but subjects who are constituted through experience"; neither is it that individuals simply decide their mobility patterns. Mobility, displacement, and migration are all constituted through politico-spatial relations.

One's mobility is an expression of power relations, but mobility also shapes power in a recursive manner. For example, many women in late-twentieth-century Europe and North America have been afraid to walk the streets at night for fear of being attacked, a fear of crime that constitutes "a spatial expression of patriarchy" (Valentine 1992, 27). The threat of sexual violence against women serves to restrict their mobility. But women also have organized to reclaim public space and make it safe again. The first "Take Back the Night" event originated in Germany in 1973 as a response to a series of sexual assaults, rapes, and murders. Take Back the Night rallies also have been held throughout the United States and Canada since 1978 (Lederer 1980). Such gatherings reclaim the streets for women and make sexual violence a visible, public issue, as opposed to a private, individual one.

In a similar vein, one's physical abilities or disabilities clearly shape everyday mobility. What is less obvious, but just as important, is the way in which the built environment both enables and forecloses particular kinds of movement. Vera Chouinard, a feminist geographer and professor, chronicled her experience of exclusion from her own office at a Canadian university (Chouinard and Grant 1995). Without access for her motorized chair, her mobility is restricted not simply based on physical disability but also because of lack of accommodation and appropriate planning and policy in relation to the university's design. The London underground (subway) and Paris metro are other examples of spaces built for people who do not use chairs, strollers, or crutches. For those who do, transportation and mobility become a major issue, shaping access to institutions, workplaces, and services.

Mobility is always constrained. The mobility of all persons is subject to the configuration of Massey's (1993) power-geometry, but conditions of highly restricted mobility, even containment, are more common for those bodies that are criminalized, displaced, and/or construed as a security threat to the state and its citizenry. Katharyne Mitchell (1997b) cautioned against representations of unfettered migrant mobility, particularly in the context of transnational migration, which claims that migrants forge social fields across international borders by living and working in distinct locations. At the other end of the mobility spectrum, migrants, refugees, and asylum seekers are liminal to states (Mailkki 1995). Their outsider status beyond the boundaries of their home country can raise suspicion and lead to their geographical containment when they seek sanctuary in a neighboring state. Somali and Sudanese refugees in Kenya, for example, are located in remote camps, as far away as possible from urban life, employment, and access to agricultural resources that might improve their condition (Hyndman 2000). Likewise, Mountz (2004) observed that groups of migrants arriving on Canadian shores by the boat from Fujian province in China are more likely to be criminalized and detained by the authorities than migrants from the same place who arrive by plane as individuals, suggesting that the optics of migrant mobility are linked to perceptions of state security.

Mobilizing the Subject in Feminist Political Geography

Poststructuralist approaches to understanding feminism offer insights into how geographers might understand mobility as constitutive of subjects. Political theorist Mouffe (1992, 382) noted,

> Feminism, for me, is the struggle for the equality of women. But this should not be understood as a struggle for realizing the equality of a definable empirical group with a common essence and identity, women, but rather as a struggle

against the multiple forms in which the category "woman" is constructed in subordination.

Implicit in Mouffe's argument is that the category "woman" is constructed differently across space and time. Likewise, the mobility and access of "woman" are produced differently across geographical and historical contexts.

Also on the issue of feminism's subject, Pratt (2004) wrote,

> Whether feminism as a social movement is successful in articulating other liberation struggles within the category, woman, is something that is decided through political struggle and not only or finally through philosophical debate. To the extent that it is successful in fulfilling this function of representing the universal, we would expect the feminist movement to be increasingly emptied of its singular focus on woman, and possibly rethought around a broader critique of the production of social difference and the multiple exclusions enacted by dominant groups and institutions. (excerpt from chap. 4)

Extending this critique further, analysis of the production of differential mobility and access to institutions, including those of the state, is vital. The state takes many forms and has been defined as a bundle of sometimes contradictory practices rather than as a unitary actor (Mountz 2004). Its treatment of women, immigrants, and noncitizens varies considerably across time and space.

Accordingly, feminism has long had an ambiguous relationship to the liberal state (Pateman 1989). Individual rights-bearing citizens are equal subjects under the law; on the ground, participation in and access to active citizenship are more problematic. Citizens, one discovers, are constituted as gendered and racialized, as well as legal, subjects. Thus, although rights may be accorded equally in a legal sense, the outcomes of such rights are not equal. Liberal geographies of people as (equal) rights-bearing individuals, in charge of their mobility and futures more generally, remain relevant (Blomley 1994), but the limits of their claims need to be specified. What is important to this discussion is that poststructuralist perspectives allow us to specify these limits by illustrating the ways in which rights operate both as an instrument for potential socio-political change within liberal states and as a mode of state monitoring and possibly its control over mobility.

When individuals press claims as members of a subordinated group, they are accepting and redeploying an often stigmatized identity to gain rights (Pratt 2004). They allow themselves to step forward and be counted and administered by the state in particular ways. "[R]ights are not simply a tool for individuals and groups to use instrumentally; they are themselves constitutive of these groups and individuals. They encourage identities to congeal around particular social characteristics" (Pratt 2004, 105). Refugees, as another example, can claim no rights as refugees until they cross an international border, seek asylum from legal authorities, and are judged to be legitimate. They are literally an embodiment of rights enshrined in international law. Once in camps, refugees tacitly consent to being counted and administered through international agencies that restrict mobility and control access to food and health (Hyndman 2000). "Refugee" is not normally a desirable way to identify oneself, except for the purpose of seeking protection or claiming rights through asylum. Claiming refugee status is also an example of "jumping scales" (Blomley and Pratt 2001), whereby a person abandons the legal rights and protection of her or his own nation-state and seeks recognition at a coarser scale, that of international law.

This example raises the question of scale, and in particular mobility across scales, for feminist political geographers. Scale is critical in structuring political action (Staeheli 1994, 388):

> To the extent that oppositional movements can move across scales—that is, to the extent that they can take advantage of the resources at one scale to overcome the constraints encountered at different scales in the way that more powerful actors can do—they may have greater potential for pressing their claims.

Swyngedouw (2000, 70) added that the "continuous reshuffling and reorganizations of spatial scales are an integral part of social strategies and struggles for control and empowerment." Analyzing individual and group mobility within the context of the state, for example, generates a different analysis than examining mobility in relation to the global economy. In describing the shortcomings of development studies and postcolonial studies, respectively, Sylvester (1999, 703) cogently stated, "Development studies does not tend to listen to subalterns and postcolonial studies does not tend to concern itself with whether the subaltern is eating." Both approaches examine disparate relations of power that render certain countries and peoples more vulnerable than others. Transposing this example to speak to the question of scale, one can say that modernization theory in development studies tends to see poverty and lack of industrialization as outcomes of deficiencies that are internal to a given country. Postcolonial studies, in contrast, tend to analyze the absence of voice that a marginalized person or country may have in narrating its own affairs, but it does so by examining geographies that incorporate global relations of power and colonial practices. Not only theory but also scale shapes the outcomes of geographical analysis.

There are, in short, several different ways to understand mobility from geographical perspectives that are both feminist and political. Despite these connections, existing analyses of mobility in feminist geography tend to focus on economic, social, and cultural relations of power (Hyndman 2001). In what follows I aim to fill this political gap in feminist geography by offering analyses of mobility as geopolitics, invoking multiple scales of inquiry both larger and smaller than the state. In so doing, I do not deny, the importance of the state in dominant geopolitical discourse but aim to make visible the everyday implications and impact of prevailing geographies of politics, using migration as the medium.

Migration: Embodied Mobility and Corporeal Access

The migrant and migration as an aggregate phenomenon together comprise a medium for understanding the (geo)politics of mobility. The migrant is an embodiment of movement, a process structured by the power-geometry of which Massey spoke. There are multiple rationales for focusing on the migrant body in particular. First, such an approach insists on embodied, situated knowledge: "These are [knowledge] claims on people's lives; the view from a body, always a complex, contradictory, structuring and structured body, versus the view from above, from nowhere, from simplicity" (Haraway 1991, 195). Despite some claims to the contrary (Katz 2001), situated knowledge shapes seeing and the selection of political struggles. Pettman (1997, 95) noted that writing in international relations has been disembodied; neither writers nor their subjects have visible bodies. How and from where knowledge is produced shapes the meanings and connotations of mobility and access as they are constituted across scale. Second, such an approach highlights the idea that bodies are "sites of performance in their own right rather than nothing more than surfaces for discursive inscription" (Dowler and Sharp 2001, 169). That is to say, migrants are not simply patterned outcomes of macropolitical and economic processes but geographically and historically constituted subjects in their own right. They are neither full authors of their actions nor mere dupes of external power relations. Third, the body is a vital starting point from which to analyze the role of the state in an era of increasing globalization and transnational flows. With claims that the nation-state is dead in an era of globalization (Ohmae 1995), scholars can use the attention to the mobility of bodies at such a fine scale to trace the remaining influence of the state, if any (Mountz 2004). Geographies initiated at the scale of the body also offer up the possibility of documenting containment practices authorized by the state at multiple scales and seek to deconstruct the state as a unified entity. Such a starting point enables one to examine the multiple performances that such bodies enact in relation to state agencies as subjects in their own right. In the following section I illustrate how migrants negotiate and inhabit multiple subject positions that, in turn, shape their mobility and experiences (Kofman and England 1997).

Theorizing mobility begins with people's embodied stories of migration and displacement (Hyndman 1997). In Xavier Koller's 1990 film *Journey of Hope,* a poor peasant family sells its meager farm assets in rural Turkey, banking on swift passage to the utopic Switzerland that it has seen on a postcard. Of their many children, the parents take only one—their youngest son, bearer of the family's name and agent of its future fortunes. Their journey is arranged by a contact whose trade and trafficking in illegal migrants is a lucrative business. In the company of a sympathetic German truck driver, the family fails in its first attempt to gain entry and is turned back to Italy, where the trio finds another agent who assures them he can help if they can pay. The business of trafficking in migrants is depicted as increasingly unsavory as the Turkish family approaches the mountainous Swiss-Italian border. The family, now part of a larger group of migrating clients, is transported to the frontier in the back of a van and is instructed to pose as political refugees as soon as they cross the border. Unprepared for the snowstorm and struggle over the Alps, some members of the group are discovered by Swiss border patrols, many near death, when they finally arrive at the border. The *Journey of Hope*, embodied by the young boy whose language dexterity enables cultural boundaries to be crossed and whose winning spirit with strangers renders new lands less daunting, culminates in the boy's death, the imprisonment of his father, and the grief of his mother. At the same time, many people along the way have been enriched by the failed journey. Migration is an embodied expression of desperation and hope in a highly unequal world characterized by disparate economic conditions of insecurity. It points to a rescaling of geopolitics, in which the prevailing political concern is no longer the security of states but the security of persons in social, economic, and political terms.

Conventional geopolitics, in both geography and political science, has been largely concerned with the security of states and the relation of states to a global political economy. Although the scales of the state and the global commons remain relevant, they are by no means sufficient in probing questions of security for civilians in a country where they are discriminated against by their own government or have little access to basic food, shelter, and health services. Security is implicitly a question of scale: security for whom? From a feminist perspective, shifting the focus of security to that of civilian safety and well-being unsettles the state-centric approaches of conventional geopolitics. If security is interpreted as protection from violence, freedom from fear and intimidation, and the right to a livelihood, as I suggest, it becomes a much more contested idea in which scale remains a central question.

Rights instantiate a battle of scale: which scale of accountability and legitimacy can be invoked? For whose benefit? The idea of "human security" has been proposed by UN organizations and governments in an attempt to address security at multiple scales. Notions of security that underscore the importance of human rights generate legitimacy for international interventions to violate the sovereignty of rogue states, where such states are unwilling or unable to respond (DFAIT 2000). Human security, in theory, disaggregates the broader notion of security to a finer scale at which smaller political constituencies and vulnerable groups become visible and their security becomes a public matter of concern (Hyndman 2001). Human security is a term introduced by Boutros Boutros-Ghali's UN *Agenda for Peace* in 1992 to highlight the atrocities and subsequent conflicts that exist within states, making the point that the governments of such states should not be able to hide behind their sovereignty. Indeed, sovereignty is up for negotiation in states that failed to provide basic food security, health security, or environmental security for its citizens. In practice, human security also has become a rationale for the selective involvement of more powerful states in less powerful ones, in which the governments of the latter fail to protect their citizens and the governments of the former care to intervene. In relation to human displacement generated by conflict, human security is intimately linked to state security. During the 1990s governments in northern countries generally agreed that an international intervention into a country affected by conflict and violence may be a way to stop the mass migration of people fleeing for their safety into neighboring countries and states. In other words, UN interventions into countries affected by conflict, such as Iraq, Somalia, and Bosnia-Herzegovina, were seen to be strategies that might prevent forced migration, relieving pressure on refugee admission obligations at home (Hyndman 2000).

Security, like mobility, can be approached from an embodied perspective. Mountz (2004) referred to corporeal geographies as the starting point for new understandings of the roles of the nation-state in relation to human smuggling. To the extent that the bodies of successfully smuggled migrants are seen as potentially diseased and criminalized, the security of the state is thrown into question. The state has a monopoly on determining who gets into its territory, but where borders prove porous to irregular migrants, state sovereignty is at risk. The threat of human smuggling also can be used to underwrite particular foreign policy, including aid disbursements and trade concessions. In a global world, the argument goes, no country is immune to the dangers associated with countries affected by conflict, unwanted migration, disease, transnational crime, and the like. To avoid such problems, individual countries must contribute to the well-being of the global commons. On the basis of this line of argument, now shared among aid agencies in the most industrialized countries, and of alarmist media representations of migrant invasion, state boundaries are unwittingly reinscribed through a discourse of insecurity. Only by examining multiple scales concurrently, in this case the scale of the migrant body and the vulnerable state, are these strategic modes of recentering state security exposed. To ensure national security, a state may refuse entry to prospective migrants, despite conditions of insecurity that may characterize the migrants' status. Mobility and access of particular bodies to a given territory are monitored by the state, whose criteria for entry remain selective. The body, as a subject of geographical inquiry, thus exposes the machinations of the state's efforts to ensure its security through the restricted mobility of unsolicited migration.

Feminist Geopolitics: Illustrating the Case

In the remaining pages of this chapter I analyze mobility, displacement, and containment at multiple scales. In so doing, I underscore a feminist geographic approach to the politics of mobility. These scenarios attempt to flesh out the ideas introduced so far and demonstrate the multiple, sometimes competing, scales at which power relations are negotiated. The first example examines patterns of immigration and exclusion in a historical context, demonstrating the way in which the Canadian state invented regulations, including the passport, not as means of enabling passage but, rather, as a way of excluding those British subjects it considered undesirable.[1] By privileging state control of borders over the obligations of empire, South Asians were effectively barred from Canada through passports and policies developed in the early part of the twentieth century. The second scenario illuminates the politics of mobility for people who are "out of place," namely refugees and internally displaced persons who are pushed involuntarily from their homes. Their relative mobility in and around camps is differentiated by gender, class, nationality, and geographical location as well as by the geopolitics of international relations and global political economy. Concern to minimize the costs of international obligations to refugees, reflected in the neoliberal policies of donor countries, also shapes the character of assistance provided to those adversely affected by such crises. Camps, states, and international law all bear on the mobility of these displaced persons. Finally, a brief analysis of migrants in and to South Africa illustrates the highly gendered and racialized legacies of colonialism and apartheid in relation to mobility. African men and women are situated very differently in relation, for example, to the current crisis of HIV/AIDS in that country; gender, race, and apartheid law have generated differential spaces of containment, contagion, and controversy. Displacement and mobility are shown to be highly gendered, politicized relations of power.

The Politics of Mobility: Immigration, Exclusion, and the Passport

Race, ethnicity, and gender mark people in particular ways that affect mobility. Although rarely officially named as criteria for exclusion, people of particular racial, ethnic, and national backgrounds have been and are still kept out of more industrialized countries, such as Canada, with women and men being affected differently (Mongia 1999). Deciding who gets in is a highly selective process. In 1885 government legislation enacted a "head tax" of $50 per person for all male Chinese migrants in Canada, making it more difficult for this group to get into and stay in Canada. Chinese women were not allowed into Canada because it was thought that together with Chinese men, they would marry, start families, and stay in the country. By 1903 the tax was raised to $500 per person. Immigration to Canada has always been a gendered and racialized project.

Beginning in the early twentieth century, South Asians from the Punjab region of India began migrating to Canada. In 1897 Punjabi Indian troops based in the British Crown Colony of Hong Kong and nearby outposts had traveled through Canada from Victoria to Halifax to assemble in London, England, for Queen Victoria's diamond jubilee. In 1902 troops again made the trek for Edward VII's coronation. These visits by British subjects of color across the settler Canadian territory inspired migration (Ralston 1999).

In 1903–1904, some forty men and four women from India came to Victoria and Vancouver. Government anxiety over the immigration of Indians to Canada began in earnest in 1906, with the arrival of about 2,000 Indian men at Vancouver (Mongia 1999). Their numbers grew quickly to 5,164 men and 15 women by the end of the fiscal year 1907–1908; the highly skewed gender ratio was only exacerbated during this period. In 1907 the government of Canada proposed the implementation of a passport system to selectively curtail migration to the Colonial Office in London and to the government of India. The Viceroy of India rejected the idea, suggesting that Canada proceed with suitably disguised methods of discrimination, requiring "certain qualifications such as physical fitness . . . and the possession of a certain amount of money" (Viceroy of India, cited in Mongia 1999, 537). Although the Canadian government was slower to act, the provincial government of British Columbia quickly found out that Indians coming to Canada departed from the Port of Calcutta for Hong Kong and then traveled on to Canada. Using this information, the British Columbia government passed a regulation, or Order in Council, stating, "Immigrants shall be prohibited landing, unless they come from their country of birth or citizenship by continuous journey, and on through tickets purchased before starting" (Viceroy of India, cited in Mongia 1999, 540). Because passage took place in two parts, with no possibility for a single prepurchased ticket, this order effectively excluded all Indians from coming to Canada. Combined with another regulation that every immigrant needs to possess $200 on arrival, the government was able to enact selective discrimination and restrict mobility without naming race as such. Between 1909 and 1913, only 27 Indians managed to enter Canada.

In 1912 the editor of the *Daily Province* argued that racial mixing should be avoided by preventing "Oriental" immigration: "We do not want a mixed breed, half Oriental, half Occidental, in this country" (cited in Ralston 1999, 33). In 1913 the editor of the *Vancouver Sun* stated that South Asian men should not be allowed to bring their wives; otherwise, permanent settlement would be established:

> The point of view of the Hindu (in wanting Canada to admit wives and families) is readily understood and appreciated. But there is the point of view of the white settler in this country who wants to keep the country a white country with white standards of living and morality. . . . [Hindus] are not a desirable people from any standpoint for the Dominion to have. . . . The white population will never be able to absorb them. They are not an assimilable people. . . . We must not permit the men of that race to come in large numbers, *and we must not permit their women to come in at all*. Such a policy of exclusion is simply a measure of self-defence. . . . We have no right to imperil the comfort and happiness of the generations that are to succeed us. (cited in Ralston 1999, 33)

The competing loyalties of empire and nationhood were finally tested on 23 May 1914, with the arrival of 376 passengers, mostly Punjabi Sikhs, on the *Komagata Maru*, which landed in the Vancouver port. The reaction among politicians was strong. Then minister of the interior, Frank Oliver, expressed veiled racist sentiments in the clothing of national sovereignty in 1914:

> The immigration law as it stands is a declaration on the part of this country that Canada is mistress of her own house and takes the authority and responsibility of deciding who shall be admitted to citizenship and the privileges and rights of citizenship within her borders. . . . This is not a labour question; it is not a racial question; it is a question of national dominance and national existence. (cited in Mongia 1999, 550)

In such cases, the state assigns nationality as the basis for exclusion, but it is little more than an alibi for race. Mobility is regulated by the state in ways that do not name country of origin but selectively control migration from these locations, nonetheless. Mongia (1999) convincingly argued that apparently objective criteria for entering a country are encoded with prohibitions of race and gender. Ironically, the government of the day also employed a gendered analogy, likening admittance to Canada to entrance to one's house. The emergence of Canadian sovereign space as domestic is interesting because it sets up a basis for exclusion of those from outside. Despite shared British subjection, the analogy frames immigration as by invitation only.

Displacement and the Politics of Mobility

Just as Sikhs from northern India were not invited in to western Canada, asylum seekers are not normally particularly welcomed by Canada and other industrialized countries. Access to such countries is highly uneven across lines of gender, class, and geographical location. The following vignettes link gender and geopolitics though mobility.

> Applications for refugee resettlement from Kenya to Australia and Canada are available at the high commissions for each country located in Nairobi. The refugee camps, where prospective refugee applicants live temporarily, are roughly six hours away by bus. Only those with the money and the time to make the trip can apply. The vast majority of women in these camps are responsible for child care, food preparation, and other labour-intensive household tasks. They cannot get away for days at a time. Besides, few have the extra funds to buy a bus ticket to Nairobi. Their restricted mobility shapes their potential emigration options. (adapted from Hyndman 2000)

> In Afghanistan, a dramatically different politics of mobility has emerged: women and girls are moving from their homes, back into employment, schools, universities, and public space more generally. Early in 2002, schools for girls opened across Afghanistan after a seven-year hiatus. Of the 22 classes offered at one Kandahar school, 13 were for grade one. Only three classes are taught above the grade three level, although many of the students are in their teens. A new government, led by Hamid Karzai, has replaced the self-declared Taliban government of 1996–2001. Under Taliban rule, women and girls were literally banned from public space, unable to hold jobs or attend schools. Their movements in public space required the male supervision of a husband, father, brother or male relative. Women who

> were sick were not allowed to be examined by a male doctor, yet female physicians were forced out of their jobs, so that there were no women physicians. Afghan women were confined to their homes. (MacKinnon 2002, 88)

Each of these scenarios depicts a kind of displacement (from home to a camp in another country, and from work and school to home, then back into public life) that is related to women's access to mobility. Lacking access to mobility restricts possibilities for citizenship in a new country, in the first scenario, and precludes the possibility of earning one's livelihood and seeking education, in the second. In each case mobility is deeply intertwined with broader geopolitical considerations. In the Kenyan camps, refugees have sought safety from the violence of conflict in Somalia and Sudan. In so doing, they find their mobility constrained by the Kenyan government's decision to locate camps in marginal border areas because of their perceived destabilizing influence. Kenya and Somalia have been geopolitical adversaries since the 1960s, when Somalia attempted to annex the Somali-occupied part of northeast Kenya. In Afghanistan, with the defeat of the Taliban late in 2001, the return of women to work and girls to school is hailed as an achievement of the U.S.-led "war on terrorism." And yet, this success was never a stated aim of the military operations in Afghanistan. Moreover, the rights of women in nearby Saudi Arabia, a major U.S. ally where women are routinely excluded from public space (e.g., they are prohibited from driving cars) and punished if they violate these codes, have never been a major issue for the United States. The United States' access to Saudi Arabian oil is geopolitically more important than women's access to public space and basic rights as citizens.

Elsewhere, I have developed the idea of the "geopolitics of mobility" to argue that international borders are more porous to global capital than to displaced persons (Hyndman 1997). The mobility of international humanitarian aid, for example, is juxtaposed with the relative immobility of migrants, especially refugees. Since the end of the cold war—during which refugees had political value to the superpowers—the industrialized countries of Europe, Japan, and particularly North America have become much less interested in resettling refugees in their own countries than in managing forced migration at a distance, closer to its source. Generous donations to multilateral organizations, such as UN agencies and nongovernmental organizations, make possible arms-length strategies of helping people who are displaced from their homes. At the same time, immigration policies restrict access to these countries, making it more difficult rather than less difficult to resettle permanently.

Employing mobility as an analytic of geopolitical power offers up possibilities for feminist politics and political geography. At a fine scale, people's mobility varies tremendously across race, gender, class, caste, nationality, immigrant status, and other dimensions. The power-geometry of gender and socioeconomic status shapes the mobility of groups and individuals in important ways, but analyzing how mobility is shaped by institutions, governments, and legislation—what might be called "mobility from above"—is equally important. Power relations that enable or restrict individual movement are embedded in political arrangements, organizations, and practices both locally and across political boundaries. Once again, the importance of jumping scales and of invoking analysis at multiple scales is emphasized.

Race, Space, and Law: The Gendered Politics of Mobility in the Apartheid State

If mobility in and around isolated refugee camps in Kenya is framed primarily by the intersection of gender, class, and geopolitics, mobility during the apartheid era in South Africa was framed primarily by the intersection of race, gender, and legislation enacted by the colonial state and then by the apartheid state. A colonial system of male migrant labor was established to operate the gold mines and to extract cheap wages from black African men from foreign, often adjacent, countries. Because such men were not accompanied by their families, employers felt justified in paying wages for a single person rather than for a family. Spatial separation of families seemingly justified social decontextualization so that migrants ceased to be part of families while working in the mines. Male migrant workers left family members behind, either in another country—such as Lesotho or Swaziland—or in one of the homelands reserved for black South Africans. Apartheid law produced distinct categories of race and assigned separate spaces for each. The sexual division of labor, whereby men were employed in wage labor and women were more likely to look after children, crosscut these legal race-based assignments.

This racialized and gendered migrant labor system was maintained under apartheid rule, a legislated system of racial and gender segregation largely enacted after 1948. Two key pillars of segregation in South Africa were the 1913 Land Act and the Natives (Urban Areas) Act of 1923. The former made it illegal for Africans to purchase or lease land from Europeans anywhere outside the reserves set aside for them. The latter established the principle of residential segregation in urban areas, giving Africans no permanent rights to live in towns and no justification for being there unless needed by whites as labor. In 1949 the Population Registration Act legislated that every South African be given a registered race classification and that every person carry such documentation. Once everyone was classified by his or her registered race, mobility could be controlled and monitored by a system of passes. The 1952 Abolition of Passes and Consolidation of Documents Act created a more comprehensive, single identity document that replaced all other papers, generating a more efficient system of controlling mobility. No (black) African could leave her or his area without a permit from local authorities, instantiating a policy of containment for black South Africans.

For black South African men who worked in cities, apartheid legislation required them to carry appropriate passes and to live in shared hostels located in townships situated within commuting distance of white cities. Employed black men lived in the townships while their families generally lived in homelands designated by the South African government. In 1986 the pass laws restricting the mobility of unemployed family members were lifted, and families joined male breadwinners in their township hostels, which quickly became overcrowded. Although legal apartheid ceased to exist after the election of Nelson Mandela and his African National Congress government in 1994, de facto segregation based on race is still in place, based now primarily on economic location rather than on racial classification as a modus operandi for differential access to resources.

Elaborating on South Africa in the contemporary period, let me turn briefly to a gender analysis of migrants in the country, a highly gendered geography of mobility and blame. The example identifies a legacy of apartheid, whereby men and women are unevenly held responsible for contracting and spreading HIV/AIDS. McLean (2002) argued that black men have been represented not as agents of their sexual geographies but as historical victims of the colonial migrant labor system and subsequent apartheid politics. Black women, on the other hand, have been cast either as passive receptacles of the disease or as its promiscuous purveyors in a geography of blame. Drawing on Patton's (1994) analysis, McLean's work provides a historically grounded description of the relationship between political rule, economic interests, migration patterns, and sexually transmitted diseases in South Africa. By focusing on male migrant workers and the women with whom they interact, she analyzed the ways in which these men and women are differentially represented and implicated in the transmission, spread, and prevention of HIV/AIDS. Specific power relations that are constructed around differences of gender, race, ethnicity, sexuality, and nation intersect with mobility and migrant identities (see Silvey and Lawson 1999).

In the context of South Africa, McLean (2002) contended that the relationship between migrancy and sexually transmitted diseases, including HIV/AIDS, refers back to the colonial encounter, in which conditions set the stage for the large-scale spread of sexually transmitted diseases through a circular migrant labor system that forced permanent geographic mobility on workers while disrupting their interpersonal and sexual relationships. State control of sexually transmitted diseases was linked to racialized assumptions regarding the African body and its sexuality. Even more critical to a newly industrializing South Africa was the preservation of a labor force capable of working long hours at low pay in dangerous conditions in the mines, factories, and farms. "Such controls were coercively enacted and tightly linked to pass laws that restricted the mobility and hence the earning capacity of already-impoverished South African blacks" (McLean 2002, 30). Under apartheid, law, gender, and race were part and parcel of containment and relative immobility.

The intersection of race and gender over colonial and apartheid pasts has given rise to distinctive patterns of migrant representation. Male migrant workers have typically been represented as historically situated victims of their social, political, and historical circumstances, acting to reclaim their power and agency in the face of historic and ongoing racism and oppression through the assertion of masculine identity. They are portrayed as

> sexual and economic actors grounded in a home, a history and a sexual geography, while at the same time being culturally absolved of blame for the epidemic and its spread. Meanwhile, black women are represented as vulnerable and powerless in terms of negotiating safer sexual practices and are otherwise divested of agency and sexual identity, save for their capacity as irresponsible vectors of disease or as the objects of prevention discourse. (McLean 2002, 23)

The migrant body is at once a site of performance and the subject of political representations that locate black women and men very differently in the prevailing narratives of HIV/AIDS. Such assumptions inform and structure both the research questions asked and the direction of policy discussions around HIV/AIDS in what is now the "new" postapartheid South Africa.

Taking McLean's analysis a step further, it is pertinent to ask if there is a relation between geopolitics and current patterns of access to health care for those affected by HIV/AIDS. U.S. Republican politician Jesse Helms recently changed his position in relation to access to treatment for HIV/AIDS, arguing that antiretroviral drugs should be made available to HIV-positive pregnant women. By specifying pregnant women, and not all women affected by HIV/AIDS, Helms made the classic "deserving victim" argument: unborn children are not at fault for contracting the disease and should not be made to suffer from it. Women who are not mothers, however, are somehow less deserving of treatment, as are men. By arguing for such limited access, Helms only serves to reinforce earlier geographies of blame, even if unborn children are to benefit. His politics beg the question, Should American women with and without children have the same access to treatment as South African women do?

The scenarios outlined—of South Asian immigration and Canadian government exclusion; of displacement, asylum, and containment among refugees; and of migrant labor as a racialized and spatialized expression of apartheid in South Africa—all speak of the intersection of geography and politics in relation to mobility. Each example speaks to the embodied practices of people on the move whose access to Canada, immigration visa posts, and health resources are highly uneven based on their gender, race, class, and nationality locations. Each of these geographies speaks to the institutional, legal, and political processes that also shape mobility and access. Government regulations in a predominantly white settler society are used to exclude South Asians from entering Canada; the location of camps for Somali and Sudanese refugees in remote areas of Kenya, far from the capital city, restrict access to visa posts for those without resources to travel or child care; and the colonial, apartheid, and even contemporary economies of South Africa have been dependent on migrant laborers who are separated from their families and represented as victims of oppressive power relations and vectors of HIV/AIDS.

Conclusion

When disparate relations of power result in violence and deprivation, both feminist and political geographies are crucial to thinking through mobility and displacement. Mobility is as much about technologies of control, containment, and separation as it is about movement and agency. The geometry of one's location, alluded to by Massey, places people, just as people may choose to travel to a particular place. One's mobility shapes and is shaped by prevailing geopolitical practices, and these occur at multiple scales. Analysis at the scale of the body augments our understanding of mobility as a site of performance as well as inscription. As a unit of geographical analysis, bodies are "sites of performance in their own right," not simply sites on which power relations are inscribed (Dowler and Sharp 2001, 169). The body as a scale of analysis, in concert with analysis at other scales, also offers insight into the ways in which scale frames explanatory narratives.

For too long, political geography and feminist geography have represented two solitudes within the discipline. One of my aims in this chapter has been to demonstrate the rich potential for analysis and for politics when connections are forged between the two. By focusing on the processes and politics of migration, and on the migrants themselves, I argue for a more embodied and accountable understanding of mobility as a critical dimension of both political and feminist geography. Such an understanding raises several new questions: how are geographical sight lines changed if power relations are analyzed at multiple scales? Retaining gender as constitutive of differential access and mobility across time and space, how can this approach be extended to include social, economic, and political locations beyond gender? How can feminist thinking about mobility, displacement, and containment influence critical approaches to geopolitics? Much remains to be done.

Note

1. By choosing a historical example, I am by no means implying that such exclusionary measures are a historical phenomenon. The act of simply being born in one country rather than another significantly shapes one's mobility. I think here of a colleague with whom I recently collaborated on a research project in Sri Lanka. We are both middle-class women born in the 1960s with Ph.D.s from North American universities. She is a citizen of Sri Lanka I of Canada. Based on where we were born and the citizenship we hold, the restrictions on our mobility are completely different. I can enter Sri Lanka on a tourist visa obtained for free at the airport upon arrival, no questions asked. She, in contrast, must buy a transit visa from the British government simply to change planes and sit in the transit lounge at Heathrow airport en route to Canada. She must apply for a visa for most international trips she takes, an enormously time-consuming, often costly, hassle that is often complicated further by the absence of a visa post or consulate in Sri Lanka for the country she intends to visit. In such cases, she flies to India to access the appropriate embassy, high commission, or consulate and get the necessary visa, then flies home before embarking once again on her intended journey. As a highly educated and employed woman, she almost always gets a visa, but the time and energy spent collecting the required paperwork represents an asymmetrical burden based on nationality. One's citizenship is embedded with specific histories and politics of where and how one can move across international borders.

13
Crossing Borders:
Gender and Migration

PARVATI RAGHURAM

Migration reconfigures many of political geography's key concepts in important ways. Both the state and its borders are essential to mainstream political geography, yet recent work by political geographers has paid little attention to the ways in which the relationship between the territorial state and the people resident in it are changing because of migration (Agnew 2002; Taylor and Flint 2000; but see Nagel 2002).

The citizenry of nation-states is altered as a result of migration. For instance, migrants may take up dual citizenship so that people's territorial allegiances become split across states (Sassen 1996).[1] The economic and political powers of migrant groups also influence the economic, cultural, and political landscapes of both receiving and sending states (Pessar and Mahler 2002). Moreover, the notion of citizenship is changing because of such migration, with some theorists claiming that we now inhabit a postnational space marked by global citizenship, or at least some form of regional citizenship (Soysal 1994). These theorists stress the deterritorializing nature of contemporary global processes marked by ease of movement of capital, goods, and ideas, as well as of people across borders, and by the development of international discourses of rights against which claims can be made by migrants (for critique see Joppke 2000; Kofman 2002).

At the same time, states have taken on the mantle of providing safe havens for their current citizens by securing the borders of the state and limiting the entry of new migrants (Her Majesty's Stationery Office 2002). State boundaries have been strengthened, as it is argued that the movement of people is not simply an addendum to the list of movable commodities; rather, migration is set within a different set of regulatory, political, and ethical discourses and therefore raises a different set of issues. The migration of some people is increasingly controlled and regulated by the state, and barriers to movement are strengthening, not decreasing. The state's territorial boundaries are regulated and have become sites of inspections and restrictions as the state determines the general conditions of entry, work, and residence of the people who live within its borders.

Changes in the territorial boundaries of states trigger refugee movements so that migration may also be deemed a consequence of changes in the territorial state. Migrants crossing borders distort borders—extending them and questioning them. But states also have used the presence of migrants, particularly refugees, to strengthen borders (see Wastl-Walter and Staeheli 2004 [this volume]). Importantly, the invocation of the language of borders has gained strength because of the perceived need to control borders. Increasingly, conflict at the borders, and therefore border control, is activated through exclusion and inclusion of "unwanted" people and goods rather than through discourses of territory. Borders have criminalized some migrants, and this has been picked up in public imaginations of migration, whereby migrants are now primarily identified by their legal status. Questions of legality and illegality of migration have become pressing in the context of such border controls.

These changes have occurred on a gendered landscape. Feminist political geographers have long argued for the need to recognize the gendered nature of the state (Kofman and Peake 1990). Although a state's immigration policies may not be constructed as overtly gendered, they do differentially foster or retard the migration of women (Kofman et al. 2000). In this chapter I explore the challenges posed to the relationship between territorial entities and its people when women migrate. I divide the chapter into two sections. In the first section I examine the ways in which a state's immigration regulations intersect with pressures from other scalar levels, from the global to the household, to differentially influence the movement of men and women. In the following section I explore how these movements have so far been theorized and the limits to current theorizations.

Women Crossing Borders: Migration Regulations and the State

State practices are an integral aspect of migratory regimes and are crucial to an understanding of flows and experiences of migrant men and women. In this section I examine some of the regulations and practices of the receiving states and the sending states. In practice these often are linked, but most current literature focuses on the receiving state and how they define the mode of entry, rights of residence, and status of migrants, and so I begin here. Although the policies are purportedly gender neutral, they play themselves out in a gendered world, differentially influencing people's ability to emigrate and to enter and their subsequent status. I then discuss some of the ways in which sending states have fostered or responded to female migration.

Migration is institutionalized at both ends; institutions allow and encourage some women to move, while limiting the movement of others. For instance, the gender breakdown of migrants may be closely related to the gendering of education received by men and women in their own countries. Donato (1992) found that differentiated levels of access to educational opportunities was the second-largest factor influencing the proportion of women among numerically limited immigrants to the United States (i.e., those who were entering on labor permits rather than for family reunification). At the receiving end, migrant experiences are mediated by immigration policies and rules, which influence men and women differently. British immigration policy between the mid-1960s and mid-1980s, for example, differentiated between men and women in the nature of the family they could bring in, the limits on employment of spouses who joined the primary migrant, and the conditions regulating their stay (J. Bhabha and Shutter 1994).

Other axes of difference such as stage of the life course, class, country of origin (a category that is usually historicized and racialized), and sexuality also operate alongside or intersect with gender differences. Stage of the life course has very different effects on men and women migrants, as women continue to take up primary responsibility for caring activities within the home. Caring responsibilities, moreover, may limit some women's movement, while forcing others to move (Chamberlain 1999).

The Receiving State

Immigration controls are usually applied on a bilateral basis, with regulations reflecting historical, political, economic, and social ties between the sending and receiving countries. Country of origin can differentially influence the gender breakdown of migration streams. For instance, significant proportions of migrants from Ireland, Australia, and the Philippines are women, with Ireland sending more women than men since the 1930s. More recently, the casting of Filipino women as global caregivers by the state policies of the government of the Philippines and the immigration policies of the states to which these women have migrated also has led to high rates of female migration from this country.

The kinds of state controls exerted on migrants usually vary by the mode of entry, differentiating between labor migrants and those who enter for the purposes of family reunification or as students, tourists, and refugees. This categorization uses the purpose of migration as the primary basis for differentiation, but feminists have argued that such categories are not necessarily appropriate to the experience of female migrants. For instance, women (possibly more often than men) may move from one category to another. This is a particularly crucial issue that needs addressing in an "age of migration" that has been marked not just by acceleration and diversification but also by the feminization of migration (Castles and Miller 1998). However, because these categories form the most common basis for immigration regulations, I use them here.

Labor Migration The number of women migrating across borders always has been high but the past two decades have seen a remarkable growth in the movement of women moving alone, for purposes other than family formation or reunification (Lim and Oishi 1996). The significance of labor market shortages in the control of migration has increased from the late 1990s, and the issue of work permits has become an important strategy for fulfilling shortages in very specific niches.[2] As a result, there is an increasing emphasis on the labor market as a locale for the selection of migrants. National governments rewrite immigration regulations to meet labor market requirements, but this is usually accompanied by restrictive immigration policies. In migrant-receiving countries, such policies do not stop migration; they simply increase the number of migrants who are clandestine.

At the same time, regionalization policies, for example, policies of the European Union, have widened the frontiers of migration, encouraging free movement of people within these boundaries but more firmly excluding those from outside. Many obstacles to movement, however, may still remain. For instance, within the European Union, the broad denial of citizenship rights to third-country nationals, issues of cross-accreditation, and linguistic and social aspects of work have prevented large-scale mobility among the highly skilled (Piexoto 2001). Historical relationships and bilateral treaties also offer other routes for relaxation of controls on labor migration. In the United Kingdom, the working holiday scheme open to young citizens of the British Commonwealth is one such example.

An important axis of differentiation that separates the experiences of labor migrants is the question of skills. Skilled migration is becoming the only acceptable form of migration into many developed countries, and states have played an important part in facilitating the migration of those with "shortage skills" (Raghuram and Kofman 2002). Many of the established settler societies, such as Canada, Australia, and New Zealand, have a long history of using a point system to facilitate skilled migration, but other, less formalized versions of such schemes have always operated (Iredale forthcoming). The language of skills often has been gender neutral, but in practice state recognition of skills meant that some (often masculine) skills have been preferred over others. For instance, in the 1960s and 1970s the U.S. Department of Labor's category "highly skilled" referred to people with medical, engineering, science or research, and informational technology training. But as these fields of study were at the time primarily male preserves, the highly skilled migrant who arrived in the United States and joined the mainstream labor market was often male (Kanjanapan 1995).

Familial ideas of the appropriate worker also meant that it was often men who became the primary migrants with spouses, who were often highly educated but were nevertheless relegated to the undifferentiated category of "wife." This does not mean that such women were all unemployed, but restrictions on spousal labor force participation often meant that the women did not work for considerable periods of time after migration, had career breaks, and then faced disadvantages when finding a job commensurate with their skills (Purukayastha forthcoming).

Gender differences in skilled labor migration take a different form when states use skilled migration to meet specific labor market shortages (Raghuram 2000). For example, a number of the new niches have occurred in the caring professions, in which the "caring ideology" conforms to oppressive notions of femininity

(Bowlby et al. 1997) and operates to gender labor in both lesser skilled sectors—such as domestic work—and professionalized occupations, such as nursing, social work, and education. Most of the existing labor market niches for women occur in such caring professions, so that women are well represented as primary migrants within these sectors. As a result of these two factors, 92 percent of nurses emigrating from the Philippines are women (Ball 1996). Moreover, because state intervention in regulating the labor market of the caring industries is guaranteed in the welfare state model (see, for instance, Seccombe et al. 1993), the state plays a greater role in the migration of women than it does in the migration of men. However, the definition of skills is itself gendered, and the caring skills developed by women are relatively undervalued, so that such jobs may be recast as semiskilled rather than skilled. State-sponsored programs, such as the Canadian domestic caregiver programs, provide one example of the deskilling of nurses who after migration are employed as social workers, caregivers, or domestic workers (McKay 1999). Importantly, increasing global inequalities have led some women to engage in circulatory migration, taking up jobs in other professional and entrepreneurial fields in order to survive economic hardship (Morokvasic 2003).

Hand in hand with the valorization and hence facilitation of skilled labor migration has been the devalorization of lesser skilled migrants with more limits on the rights accruing to them. This includes increasing restrictions on the period of stay with no access to citizenship and limits or refusal of visas to accompanying dependents. This is a pressing problem, as the thesis on the feminization of migration has primarily been based on the experiences of the large numbers of labor migrants entering relatively lesser skilled sectors of the labor market—particularly domestic work and sex work. Both forms of migration have long histories (see, for example, Cumaranatunga 1990). For instance, until 1980, the United Kingdom had specific quotas set aside for the recruitment of domestic workers in hospitals, hotels, and private homes. Filipina and Malaysian women took up the largest share of permits in this category (Kofman et al. 2000). In recent years there has been an increasing, but largely unmet, demand for such workers, as the contraction of the welfare state means a withdrawal of state services for the care of the young and the elderly. This has occurred alongside a rapid increase of women in waged work without a commensurate change in attitude toward the traditional division of labor in the home, leading to a "new international division of labor between women" (Friese 1995). The state controls such labor through quotas, and by regulating the conditions of entry and stay, it also may be implicated in establishing such flows. For instance, Huang and Yeoh (1996) argued that the Singaporean state's policy of increasing the participation of Singaporean women in the labor force, in order to secure economic development and therefore regional hegemony, has led the state to recognize the need for importing reproductive labor and, hence, commensurate changes in immigration laws. These processes also have led to "transnational mothering" or "caring at a distance" as women are separated from their own children and from others for whom they have primary caring responsibility (Hondagneu-Sotelo and Avila 1997).[3]

An expansion in the hospitality industry and the embedding of sex work in the tourist industry (Truong 1996) also have led to a growth in demand for women's labor in domestic work and sex work. However, state restrictions and the il/legality of sex work, along with its low social status, mean that nonmigrants with more labor market options are less likely to take up this work. It therefore offers employment opportunities for migrant women. Labor market controls operate in conjunction with controls over period of stay, but together they drive most sex workers into the undocumented sector of the labor market. For instance, short-term visitors from Central and Eastern European countries may enter Germany on tourist visas in order to undertake sex work, but even when women can avoid prostitution as legal "guests," they may be forced into it as overstayers. The scale of the industry often is large: an estimated fifty thousand Thai and eighty thousand Filipina undocumented women work in the Japanese sex industry, while thirty thousand migrant sex workers work in Italy, of whom approximately two-thirds are from Albania (B. Anderson 1997; Kofman et al. 2000).

Movement of undocumented labor is a pressing issue for many regions. For example, the trafficking of women from Myanmar, Cambodia, Laos, and Vietnam to Thailand and Taiwan, the "more economically developed" nations in the Greater Mekong Subregion, shows the extent to which regional disparities trigger migration (Asian Migration Centre 2002). For women in sub-Saharan Africa, the Middle East has become a major destination area (Kebede 2002). Increasing controls, however, force women to use traffickers to cross the border, many of whom may themselves belong to criminal organizations, making the women further targets of law-enforcing agencies. In recognition of the problems that the state faces in regulating entry and period of stay, some states have had regularization programs, as, for example, in the United States and some Southern European countries. In South Korea, the Voluntary Reporting Programme for Undocumented Migrants (Joint Committee for Migrant Workers in Korea 2002) has not, however, significantly altered the conditions of migrants. Rather, it has been used to perpetuate insecurities among migrants by allowing them to stay as trainees rather than stay on work permits.

Family Migration Noticeably, it is in discussions of family migration that gender issues are most explicitly recognized (see, for example, Dobson et al. 2001). This may be partly explained by the numerical significance of women in the family migration categories. *Family migration* is a broad term that encompasses family reunification (includes migration of family members who follow a primary migrant), family formation (includes migration by members in order to constitute a new family, as, for instance, through marriage), and family migration (in which the entire family migrates together) (Kofman 2004).

Institutionalized differences in the notion of family, primary carer, and social responsibilities affect who is allowed to bring whom under the broad rubric of family migration policy. For instance, in societies where the son is seen as the primary caregiver of the parents, it may be easier for men to bring their parents than for daughters to bring theirs. Gender differences in the permissible age of marriage or retirement also influence who may enter or leave a country under these categories.

Gender, sexuality, and generation form the three cornerstones in definitions of the family. Within the European Union, despite empirical evidence regarding the diminishing importance of the nuclear family, this family form is still used to define migration policy. Families are seen to include spouses and dependent children usually younger than the age of eighteen years, and spouses are identified on the basis of traditional notions of marriage. Very few countries, for example, the Scandinavian countries, the Netherlands, and, more recently, the United Kingdom and Canada (Kofman 2004), allow cohabiting or same sex couples if they form "relationships akin to a family" in the receiving society.

Entering as a spouse reinforces the dependency of migrants on their husbands or wives, as most countries limit spouses' access to employment, to public funds, and to rights to stay for at least some period after entry. As more women than men enter through the family route, the effects of such legislation particularly affect women. In the United Kingdom, however, there is increasing masculinization of the family migration category, as the children of migrants (particularly from South Asian countries) marry men from the home country and sponsor them. In addition, as women's roles as earners is becoming privileged, familial strategies for migration may well involve using women as lead migrants (George 2000; Espiritu 2002), with much less time lag between the female migrant and the male follower. However, within the migrant's own family this wage-earning role is only additional to and not replaced by women's reproductive responsibilities. Moreover, these responsibilities may well be complicated by men's emotional problems arising from the threats to their status as head of household (George 2000).

Displacement Migration and Refugees The reordering of state boundaries, such as the merger of two states, may also induce migration. The redrawing of the map of Europe with the reunification of East and West Germany and the return of Hong Kong to the People's Republic of China have sparked migration streams. In the latter case, only families that have the financial capital to move have migrated, but even here the entire family has not always moved. Men may live in the home country and maintain their assets there, while women and children move to the new country (Yeoh and Graham 2002).

The redrawing of borders has frequently been accompanied by conflict-induced population movements. Refugees, however, often are assumed to be men, despite the fact that women form a significant proportion of most movements and may form the majority in some cases, especially where the movements occur across contiguous borders. For example, 80 percent of Rohingya refugees moving from Burma to Bangladesh are purported to be women (Siddiqui 2003). The 1951 Geneva Convention guarantees the right to seek asylum to people "who owing to well founded fear of being persecuted for reasons of race, religion, nationality, membership of a particular social group or political opinion, is outside the country of his nationality." Persecution on grounds of sex is not included, and to gain refugee status, women have to claim that they had suffered rape, sexual assault, or other violations as a result of membership of one of the convention's categories.

The specificity of gender persecution was first acknowledged by the European Parliament in 1984, which called for states to recognize women who transgressed social norms of their society to be treated as a "particular social group." During the 1980s judicial authorities began to recognize gender persecution as a valid reason for granting refugee status. Some campaigners have argued for women to be classified as a social group for asylum purposes, although Adjin-Tettey (1997) argued that applicants would need to show they had suffered serious harm as a result of their gender in the same way as applicants basing their claim on membership of other social groups. Sexual violence is recognized as a form of persecution by France, Germany, and the Netherlands, whereas abortion, sterilization, and genital mutilation can be treated as forms of torture in the United Kingdom (Kuttner 1997, 18). With the collapse of communism and the rise of anti-Islamic sentiment, Western governments are more prepared to question state sovereignty of Islamic systems (J. Bhabha 1996, 18–19). However, this may bring them into conflict not only with other states but also with human rights activists in the home country who ascribe the demands for such rights as being Western-influenced and against local cultural or religious practices (Pessar and Mahler 2002). In response, many states still ignore the possibility or extent of gendered harm, so that women's asylum claims are less likely to be heard. This is particularly problematic at a time when there is a growing convergence among affluent countries to regain control of their borders through more restrictive immigration and refugee policies as well as through a general withdrawal of civil and human rights for certain categories of noncitizens. For example, quoting research by Silvey (1999), Pessar and Mahler (2002) argued that Indonesian women's greater ability to use sexual victimization as grounds for seeking asylum has made it harder to motivate Indonesian men to take up the cause against sexual victimization.

Reconfiguring the Sending State

Crucially, border controls are mostly controls over immigration. Emigration controls are insignificant or absent in most states, with only a few states facilitating the emigration of its nationals. For instance, the national government of the Philippines has responded to the global demand for nurses by liberalizing conditions affecting entry into nursing and easing restrictions on the number of nursing schools so as to increase the number of Filipino nurses who are "available for export." The setting up of state-sponsored labor-export programs has been fueled by the increasing economic problems at home and the need to secure worker remittances in order to alleviate foreign debt. As the Philippines's economy has become dependent on exporting its nationals, it also has set up regulatory bodies to ensure the welfare of those whom it "exports." Although such measures may be regarded as strengthening the national economy and looking after its diasporic populations, they also may be seen as weakening the state's ability to retain its labor force for its own developmental needs and thus as a step toward the dissolution of the state in the context of the pressures of the globalizing care industry (Ball 1996, 1997).

Official control of its overseas labor force is also important in other major labor exporting countries such as Indonesia. Between 1994 and 1999, overseas contract workers—more than two million women and approximately 900,000 men—went abroad through this scheme (Hugo 2002). However, as Hugo argued, the numbers may be much higher, as many of the workers who leave a country do not go through the official system, because it is time-consuming, expensive, and cumbersome. In some Islamic countries, women have circumvented controls over their migration by using the pretext of going to Saudi Arabia on a pilgrimage in order to migrate to other Arab countries (Kebede 2002).

The most recent attempt by states to retain control over their migrant peoples has been theorized through concepts such as transnationalism and diaspora. Contemporary feminist critiques of the relationship between gender and the nation-state highlight the extent to which women are incorporated and possessed by the nationalist project (see Mayer 2004 [this volume]). Familial narratives such as kinship, family, and descent are used in gendered ways to invoke nationhood. Transnationalism involves identification with and participation in social, economic, and political activities in more than one nation-state. Recognition of the importance of transnational migration as a phenomenon and of the diaspora as a resource to the original sender country has led many states, including Colombia, the Dominican Republic, Portugal, and Brazil, to change their laws (Fouron and Glick-Schiller 2001). The work of maintaining ties across nation-states can be a gendered process, with women often being assigned the primary role of social reproduction, maintaining social relations and caring across borders (Salaff 1997), whereas men appear to be more active in maintaining economic networks (Dicken et al. 2001). Women here are rediscovered and reinscribed into their community role, maintaining links with their old social networks while creating new networks in the destination country. Interestingly, transnational political activities seem to be less gender sensitive, as both men and women participate in social movements based both in the home country and in more global movements.

As Chamberlain (1999, 263) argued, "International migration challenges conventional loyalties and globalises the nation state." However, she found that Caribbean migrants to Britain "continue to acknowledge and adhere to a Caribbean consciousness that transcends national borders," although what is important here is to question the extent to which this consciousness can become a tool for redistributing gendered power in both sending states and receiving states.

Thinking Gender and International Migration

Despite the migration of women being more common than that of men, women often have been ignored in migration theory. When women's migration has been analyzed, it often is understood through the same lens as the movement of men. Economic theories of migration problematically assumed that migration was a result of rational decision making by individuals acting alone. This meant that the structural inequalities of gender as they operate in global (and local) labor markets, in state policy, and in the household often were ignored. From the mid- to late 1970s, there was a wave of theorizing drawing heavily on Marxist political economy, dependency theory, and world systems theory. Castles and Kosack (1973), for instance, argued that labor migration was a form of development aid given by poor countries to rich countries and that it was unrealistic to assume that individuals exercised free choice over migration, given global inequalities in economic and political power and the ways that economically dominant states controlled migration to suit their labor supply needs. Although these accounts forced migration theory to take account of the complex structures of political economy that result in global inequalities, structures of gender inequalities were not recognized.

Since the 1970s feminist interventions into migration research have been substantive, although their impact on mainstream migration theory is still limited. Early feminist work in this field came from a political economy framework and highlighted the gendered nature of the labor, which was mobilized by capitalists through the mechanisms of migration. More recent considerations of these arguments have recognized the extent to which women's migration is a response to global inequities. For instance, Sassen (2000) understood the increasing feminization of migration as a consequence of global inequalities that have been sharpened by globalizing processes, such as economic restructuring, and have increased the productive and reproductive burdens of women.

The policy focus of much feminist migration research, which targets immigration regulations and citizenship rights, has meant that the scalar level of the nation-state was crucial in such research. At the same time, feminist research has strongly argued for the recognition of noneconomic reasons for migration and has identified these primarily at subnational levels. Individual agency may be

understood within the liberal regime or as structured through households or social networks that mediate structures (including the state) and the individual.
Identifying the individual reasons for women's migration involved recognizing the
differential effects of political and economic change on men and women. For example, structural adjustment may act to increase male dependence on female income, which may lead to marital discord and physical violence and may ultimately
force female migration. These processes also may act alongside increasing rever-
sion to conservative religious legislation and practices, leading to the curtailment
of women's freedoms, which also may be accompanied by the impossibility of divorce. Even as early as the mid-1970s, research carried out by Morokvasic (1984)
pointed out the extent to which migration represented not simply an enforced response to economic hardship by single, widowed, or divorced women but also a
deliberate, calculated move on the part of individual gendered actors to escape
from a society in which patriarchy was an institutionalized and repressive force.

More recent research on Filipino women has shown how migration arises
from a wish to help the family but that this familial imperative is intertwined
with personal motivations (Asis 2002). The two actions are not necessarily
conflicting but, rather, complementary. This brings us to another level of migration research, which has been crucial for feminist researchers, particularly
those working in the South: the household. Households may offer a site for
decision making (Bruegel 1996) or for negotiating the work of migration
(Salaff 1997) or may act as a conceptual tool for understanding the ways in which
networks are used during migration (Boyd 1989), thus providing a meso-level
analytical framework for understanding migration (Portes 1997).

For many migration theorists, the household is the primary scale at which
gender has been analyzed. Portes (1997), for instance, confined his discussion
of gender and migration in his article "Immigration Theory for a New Century"
to a single page subtitled "Households and Gender." Although gender is a crucial variable within the household, its intersectionality with generation is important in structuring migration. Moreover, there is also a fear that gender
research may ultimately only be household focused. Hondagneu-Sotelo (1999,
567), writing about research on U.S. immigration, also remarked that gender
often is ignored and, when it is considered, "is somehow contained within kinship
and domestic unit boundaries." Reducing the migration decisions of women
to results of negotiations with other household members may limit their
agency in problematic ways. This is particularly important to recognize at a
time when the feminization of migration has become a common mantra. Now
that women's movement has become widely recognized, a simultaneous shift
to viewing this movement as a result of their bargaining power within households removes the possibility of seeing the individual agency of women.

Most research has so far failed to link the ways in which the household is a
site in which the labor market inequalities of sectoral employment and the
gendered nature of the workplace are played out (but see Peake and Trotz

1999; Fouron and Glick-Schiller 2001). The household mediates wider structural elements of society, including various axes of social stratification. Patriarchy within the household is related to, and interacts with, patriarchy in other sites, so that households are not only sites of gendered hierarchies but also sites of hierarchies within society as a whole (Halfacree 1995; Raghuram 2004b). Migrant women are caught between an undervaluing of their maternal and other familial roles because of the overprivileging of the public sphere (Andall 1995) and a reinscription of their paid work in the private realm because of the private nature of the workplaces in which many of them are employed.

The use of social networks as a way of understanding migration and career entry helps to overcome some of the weaknesses of other theories of migration, as it emphasizes the role of agency and aspects of the social that condition agency during the migration process (Boyd 1989). Networks partially overturn the unhelpful distinction between agency and structure by focusing on the channels of migration. However, most analyses of women's networks also have located women in the domestic sphere, often reducing the social to the familial when such networks are facilitating female migration. This strategy problematically reinscribes the private as the most significant sphere where women can form and participate in networks. Campani (1995) offered an interesting exception to this in her discussion of formalized social networks among Filipina migrants to Italy. Ultimately, networks are inscribed with power differentials between those who have achieved some stability and upward mobility after migration and those who have not. Thus, social networks may be used to exploit (Hondagneu-Sotelo 1994) as well as to support (Robinson 1991) other migrants. Hüwelmeier's (2001) analysis of nuns' participation in transnational networks suggests some ways in which women's networks extend beyond the familial but also some of the potential conflicts between those who have different commitments to the two nations implicated in the network.

Ultimately, gender-sensitive research on migration needs to "examine not just discrete activities but actual processes, such as state building and the negotiation of patriarchy, that are played out across borders" (Pessar and Mahler 2002, 9). Adopting a multiscale approach that is grounded in people's experiences and uses experience to recognize the role of structures may be one way of addressing the politics of scale in migration.

Conclusion

Rights of entry offer the first mode of control by the state on its migrant populations. Regulations around integration and citizenship offer further "points" for such control. The right to citizenship, and thus to political participation, is usually the last right that migrants accrue from the state. In fact, it may be argued that migrants cease to be migrants when they acquire citizenship because their duties to the state of adoption are now equal to those of people born in the state. Hence, migrants, and particularly migrant women, are rarely seen as political actors. Feminists, however, have long argued that the typecasting of migrant women limits the agency ascribed to them, particularly political agency. Moreover, formal political apparatuses have rarely provided a space for migrant women. This does not mean that migrant women have not been politically active. On the contrary, they have frequently spearheaded campaigns. The participation of migrant and refugee women in formal political processes, however, still remains limited, with women more often being cast as beneficiaries of policies rather than as policy makers.

As we have seen, the migration of men and women has been differentially influenced by state regulations and border controls, key categories of analysis for political geography. Feminist perspectives on women's crossing borders also have added to the theoretical insights on scales at which the movement of people may best be analyzed. Despite this, a number of lacunae remain. There is still very little direct focus in current literature in political geography on migration, and the little work that exists has primarily been done by feminists (Hyndman and Walton-Roberts 2000; Kofman 2002; Nagel 2002). Expanding their arguments and including this in the "malestream" research in political geography remain crucial tasks for the future. The integration of work on the national and global scales, along with that on households and networks, is another area that needs addressing. Relegating the household to the level of the familial, rather than recognizing the multiple ways in which the household reflects and acts as a site for strategizing at other levels, needs further work. Finally, despite increases in work on borders, even the critical analytical research on borders has usually been done by people within those "safe borders." We do not hear enough about how people in the south see these borders. Those who have been excluded by the borders, and those who have not (yet) moved, have been influenced by narratives of migration, by what Pandurang (2003) called premigration experiences. Does the state appear to be dissolving, or do we see the relative powerlessness of Third World states within the context of First World powers? How does the differential erosion of borders within states influence and lead to the reinforcement of other borders and how are these felt across genders? These are areas of research to which feminist political geographers have much to contribute.

Notes

1. In this chapter I focus only on international migration and the crossing of national boundaries. However, it must be recognized that internal migration is often more significant for women than international migration is. Another question that has not directly been addressed here is that of children of migrants who do not gain political rights in their country of settlement but accrue their citizenship from the country of origin of their parents, although they themselves have little direct contact with that country.
2. This control over the labor market may be harder to achieve when there are strong regulatory bodies with established professional criteria for recognizing and accrediting existing skills.
3. Interestingly, the countries of Southeast Asia have been marked by diverse flows of domestic workers, and the demarcation of sending and receiving countries is not very clear. Streams of migration are locationally specific, with migrants from particular villages moving to specific international locations through the use of networks (Hugo 2002).

14
Social Movements, Protest, and Resistance

JOAN FAIRHURST, MAANO RAMUTSINDELA,
AND URMILLA BOB

Until the early 1980s, general theories of collective action were largely informed by Marxist thinking and political economy analyses, and they dominated the discourses pertaining to social movements. This domination has been problematic and has narrowed what is studied in relation to the cultural, economic, and political dimensions of social movements. These analyses have thus been critiqued from several perspectives, some of the most influential of which are gender-based critiques (Engel 2001; Kuumba 2001). Postmodern perspectives also have highlighted the limitations of generalizing theories, especially the limitations of class analysis in the face of collective actions that are not reducible to class (Pieterse 1992). In this chapter we argue the need for gendered analyses of social movements from a variety of perspectives, not least because of earlier hegemonic approaches that have ignored women or have treated women as a monolithic category. Furthermore, an important challenge in terms of social movement research is that thus far the engendering of social movement debates and analyses has been conducted largely by women. It is imperative that gender as an analytical category be embraced by social movement researchers more broadly to avoid a ghettoization of the experiences and concerns of women. We start by placing these issues within the broader idiom of political geography and the different contexts in which social movements arise. Although many analyses of social movements are gendered in the sense that the participants often are women or in that the issues have gendered implications, analyses do not typically feature feminist theory. Hence, in the later portions of this chapter, we attempt to introduce a more feminist perspective on the study of gender within social movements.

Contextualizing Social Movements, Protest, and Resistance

The defining theme of this chapter and its associated notions of resistance and protest form an integral part of politics. Moreover, both informal and formal arenas must be accommodated; as such, individual and collective actions can be seen in the arenas of government-centered formal politics, the public domain

199

of authority, the noninstitutional, and the private sector of business and domesticity (Painter 1995; Doyle and McEachern 1998, 23–24). Indeed, social movements are rooted in power dynamics. As Brook (2000, 1) stated, "Where there are power differentials—and there always are—there is resistance and rebellion, or more generally collective action." Protest then implies a declaration of objection, a denial of the acceptance of a situation. Protest levels can range in degree and be short-lived and ephemeral, from a passive display of posters appealing for abolition of social practices that violate women's rights (sexual abuse, workplace discrimination, etc.), to vociferous marches and strikes. Protests often have sacrificial results for women, whether the women are breadwinners or whether they depend on others for financial support in the household. Resistance has a connotation of opposition and can be passive or active. However, it is clearly associated with some form of action and striving against something, with a determination to succeed. Resistance also implies an opposition.

In the context of protest and resistance, women can be vulnerable to violence. Violence can be described as force in action, rough or harmful, and often is used to intimidate. However, not all forms of protest and resistance engage in violence. Della Porta (1996) drew specific attention to political violence as a particular repertoire of collective action that involves physical force considered at that time as illegitimate in the dominant culture. Examples include damage to property, violent confrontation when members of opposing political groups fight with one another, clashes with the police, violent attacks directed at persons causing injury or death, random violent attacks, armed seizure of places or people (including armed trespassing), holdups, and hijacking. Women often experience incidents such as these differently than men. Think, for example, of women's exposure to sexualized violence in informal settlements, in refugee camps, in cities, in villages, and in their own homes. Numerous studies have begun to explore and expose the violence embedded in many social movements and actions of protest, as well as resistance (Mamdani 2001a). The antiabortion, antiapartheid, environmental, cultural, and ethnic movements have in specific instances adopted violent approaches to achieve their objectives. The question of whether the end justifies the means remains an important social and ethical one.

The term "social movements" implies collective effort and, by inference, concerns with human beings and their relations to each other; social movements highlight the organizational facet of protest and resistance and so also may be associated with violence. Jenkins (1981) noted that groups of people tend to coalesce at times of turmoil when protest activity intensifies, new repertoires of collective action are created, and unconventional action spreads to different social sectors. Social movements, then, imply effort on behalf of a group of people working together to achieve results that effect social change (Jordan and Maloney 1997; Doyle and McEachern 1998). From a variety of definitions of social movements, one of the most succinct is that of Neidhardt and Rucht (1991, 450, quoted in Porta 1996): "An organized and sustained effort of a collectivity of interrelated individuals, groups and organizations to promote or resist social change with the use of public protest activities."

Social Movements

Tarrow (1998) located the birth of social movements generally in the eighteenth century when nation-states, economic development, and new systems of communication made it possible to mobilize against authority in a sustained and collective manner. At that time, political opportunities and discontent created the context for social mobilization and networks within culturally and locality specific forms that challenged authority. This resulted in new forms of action and social networks as well as the potential for transformation of economic, political, cultural, and social systems. Tarrow (1998) provided illustrative examples of social movements spanning from Europe in 1848, student protests and the civil rights movement in the 1960s in the United States and Europe, as well as waves of democratization in Eastern Europe in the 1980s.

In the 1960s the literature on social movements emerged from two sources: Marxist urban sociology (such as the work of Chris Pickvance) and social action research (such as the work of Alain Touraine). Both sources were linked to the unrest, protest, and questioning within civil society. For example, women's movements and student movements were prevalent at that time, and there was a sense of historical purpose and transformation of society. Since the 1970s and 1980s, the literature of social movements was very much taken up in political sociology and political science and there is now a substantial theoretical and comparative literature. Currently, social movements such as environmentalism, feminism, and nationalism predominate. McAdam et al. (1996) indicated how ideology and belief systems, mechanisms of mobilization and locale, as well as national politics shape the development, form, and outcomes of such movements. Thus, the contexts in which these movements evolve are central to understanding the nature and purpose of these social movements. Routledge (1993), for example, showed that the nature of the geographical places in which social movements originate and evolve as they engage with space-spanning organizations, such as states and nongovernmental organizations (NGOs), is key to understanding these movements.

The development of new communication technologies also has had a dramatic impact on social systems and organizations (Buechler 1993). There are two broad positions in terms of debating the impacts that information technologies have on social mobilization (Myers 1999). The first position is that inequality of access to technology leads to the widening of the gap between the information rich and the information poor. This implies that the information rich are better able to mobilize resources and networks as well as to share information. Thus, information technology increases the concentration of power in the hands of a relatively few, powerful elites. Alternatively, pluralists argue that power has become less centralized as advances in technology provide the potential for greater democratization and increased participation in political processes. The emergence of transnational social movements and global social politics is thus becoming more pronounced as information technology and increased mobility create new spaces for communication and interaction. Myers (1999), for example, stated that social movement activists use information technology to communicate with other activists in several complementary ways. These ways range from the relatively unorganized and individualistic use of electronic mail networks to systems professionally organized specifically for activism.

Smith et al. (1997) examined the relationships between an emerging global civil society as manifested in transnational social movements and international political institutions. Smith et al. argued these relationships play a critical role in defining global governance trends, as well as promote institutional and policy changes in the international order. Hahnel (2000) asserted that in terms of transnational social movements, the protests against the World Trade Organization in Seattle announced, and the demonstrations against the International Monetary Fund and World Bank in Washington, D.C., confirmed, that a full-fledged movement opposed to corporate-sponsored globalization has finally emerged in the United States to join already well-established international movements. As members of civil society become increasingly aware of their rights, especially their right to protest, a range of social movements has become more visible and vocal. Cases in point are the disability rights movement (Adam et al. 1999; Fleischer and Zames 2001) and the emergence of gay and lesbian movements (Engel 2001). Malhotra (2001) showed how over the course of the past few decades, the political left throughout the industrialized West has been challenged by an array of activist social movements to become more inclusive.

Ekins (1992) claimed that four sustained factors provide the backdrop of current social movements: war, insecurity, and militarization; the persistence of poverty; the denial of human rights; and environmental destruction. These problems are most acute and concentrated in underdeveloped and developing countries. Common to each is that their impact can be felt at individual and societal levels and that they can bring partial or total change. In a typology of social movements, Aberle (cited in Brook 2000) differentiated these as follows: alternative, bringing about partial change at the individual level; redemptive, bringing about total change at the individual level; reformative, bringing about partial change at the societal level; and revolutionary, bringing about total change at the societal level.

In terms of social movements in underdeveloped and developing countries, conflicts often are linked to agricultural crises and high levels of under- and unemployment. The issue of land, especially in rural economies, has been the focus of much social action. The Landless Workers Movement (2000) in Brazil, for example, is one of the largest and most effective social movements in Latin America. In Africa numerous social movements have been central in mobilizing and agitating for widespread and effective land reformation.

Although these movements are sometimes organized and formally constituted, this is not always the case, as in the Zimbabwean land crisis. Social movements that are linked to struggles over resources, especially land, are most evident in countries mired by skewed distribution patterns and high levels of economic inequalities embedded in historical processes of colonialism. Geographically, these stark inequalities are clearly noticeable in the landscape at different scales, such as regional inequalities, relative rural poverty, and deprivation in urban informal settlements. Notwithstanding these insights, the struggle for resources in developing countries often is undertaken without a rigorous examination of the processes and implications of patriarchal land relations and practices.

The demands of social movements in terms of distribution and related inequalities have resulted in numerous responses from formal institutions, such as governmental departments and the NGO sector. State-led land reformation processes are noticeable in many countries. However, the inabilities of governments to respond to the needs of their people often have resulted in violent conflicts. In both Africa and Latin America, for example, violent clashes between landless people, police, and landowners have become commonplace. In countries in Africa, the prevalence of traditional authorities and the ambiguous roles of the chieftaincy in relation to local government structures often have heightened conflicts over land, especially in rural areas. However, numerous organizations have continued to resist suppression by networking and building partnerships with a broad spectrum of international organizations and movements including NGOs, human rights groups, religious organizations, and labor movements.

The attempted repression of social movements by the state also is clearly discernible (Smith et al. 1997). Generally, the state is negative toward anything that seems to interfere with its rational design of administrative and social order. In turn, that order is mediated by complex relationships between the state and its citizens. Kothari (1993, 64) elaborated on these relationships as follows: "The state and its relationship to the people emerges as a relationship not just between classes and the masses, but also between the principal carrier of modern capitalism and the social order; between the military and the civil order; between the development policies of the state and its transnational sponsors and the economic and ecological catastrophes that are affecting the masses and sheer survival of large numbers of people." Out of these relationships emerge local strategies of resistance as an effective alternative to neoliberal adjustment.

Inasmuch as "scale issues are inherent in strategies of social movement" (Miller 2000, 18), the state's responses to protests are layered from local to national to international scales. For instance, the state could regard small-scale and localized protests by ratepayers, social clubs, students, and so on simply as ways of raising issues that demand some attention without the state being obliged to meet any demand. However, such protests could have ripple effects beyond localities. This is often the case with squatter movements, in which women are often central; these movements not only create social (dis)order but also seriously challenge property relations. In many instances, the state has responded by criminalizing squatters, as under the Pinochet government in Chile (Hardoy and Satterthwaite 1989). In this context state action not only is guided by the activities of illegal citizens (i.e., squatters) but also is conditioned by the demand of global capitalism for property rights, especially when squatters invade private land. As De Souza (2001, 485) commented, "Private property rights are claimed to be superior to public rights to land, since the former is characterized as being solely responsible for the activation of economics and markets." The same comments about squatters could be made about peasant movements, such as the peasant unrest in Zimbabwe in 1948 and the Guerilla Army of the Poor in Guatemala in 1972 (Binswanger and Deiniger 1993). Officials saw these organizations as part of the network that aimed to overthrow the government; consequently, state action became brutal.

It follows that state action against social movements is framed by the objectives of organizations, their activities, and their profiles. Organizations that directly challenge the power and legitimacy of the state often are branded as "terrorists" in order to legitimize state action. Depending on one's point of view, terrorists have many colors and can transform themselves into different forms at different scales. Terrorist groups can transform themselves into transnational criminal organizations (Dishman 2001) or political organizations (Della Porta 1988). Our concern here is how notions of terrorism can be constructed by the state as symbols of alternative power or as a force that warrants state action. Such constructions were dominant during liberation struggles when the activities of liberation movements, in which women have been very active, were considered to be terrorist, as the examples of the African National Congress (South Africa), South West Africa People's Organization (Namibia), and the Palestinian Liberation Organization (Palestine) show. The designation of a group as terrorist creates conditions for state-sponsored elimination of people from public life through assassinations, life imprisonment, and the like. Though assassination is not a legal tool of state policy under the banner of international and criminal law, it became legitimized because of its usage by individual states with differing legal and criminal criteria (O'Brien 2001).

At issue here is that the state can label its opponents as terrorists through antiterrorism legislation in order to "hunt people down" and deny them a resource base. The systematic slaughter of opponents also could result from the combination of state forces and sections of the population, as has been the case during the reign of terror in Italy in the 1970s by the Red Brigade. As Della Porta (1988, 155) aptly observed, "The fact that a large number of people were believed to be involved increased the need to understand the motivations that led to the violent behavior of individuals who had been politically socialized in a consolidated democratic regime." Mamdani (2001b, 7) made a similar observation on the state-sponsored atrocities in Rwanda in 1994, where "the violence of genocide was the result of both planning and participation. The agenda imposed from above became a gruesome reality to the extent it resonated with perspectives from below. Rather than accent one or the other side of this relationship and thereby arrive at either a state-centered or a society-centered explanation, a complete picture of the genocide needs to take both sides into account."

Elimination of opposing groups also could lead to systematic slaughter of people by repressive regimes. A case in point is the killing of three-quarters of the Herero and half the Nama people in present-day Namibia by the Germans between 1904 and 1908. The unintended result of such brutality was the development of radical behavior on the part of the Herero. As Goldstein's (1983, 340) analysis of political repression in nineteeth-century Europe showed, "Those countries that were consistently the most repressive, brutal, and obstinate in dealing with the consequences of modernization and developing working-class dissidence reaped the harvest by producing oppositions that were just as rigid, brutal, and obstinate." More recent examples include the resistance to the Israelis' siege of Ramallah in Palestine. Repression there led to the emergence of the first Palestinian women suicide bombers in 2002, placing women at the forefront of the Palestinian struggle. Similarly, since 2002, women in the Chechnya uprisings against Russia have come to play a central role as suicide bombers.

Inserting Gender into the Analysis of Social Movements

Notwithstanding a long history of women's engagement in a wide range of social movements, feminist analyses of them only came to the fore in a consideration of second-wave feminism in the 1960s, when discrimination and oppression against women in the home and in the workplace fired protest. These concerns were manifest in demands for voting rights and, more recently, political leadership roles and women's visibility in the public arena.

Since the mid-1980s women have been the subject of many studies pertaining to social movements. However, many of these studies tended to be descriptive and focused primarily on women's involvement in organizations linked to survival strategies such as informal trading clubs, soup kitchens, and sewing clubs (Tarrow 1998). These studies had the effect of reinforcing traditional gender roles in social movements, tending to focus on the domain of reproduction as women's realm. Such a focus has come under sharp criticism from feminist theorists and researchers who have challenged hegemonic approaches to social life and social change. There is increasing awareness that women have long been engaged outside the domestic sphere primarily as a result of acute economic crises, forcing them into paid employment, which in turn has forced women to collaborate with others outside the home environment (Schild 1994). Interacting with others and sharing experiences often allow women to question their personal situations in a wider context, allowing them to become conscious of various dimensions of oppression and to develop a sense of solidarity based on their common interests and identities. Connections between women often have led to the development of women-centered social movements that have been at the forefront of protests and attendant violent outcomes. In contrast to long-held biases about women, women's involvement in social movements has revealed the fluidity of their positionalities and identities.

Some of the key themes in the literature that examines gender and social movements are the factors that influence why women get involved, how they participate, what they hope to achieve, and the constraining as well as enabling contexts of their involvement. Indeed, Slater (1994) asserted that gendered aspects of social movements within the contexts of grassroots development, empowerment, and democracy have received significant attention. There is a growing body of literature that shows the overwhelming presence of women in community and neighborhood organizations in many parts of the world (Jacquette 1991; Chinchilla 1992; Schild 1994; Kuumba 2001). Women's contributions, however, often are stigmatized. Kuumba (2001) used two well-known examples, the U.S. civil rights movement and the South African national liberation movement, to document the circumscribed roles of women, as well as the role of female leaders, and how gender issues influenced movement activities and results.

Differential participation among women in social movements is clearly evident. Whereas some women assume leadership roles, others attend meetings or join marches and other forms of protest action. Furthermore, women join organizations for a number of reasons. Some women join out of economic necessity to improve their quality of life, for social interaction, or to acquire information. Others feel compelled to respond to political repression and human rights violations. In some instances women join social movements to acquire tangible benefits such as participating in training workshops, sharing resources, or being given food aid. Many women join organizations to personally grow, as these are places where learning occurs. In the latter case, this is part of the politics of becoming, as well as the struggle for identity. It is worth noting, however, that in many parts of the world, the socioeconomic and political situations of the poorest segments of society have not changed significantly, even though there has been a dramatic increase in the number of women's organizations and women's involvement in them.

The previous discussion illustrates some of the contexts in which social movements evolve. This variation is important to understand and should be taken into consideration in attempts to categorize social movements. Placing protest action and social movements more generally into conceptual categories (such as environmental movements, feminism, and labor movements) can lead not only to reductionism but also to a failure to understand how movements link to other movements and to the fissures that can exist within movements. In many cases movements complement and support each other as similar power relations are embedded in the interests and concerns of different groups. However, these power lines also can be grounds for potential division. For example, in the South African struggles against apartheid, issues of ethnicity, lineage, location, gender, and class were paramount issues and concerns. The inability to resolve some of these different and conflicting interests often led to tensions within the liberation movement. Another example includes the need to integrate analyses of environmental struggles with other forms of oppression such as racism and sexism. In addition, feminists of color have identified the dissenting voices and tensions between the indigenous ecology movement and the dominant Western environmental movement rooted in biodiversity conservation (Mies and Shiva 1993; Shiva 1993a, 1993b; Merchant 1995). Thus, power dynamics within groups can result in some concerns being marginalized in relation to others. Hence, Kuumba (2001) raised pertinent questions, such as the following: Do men and women experience participation in social movements differently and are gender roles reproduced or undermined during national liberation struggles? In addition, it is important to examine the ways in which gender dynamics shape the form, intentions, and outcomes of social movements and protest action.

Goodwin et al. (2001) went further and challenged the rationalistic, structural, and organizational models that have dominated social movement studies in the past three decades. As they indicate, social movements and protest are related to moral institutions, felt obligations, and rights as well as information about expected effects. Hence, they reincorporate emotions such as anger, indignation, fear, disgust, joy, and love into research on politics and social protest. The main areas in which emotions are evident include the emergence of militant AIDS activism, the antiabortion movement, and movements against violence against women and child abuse. Given such a mandate, social movements are faced with the challenge, as articulated by Ekins (1992), of contributing to a new world order that is based on peace, human dignity, and ecological sustainability. Rethinking social movements, protest, and resistance from a gender perspective thus requires the critical insertion of the four following points.

First, there needs to be a shift away from generalizing the processes and outcomes of social protest and resistance. Social movements are embedded in a range of power dynamics inclusive of gender, race, ethnicity, location, sexuality, and other power relations.

Second, more emphasis needs to be given to the role of women in organizations as well as to the institutional configuration of political society (Slater 1994). This includes civil society structures, political parties, NGOs, and government structures. NGOs in particular play a major role as lobbying agents, often with widespread international networks. Thus, NGOs have a central role to play in globalizing social movements and issues, yet in many places their leadership is dominated by men.

Third is the issue of locality-specific cultural dimensions. For example, cultural politics often can lead to the entrenchment of patriarchal practices and social differentiation within communities at all levels and within social movements. From a gendered perspective, the widespread existence of patriarchy is rooted and reinforced by cultural traditions and practices. In the African context, for example, the role of the chieftaincy remains ambiguous. Mamdani (2001b) argued that traditional leaders and notions of ethnicity as well as identity more generally have played a central role in the violence that continues in many parts of Africa today. Slater (1994) stated that in Argentina the violence associated with state terror brought forth new forms of resistance that gave birth to other modes of political violence. These modes tended to have a destructive impact on the openness and vitality of existing social movements. Furthermore, the destructive impacts of these actions on civil society, especially women and children who often make up the most vulnerable members of society, must be examined.

Fourth, the increase in protest action throughout the world is a sign of greater awareness of human rights. However, human rights advocacy campaigns for women's rights have now extended from women's needs to an ever-increasing emphasis on the person, the individual. The impact of this on material aspects of women's lives requires more systematic attention.

Conclusion

The impact of women's participation in various forms of resistance and protest has remained largely unnoticed or taken for granted. Thus, it has been necessary to rehabilitate analyses of social movements to see women as active agents of sociopolitical changes (Lobao 1990; Einhorn 1993; Cockburn 2001). The insertion of gender into an understanding of social movements is necessary to ensure that women are not rendered "textually invisible" (Schild 1994, 60). It also constitutes part of the broader project of social movements that is to make power visible and to open up civil society by creating spaces for debates and fostering transformation.

15
A Gendered Politics of the Environment

JOSEPA BRÚ BISTUER AND MERCÈ AGÜERA CABO

The environment and nature as territorial features with clear geostrategic and political relevance traditionally have been areas of study for political geography. Interest in the natural environment has focused above all on the strategic role of specific natural resources in geopolitical conflicts. One of the oldest debates in political geography is that over natural resources of the sea, such as debates over the sovereignty over continental waters and the debate between "Mare Clausium" and "Mare Liberum," which dates back to the seventeenth century. In addition to conflicts over fishing resources, in the second half of the twentieth century, there have been conflicts over oil and metal ore deposits. The dependence of Western economies on scarce resources such as oil was made clear in the 1973 crisis, which led to the emergence of the debate about resource limitations (Nogué and Vicente 2001). The Persian Gulf conflict in 1991 and the 2003 Anglo-American-led coalition invasion of Iraq are clear examples of the consequences of limited oil resources in geopolitical struggles. In addition to territorial sovereignty over resources, there also are conflicts over rivers that mark national borders, which have increased with the growing strategic value of water as a resource in limited supply. Water, for example, has been a key factor in the analysis of conflicts in the Mediterranean region, especially in the case of Israel and Palestine and the Middle East (e.g., Feitelson 2002), and of the still ongoing debate about the transfer of the Ebro river in Catalonia, Spain. However, the environmentalization of political geography, or the development of political ecology, in the sense of placing environmental problems at the forefront of debates, is relatively recent and is growing in parallel with the increase in global and local political concerns about the environment (Nogué and Vicente 2001).

In this respect research in political geography concerning the environment is expanding and diversifying at the same time that environmental conflicts are being understood as having clear social and economic dimensions, making them key factors in global policies. In an attempt to set out what a gendered perspective offers political ecological analyses, we examine the environmental problems that generate conflict at local and global levels, as well as global policies for the environmental management of the planet. We also examine the informal environmental policies that are arising from civil society and that are based on a remapping of the world order.

We begin this chapter with an analysis of the increasingly visible role of the environment in geopolitical conflicts, and we consider the ways in which gender enters into these issues. A focus on gender makes visible the inequality in the political and management strategies being adopted by developed and developing countries. We follow this with a consideration of the official discourses of environmental management and the development of social movements around these discourses. We further expand this analysis by examining the role of women's organizations and the perspectives of women presented in the "Women's Action Agenda 21," which arose from the Earth Summit in Rio. Here we focus on the perspectives of women's groups that are concerned with environmental problems; these organizations constructed a proposal that was characterized by clear ideological differences from the official discourse of institutional management. In the final section of the chapter, we consider the potential of ecofeminism and reflect on the question of sustainability from a gendered perspective.

Environmental Geopolitical Conflicts: The Difference Gender Makes

The nature of conflicts linked to environmental problems is profoundly marked by the scales of the conflicts. These conflicts often become part of a global geopolitical analysis to the extent that they have an impact beyond the territorial boundaries of states. The impact of environmental conflicts that cross political borders leads to a consideration of territorial sovereignty as a key factor in the legitimacy of the use and management of natural resources.[1] In this respect the 1972 Stockholm Human Environment conference highlighted the conflict over national environmental responsibilities and the need for international control (Cadwell 1996). In the same context the debate generated by climate change and the consequent degradation of large forests with the loss of biodiversity and an increase in desertification of extensive areas of the planet highlights the large-scale effects of environmental problems.[2]

Conflicts that spill over national boundaries have led geopolitical analysts toward investigating crises of political legitimacy of nation-states, crises that have arisen from the lack of nation-based solutions addressing people's safety in the face of environmental hazards. They also have revealed the vulnerability of developed countries given the globalization of environmental problems, demonstrating their dependence on developing countries. The inability to provide solutions capable of integrating and managing the uncertainty and unpredictability of environmental problems also has contributed to the current crisis of confidence in, and consequently legitimacy of, science and technology and its managers.[3]

In contrast to these geopolitical analyses that revolve around the role of formal agents (institutions, international agreements, and states, for example) as managers of global policies, the inclusion of a gendered perspective has made it possible to shift attention to include informal agents—that is, the people affected—and their role in the conflict. An extensive part of feminist geopolitical thought has focused on the role of women in sustaining and caring for the family and the community, in accordance with the gender-based division of labor, as a determinant in explaining women's role as managers of natural resources (C. Jackson 1994). The active role of women as the main "victims" of environmental conflicts and degradation in the course of policies that shape everyday life—especially "reproduction policies" (Nesmith and Radcliffe 1993)—also has been underlined (Rodda 1991; Sachs 1996; Steady 1992; Agarwal 1997; Cooney 1999). The study of the women's groups in the face of environmental problems has shown how political actions focus on aspects of problems that directly affect local life, such as environmental health and air and water quality, as well as on global problems, such as climate change, the loss of tropical rainforests, and the struggle against nuclear weapons (Nesmith and Radcliffe 1993).

Another debate that has traditionally provided a focal point for geopolitical analysis of world environmental problems is that of population increase and pressure on resources as inseparable causes of worldwide environmental degradation. This discourse remains anchored in the Malthusian rhetoric of the "limits to growth" (Meadows 1972), which gives rise to demographic policies that prioritize, when they are not exclusively geared toward, reducing birth rates. Thus, the debate about resource limitations focuses especially on the demographic pressure exerted by Third World countries, forecasting a catastrophic future given exponential population growth (Keyfitz 1998), which brings with it the danger of uncontrolled pressure on resources and a greater environmental impact on the planet. In this debate poverty has been singled out as the main agent in environmental degradation; hence, demographic control is put forward as the key to halting its global impact. As an alternative to this neo-Malthusian view, environmental destruction linked to the needs generated by poverty is understood as a problem of wealth redistribution (Martínez Alier 1992).

Regardless of which analysis is followed, geopolitical analysis has focused on industrialized economies that depend on nonrenewable resources and on the overuse of renewable resources that affect extensive areas of the planet (what has been referred to as the ecological footprint). It is to the extent that the industrialized countries need resources available in the Third World that the latter have become geostrategic spaces, or sanctuaries where these resources can be exploited (García 1995).

By contrast, critical viewpoints emanating in the South make a direct link, for example, between sustainability and fairness (García 1995). Nogué and Vicente (2001) pointed out that birth control is part of the North's domination strategy designed to preserve economic and ideological hegemony, a hegemony achieved and maintained by the exploitation of human and natural resources in the South. In this respect a gendered perspective has introduced new elements, as it sees population control as just one more expression of an andro-centric ideology (Filemyr 1997). Ecofeminist perspectives, for example, have viewed birth and fertility control as a facet of patriarchy that explicitly targets women. In a somewhat maternalist vein, the abuse of nature has been linked to the control of women's reproduction and of their bodies (Mies and Shiva 1997); women's fertility has been highlighted as a natural cycle in life that should be as appreciated as the Earth's natural cycle is, and the need to respect women's cultural and local experience has been asserted (Diamond 1997).

The relationship between development and poverty also has been stressed, highlighting the central role played by women as development agents (Sen 1994) and, therefore, the need to direct political attention toward integrating women in development policies by promoting their experience, knowledge, and leadership capabilities (Jiggins 1994; Sen 1994: Silliman and King 1999).

Global Planet Management: Official Discourses and Social Movements

Action taken by official institutions in the environmental management of the planet is based on establishing agreements, recommendations, and legislation and on setting up international regulatory bodies.[4] The list of conferences and summits that aim to produce agreements about the environmental management of the planet, and that would appear to have had a turning point in the 1992 Rio Summit, is already quite long.

A number of authors have commented on the technocentric orientation of these international policies (García 1995; Brú Bistuer 1997). They circulate within a discourse based on the legitimacy of a scientific community to direct policies, which has developed an extensive research infrastructure to control and maintain the environmental order as well as a mercantile conception of the environment (Martínez Alier 1992). Underlying this orientation is a modernist faith in the ability of science and technology to shoulder the global response to environmental problems without renouncing the Enlightenment idea of progress (Brú Bistuer and Agüera Cabo 2001). These policies have been denounced as a new expression of the hegemonic countries' domination—a so-called green imperialism (J. Anderson et al. 1995; Shabecoff 1996; Shiva 1998; Mofson 1999).

Despite these critiques, local environmental policies are increasingly based on the premises laid down in international forums and, in particular, the directives set out at the Earth Summit held in Rio de Janeiro in June 1992, which were given shape in the foundation document for environmental policies, Agenda 21. The idea of sustainable development, which is the basis for Agenda 21, rests on the principle that growth is necessary but should be controlled. Once this premise has been accepted, the priority global course of action is to achieve sustainable development in all countries. However, although developed countries can build "environmental correctness" criteria into their current policies without having to change the structural basis of the prevailing growth model, developing countries are caught on the horns of a particularly tricky dilemma:

they need to achieve economic and social development that eradicates poverty (which entails environmental degradation) but they cannot use the model followed by the industrialized countries, as, according to these same countries, it has had a devastating impact on the environment. Thus, in spite of the global alliance, which has been promoted to establish such "macropolicies," the impact of Agenda 21 takes the shape of different local sustainability models depending on national economic development levels, as shown in Table 15.1.

Macroenvironmental policies map out different sustainable development models for developed and developing countries, which are presented as being complementary. However, running parallel to the development of official policies has been the increasing intervention of civil society, originally as a way of exerting political pressure but increasingly as protagonists, or as local agents for the implementation of global policies. We are thus faced with a complex scenario that can be dated to the rise of environmentalist movements in the 1970s and 1980s. During this time the interests of environmentalism and feminism at least partially coincided because they promoted alternatives to the social and economic model represented by capitalism (Taylor 1993a), which, in addition to its implications for the exploitation of some human beings by others, began to be identified as the cause of world environmental problems, often under markedly ethno- and androcentric paternalistic forms of domination. The link between feminism and ecology was subsequently strengthened by popular activism in response to environmental disasters. This movement, which is simultaneously feminist and environmentalist, has been known since then as ecofeminism.[5]

Parallel to the activity of politically organized groups of environmentalists and feminists has been the development of locally rooted social movements in different contexts in both the Third and the First Worlds. In these movements the attachment to the environment derives primarily from personal experience and everyday life. These movements have demonstrated the effects of environmental problems on less-advantaged communities and social groups. In this context, women have played decisive roles as activists and leaders. In the 1970s and 1980s, among these movements, Chipko, the Green Belt Movement, and Greenham Common stand out.

The Chipko movement took place in the Uttar Pradesh region of the Indian Himalayas during the 1970s and 1980s. In reaction to the exploitation of forest resources by a multinational firm, groups of residents led by women peacefully demonstrated by hugging trees to prevent them from being cut down. The images of the resistance of the inhabitants spread until, in 1980, Prime Minister Indira Ghandi announced a ban on the harvesting of trees by the firm for fifteen years. The participation of women in the movement and their leadership were furthered by the work of ecofeminist Vandana Shiva, who made the movement an emblem of ecofeminism, emphasizing the sensory and spiritual experience of women with respect to nature.

Table 15.1 Differences between the Models Proposed for Industrialized Countries and Developing Countries According to the Macrodirectives of the Agenda 21 Summit Meeting in Rio de Janeiro, 1992

Macrodirectives of Agenda 21	Micropolicy Priorities: Industrialized Countries	Micropolicy Priorities: Developing Countries
Sustainable development model	Adaptation of current policies to environmental criteria	Search for an alternative growth model given the unfeasibility of following the growth pattern of industrialized countries
Population resources and policies	New technology Compensatory financial measures Production and consumption of products with environmental labeling	Demographic control Health control Restrictions on use of renewable resources
Waste and pollution	Legislation and planning New technology Production and consumption of products with environmental labeling Environmentally clean management of chemical, hazardous, and radioactive waste	Transition to the use of renewable and nonpollutant energy sources based on research from industrialized countries Education of the population
Energy	Legislation and planning New technology	Use of renewable energy sources researched in industrialized countries
Agriculture	Biotechnology	World suppliers of primary products Use of sustainable techniques researched in industrialized countries
Biodiversity	Research	Conservation
Participation of individuals and social groups	Promotion of the participation of local authorities, business groups, various social groups, and nongovernmental organizations	Programs aimed at women, indigenous populations, farmers, and other marginalized groups

The Green Belt Movement also relied on media representations, largely directed by women. Created in 1977 and led by Dr. Wangari Mathia of the National Council of Women of Kenya, the movement sought to avoid the deforestation of a region of Kenya; in so doing, it also attempted to create a space of empowerment for women. The project involved a cooperative that engaged in efforts at reforestation and that attempted to teach the local population about methods and techniques that would minimize environmental impacts of various activities.

The Greenham Common movement was initiated by women in 1981 as a protest against the deployment of U.S. nuclear missiles in Europe. The mobilization began with a march from Cardiff, Wales, to the Greenham Common military base in England, where a group of women chained themselves to the mail door of the base, making known their intention to stay there until the missiles were removed. From this action the Greenham Common Women's Peace Camp grew, attracting women from a wide variety of backgrounds.

At the beginning of the 1990s, the Rio de Janeiro Summit was a historic milestone for informal political action and at the same time an example of the complex interplay between popular movement actions, political action groups, and nongovernmental organizations (NGOs). NGOs, which largely see themselves as apolitical, are increasingly playing a decisive role: they are simultaneously organized as a tool for the local implementation and popularization of official agreements (Altvater 1998) and also as a response to hegemonic discourses. In the last decade social mobilization also has given rise to another type of movement that directly opposes capitalism, the so-called antiglobalization movement.[6] It is characterized by its nonhierarchical organization and mobilization mechanisms strongly linked to the tools of the information society (Castells 1996, 1997, 1998), especially the global communication network of the Internet.

Global Environmental Policies and Women's Organizations

As the activities outlined previously demonstrate, environmental and geopolitical issues are intertwined. Responses to environmental problems often have demonstrated an ethnocentric bias, as state-led proposals to address environmental problems reflect and reinforce the inequalities between the groups affected by these problems. In response, social movements have tried to formulate alternative responses. In this section we illustrate how pressure from women's groups and organizations has shaped discourses of environmental crises and how this has been integrated into the politics and policies of international organizations.

The declaration of the Decade of Women as part of the World Action Plan of the UN conference held in Mexico in 1975 and the forum reserved for NGOs drew attention to the fact that "women's problems" were inseparable from political and economic directives in their geopolitical contexts. However, among women the division into those from developed and developing countries led to different interpretations of their problems. Whereas feminists in developed societies cited patriarchal society and its alliance with capitalism as the source of inequalities, women in developing countries pointed to imperialism, colonialism, Zionism, fundamentalism, and apartheid as the causes of their predicament (Savané 1988).

Ten years later, the 1985 Nairobi conference marked the start of the international feminist movement, not so much because of the large number of women involved but because of its globalizing stance. The earlier creation of women's associations and networks for the defense of nature and the environment was decisive in the development of this struggle. For example, the Environment Liaison Centre International had already been set up in Nairobi, Kenya, in 1972, and it played a fundamental role at the Nairobi conference by organizing a seminar on "Women and the Environmental Crisis" at which the now well-known Chipko movement was presented for the first time.[7] A little later, in 1974, ISIS (Women's International Cross-Cultural Exchange), a women's information and communication service, was established.[8] Driven by the NGO forum at the Mexico conference, in 1976 the International Women's Tribune Centre was set up with its head office in New York. This organization was geared toward women's communication and technical assistance in development projects and financed by the development agencies of the governments of Canada, Finland, the Netherlands, Norway, and Sweden, with additional funding coming from churches and private foundations in the United States and Europe.

The United Nations also established a series of bodies focusing on issues of women and development, which are gaining an environmental profile. These include the Division for the Advancement of Women, with offices in Vienna and New York, which was created to run the secretariat of the Decade of Women (1980–1990), and United Nations Development Fund for Women, a fund with the aim of implementing development projects managed by women in the poorest countries. Regional commissions also should be mentioned: the African Training Center for Women, with its head office in Ethiopia, was founded as early as 1975; the "Comisión Económica para América Latina," created at the start of the decade with its headquarters in Chile; the Asian and Pacific Center for Women and Development, set up in 1977 with its head office in Malaysia; and International Research and Training Institute for the Advancement of Women, with its head office in the Dominican Republic and which, although founded in 1975, only became operational in 1980.

At the end of the Decade for Women, the Women's Environment and Development Organization was established, with headquarters in New York. The Women's Environment and Development Organization is a dynamic NGO that tries to facilitate links between women's groups and UN policies and is close to the UN's decision-making areas; its goal is "to make women more visible as participants, experts, and leaders in public debate on international affairs, and in formulating alternative peaceful solutions to world problems" (News and Views 1992). Also in the United States, "The WorldWIDE Network" (Women in Development and Environment) was started in 1981. It focused on publicizing success stories among women in the network and on permanently expanding an international directory of women working in all environmental fields.

In Europe mention should be made of two networks also set up at the end of the 1980s: WIDE and WEN (Women's Environmental Network). WIDE's head office is in Rome and it has representatives in Germany, Belgium, Denmark, Spain, France, Ireland, Italy, Switzerland, the Netherlands, and the United Kingdom. It works to coordinate associations from the North that operate in the South and also to further connections between associations and local development projects between countries in the North and South. WEN's head office is in London and it focuses on a British and European context; it works on the premise that women are the largest group of consumers and consequently have the potential to influence companies that produce products that have environmental and health risks.

In addition to these large networks, there are a vast number of associations that coordinate organizations working in the field of women and the environment and whose work is increasingly decisive at national and regional levels.

From Miami to Rio and beyond: The Pressure to Include Women's "Voice" in Gender Policies

The 1992 Earth Summit held in Rio de Janeiro was viewed by various women's groups as a key opportunity to influence international policies and to incorporate within them feminist perspectives on sustainable development. The World Women's Congress for a Healthy Planet was held in Miami in 1991 in order to draw up women's political demands for the Earth Summit; fifteen hundred women from eighty-three countries came together at the congress from different cultures, religions, ideologies, and professional and nonprofessional occupations as representatives of UN's agencies; governments; environmental, development, women's, and religious organizations; grassroots activist groups; universities; foundations; and the media (World Women's Congress for a Healthy Planet Official Report 1992).[9] Out of this meeting came the "Women's Action Agenda 21," a statement that provides an alternative to sustainable development based on personal experiences of the problems and on the interests and values defended by women.

The vision of environmental problems set out in the Women's Action Agenda 21 decenters the order of the hegemonic political map by establishing a connection between causes and effects, constructing a global interpretation of social, economic, and ecological issues and the linkage of impacts at different levels from the global to the personal. It presents a critical, cross-cutting analysis, which introduces a gendered dimension to problems that are traditionally mapped out as independent sectors. It makes clear the necessity and, at the same time, the difficulty of incorporating this decentered, interconnected, and cross-cutting view into a political model that speaks to hegemonic discourses.[10] In spite of the pressure it exerted, Agenda 21—the plan that emerged in Rio—preserved a hegemonic order of priorities; although space has been granted to women's demands, the premise of remapping the underlying patriarchal order has not been taken on board. The original model designed in Miami implies a social, economic, and ecological revolution, consciously assumed, whereas the Rio model is merely a readjustment of the hegemonic economic growth model using environmental correctness criteria. Table 15.2 is an outline of how some environmental problems were considered by the Miami's Agenda 21 and the Rio summit's interpretation of them, especially with regard to the role of women.

Agenda 21 views women, minorities, and indigenous populations as needing educational programs, family planning, recognition of land ownership, and access to resources and inclusion in local policies, but women lost their voice when it came to determining the character of sustainability built into the model. Thus, the existence of "the other" has been recognized, but this "other" is not a subject in its own right. Even though the Platform for Action of the 4th Conference on Women in Beijing marked the consolidation of women's demands along the lines set out in Miami, the panorama of official policies has not changed in substance (Looss 2002). After the summit in Rio, work was carried on at the Rio +5 Summit and the Rio +10 Summit (in Johannesburg), but it should be pointed out that Agenda 21 is a framework document that laid down the priority courses of action from which the other summits could draw up extensions or modifications—but not changes with respect to the global policy directives set out in the document.

After the summit in Rio, it seemed that the themes of women and the environment or women and sustainable development might have been incorporated into the geopolitical agendas of international agreements, but they always remained below the focus of official policy.[11] Of them all, perhaps the World Summit on Social Development in 1995 and its revision in 2000 offered the greatest possibility for a new vision of development with a transversal understanding of environmental problems. By contrast, even though unofficially held under the guise of women's empowerment, the World Food Summit in 1996 and its revision in 2001 promoted an attitude toward aid and development that relied on women's traditional roles. It is important to emphasize that these efforts do, however, establish the need to develop indicators that permit the evaluation of proposed actions that are supposed to favor women.[12] The World Summit on Sustainable Development, convened in Johannesburg in 2002, has attempted to incorporate the ideas and movements since the Rio summit, in an attempt to actualize a women's agenda. One such effort has been presented under the Women's Action Agenda for a Healthy and Peaceful Planet, 2002–2015. Incorporating its characteristic transversal vision of environmental

Table 15.2 Differences in Interpretations around Global Environmental Themes between the Women's Action Agenda 21 and Agenda 21 of Rio de Janeiro

Issue	Women's Action Agenda 21	Agenda 21 of Rio de Janeiro
Consumption	Consumption is seen as a power that women have to drive industrial development that respects the environment and society and that may enable a world alliance to boycott current unsustainable production and consumption models.	It identifies the importance of the women's role as consumers and the impact of their purchasing power on economies. The need to implement policies to change unsustainable consumption patterns is set out and special emphasis is placed on the role of new technology in this process.
Technology	Technology often involves destruction of nature and has not been within reach of the needs of the poor nor has it been accessible to women, many of whom have been its victims. The ethical implications of technology and the need to democratize it to make it available to and beneficial for women and marginalized groups are considered.	It identifies the benefits of technology in carrying out sustainable development and the importance of reinforcing research and promoting new technology and of involving developing countries in technological development through knowledge transfer.
External debt	Industrialized countries must admit their exploitation of the resources of developing countries. It condemns the negative impact of the International Monetary Fund and World Bank's restructuring policies on the poor, especially women and children. It is a proposal for action geared toward paying off external debt, such as boycotting banks that uphold it.	It identifies the need for developing countries to pay off their external debt and the incentives for international cooperation to reduce debt.

(Continued)

Table 15.2 *(Continued)*

Issue	Women's Action Agenda 21	Agenda 21 of Rio de Janeiro
Population	The main causes of environmental degradation are military and industrial pollutants and capitalist economic systems, and not women's fertility rates. The consumption-to-waste production ratio per person, which is much higher in the industrialized countries than in the poor ones, must be corrected.	It cites population growth as an unsustainable environmental pressure. It identifies the need to implement family planning policies and provide educational programs for women, and it puts forward the need to raise the educational level of women and to promote their economic independence and their participation at decision-making levels. It also proposes a war on poverty as a key factor in reducing demographic growth.

problems and commitment to deep socioecological change, the agenda addresses the most important themes and issues on the horizon for the next decade.[13]

The Foundations of the Alternatives: Ecofeminism and a Gendered Approach to Sustainability

In the previous section, we discussed the tension between the global geopolitical environment related to ecological issues and the platforms and mobilizations presented by women's groups. These platforms constitute a distinctly radical approach to the environmental crisis. Notwithstanding this claim, women's groups are not homogeneous and they present diverse alternatives to environmental issues. To address these issues, we present in this section the ideological and political differences within ecofeminism. By way of conclusion, we reflect on the gendered nature of environmental politics and the diverse alternatives in gendered discourses on the environment.

Ecofeminism

To understand the analytical framing that has furnished the ideological and political body of ecofeminism, we need to address a basic point: the awareness that the various forms of relationships (experiential, intellectual, productive, symbolic, etc.) between human beings and the environment are deeply marked by gender differences. In this respect a common starting point for different ecofeminist stances is to show how these relationships are represented by dualisms that associate femininity with nature and masculinity with culture. However, this practice falls into two broad groups. One group, which asserts an essence of the feminine as an ahistorical reference value, is labeled "culturalist," whereas those that aim to deconstruct any gender assignment are grouped under the label sociopolitical (King 1988). For the sake of clarity and without losing sight of the fact that these are not closed ideological attitudes, we shall use these terms in the following discussion.

Culturalist stances suggest that the link between women and nature is natural and based on the ability of the female body to give birth to life and also in women's gender activities, which are closely connected with giving, maintaining, and reinforcing life (Mies and Shiva 1997, 1998). This view has enabled a revaluation of the differences between female and male values, the former alienated by androcentric cultures. The search to show the spiritual link of women with nature, and the corroboration of their direct actions to protect the environment, enabled women to become visible and, with this, to explore a new femininity identified with nature. Culturalist feminism has thus demonstrated the experiential diversity of the feminine and has given the feminist movement flexibility; it has broadened its objectives and has introduced new identification reference points that differ from those that Western feminists—mostly white and urban middle class—have traditionally put forward. The political consequences of culturalist feminism in terms of environmental management appear strongly marked by the assertion of the superiority of the feminine. Thus, alongside the critique of hegemonic management models identified as products of a megalomaniac and destructive masculinity, the establishment of a radically different socioenvironmental order based on the everyday and on prioritizing conservation and caring for people and nature is advocated.

Sociopolitical approaches, for their part, point to environmental gender differences as cultural and social facts. Neither the attributes nor the meanings given to nature or women (or all the differences associated with these categories) are seen as ontological qualities but rather as cultural constructs derived from historical processes. The political consequence of this theoretical argument is that gender differences are projected in all kinds of relationships established with the environment; they are an integral part of policies; therefore, it is through political struggle only that one can recognize the role that these differences play, as opposed to a neutral interpretation of the relationship with the environment based on the neoliberal model (Rocheleau et al. 1996).

Environmental Management Alternatives and Gender Discourses

Through awareness of the axiomatic identification between nature and femininity that characterizes modern thought, the feminist movement has attacked the androcentric nature of environmental management models and has developed global alternatives that enable a nonalienated and sustainable relationship between human beings and between them and the environment.[14] At the same time, some elements of feminist approaches have been incorporated into reformulations of hegemonic environmental management models in what has come to be known as the "gender approach to environmental change." This approach brings with it the demand to take a critical look at the successive redrawings of environmental discourses, rather than dismissing them entirely, to reveal the scope of ecofeminist narratives of environmental management. The technological and ecological efficacy that is the main feature of the official hegemonic version of sustainability (e.g., Rio's Agenda 21) does mark a change with respect to previous external environmental management paradigms in that the former takes the shape of a twin-track modernization: ecological and democratic. It is ecological in that it puts forward the protection and conservation of nature and the environment, and it is democratic as it gives an image of permeability with respect to the opinions and interests of the general public. The study of the decisions and actions of women geared toward minimizing risks and the environmental impact of consumption and, indirectly, production has been incorporated into this framework by feminists (Brú Bistuer 1993, 1996).

The efforts of women's organizations to place a gender point of view at the heart of Agenda 21 has served to make women visible as environmental agents, revealing the decisive importance of the domestic sphere in environmental management. These are crucial facts to establish when consolidating a new policy orientation, that is, getting policy makers to recognize the strategic importance of the quotidian and taking it as a reference point for the organization of environmental management. Thus, the "new feminized approach" put forward by ecofeminists poses a critique to mainstream development models. While these models highlight women's actions as environments agents, they do so in ways that rely on women's traditional domestic attributes (such as a sense of gender responsibility, perserverance, and an ability to save) and that serve to reinforce androcentric policies.

However, the fact of making women visible as environmental agents and demonstrating the environmental dimension of daily life does not by itself lead to major changes in the technological and scientific management model, as is clearly shown by the contents of Agenda 21. The goals mapped out in Agenda 21 are undoubtedly a breakthrough with respect to international policy agendas and a tool for putting pressure on national governments to include women in environmental and development policies. Nevertheless, it still remains to be seen whether the inclusion of women in decision-making bodies or in scientific and technological research will make the adoption of feminist alternatives possible, as opposed to the adoption of an androcentric model as the one that turns out to be operative in the prevailing political and scientific systems.

Furthermore, attention needs to be drawn to the nonexistence of specific gendered policies targeted at men; there are no measures to palliate the problematic social situation that reproduces a patriarchal order that profoundly degrades men as well as women. Wars, economic crises, and the lack of questioning of traditional masculine identities linked to acculturation processes and so forth are facts that seriously erode men's self-esteem without offering them new models for their participation in daily life and in caring for families and the environment.

Conclusion: Identifying Priorities

A gendered approach to environmental management is aimed at achieving environmental fairness and distributive justice—that is, at guaranteeing the right to fair access to resources and to environmental quality for all human beings. Yet the literature on environmental justice has tended to prioritize not gender but rather class components and their geopolitical dimensions, which establishes the division between rich and poor countries; its assertion of distributive justice comes from its alignment with modernist concepts of equality, citizenship, and justice. Thus, ecological thinking on the left—of a radical or social democratic hue—has been underlain by a notoriously androcentric approach in which inequalities of access to resources and environmental quality, marked by gender, are interpreted as examples of inequality brought about by capitalist oppression and rarely as forms of the specific oppression of women that develop and survive both inside and outside capitalism (Bondi 1990; McDowell 1992b; Women and Geography Study Group 1992).

However, seeing women as legal subjects in terms of work and property and as social and economic agents distinct from men has changed measures adopted in development policies and clearly made them more efficient. Proof of this are the outcomes attained in the recovery of agricultural loans when the receivers have been women or groups of women, the success of production by women's cooperatives, and the efficacy and maintenance of women's forestry and soil conservation initiatives, among other examples (Joeckes et al. 1996; Leach 1996; Rao and Rurup 1997; Rocheleau et al. 1996; Wickramasinghe 1995).

Nevertheless, and in spite of the importance of making women visible and the emphasis placed on the environment, feminists should not trust that structural changes in policies are capable of questioning the narrowness of the sense of justice on which alternative approaches have been based. Even progressive political projects have adopted the modernist interpretations of the gender approach. They praise women and recognize the importance of the changes brought about by them, and they demand their active commitment to the building of a better society, but they do not start from questioning the androcentric discourse of hegemonic powers. Thus, as long as fundamental changes capable of breaking down the socialization mechanisms that establish gender identifications at an individual and collective level do not take place, women's struggle for better environments for all humankind will have to maintain its own profile, distinct from neoliberal environmentalism and progressive ecology.

The present seems to be a decisive moment. The rapid growth of the clearly antiauthoritarian antiglobalization movement—which, with its recent mobilizations in Porto Alegre and Barcelona, is showing itself to be extremely vigorous and increasingly rooted in civil society—is shaping up as a new intercultural framework in which to rethink relationships between men and women and their roles in the design of new environmental policies with a global reach.[15]

Notes

1. For example, the accident at the Chernobyl nuclear power station in 1986 sparked a wide-ranging social and political debate in the West about the risk posed to the planet by nuclear energy.

2. See Funtowicz and Ravetz (2000), who developed an analytical model regarding the credibility of arguments exclusively based on scientific and technological data in the generation of environmental risk management policies.

3. Worthy of mention as framing documents for the implementation of international agreements are the following: the Bru Bistuerndlant Report "Our Common Future," produced by the World Commission on Environment and Development (1987), which propagated the concept of sustainable development, and Agenda 21, based on the UN conference on the Environment and Development at the Rio Summit in 1992, which has become the primary framework guiding local policies toward sustainable development.

4. The United Nations, through the United Nations Environmental Programme, has the main responsibility for the implementation of global environmental policies. Institutions such as the Worldwatch Institute, the World Wide Fund, and the World Resource Institute have been set up to research and issue reports on the global environmental situation.

5. The term was originally coined by Françoise D'Eaubonne in her book *Le Feminisme ou la mort!* (D'Eaubonne 1974). For a panoramic view of the various positions in ecofeminism, see Caldecott and Leland (1983), Plant (1989), Diamond and Orenstein (1990), and the Spring 1992 issue of *Hypatia* (Indiana University Press) dedicated to ecological feminism.

6. Some of the most significant antiglobalization activities took place in 1999 in Seattle; in 2000 in Bangkok, Washington, D.C., and Prague; in 2001 in Gothenburg, Barcelona, Salzburg, and Genoa; and in 2002 in Porto Alegre.

7. When Environment Liaison Centre International documents are translated into Spanish, its initials are changed to CEMA-I to fit the translation of its name as "Centro de Enlace para el Medio Ambiente Internacional."

8. In 1983, when it had almost ten thousand contacts in 130 countries, it split into two: ISIS-wice in Geneva and ISIS International with offices in Rome and Santiago de Chile .

9. The congress was called by the Women's International Policy Action Committee, a committee made up of fifty-three women from thirty-one countries (World Women's Congress for a Healthy Planet Official Report 1991).

10. The contents of Agenda 21 had to be negotiated so that instead of confining gender questions to a single chapter, aspects that affect women also were included in the chapters on Education, Legal Institutions, Promoting Human Settlement Development, Combating Poverty, Changing Consumption Patterns, Demographic Dynamics, Human Health Conditions, Sustainable Agriculture and Rural Development, and Managing Fragile Ecosystems: Combating Desertification and Drought.

11. Bisi Ogunleye and Minu Hemmati, of the Country Women's Association of Nigeria, presented an excellent summary of women's groups' contributions to UN conferences during the meeting of the Intersessional Working Group of the UN Commission on Sustainable Development in May 2000. Their report is available at http://www.earthsummit2002.org/wcaucus/meetingreports/csd8%20report.htm.

12. In this respect the issues raised by the German delegation in the preparatory meetings for the Johannesburg summit are interesting. See, for instance, Corral and Ransom (2002).

13. It addresses issues in ten different sections: (1) Governance and Sustainable Development; (2) Globalization and the Claim for Transparency and Accountability in the Institutions of the Global System; (3) Gender and Environmental Dimensions of Conflicts and Militarization; (4) Impacts of Market, Production, and Consumption on Sustainable Development; (5) Women's Rights and Control of Natural Resources; (6) Women's Sexual and Reproductive

Health Rights and the Environment; (7) Environmental Security: Protecting the Health of Present and Future Generations; (8) Threats to Biodiversity and Indigenous Knowledge; (9) The Gender Dimension of Sustainable Cities, Urbanization, and Migration; and (10) Gaps and Opportunities in Education Communication and Information Technologies.

14. There is an ambiguity to the term *sustainability*. In social and political terms it is configured as a way of rethinking the crisis of the idea of progress, which in the environmental field is focused on the discussion toward the limits of growth (Brú Bistuer and Agüera Cabo 2001). Sustainable development has diverse ideological orientations and provides a frame of reference for different models of negotiation, from those who pose a complete reformulation of the relationship between nature and society to those who merely wish to adapt growth models and the discourse of technological efficiency.

15. We are referring here to the World Social Forum, held in Porto Alegre, Brazil, in February 2002, and the social summit, which ran in parallel to the meeting the European Union heads of state held in Barcelona, Spain, in March 2002.

16
Making Feminist Sense of the State and Citizenship

VERA CHOUINARD

In the *longue duree* of struggles to make sense of human societies and spaces of life, few entities have been as conceptually and practically pivotal, perplexing, and elusive as "the state." Conceptions of the state have ranged from ancient views of it as the epicenter of empire building and elitism to classical visions of states as institutions through which reason, democracy, and justice might prevail in an otherwise brutal and individualistic world and to radical conceptions of the state as modes of regulation and governance that too often, oppress many and empower few.

In political geography the state and local states have been defined in relatively conventional ways, as sets of government institutions operating over space and, in more radical ways, as having functions and forms intimately linked to the reproduction of capitalist societies and spaces of life (Johnston 1982; Clark and Dear 1984). For most political geographers, apart from those drawing on world systems frameworks, the nation-state has been the primary unit of analysis. Geographers have, then, wrestled with what the state is, how it shapes our lives and life spaces, and how relations and practices of power within its realm might be contested. However, the role of states as sites of struggle over gendered relations of power has tended to be ignored, even in much of the radical literature. Exceptions to this, such as work by Jessop (2001) on gender relations and the state and by Connell (1990) on political regulation of socio-sexual regimes and masculinities, are rare.

In this chapter I focus on how feminist geographic research has challenged views of what the state is, how it places us in society and space, and how we might struggle for more inclusive, empowering societies. This work is part of an innovative interdisciplinary literature examining how differences such as class, gender, sexuality, and race are regulated by the state and contested by those subject to its power.

I begin by discussing how feminist scholars have helped to redefine what the state is and why and how it shapes our lives. Next, I discuss how feminist geographers have advanced our understanding of why, how, and where state power transforms our lives at local through global scales. Recently, this research has focused on social and spatial differencing among subjects of the state, including those "others" whose claims to citizenship rights and other entitlements are particularly tenuous. Such studies tell us a great deal about how diverse women, children, and men are differentially situated as subjects of state power. It has less to say about the dynamics of state formation in particular places and times because the state as a unit of analysis has been decentered in favor of focusing on the impacts that the exercise of state power has on diverse subjects (e.g., through changes in laws, social programs).

I conclude the chapter by considering whether feminist geographies of state power are moving in directions that are, in some ways, paradoxically out of step with the dramatic changes in state power and relations of ruling we are witnessing in an increasingly global world. Do we, once again, need feminist geographic perspectives that help to bring more clearly into view the causes, and not merely the consequences, of state intervention in our lives and places of life?

Conceptualizing and Contesting the State:
Feminist Geographic Perspectives

The state has always been a contested concept. One reason is that so much is at stake: explaining, justifying, or criticizing ways of deploying state power and governing people and places. It is also because how we understand state power influences how we engage with it. It is not surprising, then, that debates about the state have raged inside and outside academia.

In political geography the state has usually been seen as a relatively neutral set of government institutions that are spatially manifest in phenomena such as electoral districts and national boundaries. From the late 1970s, however, geographers began to develop alternative, radical perspectives on state power. Clark and Dear (1984) encouraged geographers to understand the forms and functions of the state as arising from its role in perpetuating capitalist class relations and ways of life. They defined the state apparatus not as politically neutral but as "the set of mechanisms through which state power is exercised and state functions realized" (p. 49). Such conceptions promised to advance our understanding of state intervention in cities and regions, helping us to explain why, for instance, investment in urban-built environments almost invariably works to empower already privileged groups such as developers at the expense of vulnerable people (e.g., low-income people displaced by urban redevelopment schemes) (Johnston 1982; Dear and Wolch 1987).

These conceptions of the state as embedded in capitalist society and space were not without problems. They tended to give a rather top-down impression of how state power was exercised, which seemed to leave little room for popular resistance. They also tended to conceive decision making within the state as necessarily rational. Still, theories of the capitalist state inspired scholars to critically examine the social relations of power and ruling through which states intervened in different places (Fincher 1989b; Dear and Wolch 1987; Chouinard 1989). As in the interdisciplinary literature, the emerging radical geographic literature remained, apart from geographers' taking world-systems approaches, primarily focused on nation-states and local states. Comparatively little attention was paid to political-economic and cultural changes at transnational and global scales, such as the emergence of the European Union. Such matters have started to receive more attention today as feminist and social geographers seek to advance our understanding of globalization and the worldwide development of neoliberal modes of governance (Gibson-Graham 1996; Peck and Tickell 2002; Peake and Trotz 1999).

Feminist challenges to Western conceptions of the state as a gender-neutral but implicitly masculine site of power have gone on for a long time. As early as 1792, Mary Wollstonecraft published a withering critique of conceptions of the state as the exclusive domain of men and protector of men's rights. During the late nineteenth century to the mid-twentieth century, women protested their exclusion from citizenship and demanded the vote and an end to their status as the property and dependents of men. Contemporary struggles to advance women's rights, for instance, to equity in employment, are still challenging gender-neutral views of nation-states and indeed supranational states—views that fail to acknowledge laws, policies, and implementation practices working to keep diverse women in disempowered places of political-economic and cultural life. Although, at present, some women's struggles for voice, representation, rights, and empowerment vis-à-vis the state may seem only distant memories, these are recent chapters in the *long duree* of women's history. Today, as neoliberal states deepen the oppression of growing numbers of women, it is clear that women's struggles in and against the state are far from over.

Decentering the State in Feminist Geographic Research: From Perspectives on the State to Gendered Geographies of Differencing and Citizenship

Over the past two decades, very significant changes have occurred in feminist geographies of the state's role in transforming society and space. Whereas during the late 1970s and 1980s, feminist scholars focused on the state as a terrain of struggle over gendered political-economic power, from the 1990s onward feminists concentrated on the implications of state policy and law for diverse subjects' access to the rights and entitlements of citizenship. The state, as a site of struggle over gender, class, and other divisions of power in capitalist societies, was decentered, as attention turned to the sociospatial consequences of state regulation and away from the causes of changes in state intervention in people's lives. Questions about how different individuals and groups, such as welfare moms, were being represented in policy discourses and disciplined in society and space through policy practices took center stage, while questions about the state, as a complex causal terrain of struggle over power, began to recede from view (Cockburn 1977; MacKinnon 1989; Walby 1990; Fraser 1989; Chouinard and Fincher 1987).

Why did such a fundamental shift in thinking about the state occur? And what were its consequences for feminist geographic research?

Theorizing the State

From the late 1970s feminists theorized the state as a key site of struggles over class and gendered divisions of power in society. Conceptions of the state as a "contested terrain" built on various feminist traditions. Liberal feminists conceptualized the state as a set of institutions through which equality between the sexes could, in an enlightened democracy, be realized (Z. Eisenstein 1981; Bryson 1992). From this vantage point, the state was a neutral site through which to promote equality between women and men. This perspective informed a range of debates about women's inequality. However, most feminist theorists, influenced by Marxist and radical literatures, took much less benign views of state institutions and power. They insisted that the state and local states played central, causal roles in perpetuating societies and spaces of life in which class and gender divisions of power sustained social relations and practices oppressive to women. The state was necessarily implicated in women's marginalization, a role inscribed within its very institutional organization, policies, and implementation practices. Gender, class privilege, and power, such as the corporate capitalist male elite's hold over urban redevelopment, signaled that states were in many ways embedded within and captives of particular sociospatial orders (e.g., Cockburn 1977; Walby 1990; Watson 1990).

Other feminist theories of the state drew on tenets of radical feminism and argued that women's oppression was rooted in men's control over women's biology, reproductive capacities, and sexuality. MacKinnon (1989) argued that the violent sexual oppression of women by men was materialized through the institutional structures, laws, policies, and procedures of so-called democratic states. States perpetuated women's oppression by men through, for example, rape laws and judicial proceedings, which revictimized women (e.g., using past sexual histories to discredit women's testimonies about being raped).

Feminist geographers' theorizations of the state and local state during the 1980s drew primarily on Marxist and socialist-feminist traditions (Bowlby 1984; Fincher 1989b), which reflected close ties between scholars working in radical, Marxist approaches to urban and regional change and those arguing for feminist perspectives that could help make sense of gender as well as class differences in cities and regions. Some of this early work took a liberal feminist perspective, for instance, attributing gender inequalities in access to transportation and job opportunities in cities to planning policies, which did not take these inequalities into account (Wekerle and Rutherford 1988). Others conceptualized the state as simultaneously a "creature of capitalism" and as a terrain of conflict over the extent to which prevailing class and gender divisions of power would be perpetuated. Chouinard and Fincher (1987) advocated a conjunctural approach to conceptualizing the state as contradictory, geographically specific, and historically specific terrains of class struggle. This perspective recognized that state institutions, laws, and policies were necessarily limited by the dynamics of the wider capitalist sociospatial order but also that state intervention reflected contingent conditions of life in specific places and times (i.e., conjunctures). Fincher's (1981) analysis of struggles over urban renewal in central Boston neighborhoods is a good example of this approach. She argued that this city's urban planning and redevelopment policies were constrained by the class structure through which urban-built environments were produced, most notably the footloose corporate capital forcing cities to compete for investment through progrowth policies. But these environments also were shaped by conditions in particular cities, such as citizens' activism around neighborhood redevelopment issues.

Contemporary feminist geographic conceptions of the state have built on these theories of what the state is and how it regulates, governs, and changes lives. Traces of liberal feminist theories can be detected in the importance attached to issues of women's rights, political representation, and status as citizens. Socialist and radical feminist perspectives surface, for instance, in resistance to poststructural explanations of state power as abstract outcomes of policy discourses divorced from struggles over state power in places. Although feminist geographers acknowledge that discursive struggles matter, their accounts of phenomena such as welfare policy reform also have insisted, at least implicitly, that the state is materially embedded in particular sociospatial orders and that the material consequences of state intervention in people's lives in places matter in understanding people's subjection to state power (Cope 1997; McDowell 1999; Rose and Blunt 1994). Class and other differences matter in making sense of why some people are empowered through their engagements with the state and others are disempowered. Where (and how) a person lives, as well as the meanings others assign to this, has implications for whether they are judged as entitled to such aspects of citizenship as occupying urban public spaces. This is why local state agencies, including police, often forcibly remove and exclude "undesirables" such as street youth from urban spaces designated for more privileged users (e.g., displacing them from parks and convention center grounds). To some extent, then, contemporary feminist geographers have retained the materialism of earlier socialist-feminist and radical accounts of the state.

Given these various influences, it is important not to assume that contemporary feminist geographic explanations of phenomena, such as differences in entitlement to citizenship in global cities, follow in any neat way from theories that have helped to challenge earlier radical conceptions of state power. Rather, feminist geographers are building on some aspects of these more recently popular perspectives and are discarding and modifying others as they try to understand state power in particular places and times. Still, it is clear that feminist geography's present focus on citizenship and the sociospatial outcomes of exercising state power has decentered concerns with why states are deploying power in ways that are deepening class, gender, and other divisions in society and space. However, in an era of rapid transformations in citizenship, when more people are finding themselves with little or no influence over state intervention in their lives, perhaps this shift away from feminist theories of the causes of changes in the state and relations of ruling has gone too far.

From the State to Gendered Geographies of Differencing and Citizenship

During the 1990s feminist scholars turned their gazes toward the consequences that state rule had for diverse peoples' lives and away from the state. This shift was evident in the literature, as the number of works explicitly dealing with why, as well as how, power was being deployed declined. *Playing the State* (Watson 1990), one of the last major edited collections to be published, posed critical questions about the state and power, asking, for instance, why having more "femocrats" working within the Australian state did not seem to be translating into policies and practices that were making society less oppressive for diverse women. Such questioning brought feminist scholarship and activism together by encouraging assessment of what feminist struggles over state power had (and had not) achieved. Before scholars could answer these questions, however, other questions came to the fore—questions about justice and ways of negotiating differences among citizens (Young 1990), how subjects of the state were constructed through policy discourses (Fraser 1989), and how differences in citizenship status, practices, and geographies of political life influenced women's and men's capacities to claim entitlement to citizenship rights and to places within global cities (Kofman 1998).

Why were feminist geographers caught up in this intellectual and political shift away from critical analyses of the state? And what were the consequences of this for our understanding of, and engagement with, state power?

Part of the answer lies in wider shifts in critical social theory. Poststructuralist, postmodern, and postcolonial theorists criticized earlier radical and feminist theories for encouraging grand metanarrative explanations, arguing that these falsely claimed to provide a total account of processes of sociospatial change. The aim of "post" theories was to develop less totalizing explanations, which allowed for the partiality and incompleteness of all knowledges and challenged Western ways of understanding the world (Spivak 1988; Barrett and Phillips 1992). But, ironically, these critiques were in some ways as totalizing and dismissive in their portrayal of radical scholarship as they alleged earlier radical scholars had been in making sense of the world. Although feminist scholars were among those who engaged with the "posts" in especially thoughtful ways, the sweeping, dismissive style and tone of these critiques helped sustain, if not trigger, the shift away from theories of the state in feminist work. The problem with prior critical theories, according to commonsense "post" wisdom, was overly binary ways of categorizing and thinking about entities such as women or the state. Although there were grains of truth in such claims (e.g., witness feminists' own critiques of categorizations of "women" based on privileged women's lives), the danger was that these theories would be conflated with the problematic notion that all pre-post theories were necessarily tainted by binarism. If this idea were accepted, then the mere project of theorizing the state was suspect.

This is not to suggest that these critiques were without some validity with respect to feminist theory and explanation. Calls for greater attention to diversity and the situatedness of knowledges resonated with many feminists' critiques of their own scholarship as produced from privileged positions of whiteness and class. They also resonated with feminists' struggles to grapple with diversity and exclusion within the women's movement. As critical scholars, feminists were also among those who were more sympathetic to notions that whose knowledges count should be open to questioning and that it is often useful to unsettle the authority granted to academic knowledges. In this they joined postpositivist philosophers of science who also had been raising such matters long before the turn to poststructuralist ways of thinking.

It was in the context of these debates, and a rapidly changing world, that feminist scholars began to conceptualize state power as more contradictory, uneven, partial, and incomplete than structural explanations of it sometimes allowed. Attention turned to what Fraser (1989) termed "unruly practices" of the state: from discursive representations of those dependent on state assistance, through to how these images shaped diverse peoples' locations in relations and practices of citizenship. There is an intriguing resonance but also tension between these partial, "post" accounts of state power and real and imagined declines in the power of nation-states to influence what happens within their borders in a rapidly globalizing world. The resonance lies in an overwhelming sense that, as subjects of state power, we are immersed in a present that is so quickly becoming the past that we can only hope to catch fleeting glimpses of how our political places are changing and have scarcely a moment to wonder why. The tension lies in the sense that although we urgently need to understand why more and more of us are becoming disempowered in our relations with states, in trying to make sense of why this is happening we seem to be constantly kept off balance by the pace of political change and by the blurring of boundaries between what is real and imagined about state practices and our subjection to state power.

There has been a synergy, then, between "post" ways of thinking about the world and the dizzyingly rapid transformations in which we are caught up in our societies and spaces of life. Feminists thus began to theorize state intervention not as necessarily coherent, rational responses to the logical requirements of a global, capitalist, and patriarchal sociospatial order (e.g., the need to maintain gender divisions of labor) but as inconsistent, contradictory outcomes of forces of change—forces that are real and imagined, discursive and material, lived but beyond more than partial comprehension. If state power were much less unified in its causal dynamics than feminist theorists had previously imagined and if different subjects of state power were ruled in similarly inconsistent, contradictory, and confusing ways, then feminists needed to grapple in greater detail with the discourses and practices of ruling through which particular citizens were subjected to and resisted state power in their daily lives.

Closely associated with these shifts in theory and explanation was the so-called cultural turn through which scholars became eager to address issues of identity, difference, representation, and meanings inscribed on diverse people and places (e.g., what it means to be "queer" and disrupting heterosexist ways of being in place). Critical scholars' engagements with cultural aspects of global capitalist societies also gained momentum from the political struggles of marginalized groups, such as gay women and men, who often used public performances of transgressive identities to challenge oppressive images and assumptions about their lives and places in the world (Bell 1995; Brown 1997).

It is always hard to say, definitively, how these forces combined to shape feminist theory and research on the state. I suspect many of us drifted with certain aspects of these wider scholarly turns and, deliberately or not, resisted others. What is pretty clear is that feminists' turns away from theorizing the state have been too widespread and too coincidental with these currents to be unrelated. This is particularly intriguing because it would be hard to make a convincing case that most feminist theories of the state were so flawed that they could not have been refined in ways that further advanced our understanding of state power. Although by the 1990s feminists such as J. Allen (1990) were expressing skepticism about the need for a theory of the state, it remains unclear that theorizing the state from a feminist perspective was an inherently flawed project. In fact, during the present era of rapid changes in states—changes particularly oppressive to women "of difference"—one could argue that feminist theories and explanations of state formation and geography of state rule have never been so urgently needed.

Clearly, feminist scholars and geographers began to focus on how different subjects of the state experienced and contested state power in their everyday lives and life spaces. This included examining how differences among individuals and in their representation as subjects of state power within policy discourses altered their entitlements to citizenship. This work shed light on how people are differenced in their engagements with state power and how particular female subjects, such as single mothers, become entrapped by negative identities inscribed on them through government discourses and policy (Fraser 1989; Gilbert 1997).

These studies of the diverse consequences of state rule challenged, at least implicitly, conceptions of state power as exercised, interpreted, and contested primarily in public, historically male, spaces of life, such as government legislatures, and encouraged feminist geographers to explore state power as more diffuse, pervasive, and sociospatially uneven in its implications for diverse subjects negotiating both private and public spaces of life. This helped to open our eyes to formerly personal and private aspects of state regulation, such as how antigay legislation in some U.S. states disciplines nonheterosexual persons metaphorically into the closet and literally into the home. Furthermore, as D. Cooper (1995) emphasized, these more fluid, decentered conceptions of the state—in which power is understood to be manifest and encountered along multiple sociospatial dimensions through discourse and representation, regulation, and resistance, and spaces of engagement beyond the institutional boundaries of the state—help to reveal inconsistencies and ambiguities in state power in far more sophisticated ways than would radical theories presupposing that state projects are unified and coherent. Such theories allow scholars to entertain possibilities that states respond to activism around issues, such as AIDS, in geographically uneven and contradictory ways, reflecting the specificities of power and struggle at diverse sites and the prevailing conditions of political life in particular places and times.

Feminist Geographies of Differencing and Citizenship

Issues of diversity and citizenship and the impacts of state regulation on people's lives and places in society and space have been of growing concern in recent feminist political geographic research. A key focus is on what Kobayashi (1997) termed *differencing*, that is, complex sociospatial processes of empowering and enabling some people and marginalizing and oppressing others on bases of the differences they embody. In accord with postmodern and poststructuralist influences, our understanding of how state power is deployed and contested through differencing encourages us to think about how engaging with state power is a fluid, shifting, and often confusing experience.

As women, for example, we are caught up in relationships to state power through multiple identities, roles, and embodiments of differences such as class and race. Women relate to state power, simultaneously and alternatively, as female citizens, mothers, daughters, activists, caregivers, paid or unpaid workers, or union supporters or opponents, or as rich or poor, old or young, gay or heterosexual, and so on. Thus, the identities and lived relations most central to women's engagements with state power shift as they negotiate different identities, roles, spaces of life, and ways of being in place. The related acknowledgment that political identities are gendered but in diverse, embodied, and spatially uneven ways focuses attention on people's diverse locations within relations and practices of citizenship. This can help us to better understand why it is, for example, that being a woman of color or with an impaired body or mind often means being much less able to exercise legal rights than women who are privileged by ableness and whiteness (Chouinard 2001).

Among the interesting examples of feminist geographies of the state as a terrain of differencing is Fincher's (1993) account of how femocrats' definitions of female citizens' service needs as similar to their own (i.e., white working women with able-bodied preschool and school-age children) have translated into patterns of service delivery in the city of Melbourne, Australia, which targets day care services to middle-income neighborhoods and neglects women with other needs and in other locations in the city (e.g., women caring for disabled children or aging relatives). This research shows where and how women's subjection to state power influences their capacities to perform different roles in place, how, for instance, racialized inscriptions of what it means to be a "welfare mom" disadvantage many women struggling for more empowering locations within relations of citizenship (Cope 1997). Such work demonstrates that the state is neither unitary nor coherent but tension ridden and contradiction laden, as struggles over who will be empowered, and who will not, are fought out.

A recurrent theme in this work is that differencing through subjection to state power occurs in real and imaginary ways. Cope (1997), among others, showed that recent welfare policy reforms in the United States are fuelled by images of single mothers as part of a dependent urban underclass, a situation that reinforces their marginalized status as citizens. Similarly, Miranne (2000) explained how state restructuring in Canada has had profound implications for the lives of single mothers receiving welfare benefits, leading to their growing sociospatial emboundedness within a workfare system that keeps them in poverty and despair.

Bringing Geographies of Citizenship into View

Feminist geographers are thus demonstrating that becoming gendered and otherwise differenced subjects of the state is a geographic process that cuts across public and private spaces of life and is about being put into real and imagined places of relative power and powerlessness.

Historical geographies of transformations in women's lives are among the recent studies helping us to understand women's subjection to different forms of state power in places. Litoff and Smith (1994), for instance, explained how women's identities and political geographic horizons as citizens of the United States changed during World War II as many women became, for the first time, employed in traditionally male occupations (e.g., shipyard and factory workers), financially independent, and engaged with news of the war and world politics.

Feminist geographers also have drawn attention to how geographic representations of political action, as unfolding exclusively within public spaces of state power, have overlooked gendered differences where challenges to state power and policy occur. In the West and developing regions of the world, images of politics as unfolding in public spaces of political life traditionally dominated by men have helped to render women's organizing and action in spaces such as the home invisible in geographic accounts of struggles over state power (Staeheli and Cope 1994; Radcliffe 1993; Fincher and Panelli 2001).

Challenging Western Perspectives on State Power and Citizenship: Postcolonial and Transnational Feminist Geographies

Feminist geographers also are drawing in very creative ways on postcolonial theory and activism to challenge Western conceptions of state power and citizenship and are giving voice to the realities of being postcolonial subjects. These include being caught up in racialized and gendered spaces of military brutality, violence, terror, destruction, and displacement. An unsettling example of such work is Nolin Hanlon and Shankar's (2000) moving account of the thousands of *testimonios* submitted to the United Nations and church-based commissions working with survivors (and some perpetrators) of assaults and massacres in Guatemala, massacres that led to the deaths of more than 400,000 people, destruction of entire communities, and sexual assaults against more than 6,000 women.

Feminist geographers, building on postcolonial theories, also have drawn attention to discursive representations of the nation-state and to real and imagined processes of nation building, which situates diverse peoples inside and outside relations of citizenship. This work aims to unsettle geographies of the state, nation, and diverse political subjects (Sharp 1996; Radcliffe 1993; see also Mayer 2004 [this volume]). Deconstructing fictitious accounts of nation building is a related goal. Schaffer (1994) showed how postcolonial conceptualizations of the "nation as narration" reveal the gendered nature of the "foundational fiction" of the state in settler nations such as Australia, where only heroic, civilized white male settlers led territorial expansion.

Kay Anderson (2000) suggested that a transnational perspective that focuses on nation building as a sociospatial process of putting differenced citizens in relatively more and less empowered places is a promising direction for future feminist geographies of state power and citizenship. Nations and nation-states are being forged in an increasingly transnational world of international migration and investment, and it is hence problematic to assume that differences in citizenship in particular nations can be fully explained by the dynamics of racism. She pointed to other processes of nation-building, such as reviving images of settlers as founders of the nation and constructing transient businesspersons as outsiders, which may be just as important in forging a nation and its citizens out of an increasingly global society.

Back to the Future? Directions and Challenges in Feminist Geographies of State Power

Clearly, feminist geographers have contributed to rethinking and remapping state power in more poststructural and postcolonial ways. Postmodern social theory has had a less obvious impact on these feminist geographic studies, although concerns with unsettling discourses about state power and diverse citizens certainly parallel postmodern concerns.

By challenging conventional political geographic understandings of the state, feminist geographers have been at the forefront of understanding how states difference those they rule. They have shown how embodied differences, such as in gender, race, sexuality, and age, give rise to differences in citizenship (Gilbert 1997; Elder 1998; Fincher 1993). Studies of the political status and experiences of immigrants in regions such as Europe (Kofman 1998) have helped us to understand transnational, gendered processes of subjection to state power, which are marginalizing groups such as migrant women. Work on women's experiences of living in refugee camps, such as those in Somalia, also reveals how women are caught up in spaces of transnational political and cultural engagement, where they struggle with gendered differences in power that are refracted and played out through collisions between Western and non-Western ideas and ways of life (Hyndman 2000).

Making Connections: From Embodied Life to a Global World and Back Again

A key strength of these studies is the skill with which connections are made between forces of political-economic and cultural change operating at different geographic scales. Pratt's (1998) analysis of how political power is welded over Filipina nannies within the private spaces of Vancouver households might, initially, seem to have little to do with transnational or national processes of state rule. Indeed, a conventional political geographic understanding of politics as exclusive to spaces such as electoral districts or legislatures would almost certainly disregard such places as important terrains of political power. However, Pratt's study skillfully connected the politics of this local sphere with national and transnational realms of state power. We learn how lack of access to immigrant status places Filipina nannies in Canada in precariously dependent relationships with their employers and allows the latter to exploit nannies' fears of losing the employment (needed to remain in Canada) in order to dictate work hours and duties and to breach human rights, such as rights to privacy, within the home. Negotiations over such seemingly mundane matters as whether a nanny is allowed to cook her favorite dishes from her country of origin are thus revealed as gendered and racialized terrains of struggle over these women's places within national and transnational relations of state formation.

Complementing such advances are feminist geographic studies that challenge scholars to rethink processes of sociospatial polarization in contemporary global cities as processes of differencing in rights to urban space, who does and does not have rights to be in spaces of global finance, for instance. As Kofman (1998) reminded us, the questions of "whose city is this?" and who does and does not count as a citizen have scarcely begun to be addressed. This is not only because gender is still often overlooked as a significant factor in polarization in global cities but also because questions about how different urban spaces are governed, who is entitled to those spaces, and why receive insufficient attention. Yet, as Kofman (1998) pointed out, we cannot hope to understand the forces shaping global cities today without attending as much to politics of struggle over rights to be in urban space as we do to economic forces, such as the rise of informational industries and escalating class polarization as a result of losses in manufacturing jobs and growth of low-paying unskilled service sector ones.

Feminist geographers are then taking up the challenge of examining the politics of inclusion and exclusion in a global world. This is vital in a world in which different peoples' fates are governed by an increasingly intricate, globally intertwined web of institutions through which state power is deployed (e.g., war crime tribunals, the European Union, United Nations, and World Court).

Feminist geographers are expanding our understanding of how and where we are engaging with and contesting prevailing relations of state rule. Recent work on whiteness (Kobayashi and Peake 2000; Peake and Ray 2001) promises to push our geographic understanding of racialized places of citizenship and engagement with state power in exciting directions. Feminist geographers provide a framework for understanding how places that differ from privileged norms of whiteness—poor inner-city neighborhoods, for example—become constructed as negative, other spaces of life within a nation, representationally and literally as, for example, when states direct services to "normal" and valued white neighborhoods. Differencing of citizens in and against the state thus emerges as being as much about privileging some as it is about marginalizing and excluding others. Finally, this research expands our understanding of geographies of engagement with state power and how everyday practices in civil society influence whose rights do and do not count.

Another exciting direction in feminist geography is studies of the sexualization of state power and policy practices and the sociospatial consequences of this. Elder (1998) explored why and how the South African apartheid state targeted white gay male urban enclaves for surveillance as part of a racist and homophobic mode of governance. Drawing on narratives about this urban problem and accounts of policing practices, Elder showed that white gay male neighborhoods were targeted by authorities because of fears that the white heterosexual masculine foundations of apartheid rule were threatened when affluent white men lived in nonheterosexual, nonnuclear family households. Interestingly, officials were generally not concerned about lesbian white women living in urban areas because, under this patriarchal form of state rule, sexually transgressive women were presumed to be less significant participants in political life than men and, as a result of being more residentially dispersed, a less visible gay threat to the prevailing urban order. Citizenship is then, as Bell (1995) put it, sexual; that is, it locates different subjects of state power within relations of sexualized processes of ruling, which privilege citizens who embody valued sexual identities and marginalize those who do not.

As feminist geographers broaden the range of differences—social and spatial—considered in explanations of state power and citizenship to include, for instance, bodily ability and ableness, we can anticipate further exciting advances in our understanding of past and present geographies of state power. Indeed, feminist geographers are already exploring aspects of differencing, such as the uneven provision of services to aboriginal and nonaboriginal urban residents (Peters 2000); gendered, raced, and sexualized ways of governing transnational migration and citizenship (Kofman and England 1997); and the sociospatial conditions under which female citizens are translating local activism into national and international forms of engagements with state power (what Staeheli and Cope [1994] and Fincher and Panelli [2001] referred to as jumping scale). These studies are opening up new horizons in feminist geographies of state power.

Dis-Abling Geographies of State Power and Citizenship

Emerging horizons in feminist geographies of state power also include a small but growing number of studies examining why and how "ableness," a regulatory regime, which values and privileges individuals who are able over those with physical or mental impairments, informs state intervention in our lives. Ableist modes of ruling assume that citizens who embody ableness are better able to fulfill responsibilities of citizenship, including maintaining economic independence from the state and society. As with other forms of differencing in and against the state, being able is so taken for granted as the only valuable way of being in the world that those privileged by it (e.g., enjoying easy access to important spaces in global cities and not having their productivity as workers doubted) are generally oblivious to the advantages they enjoy. To date, much of this literature has raised issues of state power and citizenship only in passing, rather than treating disablement as integral to state governance of society and space. Nonetheless, it is encouraging that issues of disability and citizenship are emerging on feminist geographers' agendas (e.g., R. Butler 1999; Chouinard 2001; Skelton and Valentine 2003). An important challenge for those doing future research is to explore the many ways in which personal experiences of disablement are deeply and inextricably political—the outcomes of real and imagined relations of ruling in which only those who can perform themselves "able-ly" matter. Among the signs that such a politicized feminist geography of disability and chronic illness is beginning to emerge is Brown's (1997) study of the role of AIDS activism in opening up new (and contradictory) spaces of engagement and citizenship in and against the state in Vancouver.

Another key challenge for future feminist geographies of disability and chronic illness is to advance our understanding of why so many disabled women throughout the world continue to experience the state as an oppressive, disempowering terrain of engagement with power. We need to understand, for example, why it is that so many disabled women are condemned to chronic poverty and exclusion even in the most affluent of countries and how these underclass locations diminish disabled women's rights to justice and well-being. The decentered conceptions of the state as a terrain of differencing that feminist geographers have helped to advance promise to enrich our understanding of the outcomes of such situated engagements with state rule (e.g., their human costs) in ways that conventional political geographic frameworks simply could not. What is less clear is whether they will help us to explain why ableness, as a regime of corporeal power, remains such a pervasive basis of negative differencing in relation to states, society, and space.

What Next? Replacing the State?

Feminist geographies of state power have in some ways become as richly diverse as subjects of differencing themselves. They are helping us better understand why some people in our frenetic global capitalist world thrive while so many others suffer. And they are alerting to us to how even our most mundane acts, such as refusing to accommodate a disabled worker, make political differences in how we are diversely subject to state power.

What is less clear is whether the decentered conceptions of state power, which feminist geographers have recently been developing, can help to explain why we are experiencing dramatic changes in relations of ruling today. To what extent, for example, do they help us make sense of why it is that arrogant and indifferent privileged white men govern and cling to power in regions such as the province of Ontario, Canada? Questions like these are crying out for answers, given the openly corrupt and cynically manipulative practices in which representatives of such governments are engaging. In the Ontario case these practices include blatantly misspending public funds on television advertisements that support conservative rule by misrepresenting government policies and practices to the public, excluding most citizens and particularly disadvantaged groups such as disabled people from policy consultation. At the same time, these representatives are catering to the corporate business elite and providing tax breaks to the well-to-do and so drastically cutting government social support to vulnerable people who need assistance (e.g., groups such as psychiatric survivors) that they are driven to desperate measures, including suicide. Similarly, we need to better understand why it is that widespread local experiments in "direct democracy" in Brazil recently translated into a left-wing national government and how disadvantaged groups, such as women, contributed to this very significant change in the nation-state. Theories that recenter the causal dynamics of such transformations in the state may help us explain such geographically uneven transformations in states and relations of ruling and, in doing so, help those of us fighting neoliberal corporate modes of governance in other parts of the world do so more effectively. Feminist geographies of the state have certainly been enriched by the decentered perspectives on the state that I discussed in this chapter. But pressing questions about transformations in states at local through global scales, such as those noted previously, suggest that it is time to develop theoretical perspectives on the state that are simultaneously centered and decentered: concerned with subjection to state power in diverse public and private spaces of life but also helpful in explaining why and how it is that we are witnessing the development of more exclusionary, ruthless, and unaccountable states—locally, nationally, and transnationally—in so many places in the world today.

Without such nonbinary feminist theories of the state—theories that can help us to pinpoint the causes of gendered and other transformations in the state and relations of ruling as well as the implications of these for diverse peoples' lives—it is difficult to know where to begin to explain the rapidly changing geographies of state power and rule in which women, children, and men are enmeshed in the world today. And one wonders whether it is more than coincidental that precisely at the time feminist and other critical scholars began to turn their gazes away from the state, reactionary forces were claiming the state and state power as their own for harsh, corrupt, neoliberal modes of ruling our lives. Whatever the potential connections between such shifts in feminist and radical theories of the state and transformations in geographies of state rule, "taking back the state" theoretically and politically seems likely to be as important for feminist politics as it appears to be for making sense of the complex politics of our global world. There are signs that feminist scholars and activists are taking these possibilities increasingly seriously. Influential feminist scholars concerned with issues such as the implications of globalization and work for women are turning their attention toward the state once again (Alexander and Mohanty 1997). Feminist and radical geographers also are voicing renewed interest in understanding state formation and relations of ruling. Katharyne Mitchell et al. (2003) called for conceptions of the state not as an abstract, relatively autonomous realm of power in global capitalism but, rather, as a socially and spatially diffuse and uneven set of relations and practices materialized through people's engagements with the state in diverse spaces of everyday life. The key challenge, they argued, is to discover why and how norms and practices of state rule are reproduced or disrupted as people negotiate their relations with the state through everyday practices in the places they work and live. Understanding why people live out their relations with the state in particular ways and spaces of everyday life is undoubtedly important, particularly when we acknowledge how little influence most people have over state intervention in their lives at local through transnational scales. What is less clear is how such feminist, Marxist, and poststructural theories of the state will advance our understanding of why the state is transforming our lives through harsh, neoliberal relations and practices of ruling. If we are to challenge these relations and build a more humane, inclusive, and tolerant world, we will need causal theories of the state that help to explain why sustaining neoliberal political cultures is central to life under global capitalism and the implications this has for understanding state intervention, in various forms, in local and global political economies. This will, in turn, necessitate that we employ theories of the state that allow us to see beyond differences in subjection to state power to why and how such differences are reproductive of particular state formations locally and globally. I am not calling, of course, for abstract theories of the state divorced from the messy realities of engagements in its relations and practices in place. What I am suggesting is the need for theories of state power that can help us grasp not only how the state is lived in places but also what this tells us about why contemporary states are ruling most people's lives in diverse but nonetheless harsh, disempowering ways. In a postmodern age in which we are encouraged to think about ourselves and our places in the world in highly individualistic and divisive ways, developing feminist theories that can help us understand both why we must and how we can work together to challenge the oppressive practices of neoliberal states just might be one of the most radically empowering things we ever do.

17
Framing Feminist Claims for Urban Citizenship

GERDA R. WEKERLE

There has been a resurgence of interest in the local state, as demonstrated by the proliferation of recent texts on the global city (Sassen 1998), neoliberal urbanism (Brenner and Theodore 2002), the politics of scale (Swyngedouw 1997; Marston 2000), urban politics and the local state (Kirby 1993; Magnusson 1996), urban citizenship (Isin 2002; Holston 1999), and urban movements (Hamel et al. 2000). In these diverse literatures, scholars have begun to direct their attention to the cracks in the totalizing narrative of globalization and to focus on themes of civil society, emancipatory politics, the politics of place, and the mobilization of local struggles and transnational networks. Gender and the struggles of women, however, are largely absent in these discussions. Yet in cities of the North and South, women's experiences over the past thirty or so years provide us with cases of how urban citizens have mobilized movements to meet the needs of everyday life in response to neoliberal restructuring and structural adjustment, how they have created spaces within the local state for feminist policies, and how they have forged transnational networks to link movements in a global civil society.

In this chapter I start by discussing the concept of the local state and current issues that emerge in the restructuring of governance under neoliberalism. I then discuss the diverse ways in which women, as citizens, have made claims on the local state over the past thirty years. In these two sections I present a review of some of the arguments about the local state and citizenship that I use to provide a context for understanding how citizens, and women citizens in particular, mobilize to effect political and social change. In the third section I outline how the concept of social movement frames might be useful in understanding the multiple and shifting strategies and points of engagement between women's groups and the local state. Invoking a diversity of overlapping identities of race, class, sexuality, and gender, women have engaged three frames based on concepts of citizenship that women's urban movements and activists have used to forward their claims: rights to livelihood and resources, rights to representation and democratic participation, and alternative and expanded concepts of citizenship that articulate an approach to radical democracy

(Mouffe 1993). In making these claims, women's movements have taken stances from outside the local state that are oppositional, they have attempted to create policy change through electoral politics and women's initiatives located within the structures of the local state, and, finally, women's justice claims have been articulated through a mobilized civil society, engaged in democratic practices. Many, though by no means all, of the literature I review draws from case studies in the United States, United Kingdom, and Canada. These examples provide further grounding and complement the examples discussed in several other chapters of this book (see especially Cope, Fincher, Chouinard, and Fairhurst et al.).

The Local State and the Restructuring of Urban Governance

Definitions of the local state vary considerably. Cockburn (1977), for example, never explicitly defined the local state but referred to British local authorities as the local state. Some urban theorists (e.g., Dear 1981) have equated any level of subnational government with the local state. A recent book on urban governance defines the local state as "the local government organizations that interact with the voluntary and private sectors for the purpose of urban governance. The two basic components of the local state are municipal government and special purpose bodies" (K. Graham et al. 1998, 289). Given these varied definitions, how can we approach the local state?

Cockburn (1977) initially introduced the concept of the local state in her analysis of the restructuring of local government under conditions of urban fiscal crises in the United Kingdom in the mid-1970s. She presented a view of the local state that is multidimensional, linking production and reproduction, state, economy, and civil society. She emphasized the role of the local state in capitalist reproduction as providing state services and employment. In so doing, she demonstrated that the local state is centrally involved in reproducing the labor force through its responsibilities for housing, public health, education, and related services. She argued that through this role, the local state is the new terrain of class and gender struggles, and she outlined collective actions around provision and access to services, especially on the part of women. She also examined several issues, including the relationship between councillors, particularly those on the Left, and their engagement with urban movements; the radicalization of municipal staff and the conditions under which they make common cause with poor clients, using their insider knowledge against urban authorities; and the local state as employer, particularly of women, engaged in cutbacks and the deskilling of jobs.

Other theorists have tried to substantially expand the theoretical terrain of the local state. Kirby (1997) argued that the predispositions of urban theorists have, in the past, been an impediment to viewing the local state as an important political site. Urban theorists, according to Kirby, often are opposed to localism as a site of "self-interest, bigotry and intolerance." Instead, Kirby (1997, 35) argued, "The local state has both analytical power and social meaning as a locus of political expression; as Hegel indicated, it is both part of the state and of civil society." Thus, the local state occupies a place between the state, economy, and civil society; it is where civil society and the state meet. Similarly, Magnusson (1996)—who tends to interchange the municipality and the local state—argued that the municipality is at a boundary between state and civil society and the space of everyday life. He argued that the local state is a focus for an alternative political space, enabling different movements to come together and develop new alternative practices (Magnusson 1996; see also Fincher 2004 [this volume]).

Urban theorists also have refocused on the local in discussions of the politics of scale. Veering away from associating the local state with the bottom of a hierarchy of scales or as one end of the bimodal local-global, theorists have suggested that scale is socially and politically constructed. Swyngedouw (1997, 137) coined the term "glocal" to suggest that "the local and the global are mutually constituted." According to Neil Smith (1993), movements and economic actors "jump scales" in a globalized world. This suggests that the local state can no longer be seen as a static site for local government, as the grounded anchor for the global, but must be viewed as a potentially more dynamic actor, with the potential to jump scales and engage in glocal actions.

From a feminist geography perspective, Marston (2000) argued that we must reconceptualize scale and the local state. Marston noted that scale is important to the strategies chosen by social movements and state actors and wrote, "Social movements have multiple scales of opportunity for mobilization, as do institutional political actors. The state, at different scales, enables or constrains these opportunities based on the particulars of the historical moment in which social movements emerge" (2000, 224). She pointed out that the literature on the social construction of scale focuses primarily on production and capitalist domination and pays less attention to social reproduction and consumption, the household scale, or gender, race, and class domination. A more complete understanding of the local state, then, needs to better situate the state within a fuller range of scales than has been common.

Recognizing the importance of scale (though not necessarily the importance of Marston's expanded notion of scale), a new literature is emerging that focuses on the strategic role of cities in the neoliberal restructuring of political and economic space (see Brenner and Theodore 2002 for a review). Within this literature is a concern for the restructuring of urban governance and its implications for local democracy. The argument is that neoliberal restructuring forces the replacement of local government by local governance, specifically the replacement of local government structures and procedures with a more fragmented system, including appointed special purpose bodies, marketization of public services, and the introduction of a consumer model for the delivery of local services. Several authors (Andrew and Goldsmith 1998; Clarke 1993) have argued that the restructuring of urban governance subverts local democracy and contributes to the political and economic exclusion of marginalized communities.

In much of the recent literature on the local state, including the literature on neoliberal restructuring, gender is absent. One of the most notable exceptions is a paper by Chouinard (1996; see also 2004 [this volume]) in which she examined how dynamic relationships between multiple levels of the local state are constructed through class and gender, arguing, "State subjects actively participate in the creation of particular manifestations and representations of the local state in their lives and, in doing so, help to create particular forms and sites of engagement with state agencies" (1996, 1486). With detailed case studies of the interactions between the local state and a women's legal clinic and housing cooperative, Chouinard suggested a process in which the local state is a site of political struggles over agendas and discourses on the part of women's movements, where outcomes change over time and may include incorporation, co-optation, neutralization, marginalization, and rejection. She suggested that not only the policies and practices of the local state but also the political strategies and practices of women's movements actively engaged with the state must be addressed. Her argument demonstrates the importance of thinking about the ways in which women, and those social movements in which women play large roles, reconceptualize the local state, citizenship, and political subjectivity.

The Local State and the Construction of Citizenship

Feminist theorists have argued that the concept of citizenship is fragmented, culturally constituted, and actively constructed. For Yuval-Davis (1997) citizenship means full membership in a community; such a membership is not just political but multilayered and located in multiple spheres. Rather than endorsing a single, abstract idea of citizenship in which all citizens are the same, feminist theorists have argued for a version of pluralistic citizenship that uses differences "both to analyze unequal power relations that impede an inclusive politics of diversity and to give voice to those who are usually underrepresented" (Savarsy and Siim 1994, 254). This notion of a pluralistic citizenship acknowledges several elements of women's citizenship: that women participate in a variety of arenas in public life, the diversity of identities, interests, and ideologies that exist within the category "women," the number of roles and identities that each woman has, and the number of formal levels within political institutions and organizations in which women participate (Savarsy and Siim 1994).

Recognizing the ways in which citizenship is a concept that extends beyond the state, various authors have connected attempts to reinvent citizenship to a revival of civil society (Friedmann 1998; Magnusson 1996). The discourse of civil society, according to Friedmann (1998, 21), introduces several possibilities for action as citizens, including resistance, participatory democracy, social citizenship, and justice. According to these authors, social movements that operate at the intersections of civil society and the local state actively construct citizenship by laying claim to new political spaces (Magnusson 1996). For example, Holston (1999) coined the term "spaces of insurgent citizenship" to describe how urban movements introduce into the city new identities and practices that disturb the status quo. He posited "the possibility of multiple citizenships based on the local, regional and transnational affiliations that aggregate in contemporary urban experience" (Holston 1999, 169). This includes the protests, riots, and campaigns that lesbian, gay, and transgendered citizens have used to push at the limits of the private and public spaces of sexual citizenship (Bell 1995). It also includes poor people's struggles, particularly those of women's urban movements, for rights and entitlements obtained through access to the resources of the state, such as low-cost housing, affordable child care, mass transit, and the cleanup of toxic and polluted neighborhoods. Isin (2002, 265) and others argued that the ways these urban problems are transformed into claims to citizenship are new because they make rights claims based on lived experience.

By explicitly including lived experience as a basis for the development of political subjectivities and citizenship claims, new ways of understanding citizenship are identified. These new forms of citizenship are not defined purely by legal standings but are shaped by—and to some extent challenge— norms and expectations of citizenship and of the ideal citizen. Some geographers, for example, have begun to theorize the relationship between sexualities and the state and to articulate the various dimensions of sexual citizenship, including rights to public space, legal rights, and the rights of lesbian, gay, and transgendered citizens in the context of international migration (Bell 1995; Brown 1995; Binnie and Valentine 1999; Bell and Binnie 2000). Bell (1995, 150) suggested that claims of sexual citizenship are simultaneously a tactic of survival and sites of resistance that "challenge the transparent and hegemonic geography of 'citizenship.'"

Many feminists hope to use the new spaces and forms of insurgent citizenship to build a commitment to the politics of diversity and to address structural transformations in the world political economy that deprive people of basic survival needs (Lister 1997). K. B. Jones (1994, 269), for example, described this commitment as the desire "to situate citizenship as civic-minded world transformation within the context of justice, responsibility and care." Sevenhuijsen (1998, vi) argued that this concept of citizenship should incorporate "a new approach to justice morality and politics." To do this, she suggested locating the ethics of care within notions of citizenship, as this takes the dual stance of breaking down patterns of domination associated with caring activities and also of transforming systems of instrumental rationality. The ethics of care, in this sense, are fully political.

The commitment to linking social needs to democracy has been a hallmark of women's activism and understanding of the rights of citizenship. Temma Kaplan (1997, 1) argued, "All over the globe women have been asserting collective rights to protect their children against pollution, disease, and homelessness. Not content merely to fight for improvements in the lives of their families and communities, many of these women justify their action by making broad claims about human needs and rights according to an interpretation of justice that they themselves are developing through their actions." After reviewing the activism of grassroots women's groups, Kaplan (1997, 7) concluded that they "have attempted, through moral claims for justice and human rights, to transform politics in far more democratic directions than ever seemed possible. . . . These women move back and forth between specific requirements for survival and principled demands for general goals such as justice. . . . By justice, they often mean more balanced behavior, an end to violence and equal distribution of social necessities." It is to women's role in movements linking social needs, citizenship, and the local state that I now turn.

Women, Social Movements, and the Local State

Women are actively engaged in asserting and renegotiating their rights as urban citizens whose standpoint and gendered experiences have been excluded and denied by the decision makers, politicians, and corporations that shape cities. Women's claims for urban citizenship are framed on their own behalf as gendered subjects, in their roles as mothers and as members and guardians of their communities. Increasingly, in cities of the industrialized North as in cities of the South, women's acts of resistance challenge globalization, which has increased women's and their family's unemployment, poverty, homelessness, and hunger. Women's urban movements are not a unitary phenomenon; they are diverse and shifting. Mobilizations are based on women's multiple identities—identities that are mutable rather than fixed (see also Fairhurst et al. 2004 [this volume]).

In the context of the local state, women's movements have strategically used three overlapping, and often simultaneous, collective action frames[1] to make claims on and in the local state. Within cities, women have been engaged in the creation of new forms of political action through informal politics in everyday struggles for survival and leadership in community-based protests, in struggles to increase women's access to public resources and participation in urban governance, and through coalitions and networks for global and urban justice. Their claims to citizenship and rights have been framed as rights to livelihood, space, and belonging; rights to representation and participation; and rights to the city based on an ethic of care and justice.

Frame One: Women's Urban Movements' Claims to Livelihood and Belonging

Instead of dismissing the politics of daily life, participants in women's urban movements have given it a high priority (see Cope 2004 [this volume]). The reasons for this include the importance of the material conditions of daily life—including livelihood—for social reproduction but also for the ways in which a politics of daily life can reshape ideas of social democracy. As Rowbotham and Linkogle (2001, 5) argued, "Movements around livelihood can carry ideas of possibilities beyond the known and contain both practical and transformational elements." In the same spirit, Gilbert (1999, 106) argued, "Bringing together feminist understandings of identity, community and place provides the basis for a progressive politics based, in part, on place-based communities to challenge power relations operating at a variety of scales in which growth machines are embedded."

For example, Susser's (1982) study of working-class women in Greenpoint-Williamsburg, New York, portrayed the women as engaged in community caring and neighborhood organizing. Because of cutbacks to service by the city of New York, they lobbied the state to meet its responsibilities. Centered on the neighborhood, women took on leadership roles and mobilized neighbors and kin in block associations, demonstrations, and dealings with politicians. Similarly, Feldman and Stall (1994) documented how African American women living in Chicago public housing extended their domestic role to community organizing in order to transform their housing environment. However, these women also jumped from the scale of home to the city when they opposed stadium construction by lobbying the legislature and waging a lawsuit against the city (Feldman and Stall 1994). This transition from the politics of daily life to lobbying or seeking formal political representation also is documented by Hardy-Fanta's (1993) study of Latina women's mobilizations in Boston, which challenges the portrayal of women's place-based urban activism as limited to the microscale. This pattern is repeated in Gilbert's (1999) study of poor racialized minority women in Worcester, Massachusetts. Women's activism to better their daily lives and economic and political marginalization was sometimes neighborhood based but also used citywide organizing focused on housing, transportation, and employment. Even women with extremely limited resources have successfully mobilized and gained support from the local state. In downtown Los Angeles, Dora Alicia Alarcon started the Street Vendors Association in the mid-1980s to lobby the city to legalize street vending (Pincetl 1994). With two hundred members—70 percent of them Latina women, many of whom were undocumented migrants—the association obtained city council support in 1993 for legalized vending in some areas.

There are some parallels between women's survival politics in U.S. cities and women's popular mobilizations in Latin American cities. In a recent book on women's resistance to globalization, Rowbotham and Linkogle (2001) argued that women in the South have been preoccupied with struggles around livelihood. So, for example, Jacquette (1994) described the growth of women's popular organizations in rapidly expanding cities since the 1980s in response to the economic crisis and cuts in social safety nets. In Peru and Chile militant mothers developed neighborhood organizations to provide communal kitchens,[2] health care, and child care. In Lima women engaged in collective action to demand state provision and resources to meet neighborhood needs. According to Jelin (1990), mothers' clubs and collective kitchens represent a new form of female organization and public activity by forcing political recognition of the public face of reproduction. Over time, some of these initiatives in civil society have been taken over as functions of the local state; an example is Lima's Glass of Milk program, which was developed by grassroots women's organizations.

Although many women's urban movements have focused on livelihood, others have focused on the environments and communities in which families live and children are raised. Significantly, these movements are cast not just as environmental movements but also as justice movements that take a goal of working to ensure safe communities in which all residents can participate and live without putting their health and lives in jeopardy. According to Krauss (1993), in the 1980s women of color in U.S. cities were politicized in response to concrete dangers to communities and health. Challenging the siting of waste and polluting industries in neighborhoods with a preponderance of poor people and people of color, women organized in communities like East Los Angeles (Pardo 1998). Krauss (1993, 248) argued that these protests were framed as "part of work mothers do" and that they developed "an environmental discourse that is mediated by subjective experience and interpretations. It is rooted in the political truths women construct out of their identities as housewives, mothers and members of communities, racial and ethnic groups." Naples (1998b) argued for the centrality of motherhood as a standpoint for community activists. She argued that this cannot be separated from race, class, and gender identities. According to Naples, working-class women and women of color often are politicized through caring for their families, and this in turn reshapes their gendered identities and political subjectivity.

Feminists also organized in cities to make claims on the local state for resources that ensured the well-being of their families; they demanded funding for battered women's shelters, rape crisis centers, violence against women initiatives, and child care (Flammang 1997; Reinelt 1995; Wekerle 1999, 2000). An understudied topic is the ways in which lesbian feminists formed the backbone of the feminist service structure that developed in larger cities and the volunteer labor they provided for feminist services after cutbacks in state funding. Verta Taylor and Leila Rupp (1993) have documented this form of lesbian feminist activism in Columbus, Ohio.

Frame Two: Urban Citizenship as Democratic Participation

Women's claims on the local state for democratic participation have taken two forms: formal political representation—particularly attempts to get feminists and women's community activists elected to local government—and organizing to gain space within the local state for women's units in order to obtain better access to local state employment, funding for women's projects, and greater participation in policy making. These women's initiatives in the local state, which emerged in the United Kingdom, Germany, and North American cities about twenty years ago, provide case examples of how the local state and social movements are mutually constituted. They offer details on how shifts in political opportunity structures created spaces within the local state for women's movements and, conversely, how these movements constructed the local state. This is particularly important for women. As Marston (1995, 195) pointed out, "Local governance restructures the rights and opportunities of citizens, particularly with respect to the question of who governs at the local level." Local government has been identified as the point of entry for women into the formal political arena and where women have made the most gains. Despite this belief in the importance of political participation, there remain deep questions about the political implications and utility of strategies to elect women and to install women's commissions, as they may carry the tendency to essentialize women's interests.

Formal Political Representation Secor (2004 [this volume]) demonstrated the great strides that have been made in the election of women and feminists to national positions in many countries. This success also is seen at the local level; here I focus primarily on elections within Canada, the United States, and the United Kingdom. In Canada, the number of women elected to political office at the municipal level is growing much faster than at either the federal or the provincial levels (Maille 1997, 54). In the ten largest Canadian cities in 1992, women held an average of 31 percent of all council seats (Sharpe 1994, 207).[3]

In the United States women held 19 percent of all local council seats in 1991, with a higher percentage in urban areas. There also has been a marked increase in the number of Latinas serving in city government and an increase in African American women elected to local office. In 1993, 18 percent of all mayors in the United States were women; 175 women were mayors of cities with populations greater than thirty thousand (McManus and Bullock 1995). In some cities, including Seattle, Washington, and Minneapolis, women have formed the majority of city councillors in recent years.

The significance of women's electoral success is sometimes argued to be in the possibility that they will forward feminist or women-friendly agendas. In one of the few empirical studies of this topic, Boles (1991, 44) argued that women bring a different viewpoint to policy making. In a comparison of male and female local councilors in Milwaukee, Wisconsin, Boles (2001, 72) found that women took a leadership role in developing policies and programs related to day care, domestic violence, and sexual assault. These local women officials often played an advocacy role for women in the civic bureaucracy. A paradox, however, is that women are more likely to be elected at the local level, yet these women, at least in the United States, have the lowest level of feminist consciousness of all elected officials (Boles 2001).

Women's Commissions and Initiatives There have been ongoing attempts to institutionalize feminist policy agendas and women's participation in policy decisions within the structure of the local state. This has been dubbed the "femocrat strategy," borrowing from the term coined by

Australian feminists to describe feminists employed as administrators and bureaucrats advocating gender equality programs within the national state (H. Eisenstein 1991; Watson 1990; Yeatman 1990). In what follows I again focus my remarks on gender initiatives within Northern, industrialized countries, even though these initiatives have been instituted elsewhere, particularly in Latin America.

Much of the feminist literature on women and the local state has focused on a brief period of time in the 1980s when local authorities in Britain created women's committees to implement equal opportunity policies (Goss 1984; Halford 1989; Wainwright 1989; Brownill and Halford 1990; Little 1994). As several authors have noted, this was a period in the United Kingdom when community-based movements allied with left-controlled local councils to mobilize opposition to the central conservative government over restructuring of the welfare state. The initial establishment of formal women's initiatives in local authorities was the result of a complex interplay between local political cultures and the strength and organization of local feminist political organizing (Brownill and Halford 1990).

For a time, these commissions often were quite successful in introducing policy initiatives related to family, welfare, and health issues, as well as policies that were specific to women; many of these initiatives acted on the livelihood issues raised by women's urban movements described previously. But the success of these initiatives is in doubt. Focusing on the gender system of London, Abrar et al. (1998) concluded that wider political and economic changes shaped the political environment of the local state in such a way that social movements, particularly feminist movements, had reduced political opportunities to influence policy. A critical element in this shift was the restructuring of local authority governance. This included more appointed boards and offices, contracting out and privatization of public services, all of which could bypass equal opportunity legislation. Within local authorities, the shift to more part-time workers reduced women's jobs and incomes more than men's (Abrar et al. 1998, 154). By the mid-1990s the number of women's committees in U.K. local authorities had declined and many were downgraded or restructured as generic equal opportunity programs (Little 1994).[4]

Questioning the Effects of Women's Participation Among feminist scholars, there is a tendency to dismiss these municipal feminist initiatives as short-lived and elitist. This may be too harsh. These initiatives created an opening for women in the local state and provided critical funding for women's programs and projects. Abrar et al. (1998) concluded that women's committees left an institutional residue of gender equality policies and created an institutional base for feminist politicians and administrators. These women's initiatives within the structure of the local state also contribute examples of the institutionalization of social movement agendas and of a relationship between movement and local state that is mutually constituted. Currently, gender policies in local states are being further transformed. A recent study (Greed et al. 2002) on the mainstreaming of gender policies in British local authorities found that these are now being implemented in response to European Union equal opportunity legislation and as a condition for receiving European Union funding for regional regeneration projects. In this way, the regional scale is influencing the restructuring of local governance and its gendered policies.

Furthermore, even though women's local state initiatives may be declining in one country, they may be robust in another. In Germany the first Affirmative Action Office for city government was opened in Cologne in 1982, followed by one in Hamburg in 1984. In 1989 there were six hundred women's affairs offices in German cities and towns (Ferree 1995). Particularly in cities with Social Democrat local governments, including Frankfurt, Hamburg, and Berlin, women's offices have become well established; they are a bridge between the autonomous women's movement and the local state. Regionally, the European Union also has focused more attention on women and cities through the European Charter for Women in the City (European Commission 1994). Regional funding from the Organization for Economic Cooperation and Development and the European Union has been provided for women's projects in countries throughout Europe and to women's groups within nation-states that are less supportive of gender policies. These regional initiatives also have supported the formation of networks and information sharing among women and city projects transnationally (Eurofem-Gender and Human Settlements 1995, 1996, 1998; Organization for Economic Cooperation and Development 1995).

The creation of women's commissions, committees, and offices in the local state is not the focus of women's mobilizations today. Since these were created more than twenty years ago, feminist theorists and activists have rethought and challenged the very concept of representing women's interests. The conception of women's interests forwarded by feminist activist organizations was challenged by nonwhite, non-middle-class, nonheterosexual women who disputed the power of women in elite positions within the state to represent all women's interests. The local state also rethought its commitment to women's committees as it became subject to new claims for democratic representation and resources framed in terms of race, class, sexuality, and disability issues (Little 1994).

Feminist theorists also critiqued the political project of increasing women's representation as elected local officials, arguing that it presupposes women have interests best represented by other women (Squires 1999, 173) and that women in office will support what might be construed as women-friendly policies. Feminist scholars argued for the need to address the diverse—and often conflicting—interests of women; women, by virtue of being women, cannot be assumed to represent the gendered interests of all women. Feminists argue that identities are constructed and plural and that to focus on a singular female identity ignores significant differences among women (Squires 1999, 176). According to this argument, the very notion of women's groups supporting the election of women to public office or establishing women's units in the local state may be construed as exclusionary and reifying difference.

Instead, feminist scholars argue that gender cannot be isolated from race, class, nationality, sexuality, or other identities and that women often are situated in multiple communities. According to feminist political scientist Phillips (1996, 253), the feminist policy process must be based on a politics in which participation "includes some measure of power. The mode of representation under a politics of difference shifts from representation by elites, whether elected, state, or interest group elites, to direct representation and participation by people who personally share in the experiences of the social and cultural groups for whom they claim to speak." She concluded, "Through such politics, emphasis is being shifted from *what* is being claimed to *how* and by *whom* claims are made" (Phillips 1996, 254). This suggests radically altered and more pluralistic democratic practices and models of political inclusion.

Frame Three: Rights to the City—Inclusion and Justice

As a result of the restructuring of the local state under neoliberalism, spaces for women within and in relation to the local state have shrunk. Women's units within local government and women's advocacy groups in civil society were labeled as "special interests" and not representative of key community or public interests. In these ways, women's initiatives—which had taken decades to institutionalize into city programs, policies, funding arrangements, and legislation— were deinstitutionalized and tossed back into civil society, again largely dependent on volunteer labor and charitable donations. As Magnusson (1996, 144) pointed out, the new focus on public-private partnerships creates favorable conditions for business; the emphasis on the city as site for investment disempowers local government and ignores disadvantaged groups and popular resistance.

The new focus on urban growth, downtown redevelopment, and gentrification embodies specific forms of masculinity and domination. The militarization and privatization of public space contrast with women's claims for rights to the city, especially its public spaces. As Neil Smith (1996, 211) said, "More than anything the revanchist city expresses a race/class/gender terror felt by middle- and ruling-class whites . . . [who] face the threat of women, minority and immigrant groups as powerful urban actors."

Losing state funding and being labeled as special interests have not made women's urban movements disappear. After more than a decade of working with and through the local state, women's organizations have learned how the system works, and they have developed networks within the state and across movements. Although outsiders again, women's movements now include former insiders. These are the "citizen experts," capable not only of critiquing government policies but also of developing alternative policies and mobilizing communities. They form the backbone of an invigorated and increasingly mobilized civil society that links labor, antiracist movements, women's movements, gay and lesbian movements, environmental movements, and the antiglobalization movement.

Within civil society, citizen mobilization has become more visible and widespread, challenging global economic restructuring and its localized impacts. Women are often the key agents in organizing citywide and national food security projects and coalitions (Field 1999). Women are establishing urban community gardens and land trusts and mobilizing legal challenges and direct action when cities attempt to sell these sites for development, as happened in New York City in 2000. Grassroots women of color and working-class women continue to mobilize against transnational polluters that dump wastes and pollute rivers. These women challenge expert knowledge and the state, drawing on women's local knowledges and community networks to mobilize opposition and generate alternatives. On another front, public sector workers in female-dominated professions, especially teachers, nurses, and public servants, have engaged in strikes to protest low salaries and deterioration of working conditions. At the same time, they are publicizing the decline of public services. Feminist researchers have found, in cities in the North and in the South, that women often take on the role of community guardians, practicing an ethic of care, when the survival of families and communities are threatened. There are new variations on this theme. For example, public interest advocacy groups led by women, such as Parents for Education in Ontario, have emerged to do research and public education on the implications of cutbacks in public sector funding and school voucher programs. This group exemplifies a new trend: with the downsizing of the public sector, civil society has become a primary source of policy documents and alternative proposals to solve current urban problems.

Antipoverty groups have challenged work-for-welfare legislation, pushed for municipal living wage laws, and created food security coalitions to deal with increasing hunger in U.S. and Canadian cities. In many cases these movements are not labeled feminist or women's movements, even though women are often the founders or leaders and the core membership. In addition, there is a focus on developing collective strength through coalitions among labor, antipoverty, and women's movements (Naples 1998b). Although many of these mobilizations are directed at calling attention to and changing local conditions, there are also attempts to link local injustices to the wider issues of globalization and economic restructuring that affect women worldwide.

Women also continue to build transnational networks that link local and global activism. Since the first UN Conference on Women in 1975, and at an accelerating pace in the 1990s, women in the North and South have used international conferences to forge transnational networks and campaigns. UN agreements on human rights have been used to call national and local states to account for their infringement of international agreements due to cutbacks in social welfare (Wekerle 2000). Antiglobalization movements and protests in Seattle, Washington, Quebec, and other parts of the world have created new transnational networks linked with local activism. For example, in Canada, young women of color have formed a new organization, Colours of Resistance, with chapters and affiliated groups in cities across North America (see http://colours.mahost.org). They ask, What does it take to create a multiracial, antiracist movement for global justice and against global capitalism? This organization, and others that developed out of the antiglobalization movement, focus on the creation of a socially responsible economy and the well-being of people and the planet. Part of this agenda is the fostering of local democracy and a focus on antiracist organizing, the needs of immigrant and refugee women in cities, and the impacts of police brutality and state repression.

In her elaboration of a concept of radical democracy, Mouffe (1993) argued for the creation of new subject positions that would not only link but also develop a democratic equivalence between anticapitalist, antiracist, and antisexist struggles. According to Mouffe (1993, 19), "It is only under these circumstances that struggles against power become truly democratic." In seeking to simultaneously address gender, race, and class domination, both in relationships with the local state and in practices within and across movements, women urban activists have sought to address issues of overlapping identities and shifting concepts of a pluralistic citizenship within a politics of place. At the same time, they have sought to link movements rooted in the local state with the transnational networks for social justice. Critical development scholar Appadurai (2001) forwarded a framework that simultaneously addresses urban movements, restructuring governance, democracy, and place. He challenged us to think of place-based movements as exercises in deep democracy, arguing that the emergence of new forms of "governmentality from below" challenges the totalizing globalization narrative and that transnational advocacy networks of the urban poor reflect "new horizontal modes for articulating the deep democratic politics of the locality" (Appadurai 2001, 26). In Mumbai, India—where Appadurai studied poor women's activism around access to housing, credit, sanitation, and the informal economy—and in cities of the North, women have engaged with the local state for resources and participation and created alternative community structures to support their livelihoods and international networks focused on social justice.

Conclusions

Although the topic of women and the local state has not had a high degree of visibility in the feminist geography, political geography, or urban geography literatures, the case studies that have accumulated on women's community-based activism, the institutionalization of feminist policies within the local state, and women's coalition building and translocal networks provide a very rich body of work that can inform current debates on urban citizenship, the politics of scale and place, social movements and their relationships with the local state, and the shifting terrains of struggle against globalization and neoliberal urbanism within civil society. In this review I do not suggest that the frames women's groups and urban movements have used have been sequential or mutually exclusive; often these frames are used simultaneously. I do suggest, however, that some feminist groups turned their attention to the scale of the local state when restructuring of the national welfare state closed down political opportunities. As the local state was subjected to neoliberal restructuring, women's groups turned to the regional, international, and global scales and mobilized through translocal networks. If we examine women's community activism closely, we also discern that even very localized movements often jump scales to citywide, statewide, or national initiatives as activists gain political experience and political opportunities. Within a globalized world and talk of the potential emergence of a global civil society, a focus on women and the local state may seem anachronistic. However, with the current focus on "reasserting the power of the local" (Cox 1997), governance from below, and the local state as the site of critical urban conflicts (Keil 1998), perhaps feminist scholars should not be too quick to dismiss this body of work. Women's claims for urban citizenship, the urban movements that frame these claims, and the new forms of governmentality that emerge all contribute to urban theory and to feminist imaginaries of urban alternatives.

Notes

1. Gamson (1995, 89) defined collective action frames as "action-oriented sets of beliefs and meanings that inspire and legitimate social movement activities and campaigns." Frames are powerful when they reflect existing culture, direct action, organize discourse, and construct meaning, according to social movement scholar Tarrow (1998, 21).
2. Community kitchens, inspired by Latin American women's movements, have been started in Toronto and Montreal. Small groups of women buy food in bulk, cook it collectively, and share their knowledge. Collective kitchens also may be linked to alternative food systems that bypass agrobusiness and supermarket chains.
3. Most recently, there has been a decline in the number of women city councillors in Canadian cities. In response, the Federation of Canadian Municipalities has established a Taskforce on Issues for Canadian Women in Municipal Government to promote the participation of women and also has funded a project to develop a tool kit of gender-inclusive public participation tools for municipal governments and women's groups.
4. In the United States in 1994, there were 265 local women's commissions, most of them set up as advisory bodies to county executives, boards of supervisors, or mayors. In Canada only six cities have had Status of Women Committees within local government, although at least eight cities have had women's advisors or targeted taskforces on women's issues (Wekerle 1997).

18
Feminizing Electoral Geography

ANNA J. SECOR

The geography of elections has figured prominently in political geography since the 1970s (Taylor and Johnston 1979). Indeed, a survey of the journal *Political Geography* shows that between 1982 and 1996, 12 percent of all articles published were specifically on voting and political parties (Waterman 1998). Topics in electoral geography have included geographies of representation and the effect of place on political behavior. Research has focused on practices of malapportionment, gerrymandering, pork barrel politics, and electoral reform (Morrill 1976; Archer and Shelley 1986) as well as debates about the neighborhood effect and the influence of place on voting and political activities (Cox 1983; Agnew 1987; Johnston 1991).

More generally, studies of electoral geography have explored how political cleavages and the social bases of geographies of voting have been translated into political power. Such studies have frequently taken as a starting point the framework put forward by Lipset and Rokkan (1967), who argued that the structure of European party systems derived from patterns of social cleavages in the nineteenth and early twentieth centuries and the effects of national and industrial revolutions on long-standing territorial and economic divisions. After Taylor and Johnston (1979) introduced this model to political geography, electoral geographers have looked at how social cleavages and geographies of party support interact to produce particular constellations of power and support in a society (Peake 1984; Johnston et al. 1990; O'Loughlin et al. 1994; Flint 1998; Secor 2001). In that political parties act to pursue policies that promote particular interests in the pursuit of capital accumulation—"the politics of power"—but also must put together broader packages of policies that are designed to appeal to voters—"the politics of support"—every election can be seen as a negotiation between these two imperatives and their associated processes (Taylor and Flint 2000). Place, political behavior, and the ways in which they shape one another have thus been central to frameworks of electoral geography, which also have extended to world-systems analyses of how electoral politics are shaped by economic inequality at the global scale (Taylor 1990).

Until the past thirty years, women have been nearly invisible to political scientists and political geographers. Important questions, concerning whether gender acts as a fundamental social-political cleavage in society, the significance of women's relative lack of political representation, or whether locality has different effects on political behavior for men and women, for a long time went unasked. In the 1970s and 1980s, however, the rise of feminism in the academy led to an increasing awareness of male biases in political geography and political science (regarding political geography, see Drake and Horton 1983). As a result of feminist critiques and the increasing presence of women in academia, a new literature on women in politics, much of which tended to follow the established methods of political science, addressed questions about women's voting and electoral behavior, their participation in political parties, and the links between women's representation and the promotion of women's interests or issues. Although many of the early studies adopted a behavioralist approach that concentrated on the extent and impact of women's participation in traditional political activities, some scholars began to critique the exclusion and subordination of women and to argue for the recognition of the gendered nature of political worldviews, policy agendas, and institutional rules. By confining the forms of participation studied to formal institutions and focusing on voting and representatives, some feminists argued, scholars were erasing the everyday political engagement of women and others.

In this chapter I seek to weave together these multiple strands of feminist electoral studies, from within and without the discipline of geography. The larger questions that I address in this chapter are about the implications of women's underrepresentation in government for the politics of power and support in party systems, and the role of gender as a political cleavage. These questions are explored through a review of three specific areas of research: (1) women's representation in political office and its geography and significance, (2) women's voting behavior and the construction of women's interests, and (3) feminist approaches to refiguring political geographies of participation. This third theme raises questions about how political participation has been spatialized through the division between public and private spheres and also leads us to examine the ways in which networks and informal politics provide alternative sites of political participation beyond the vote and formal representation in political offices.

Much of the work that has been done on women's participation in electoral politics has focused on Western Europe and North America. Throughout this chapter I use findings from the United States and the United Kingdom to illustrate the shifting relationships between gender and political participation that are at the core of our subject matter. However, as feminist political geographers, we recognize that women's participation is contextually embedded and contingent on different conceptions and performances of gender relations. My strategy in this chapter is, by integrating work that too often has been marginalized, to subvert approaches that hold up European and U.S. patterns of women's political participation and electoral politics as the norm. Although this poses a significant challenge, in that the literature on women in politics is regionally biased, it is an important methodological point. Just as feminists have critiqued the male bias in studies of politics that have treated women as anomalous by focusing on women's failure to conform to norms based on male behavior, in this chapter I seek to bring Middle Eastern women into discussions of women in politics on an equal footing. To this end, I interweave studies and examples from the Middle East[1] with research from, mainly, the United Kingdom and the United States, and the conclusions I draw are based on this heterogeneous literature and a recognition that the meaning, significance, and form of women's electoral behavior and political engagement are historically and culturally constructed.

Women and Representation

In its most general formulation, the major finding of this book comes as no surprise: *in no country do women have political status, access or influence equal to men's.* (Chowdhury and Nelson 1994, 3)

This statement is based on evidence derived from the forty-three country studies that comprise the edited volume *Women and Politics Worldwide* (Nelson and Chowdhury 1994). Global and discouraging, this observation proves to be the most consistent fact of feminist political geography. Its corollary might well be the frequently made observation that the greater the power associated with the position, the less likely it is a woman will occupy it. Women thus gain entry more commonly to the lower rungs of party echelons than to elite circles, and they more often win local political offices than national ones (Phillips 1991; Norris 1994). In the United States, for example, in 2002 women occupied more than 22.4 percent of state legislative seats, compared with 13.6 percent of congressional seats.

A global perspective reveals the uneven nature of women in legislative bodies (see Table 18.1). Worldwide, women occupy a very small fraction of national offices. Only in Sweden, where women comprised 42.7 percent of the parliament after the 1998 elections, do women even come close to proportionate representation in a national legislative body. Certainly, one could go on with statistics about women's representation in politics around the world, but, more interestingly, feminist scholars have raised questions about the underlying processes and overarching structures that shape women's underrepresentation within political offices.

"Male gender bias," and the way it functions through institutions and social norms, has been a topic of debate among feminists and others who seek to understand how formal and informal rules of the game reproduce gender imbalances in representative, electoral systems (Lovenduski 1996). In their introduction to *Women and Politics Worldwide*, Chowdhury and Nelson (1994, 16) stated, across the forty-three countries studied, "the culture and processes of formal political institutions—especially parties, their affiliated labor or employer

Table 18.1 Regional Averages of Percentage of Women in Parliament, February 2002

Region	Single House or Both Houses Combined: Mean Percentage of Women Representatives as of February 2002
Nordic countries	37.6
New Zealand and Australia	28.7
Western Europe (not Nordic countries)	18.8
United States, Canada, and Mexico	17.8
Caribbean	16.2
Central and Latin America	12.7
Sub-Saharan Africa	12.8
Asia (subcontinent, China, and Southeast)	12.3
Central and Eastern Europe (including Russia)	12.2
Central Asia	10.5
Middle East and North Africa	4
Oceania	1.8
Average for regions	15.4

Note. Data compiled by the Inter-Parliamentary Union for 179 countries (Inter-Parliamentary Union 2002); data for regions compiled by author.

groups, their youth wings and even their women's auxiliaries—are major barriers to women's equal participation in institutional politics." They argued that women's underrepresentation in elected offices can be attributed to the ingrained biases and rules of these institutions, what they called the "male culture and ethos of formal politics" (p. 16). Focusing on how institutionalized male biases push women and the issues affecting women to the sidelines of the formal political arena, feminist research has thus begun to reveal the processes that undergird the phenomenon of persistent underrepresentation of women in elected offices.

The work of political geographers provides insight into how and why constraints on women's political advancement operate unevenly across space. In the case of the United States, marked regional differences in the election of women to state legislatures—such that, for example, 5 percent of Alabama's state legislative seats are held by women, whereas the proportion is 40 percent in Washington—have been associated with the historical geography of political culture in the United States (Brunn 1974; Shelley et al. 1996; Webster 1997, 2000). Studies of women's underrepresentation in the South have attributed this phenomenon to the traditionalist political culture of the region and to the regional dominance of the individualistic Democratic Party, though the latter association (both between the Democrats and the South and the Democrats and low numbers of women politicians) has broken down since the 1980s

(Darcy et al. 1987; Rule 1990). Webster (2000, 8) suggested that the "high-intensity fundamentalist religious orientation" of the South also contributes to the region's resistance to women in elected offices. Such studies, though perhaps too general at the regional level, point toward a gendered political geography that would explore the links between political culture, patriarchal structures, and patterns of women's representation in particular settings.

When the geography of representation is examined at the global scale, the paucity of women in political office in the Middle East stands out. Any explanation of this phenomenon must take into account the specific contexts of Middle Eastern societies and polities. Kandiyoti (1997) cautioned that it is insufficient merely to point toward Islam or patriarchy as explanatory factors without looking more closely at how gender relations are naturalized and gender differences construed in local settings. To this end, Kandiyoti called for "ethnographic specificity" to make clear the local basis of women's political participation. As Joseph (2000) pointed out in the introduction to her edited volume *Gender and Citizenship in the Middle East,* close case studies offer the possibility of understanding the ways in which local patterns of gender relations are shaped by the dynamic interaction of religion, family structures, class, tribe, ethnicity, nationalism, and colonialism.

Political Systems and Women's Representation

The global geography of women's representation is ultimately an outcome of historically contingent processes that continue to operate at multiple scales, from the local to the global, to produce a range of different kinds of gender relations and polities across the globe. Today, at the national scale, differences in political system, party policies, and state laws have become associated with this gendered geography of representation. Comparative work has shown that the form of electoral systems has an impact on women's electoral success. For example, Darcy et al. (1987) found that women candidates are more likely to succeed in larger, multiseat districts in U.S. state and local elections than in smaller ones. Similarly, in a comparative study of the lower houses of the national legislatures of twenty-three Western democracies in the early 1980s, Rule (1987) found that the proportion of women elected was significantly higher in districts with multiple seats, proportional representation, and a party list of candidates. In the party-list system of proportional representation, the number and selection of legislators from a particular party depend on the proportion of the vote garnered by that party; the higher the proportion of the vote the party wins, the further down the candidate list they are able to go in seating their legislators. Because parties are likely to include some women candidates toward the top of their candidate lists in order to attract women voters and feminists, and because even those parties that do not glean the majority of votes are able to seat some legislators, the party-list system results in the entry of more women and other traditionally underrepresented groups into legislative seats. However, if parties do not place women candidates high enough on their lists, as in the case of Turkey, proportional representation may not lead to increased numbers of women in political office (Arat 1989).

In an attempt to correct gender biases in proportional electoral systems, quota or parity systems have been adopted in some European parties and polities. Quota systems implemented by internal party rules can require that all-women short lists be drawn up for particular seats or that a number of women need to be included on candidate lists (see Short 1996). In France a more comprehensive parity system has been adopted, requiring by law that all parties put forward equal numbers of men and women candidates (and alternate them on the lists) or pay financial penalties (Lenoir 2001). Quota or parity systems have proved to be effective means of tipping gender balances within representative bodies—but at the same time, they raise important issues about the meaning of representation and difference. Why does it matter whether there are more or fewer women serving in political offices? Is there any reason to assume that the mere presence of more women (regardless of their political affiliations) in a legislature will affect either the political institutions or policy outcomes?

An argument for the importance of bringing more women into public office can be made without presuming anything about representation or women's difference. From what Phillips (1996) called the "justice" perspective, it is not assumed that women legislators represent women better than male legislators or that women bring particular values or issues to political processes and debates but only that barriers to women's entrance into the field of politics must be identified and dismantled in the name of justice and equal opportunity. More often than not, however, arguments regarding the importance of rectifying gender imbalances go beyond questions of justice to suggest that increasing numbers of women in public offices are necessary to combat male biases in political structures, institutions, and policies. Phillips argued that although democratic ideals have privileged what she called "the politics of ideas," in which political interests and ideologies are thought to be detachable from experience and identities, and so women need not be represented by women, the experiences of politically marginalized groups are not adequately addressed under these conditions. Only by supplementing the politics of ideas with a "politics of presence" will orthodoxies of democratic systems be challenged and alternatives be rendered visible.

Entering a system delimited by rules and agendas set by men, women may transform political structures by operating through them in particularly gendered ways, such as by employing collaborative or network-based strategies or other gendered behaviors (Ackelsberg 1984). Although some feminists have argued that women are more likely than men to value caring, nurturing, and cooperation in their interactions and worldviews (Chodorow 1978; Elshtain 1982; Gilligan 1982; MacKinnon 1989), others have emphasized the relationship between experience and interests. From the latter perspective, structural differences in men's and women's lives lead to the development of a distinctive women's perspective on issues such as reproductive rights, women's health care, child care, public transportation, the environment, and others (Norris 1996). Women legislators are thus expected to represent women in the general population, acting as "surrogate representatives" for women who live beyond the borders of their geographically defined districts (Mansbridge 1999). One of this argument's implications, and one that I interrogate in the following section on women and voting behavior, is that gender represents a salient, interest-based social cleavage.

Women's Interests: A Gender Cleavage?

The question of whether gender represents a political cleavage can be addressed from two angles. First, do women politicians represent women's interests in any broadly identifiable sense? Second, does women's voting behavior betray significant or consistent gender differences? These two questions focus on the role of gender in political behavior and electoral support and together provide insight into the ways in which women's political participation may or may not affect political party systems.

Many feminists remain skeptical about whether the practices of women politicians diverge significantly from their male counterparts' practices or share salient characteristics with one another; studies of women political leaders (such as Benazir Bhutto, Corazon Aquino, Margaret Thatcher, and Tansu Ciller) have tended to reveal more differences than similarities within the category of "women leaders" (Genovese 1993; D'Amico 1995). At the same time, in the United States and the United Kingdom, most studies have indicated that women politicians do differ from men in their policy attitudes and political procedures, although there is conflicting evidence as to the significance of these differences. In the United States studies of women representatives at both state and national levels have shown that women in Congress and state legislatures are more supportive of women's rights and more likely to sponsor bills on health, education, and the family and child welfare (e.g., Reingold 1992; Carroll 1994; Thomas 1994; Flammang 1997). In the United Kingdom Norris's (1996) analysis of a 1992 survey of politicians and party members, *The British Candidate Study,* showed that women were consistently more in favor of women's rights (as indicated by views on domestic violence, marital rape, abortion rights, and equal opportunities for women) than were male politicians, with the largest gender gap evident in the Conservative Party. Women politicians and party members also were more likely to give priority to social policy issues, such as welfare services and health care—though party remained the strongest predictor of political attitudes and policy priorities (Norris 1996).

Do women legislators promote similar issues in non-Western contexts? A different set of issues and challenges face women in Iran,[2] where female legislators have struggled to come together around women's issues in parliament (the *Mejlis*). Although women in Iran have the right to vote and to be elected to office at local and national levels, informal barriers make it difficult for women to enter formal politics and to pursue their interests once elected. Nonetheless, in the sixth *Mejlis*, which was seated in 2000, women representatives (who comprise 11 out of the 290 elected parliamentarians) have succeeded in creating the "women's fraction," a subgrouping concerned with women's issues. In the context of Iran, these issues have included education for girls and women, revision of divorce laws, the criminalization of honor killings, provisions for war widows and orphans, the recognition of women-headed households, and the provision of custody rights for mothers of young children. One success of the sixth *Mejlis* has been to put an end to discrimination between men and women for scholarships to study abroad (Afshar 1998).

Findings from the United States, the United Kingdom, and Iran support the idea that women in politics make a difference and potentially make a difference for women. It is nonetheless important to point out that the idea of universal women's issues runs the risk of belying the multitude of salient ideological, social, cultural, and economic cleavages that the category "woman" masks. The finding that women candidates are responsive to a particular set of issues, even cross-nationally, is not evidence of a universal woman's platform but instead reveals the institutionalization of gender relations and norms. To learn from studies of women in politics in the Middle East and to build comparative studies of women's representation and interests, researchers must recognize that these concepts and practices are shaped by processes occurring at multiple scales. Thus, comparative work will need to take into consideration the colonial and imperial history of "state feminism" in the Middle East, the resulting association between feminism and political elites, and the role of local idioms, such as Islamist politics, in both naturalizing and contesting gender relations in particular contexts. As Peake and Trotz (1999) illustrated through their study of gender, race, and politics in Guyana, gender, identities, and women's empowerment are produced contingently and historically and are constantly being created and recreated through shifting social relations. Women representatives may make a difference, but how they do so will likely be contingent on their particular experiences, identities, and social contexts.

Women and Voting

In the 1960s and 1970s, conventional wisdom was that women were less likely to vote than men and more likely to vote conservatively (see Almond and Verba 1963). Although the gender gap in voter turnout has disappeared in most Western democracies, discrepancies continue in other parts of the world. In the Middle East, although in Turkey women turn out to vote in equal numbers to men (Günes-Ayata 1995), significant gender gaps in voter turnout remain in Arab countries where women have the right to vote (Abu-Khalil 1994).

Gender gaps in voting behavior remain in Western democracies, though in many cases the nature of the relationship between gender and political preferences has either shifted or disappeared over time. In Britain, Germany, Italy, and France, the electoral gender gap converged by the 1980s (N. J. Walker 1994). In the United States, while the 1950s and 1960s showed that more women supported Republicans, in the 1980s and 1990s women became more likely than men to support Democratic candidates. Internationally, gender differences in political values have been demonstrated with regard to particular issues, such as welfare, religious issues, and the use of force, with women tending to be less keen on violence, more in favor of religious initiatives (such as prayer in schools), and more supportive of social welfare programs (Conover 1994; N. J. Walker 1994). Inglehart and Norris (2003), in their seventy-country study of gender differences in voting behavior and ideological self-placement (along a left-right continuum), confirmed that in many countries women today are more left-leaning than men are in their attitudes toward social welfare and the role of the state.

Why does gender matter in the construction of political interests? Bondi and Peake (1988) argued that, in the case of urban politics in Western countries, gender cleavages arise from two arenas of difference between men and women. First, men and women experience differential access to consumer goods and services, ranging from mortgage loans to the use of the household vehicle. Second, inequalities in the household division of labor that position women as primarily responsible for dependents and the domestic environment affect women's work patterns, frequently keeping them closer to home and more likely to seek home-based work (Bondi and Peake 1988). Taken together, these factors influence women's political, economic, and social interests, frequently leading women to focus on issues that affect their local communities and the distribution of urban resources. However, Bondi and Peake pointed out that even when gender thus marks a political cleavage in society, these interests have not always translated into the political party system. There is, in effect, a gap between the "politics of support" and the "politics of power," between the interests that define gender cleavages in society on one hand and party platforms and policy outcomes on the other.

Given that gender differences in voting behavior and ideological leanings are not static but instead represent fluid configurations of issues, interests, and party platforms in particular national polities, feminist political geographers have come to focus on the processes that shape women's choices, issues, and modes of political participation (Staeheli 2001). Feminist electoral geography can use research into gendered voting patterns to reveal differences in how men and women experience political choices in their own lives. In the case of Arab countries, Abu-Khalil (1994) argued that legal voting rights do not guarantee that men and women enjoy equal opportunities to exercise choice in the electoral arena. Instead, women may be constrained in their voting choices by the dominant social norms of their societies, by male family members, by virtue of the discrepancy in literacy rates between men and women, or even by state policies that encourage or make mandatory the registration of male voters but not of female voters.

Finally, feminists have offered a critique of studies that assume voting to be the most significant measure of political participation, especially for women. Instead of seeing voting as a gateway to political engagement, feminists have argued that voting is a unique activity that shares little with other types of political participation, from protest activities and community organizing to informal ad hoc political activities pursued through familial or local networks. In conclusion, I turn to some of these critiques that broaden and recalibrate the definition of politics in order to include a range of informal activities.

Conclusions: Redefining the Political

In the previous discussions, I focused on women's participation in traditional political activities: those that revolve around parties, voting behavior, and political office. Although contributing to our understanding of women's activities within these arenas, studies that aim to generate information about women in conventional politics have tended to take the theoretical parameters of political science for granted (Githens et al. 1994). Feminists also have pointed out, however, that such studies privilege particular arenas and forms of politics in which men are more likely to engage than women, such as political campaigns, party meetings, trade unions, or other interest organizations (Randall 1987). When social scientists locate power exclusively in the machinations of political parties, government institutions, and legislative offices, they tend to reproduce the gender biases and hierarchies that work to marginalize women in the political arena in the first place. In particular, this privileging of formal, state politics rests on a dualistic worldview that divides society into public and private spheres, where the public is assumed to be the locus of legitimate and significant politics and of male dominance, whereas women are relegated to the private domestic sphere (Pateman 1988). Thus, as a result of what Kathleen Jones (1997, 2) called the "masculinization of political discourse," women and other subordinate groups have appeared to be politically inactive and disengaged while their everyday and informal political activities go unnoticed (Lovenduski and Hills 1981; Ackelsberg 1984; Randall 1987).

The assumption that men and women occupy dual and separate private and public worlds has permeated many studies of Middle Eastern politics that have emphasized female seclusion and the dominance of men in formal political institutions and associations. Feminist interventions, however, offer a new lens through which to view space, gender, and power in Middle Eastern contexts. In general, feminists have argued that the transposition of Western spatial imaginings into non-Western and postcolonial contexts runs the risk of overlooking the historically and culturally embedded production of the public-private divide and its potential variability (Chatterjee 1993; Werbner 1999). Feminist rereadings of political participation and the public-private divide have proved fruitful for the study of women's power in the Middle East. Such studies have shown that, rather than being confined to distinct spatial and social realms, men and women engage in contests over resources and position that put the domestic private sphere in constant dialogue and negotiation with the public sphere of supposed male authority in Middle Eastern contexts (e.g., Singerman 1995). Decentering the public-private dichotomy helps to reveal the political structures and processes of Middle Eastern societies more broadly and allows us to move beyond myopic models that, by privileging formal party politics, have previously rendered women's political participation invisible.

In this chapter I reviewed the contributions of feminist geographers and others to electoral studies, and I showed how electoral geography's concerns with representation, political cleavages, and voting behavior can be reworked through feminist approaches. By integrating studies from the Middle East with studies of Western Europe and the United States, I also aimed to destabilize normative hierarchies that have plagued political science and geography. Studies of Middle Eastern women's representation and participation reveal the commonalities and differences that mark different contexts of male-female and state-society relationships and that point toward the necessity of following Kandiyoti's (1997) call for close ethnographic attention to the local construction of women's political participation. At the same time, feminist political theory, with its attention to the dominant definitions of "politics" and to the ways in which these are reproduced through the representation of public and private spheres in particular settings, proves useful for understanding the modes, bases, and idioms of the political participation of women and other subaltern groups in the Middle East.

Many questions remain unanswered and point the way for future research in the area of feminist electoral geography. First, studies of women's representation and political participation have yet to address, in a broad comparative perspective, the question of when women's representation and political participation matter. When does the presence of women in formal or informal politics transform political structures? Under what conditions do women in politics subvert male privilege and the masculine norms of politics, and when do they serve to reproduce the status quo? This issue represents an ongoing question for studies of women's involvement in Islamist politics and promises to yield important insights into the relationships between gender, power, and politics. Second, although evidence suggests that gender may indeed act as a shifting political cleavage in many societies, in many cases the local processes by which gender-based interests are constructed remain to be explored and cross-culturally compared. Third, although feminists have produced a rich literature on the construction of the public and the private spheres in various contexts and its impact on women's political participation, this remains an important research area and one in which greater attention to cross-cultural differences and similarities promises to illuminate some of the basic dynamics of both women's subordination and their power.

Notes

1. I am using the term "Middle East" to indicate a debatable region that includes the area around the eastern Mediterranean, from Turkey to North Africa and eastward to Iran.
2. Iran provides an interesting example of women in politics struggling to represent women's interests in an environment of male bias. Iran is not usually defined as a democracy, because its elected officials, including the president, are beholden to the country's religious leader and the appointed Islamic Consultative Assembly.

References

Abdullah, Hussaina. 1995. Wifeism and activism: The Nigerian women's movement. In *The challenge of local feminisms: Women's movements in global perspective*, edited by Amrita Basu, 209–25. Boulder, Colo.: Westview Press.

Abrar, Stefania, Joni Lovenduski, and Helen Margetts. 1998. Sexing London: The gender mix of urban policy actors. *International Political Science Review* 19:147–71.

Abu-Khalil, A. 1994. Women and electoral politics in Arab states. In *Electoral systems in comparative perspective: Their impact on women and minorities*, edited by W. Rule and J. F. Zimmerman, 127–38. Westport, Conn: Greenwood Press.

Ackelsberg, M. A. 1984. Women's collaborative activities and city life: Politics and polity. In *Political women: Current roles in state and local government*, edited by J. A. Flammang, 242–59. Beverly Hills, Calif.: Sage.

Adam, B. D., J. W. Duyvendak, and A. Krouwel. 1999. *The global emergence of gay and lesbian politics*. Philadelphia: Temple University Press.

Adjin-Tettey, E. 1997. *Defining a particular social group based on gender*. North York, Canada: York University, Refuge.

Afsaruddin, Asma, ed. 1999. *Hermeneutics and honor: Negotiating female "public" space in Islamic/Ate societies*. Cambridge, Mass.: Harvard Institute for Middle Eastern Studies.

Afshar, H. 1998. *Islam and feminisms: An Iranian case study*. London: Macmillan Press Ltd.

Afshar, Haleh, and Stephanie Barrientos, eds. 1999. *Women, globalization and fragmentation in the developing world*. London: Macmillan Press Ltd.

Agarwal, Bina. 1997. Environmental action, gender equity and women's participation. *Development and Change* 28:1–44.

Agnew, John. 1987. *Place and politics: The geographical mediation of state and society*. Boston: Allen and Unwin.

———. 1989. The devaluation of place in social science. In *The power of place: Bringing together geographical and sociological imaginations*, edited by John Agnew and James Duncan. Boston: Unwin Hyman.

———. 1998. *Geopolitics: Re-visioning world politics*. London: Routledge.

———. 2002. *Making political geography*. London: Arnold.

Aiken, Susan Hardy, Ann E. Brigham, Sallie A. Marston, and Penny M. Waterstone, eds. 1998. *Making worlds: Gender, metaphor, materiality*. Tucson: University of Arizona.

Alcoff, Linda. 1995. Democracy and rationality: A dialogue with Hilary Putnam. In *Women, culture and development: A study of human capabilities*, edited by Martha C. Nussbaum and Jonathan Glover. Oxford: Clarendon Press.

Alexander, M. J., and C. T. Mohanty. 1997. *Feminist genealogies, colonial legacies, democratic futures*. London and New York: Routledge.

Allen, Beverly. 1996. *Rape warfare: The hidden genocide in Bosnia-Herzegovina and Croatia*. Minneapolis and London: University of Minnesota Press.

Allen, J. 1990. Does feminism need a theory of "the state"? In *Playing the state: Australian feminist interventions*, edited by S. Watson. London and New York: Verso.

Almond, G., and S. Verba. 1963. *The civic culture*. Princeton, N.J.: Princeton University Press.

Altman, D. 2001. *Global sex*. Chicago: University of Chicago Press.

Altvater, Elmar. 1998. Global order and nature. In *Political ecology: Global and local*, edited by R. Keil, L. Fawcett, P. Penz, and D. Bell. London: Routledge.

Alvarez, Sonia. 1998. Introduction: The cultural and the political in Latin American social movements. In *Cultures of politics and politics of culture: Re-visioning Latin American social movements*, edited by Sonia E. Alvarez, Evelina Dagnino, and Arturo Escobar. Boulder, Colo.: Westview Press.

———. 1999. What state is feminism in? (An)other American perspective. Paper presented at the conference, Challenging the American Century, at Loughborough University.

Alvarez, Sonia, Evelina Dagnino, and Arturo Escobar, eds. 1998. *Cultures of politics and politics of cultures: Re-visioning Latin American social movements*. Boulder, Colo.: Westview Press.

Amin, Ash, and Nigel Thrift. 2002. *Cities: Reimagining the urban*. Cambridge, Mass.: Polity Press.

Andall, Jacqueline. 1995. Migrant women and gender role redefinitions in the Italian context. *Journal of Area Studies* 6:203–15.

Anderson, Benedict. 1991. *Imagined communities: Reflections on the origins and spread of nationalism.* London: Verso.

Anderson, Bridget. 1997. Servants and slaves: Europe's domestic workers. *Race and Class* 39:37–49.

Anderson, James. 1996. The shifting stage of politics: New medieval and postmodern territorialities? *Environment and Planning D: Society and Space* 14:133–53.

Anderson, James, Chris Brook, and Allan Cochrane, eds. 1995. *A global world? Re-ordering political space.* Oxford: Oxford University Press.

Anderson, Kay. 2000. Thinking "post-nationally": Dialogue across multicultural, indigenous, and settler spaces. *Annals of the Association of American Geographers* 90:381–91.

Anderson, Kay, and Jane M. Jacobs. 1999. Geographies of publicity and privacy: Residential activism in Sydney in the 1970s. *Environment and Planning A* 31:1017–30.

Andrew, Caroline, and Michael Goldsmith. 1998. From local government to local governance— and beyond? *International Political Science Review* 19:101–18.

Anzaldua, Gloria, ed. 1990. *Making face, making soul/haciendo caras: Creative and critical perspectives by feminists of color.* San Francisco: Aunt Lute Books.

Apffel-Marglin, F., and PRATEC, eds. 1998. *The spirit of regeneration: Andean culture confronting western notions of development.* London: Zed Books.

Appadurai, Arjun. 1990. Disjuncture and difference in the global cultural economy. *Public Culture* 2:1–23.

———. 2001. Deep democracy: Urban governmentality and the horizon of politics. *Environment and Urbanization* 13 (2) :23–43.

Arat, Y. 1989. *The patriarchal paradox.* London: Associated University Presses.

Archer, J. C., and F. M. Shelley. 1986. *American electoral mosaics.* Washington, D.C.: Association of American Geographers.

Arrighi, Giovani. 1994. *The long twentieth century: Money, power and the origins of our times.* London: Verso.

Asian Migration Centre. 2002. *Migration needs, issues and responses in the greater Mekong subregion.* Hong Kong: Author.

Asis, Maruja. 2002. From the life stories of Filipino women: Personal and family agendas in migration. *Asian and Pacific Migration Journal* 11:67–93.

Aslanbeigui, Nahid, Steven Pressman, and Gale Summerfield, eds. 1994. *Women in the age of economic transformation: Gender impacts of reforms in post-socialist and developing countries.* New York: Routledge.

Aslanbeigui, Nahid, and Gale Summerfield. 2000. The Asian crisis, gender, and the international financial architecture. *Feminist Economics* 6:81–103.

Association of American Geographers. 2002. *The geographical dimensions of terrorism: Action items and research priorities.* Retrieved from http://www.aag.org/News/godt.html

ATTAC, Action pour une Taxe Tobin d'aide aux Citoyens (Association for the Taxation of Financial Transactions for the Aid of Citizens). 2003. *Platform of the association ATTAC, Adopted by the Constituent Assembly June 3rd 1998.* Retrieved from http://attac.org

———, Austria. 2003. *Website of Austrian ATTAC affiliate.* Retrieved from http://attac-austria.org

Australian Domestic and Family Violence Clearinghouse. 2001. *Pathways to safety: An interview about indigenous family violence* (Issues paper 5). University of New South Wales, Sydney. Retrieved from www.austdvclearinghouse.unsw.edu.au

Bachrach, P., and M. Baratz. 1970. *Power and poverty: Theory and practice.* New York: Oxford University Press.

Baldwin, Elizabeth, and Kenneth Friedman. 1994. *Breastfeeding legislation in the United States.* Retrieved from http://www.lalecheleague.org/Law/NBNovDec94p164.html

Ball, Rochelle. 1996. A nation building or dissolution: The globalization of nursing—The case of the Philippines. *Pilipinas* 27:67–91.

———. 1997. The role of the state in the globalization of labour markets: The case of the Philippines. *Environment and Planning A* 29:1603–28.

Bammer, Angelika. 1994. Introduction. In *Displacements: Cultural identities in question,* edited by A. Bammer. Bloomington/Indianapolis: Indiana University Press.

Barnett, T. 2003. The Pentagon's new map. *Esquire.* http://www.nwc.navy.mil/newrulesets/ThePentagonsNewMap.htm

Barrett, M., and A. Phillips. 1992. *Destabilizing theory: Contemporary feminist debates.* Stanford, Calif.: Stanford University Press.

Barrig, M. 1999. El feminismo de la diferencia desde un país Andino. Paper presented at the Seminario Internacional: Género, Etnicidad y Educación en América Latina, 23–27 August, at Cochabamba.

Bartky, S. L. 1997. Foucault, femininity, and modernization of patriarchal power. In *Writing on the body: Female embodiment and feminist theory*, edited by Katie Conboy, Nadia Medina, and Sarah Stanbury. New York: Columbia University Press.

Bassett, T. 2002. Women's cotton and the spaces of gender politics in northern Côte D' Ivoire. *Gender Place and Culture* 9:352–70.

Basu, Amrita. 1995. Feminism inverted: The gendered imagery and real women of Hindu nationalism. In *Women and right-wing movements: Indian experiences*, edited by Tanika Sarkar and Urvashi Butalia. London: Zed Books.

Bell, David. 1995. Pleasure and danger: The paradoxical spaces of sexual citizenship. *Political Geography* 14:139–53.

Bell, David, and Jon Binnie. 2000. *The sexual citizen, queer politics and beyond.* Cambridge, Mass.: Polity Press.

Bell, David, and Gill Valentine, eds. 1995a. *Mapping desire: Geographies of sexualities.* London: Routledge.

———. 1995b. The sexed self: Strategies of performance, sites of resistance. In *Mapping the subject*, edited by S. Pile and N. Thrift. London: Routledge.

Bell, James, and Lynn A. Staeheli. 2001. Discourses of diffusion and democratization. *Political Geography* 20:175–95.

Bell, M., R. Butlin, and M. Heffernan, eds. 1995. *Geography and imperialism 1820–1940.* Manchester: Manchester University Press.

Benería, Lourdes. 1999. Globalization, gender and the Davos Man. *Feminist Economics* 5:61–83.

Benhabib, Seyla, ed. 1996. *Democracy and difference: Contesting the boundaries of the political.* Princeton, N.J.: Princeton University Press.

———. 1998. Models of public space: Hannah Arendt, the liberal tradition, and Jürgen Habermas. In *Feminism: The public and the private*, edited by Joan B. Landes. Oxford and New York: Oxford University Press.

Berg, Lawrence, and Robyn Longhurst. 2003. Placing masculinities and geography. *Gender, Place and Culture* 10:351–60.

Bergeron, Suzanne. 2001. Political economy discourses of globalization and feminist politics. *Signs: Journal of Women in Culture and Society* 26 (4): 983–1006.

———. 2003. Challenging the World Bank's narrative of inclusion. In *World Bank literature*, edited by Amitava Kumar, 157–81. Minneapolis: University of Minnesota Press.

Berndt, Christian. 2001. El Paso Del Norte . . . Modernisierungskurse, Grenzziehungen Und Management-Praxis in Der Maquiladora-Industrie. *Erdkunde, Band* 55:244–55.

Bhabha, Homi. 1990. *Nation and narration.* New York and London: Routledge.

Bhabha, J. 1996. Embodied rights: Gender persecution, state sovereignty, and refugees. *Public Culture* 9:3–32.

Bhabha, J., and S. Shutter. 1994. *Women's movement: Women under immigration, nationality and refugee law.* Stoke-on-Trent: Trentham Books.

Biemann, Ursula. 1999. *Performing the border.* Switzerland. Video essay.

Billig, M. 1995. *Banal nationalism.* London: Sage Ltd.

Binnie, Jon, and Gill Valentine. 1999. Geographies of sexuality—A review of progress. *Progress in Human Geography* 23:175–87.

Binswanger, P. Hans and Klaus Deininger. 1993. South African land policy: The legacy of history and current options. *World Development* 21 (9):1451–75.

Blee, Kathleen M., ed. 1998. *No middle ground: Women in radical protest.* New York and London: New York University Press.

Blomley, Nicholas. 1994. Mobility, empowerment and the rights revolution. *Political Geography* 13 (5):407–22.

Blomley, Nicholas and Geraldine Pratt. 2001. Canada and the political geographies of rights. *The Canadian Geographer* 45 (1):151–66.

Blumberg, R. L., and G. West. 1990. *Women and social protest.* New York: Oxford University Press.

Boles, Janet. 1991. Advancing the women's agenda within local legislatures: The role of female elected officials. In *Gender and policymaking: Studies of women in office*, edited by D. Dodson. Rutgers, N.J.: Center for the American Woman and Politics.

———. 2001. Local elected women and policy-making: Movement delegates or feminist trustees? In *The impact of women in public office*, edited by Susan J. Carroll. Bloomington: Indiana University Press.

Bondi, Liz. 1990. Feminism, postmodernism and geography: Space for women? *Antipode* 22:156–67.

Bondi, Liz, and Mona Domosh. 1998. On the contours of public space: A tale of three women. *Antipode* 30:270–89.

Bondi, Liz, and Linda Peake. 1988. Gender and the city: Urban politics revisited. In *Women in cities: Gender and the urban environment*, edited by Jo Little, Linda Peake, and Pat Richardson. New York: New York University Press.

Bordo, S. 1989. The body and the reproduction of femininity: A feminist appropriation of Foucault. In *Gender/body/knowledge feminist reconstructions of being and knowing*, edited by Alison Jaggar and Susan Bordo. New Brunswick and London: Rutgers University Press.

Bowlby, Sophie. 1984. Planning for women to shop in postwar Britain. *Environment and Planning D: Society and Space* 2:179–99.

Bowlby, Sophie, Susan Gregory, and Linda McKie. 1997. "Doing home," patriarchy, caring and space. *Women's Studies International Forum* 20:343–50.

Boyd, Monica. 1989. Family and personal networks in international migration: Recent developments and new agendas. *International Migration Review* 23:638–70.

Bracewell, Wendy. 1996. Women, motherhood, and contemporary Serbian nationalism. *Women's Studies International Journal* 19:25–33.

Breitbart, Myrna. 1981. Peter Kropotkin, the anarchist geographer. In *Geography, ideology and social concern*, edited by D. Stoddart, 134–53. Oxford: Blackwell.

Brenner, Neil, and Nik Theodore. 2002. Cities and the geographies of "actually existing neoliberalism." *Antipode* 34:349–79.

Breuilly, John. 1996. Approaches to nationalism. In *Mapping the nation*, edited by G. Balakrishnan, 146–74. London: Verso.

Brook, D. 2000. The continuum of collective action. American Sociological Association's Section on Collective Behavior and Social Movements: Working Paper Series Volume 3.

Brooks-Higginbotham, E. 1993. *Righteous discontent: The women's movement in the black Baptist church, 1880–1920.* Cambridge, Mass.: Harvard University Press.

Brown, Michael. 1995. Sex, scale and the "new urban politics": HIV prevention strategies from Yaletown, Vancouver. In *Mapping desire*, edited by D. Bell and G. Valentine, 245–63. London: Routledge.

———. 1997. *Replacing citizenship: AIDS activism and radical democracy.* New York: Guilford.

———. Forthcoming. *Local political geographies.* New York: Guilford.

Brown, Michael, and Lynn A. Staeheli. 2003. "Are We There Yet?" Feminist political geographies. *Gender, Place and Culture* 10:247–55.

Brownill, Susan, and Susan Halford. 1990. Understanding women's involvement in local politics: How useful is a formal-informal dichotomy? *Political Geography Quarterly* 9:396–414.

Brownmiller, Susan. 1975. *Against our will: Men, women, and rape.* New York: Simon and Schuster.

Brú Bistuer, Josepa. 1993. Medi ambient i equitat: La perspectiva del gènere. *DAG* 22:117–30.

———. 1996. Spanish women against industrial waste: A gender perspective on environmental grassroots movements. In *Feminist political ecology*, edited by D. Rocheleau, B. Thomas-Slayter, and E. Wangari. London: Routledge.

———. 1997. *Medio ambiente: Poder y espectáculo. Gestión ambiental y vida cotidiana.* Barcelona: Editorial Icaria.

Brú Bistuer, Josepa, and Mercè Agüera Cabo. 2001.*Discursos i imatges de la sostenibilitat. Papers de sostenibilitat.* Barcelona: Ecocondern.

———. 2004. A gendered politics of the environment. In *Mapping women, making politics: Feminist perspectives on political geography*, edited by Lynn A. Staeheli, Eleonore Kofman, and Linda Peake. New York: Routledge.

Bruegel, Irene. 1996. The trailing wife: A declining breed? Careers, geographical mobility and household conflict in Britain 1970–89. In *Changing forms of employment: Organizations, skills and gender*, edited by R. Crompton, D. Gaillie, and K. Purcell. London: Routledge.

Brunn, S. D. 1974. *Geography and politics in America.* New York: Harper and Row.

Bryson, V. 1992. *Feminist political thought: An introduction.* Basingstoke: Macmillan.

Buechler, Steven. 1993. Beyond resource mobilization? Emerging trends in social movement theory. *The Sociological Quarterly* 34:217–35.

Bush, Julia. 2000. *Edwardian ladies and imperial power.* London: Leicester University Press.

Buss, Doris, and Didi Herman. 2003. *Globalizing family values: The Christian right in international politics.* Minneapolis: University of Minnesota Press.

Butler, Judith. 1990. *Gender trouble, feminism and the subversion of identity.* London and New York: Routledge.

———. 1995. Contingent foundations. In *Feminist contentions: A philosophical exchange*, edited by Selya Benhabib. London and New York: Routledge.

Butler, R. 1999. Double the trouble or twice the fun? Disabled bodies in the gay community. In *Mind and body spaces: Geographies of illness, impairment and disability*, edited by R. Butler and H. Parr. New York and London: Routledge.

Butler, Ruth, and Hester Parr, eds. 1999. *Mind and body spaces*. London: Routledge.

Cadwell, Lyton K. 1996. *International environmental policy*. Durham, N.C.: Duke University Press.

Caldecott, Leonie, and Stephanie Leland, eds. 1983. *Reclaim the earth*. London: Women's Press.

Caldeira, Teresa. 1999. Fortified enclaves: The new urban segregation. In *Cities and citizenship*, edited by James Holston. Durham, N.C.: Duke University Press.

Calla, P. 2000. Gender, ethnicity and intercultural education. Paper presented at the conference, Current Challenges to the Bolivian State: Issues of Gender, Ethnicity and Citizenship, 11 November, University of Newcastle Upon Tyne, United Kingdom.

———. 2001. The feminine as less national: Indigenous virilities in intercultural and bilingual educational processes. Paper presented at the Annual American Anthropological Association Meetings, Washington, D.C.

Calla, P., and Y. G. Rojas. Producir, dar y proteger: Crisis del estado Padre Boliviano. Paper presented at the conference La Figura del Padre, Asociación del Campo Freudiano de Bolivia, Cochabamba, Bolivia.

Campani, Giovanni. 1995. Ethnic networks and associations, Italian mobilization and immigration issues in Italy. *Ethnic and Racial Studies* 18:143–47.

Canclini, N. G. 1992. *Culturas híbridas: Estrategias para entrar y salir de la modernidad*. Buenos Aires: Editorial Sudamericana.

Capron, Guénola. 2002. Accessibility to "modern public spaces" in Latin American cities: A multidimensional idea. *GeoJournal* 58 (2): 217–23.

Carroll, S. J. 1994. The politics of difference: Women public officials as agents of change. *Stanford Law and Policy Review* 5:11–20.

Castells, Manuel. 1996. *The rise of the network society*. Oxford: Blackwell.

———. 1997. *The power of identity*. Oxford: Blackwell.

———. 1998. *End of millennium*. Oxford: Blackwell.

Castles, Stephen, and G. Kosack. 1973. *Immigrant workers and class structure in Western Europe*. Oxford: Oxford University Press.

Castles, Stephen, and Mark Miller. 1998. *The age of migration*. 2nd ed. London: Macmillan.

Chamberlain, Mary. 1999. The family as model and metaphor in Caribbean migration to Britain. *Journal of Ethnic and Migration Studies* 25:251–66.

Chang, Kimberly A., and L. H. M. Ling. 2000. Globalization and its intimate other: Filipina domestic workers in Hong Kong. In *Gender and global restructuring: Sightings, sites and resistances*, edited by Marianne H. Marchand and Anne Sisson Runyan. New York: Routledge.

Charlesworth, Hilary. 1996. Feminist approaches to international law. *American Journal of International Law* 85:613–45.

Charnay, Jean Pierre. 1994. *Stratégie générative: De l'anthropologie à la géopolitique*. Paris: Presses Universitaires de France.

Chatterjee, Partha. 1993. *The nation and its fragments: Colonial and postcolonial histories*. Princeton, N.J.: Princeton University Press.

Chinchilla, N. S. 1992. Marxism, feminism and the struggle for democracy in Latin America. In *The making of social movements in Latin America: Identity, strategy and democracy*, edited by S. E. Escobar and S. E. Alvarez. Boulder, Colo.: Westview Press.

Chodorow, N. 1978. *The reproduction of mothering: Psychoanalysis and the sociology of gender*. Berkeley: University of California Press.

Chouinard, Vera. 1989. Explaining local experiences of state formation: The case of cooperative housing in Toronto. *Environment and Planning D: Society and Space* 7:51–68.

———. 1996. Gender and class identities in process and in place: The local state as a site of gender and class formation. *Environment and Planning A* 28:1485–506.

———. 1999. Disabled women's activism in Canada and beyond. In *Mind and body spaces*, edited by R. Butler and H. Parr. London: Routledge.

———. 2001. Legal peripheries: Struggles over disabled Canadians' places in law, society and space. *Canadian Geographer* 45:187–92.

———. 2004. Making feminist sense of the state and citizenship. In *Mapping women, making politics: Feminist perspectives on political geography*, edited by Lynn A. Staeheli, Eleonore Kofman, and Linda Peake. New York: Routledge.

Chouinard, Vera, and Ruth Fincher. 1987. State formation in capitalism: A conjunctural approach to analysis. *Antipode* 19:329–53.

Chouinard, Vera, and Ali Grant. 1995. On being not even anywhere near "the project": Ways of putting ourselves in the picture. *Antipode* 27:137–66.

Chowdhury, Najma, and Barbara J. Nelson. 1994. Redefining politics: Patterns of women's political engagement from a global perspective. In *Women and politics worldwide*, edited by Barbara J. Nelson and Najma Chowdhury, 3–24. New Haven, Conn.: Yale University Press.

Christiansen, Thomas. 1998. Borders and territorial governance in the new Europe. In *Changing borders: Legal and economic aspects of European enlargements*, edited by R. Kicker, J. Marko, and M. Steiner. Frankfurt (Main): Peter Lang.

Christiansen, Thomas and Pertti Joenniemi. 1999. Politics on the edge: On the restructuring of borders in the north of Europe. In *Curtains of iron and gold: Reconstructing borders and scales of interaction*, edited by H. Eskelinen, I. Liikanen, and J. Oksa. Aldershot, UK: Ashgate.

Christopher, A. J. 1994. *The atlas of apartheid*. London and New York: Routledge.

Chua, P., K. Bhavnani, and J. Foran. 2000. Women, culture, development: A new paradigm for development studies? *Ethnic and Racial Studies* 23:820–41.

Chun, Lin. 1997. Finding a language, feminism and women's movements in contemporary China. In *Transitions, environments, translations*, edited by Joan Scott, Cora Kaplan, and Debra Keates. London and New York: Routledge.

Clark, Gordon, and Michael Dear. 1984. *State apparatus: Structures and language of legitimacy*. Boston: Allen and Unwin.

Clarke, Susan E. 1993. The new localism: Local politics in a global era. In *The new localism: Comparative urban politics in a global era*, edited by Edward G. Goetz and Susan E. Clarke, 1–21. Newbury Park, Calif.: Sage.

Claval, Paul. 1994. Playing with mirrors: The British Empire according to Albert Demangeon. In *Geography and empire*, edited by Anne Godlewska and Neil Smith, 228–43. Oxford: Blackwell.

Clayton, David. 2002. Critical imperial and colonial geographies. In *Handbook of cultural geography*, edited by M. Anderson, S. Domosh, Steve Pile, and Nigel Thrift. London: Sage Ltd.

Clean Clothes Campaign. 2001. Newsletter No. 14, July. A victory in Nicaragua! Full text available at http://www.cleanclothes.org/news/newsletter14-chentex.htm

Cockburn, Cynthia. 1977. *The local state: Management of cities and people*. London: Pluto Press.

———. 1998. *Space between us: Negotiating gender and national identities in conflict*. London and New York: Zed Books.

———. 2001. The gendered dynamics of armed conflict and political violence. In *Victims, perpetrators or actors? Gender, armed conflict and political violence*, edited by C. O. N. Moser and F. C. Clark. London: Zed Books.

Cohen, Jean. 1995. Rethinking privacy: The abortion controversy. In *Public and private in thought and practice: Perspectives on a grand dichotomy*, edited by J. Weintraub and K. Kumar. Chicago: University of Chicago Press.

Cohen, R., and S. Rai. 2000. Global social movements: Towards a cosmopolitan politics. In *Global social movements*, edited by R. Cohen and S. Rai, 1–17. London: Athlone Press.

Collins, Patricia Hill. 1990. *Black feminist thought: Knowledge, consciousness, and the politics of empowerment*. Boston: Unwin Hyman.

———. 1998. *Fighting words: Black women and the search for justice*. Minneapolis and London: Minnesota University Press.

Connell, Robert W. 1990. The state, gender, and sexual politics: Theory and appraisal. *Theory and Society* 19:507–44.

Connor, Walker. 1994. *The quest for understanding*. Princeton, N.J.: Princeton University Press.

———. 2001. Homeland in a world of states. In *Understanding nationalism*, edited by M. Guibernau and J. Hutchinson. Cambridge, Mass.: Polity Press.

Conover, P. J. 1994. Feminists and the gender gap. In *Different roles, different voices: Women and politics in the United States and Europe*, edited by M. Githens, P. Norris, and J. Lovenuski, 51–60. New York: HarperCollins College Publishers.

Cooney, Catherine M. 1999. Still searching for environmental justice. *Environmental Science and Technology* 33:200–4.

Cooper, Annabel, Robin Law, Jane Malthus, and Pamela Wood. 2000. Rooms of their own: Public toilets and gendered citizens in a New Zealand city 1860–1940. *Gender Place and Culture* 7:417–34.

Cooper, D. 1995. *Power in struggle: Feminism, sexuality, and the state.* New York: New York University Press.

Cope, Meghan. 1996. Weaving the everyday: Identity, space, and power in Lawrence, Massachusetts, 1920–1939. *Urban Geography* 17:179–204.

———. 1997. Responsibility, regulation and retrenchment: The end of welfare? In *State devolution in America: Implications for a diverse society*, edited by L. Staeheli, J. Kodras, and C. Flint. Thousand Oaks, Calif.: Sage.

———. 2004. Placing gendered political acts. In *Mapping women, making politics: Feminist perspectives on political geography*, edited by Lynn A. Staeheli, Eleonore Kofman, and Linda Peake. New York: Routledge.

Cope, Meghan, and Melissa R. Gilbert. 2001. Geographies of welfare reform. *Urban Geography* 22:385–90.

Corral, Thais, and Pamela Ransom. 2002. Women and information for participation and decision-making in sustainable development in developing countries. Paper presented at the International Workshop on Gender Perspectives for the Earth Summit. Retrieved from http://www.earthsummit2002.org/workshop/bpinformation s.htm

Costa, Lascoux. 1999. L'illusion de la maitrise, la politique migratoire en trompe l'oeil. In *Sans-papiers: L'archaisme fatal*, edited by E. Balibar et al. Paris: La Déouverte.

Cox, Kevin. 1983. Residential mobility, neighborhood activism and neighborhood problems. *Political Geography Quarterly* 2 (2):99–117.

———, ed. 1997. *Spaces of globalization: Reasserting the power of the local.* New York: Guilford.

———. 2003. Political geography and the territorial. *Political Geography* 22:607–10.

Crang, Mike. 1998. *Cultural geography.* London: Routledge.

Crenshaw, Kimberle. 1991. Mapping the margins: Intersectionality, identity politics, and violence against women of color. *Stanford Law Review* 43:1241–99.

Cresswell, Tim. 1996. *In place/out of place: Geography, ideology and transgression.* Minneapolis: University of Minnesota Press.

Cribb, Jo, and Ross Barnett. 1999. Being bashed: Western Samoan women's responses to domestic violence in Western Samoa and New Zealand. *Gender, Place and Culture* 6:49–65.

Cubitt, Tessa, and Helen Greenslade. 1997. Public and private spheres: The end of dichotomy. In *Gender politics in Latin America: Debates in theory and practice*, edited by Elizabeth Dore. New York: Monthly Review Press.

Cumaranatunga, Lakshmi. 1990. Coping with the unknown: Sri Lankan domestic aides in West Asia. In *Women at the crossroads: A Sri Lankan perspective*, edited by V. Samarasinghe and S. Kiribamuni. New Delhi: Vikas.

Dalby, Simon. 1988. Geopolitical discourse: The Soviet Union as other. *Alternatives* 13:415–42.

———. 1990. *Creating the second cold war.* New York: Guilford.

———. 1994. Gender and critical geopolitics: Reading security discourse in the new world disorder. *Environment and Planning D: Society and Space* 12:1–24.

———. 1996. The environment as geopolitical threat. *Ecumene* 3:472–96.

———. 1998. Environmental geopolitics: Introduction. In *The geopolitics reader*, edited by G. Ó Tuathail, S. Dalby, and P. Routledge. London: Routledge.

D'Amico, F. 1995. Women national leaders. In *Women in world politics*, edited by F. D'Amico and P. Beckmen. Westport, Conn.: Bergin and Garvey.

Darcy, R., Susan Welch, and Janet Clark. 1987. *Women, elections and representation.* New York: Longman.

Davidoff, L. 1998. Regarding some "old husbands' tales": Public and private in feminist history. In *Feminism, the public and the private*, edited by Joan B. Landes. Oxford and New York: Oxford University Press.

Davidson, Joyce. 2000. The world was getting smaller: Women, agoraphobia and bodily boundaries. *Area* 32:31–40.

Dear, Michael. 1981. A theory of the local state. In *Political studies from spatial perspectives*, edited by A. D. Burnett and P. J. Taylor. New York: John Wiley.

———. 1988. The postmodern challenge: Reconstructing human geography. *Transactions of the Institute of British Geographers* 13:262–74.

———. 1999. Telecommunications, gangster nations and the crisis of representative democracy: An editorial comment. *Political Geography* 18:81–83.

Dear, Michael, and Jennifer Wolch. 1987. *Landscapes of despair: From deinstitutionalization to homelessness.* Princeton, N.J.: Princeton University Press.

D'Eaubonne, Françoise. 1974. *Le feminisme ou la mort!* Paris: Pierre Horay.

Deere, Carmen Diana, and Magdalena Leon. 2003. The gender asset gap: Land in Latin America. *World Development* 31:925–47.

Della Porta, D. 1996. Social movements and the state: Thoughts on the policing of protest. In *Comparative perspectives on social movements: Political opportunities, mobilizing structures, and cultural framings,* edited by D. MacAdam, J. D. McCarthy, and N. Z. Mayer, 62–92. Cambridge: Cambridge University Press.

Demangeon, André. 1923. *L'empire Britannique: Etude de géographie coloniale.* Paris: Librairie Armand Colin.

Department of Foreign Affairs and International Trade, Canada. [cited October 10, 2000]. *Freedom from fear: Canada's foreign policy for human security.* http://www.dfait-maeci.gc.ca/foreignp/HumanSecurity/HumanSecuritysBooklet-e.asp 2000

Derrida, J. 1978. *Writing and difference.* Chicago: Chicago University Press.

De Souza, and A. M. Flavio. 2001. The future of informal settlements: Lessons in the legalization of disputed urban land in Recife, Brazil. *Geoforum* 32 (4):483–92.

de Wenden, Wihtol. 1994. Immigrants as political actors in France. *Western European Politics* 17:91–109.

Dezalay, Yves, and Bryant G. Garth. 2002. *The internationalization of palace wars: Lawyers, economists, and the contest to transform Latin American states.* Chicago: University of Chicago Press.

Diamond, Irene. 1997. *Fertile ground: Women, earth, and the limits of control.* Boston: Beacon Press.

Diamond, Irene, and Gloria Orenstein, eds. 1990. *Reweaving the world: The emergence of ecofeminism.* San Francisco: Sierra Club Books.

Dicken, Peter. 1998. *Global shift: Transforming the world economy.* 3rd ed. New York: Guilford.

Dicken, Peter, Philip F. Kelly, Kris Olds, and Henry Wai-Chung Yeung. 2001. Chains and networks, territories and scales: Towards a relational framework for analyzing the global economy. *Global Networks* 1:89–112.

Dietz, Mary. 1987. Context is all: Feminism and theories of citizenship. In *Learning about women: Gender, politics, and power,* edited by J. Conway, S. Bourque, and J. Scott. Ann Arbor: University of Michigan Press.

Dishman, Chris. 2001. Terrorism, crime and transformation. *Studies in Conflict and Terrorism* 24 (1):43–58.

Dobson, Janet, et al. 2001. *International migration and the United Kingdom: Recent patterns and trends.* Home Office, RDS Occasional Paper No. 75.

Dodds, Klaus. 2001. Political geography III: Critical geopolitics after ten years. *Progress in Human Geography* 25:469–84.

Dodds, Klaus, and David Atkinson, eds. 2000. *Geopolitical traditions: A century of geopolitical thought.* London: Routledge.

Domosh, Mona. 1991a. Beyond the frontiers of geographical knowledge. *Transactions of the Institute of British Geographers* 16:488–90.

———. 1991b. For a feminist historiography of geography. *Transactions of the Institute of British Geographers* 16:95–104.

Domosh, Mona, and Joni Seager. 2001. *Putting women in place: Feminist geographers make sense of the world.* New York: Guilford.

Donato, Kathleen. 1992. Understanding U.S. immigration: Why some countries send women and others send men. In *Seeking common ground: Multidisciplinary studies of immigrant women in the United States,* edited by D. Gabaccia. Westport, Conn.: Greenwood.

Dowler, Lorraine. 1998. "And they think I am just an old lady": Women and war in Belfast, Northern Ireland. *Gender, Place and Culture* 5:159–76.

———. 2001. Fieldwork in the trenches: Participant observation in a conflict area. In *Qualitative methods for geographers,* edited by C. Dwyer and M. Limb. London: Arnold.

———. 2002. Women on the frontlines: Rethinking war narratives post 9/11. *GeoJournal* 58 (2): 159–65.

Dowler, Lorraine, and Joanne Sharp. 2001. A feminist geopolitics? *Space and Polity* 5:165–76.

Dowling, Robyn. 1998. Suburban stories, gendered lives: Thinking through difference. In *Cities of difference,* edited by R. Fincher and J. Jacobs. New York: Guilford.

Doyle, Timothy, and Doug McEachern. 1998. *Environment and politics.* London: Routledge.

Drake, C., and J. Horton. 1983. Comment on editorial essay: Sexist bias in political geography. *Political Geography Quarterly* 2 (4): 329–37.

Driver, Felix. 2001. *Geography militant: Cultures of exploration and empire.* Oxford: Blackwell.

Dunbar, Gary. 1981. Elisee Reclus: An anarchist in geography. In *Geography, ideology and social concern,* edited by D. Stoddart. Oxford: Blackwell.

Duncan, Nancy. 1996. Introduction: (Re)placings. In *BodySpace: Destabilizing geographies of gender and sexuality,* edited by Nancy Duncan. London and New York: Routledge.

Dwyer, Claire. 1999. Veiled meanings: Young British Muslim women and the negotiation of differences. *Gender, Place and Culture* 6:5–26.

Eade, Deborah, and Ernst Ligteringen, eds. 2001. *Debating development.* Oxford: Oxfam GB.

Eatwell, John, and Lance Taylor. 2000. *Global finance at risk: The case for international regulation.* New York: New Press.

Einhorn, Barbara. 1993. *Cinderella goes to market: Citizenship, gender and women's movements in East Central Europe.* London: Verso.

Eisenstein, Hester. 1991. *Gender shock: Practicing feminism on two continents.* Boston: Beacon Press.

Eisenstein, Zillah. 1981. *The radical future of liberal feminism.* New York: Longman.

———. 2000. Writing bodies on the nation for the globe. In *Women, states, and nationalism: At home in the nation?,* edited by S. Ranchod-Nilsson and M. A. Téreault. London and New York: Routledge.

Ekins, P. 1992. *A new world order: Grassroots movements for social change.* London: Routledge.

Elder, G. S. 1998. The South African body politic: Space, race and heterosexuality. In *Places through the body,* edited by Steve Pile and Heidi J. Nast. London and New York: Routledge.

Elman, R. Amy. 2001. Unprotected by the Swedish welfare state revisited: Assessing a decade of reforms for battered women. *Women's Studies International Forum* 24 (1): 39–52.

Elshtain, Jean Bethke. 1981. *Public man, private woman.* Princeton, N.J.: Princeton University Press.

———. 1982. *The family in political thought.* Amherst: University of Massachusetts Press.

———. 1987. Against androgyny. In *Feminism and equality,* edited by Anne Phillips. Oxford: Blackwell.

———. 1995. The displacement of politics. In *Public and private in thought and practice: Perspectives on a grand dichotomy,* edited by J. Weintraub and K. Kumar. Chicago: University of Chicago Press.

Elson, Diane. 1998. Talking to the boys: Gender and economic growth models. In *Feminist visions of development: Gender, analysis and policy,* edited by Cecile Jackson and Ruth Pearson. New York: Routledge.

Engel, S. M. 2001. *The unfinished revolution: Social movement theory and the gay and lesbian movement.* Cambridge: Cambridge University Press.

Enloe, Cynthia. 1983. *Does khaki become you? The militarization of women's lives.* London: Pluto Press.

———. 1989. *Bananas, beaches and bases: Making feminist sense of international politics.* Berkeley: University of California Press.

———. 1993. *The morning after: Sexual politics at the end of the cold war.* Berkeley: University of California Press.

———. 2000. *Maneuvers: The international politics of militarizing women's lives.* Berkeley: University of California Press.

Eschle, Catherine. 2001. *Global democracy, social movements, and feminism.* Boulder, Colo.: Westview Press.

Escobar, Arturo. 1995. *Encountering development: The making and unmaking of the Third World.* Princeton, N.J.: Princeton University Press.

Escobar, Arturo, and Sonia Alvarez, eds. 1992. *The making of social movements in Latin America: Identity, strategy and democracy.* Boulder, Colo.: Westview Press.

Espiritu, Yen Le. 2002. Filipino navy stewards and Filipina health care professionals: Immigration, work and family relations. *Asian and Pacific Migration Journal* 11:47–66.

Eurofem-Gender and Human Settlements. 1995. *Proceedings from the second working meeting.* The Hague, the Netherlands: Ministry of the Environment.

———. 1996. *Proceedings from the third working meeting.* Aosta, Italy: Ministry of the Environment.

———. 1998. *Proceedings of the Eurofem Gender and Human Settlements International Conference.* Hameenlinna, Finland: Ministry of the Environment.

European Commission. 1994. *European charter for women in the city.* Brussels: Author.

Fabian, Wendy. 1993. Globalization and feminism in New Zealand. In *Feminism and the politics of difference,* edited by S. Gunew and A. Yeatman. Boulder, Colo.: Wesview Press.

Fairhurst, Joan, Maano Ramutsindela, and Urmilla Bob. 2004. Social movements, protest, and resistance. In *Mapping women, making politics: Feminist perspectives on political geography*, edited by Lynn A. Staeheli, Eleonore Kofman, and Linda Peake. New York: Routledge.

Fanon, Franz. 1967. *Black skin, white mask*. New York: Grove Press.

Fawcett, Charles. 1933. *Political geography of the British Empire*. London: University of London Press.

Feitelson, E. 2002. Implications of shifts in Israeli water discourse for Israeli-Palestinian water negotiations. *Political Geography* 21:293–318.

Feldman, Roberta, and Susan Stall. 1994. The politics of space appropriation: A case study of women's struggles for homeplace in Chicago public housing. In *Women and environments*, edited by I. Altman and A. Churchman. New York: Plenum.

Fernandez Poncela, Anna M. 1997. Nicaraguan women: Legal, political, and social spaces. In *Gender politics in Latin America: Debates in theory and practice*, edited by Elizabeth Dore. New York: Monthly Review Press.

Ferree, Myra Marx. 1995. Making equality: The women's affairs offices in the Federal Republic of Germany. In *Comparative state feminism*, edited by D. Stetson and A. Mazur, 95–113. Thousand Oaks, Calif.: Sage.

Field, Debbie. 1999. Putting food first: Women's role in creating a grassroots system outside the marketplace. In *Women working the NAFTA food chain: Women, food and globalization*, edited by Deborah Barndt. Toronto: Second Story Press.

Filemyr, Ann. 1997. Unmasking the population bomb: Analyzing domination at the intersection of gender, race, class, and ecology. *NWSA Journal* 9:138–55.

Fincher, R. 1981. Local implementation strategies in the urban built-environment. *Environment and Planning A* 13:1233–52.

———. 1989a. Class and gender relations in the local labour market and the local state. In *The power of geography: How territory shapes social life*, edited by J. Wolch and M. Dear. Boston: Unwin Hyman.

———. 1989b. The political economy of the local state. In *New models in geography*, edited by Richard Peet and Nigel Thrift. London: Routledge.

———. 1991. Caring for workers; dependents: Gender, class and local state practice in Melbourne. *Political Geography Quarterly* 10:356–81.

———. 1993. Women, the state and life course in urban Australia. In *Full circles: Geographies of women over the life course*, edited by Cindi Katz and Janice Monk. London and New York: Routledge.

———. 1996a. The demanding state: Volunteer work and social polarisation, in restructuring difference: Social polarisation and the city. In *Working paper 6*, edited by K. Gibson et al. Melbourne: Australian Housing and Urban Research Institute.

———. 1996b. The state and child care: An international review from a geographical perspective. In *Who will mind the baby? Geographies of child care and working mothers*, edited by Kim England. London: Routledge.

———. 2004. From dualisms to multiplicities: Gendered political practices. In *Mapping women, making politics: Feminist perspectives on political geography*, edited by Lynn A. Staeheli, Eleonore Kofman, and Linda Peake. New York: Routledge.

Fincher, Ruth, and Jane M. Jacobs, eds. 1998. *Cities of difference*. New York: Guilford.

Fincher, Ruth, and Ruth Panelli. 2001. Making space: Women's urban and rural activism and the Australian state. *Gender, Place and Culture* 8:129–48.

Fine, Ben. 2002. Economics imperialism and the new development economics as Kuhnian paradigm shift. *World Development* 30:2057–70.

Flammang, Janet. 1997. *Women's political voice: How women are transforming the practice and study of politics*. Philadelphia: Temple University Press.

Fleischer, Doris Zames and Frieda Zames. 2001. *The disability rights movements: From charity to confrontation*. Philadelphia: Temple University Press.

Fleming, Marie. 1979. *The anarchist way to socialism: Elisée Reclus and nineteenth century anarchism*. London: Croom Helm.

Flint, Colin. 2002. Political geography: Globalization, metapolitical geographies and everyday life. *Progress in Human Geography* 26:391–400.

Floro, Maria Sagrario. 1995. Economic restructuring, gender and the allocation of time. *World Development* 23:1913–29.

Foucault, Michel. 1980. Questions on geography. In *Power/knowledge: Selected interviews and other writings 1972–1977*, edited by C. Gordon. Brighton: Harvester Press.

Fouron, Georges, and Nina Glick-Schiller. 2001. All in the family: Gender, transnational migration, and the nation-state. *Identities: Global Studies in Culture and Power* 7:539–82.

Frankenberg, Ruth, and Lata Mani. 1996. Crosscurrents, crosstalk: Race, "postcoloniality" and the politics of location. In *Contemporary postcolonial theory: A reader*, edited by Padmini Mongia. New York: Arnold.

Fraser, Nancy. 1989. *Unruly practices: Power, discourse and gender in contemporary social theory*. Minneapolis: University of Minnesota Press.

———. 1990. Rethinking the public sphere: A contribution to the critique of actually existing democracy. *Social Text* 25/26:56–80.

———. 1995. From redistribution to recognition? Dilemmas of justice in a "post-socialist" age. *New Left Review* 212:68–93.

———. 1997. *Justice interruptus, critical reflections on the "postsocialist" condition*. London and New York: Routledge.

Freedom House. 1999. *Freedom in the world, 1998–1999*. Retrieved from http://www.freedomhouse.org/pfs99

Freeman, Carla. 2001. Is local:global as feminine:masculine? Rethinking the gender of globalization. *Signs: Journal of Women in Culture and Society* 26:1007–37.

Freidman, Milton, and Rose D. Friedman. 1980. *Free to choose: A personal statement*. New York: Harcourt.

Friedman, Susan. 1998. *Mappings, feminism and the cultural geographies of encounter*. Princeton, N.J.: Princeton University Press.

Friedman, Thomas L. 1999. *The Lexus and the olive tree: Understanding globalization*. New York: Random House.

Friedmann, John. 1998. The political economy of planning: The rise of civil society. In *Cities for citizens*, edited by M. Douglass and J. Friedmann. New York: John Wiley.

Friese, Marianne. 1995. East European women as domestics in Western Europe—New social inequality and division of labour among women. *Journal of Area Studies* 6:194–202.

Frohmann, Alicia, and Teresa Valdés. 1995. Democracy in the country and in the home: The women's movement in Chile. In *The challenge of local feminisms: Women's movements in global perspective*, edited by Amrita Basu. Boulder, Colo.: Westview Press.

Fukuyama, Francis. 1992. *The end of history and the last man*. New York: Fress Press.

Funtowicz, Silvio, and Jerome R. Ravetz. 2000. *La ciencia potnormal. Ciencia con la gente*. Barcelona: Icaria Antrazyt.

Gal, Susan, and Gail Kligman. 2000. *The politics of gender after socialism*. Princeton, N.J.: Princeton University Press.

Gamson, William. 1995. Constructing social protest. In *Social movements and culture*, edited by Hank Johnston and Bert Klandermans. Minneapolis: University of Minnesota Press.

García, Ernest. 1995. *El Trampolí Fàustic*. Alzira: Germania.

Garcia-Ramon, Maria, and Joan Nogué-Font. 1994. Nationalism and geography in Catalonia. In *Geography and national identity*, edited by David Hooson. Oxford: Blackwell.

Gautier, Arlette. 2003. Femmes et colonialisme. In *Le livre noir du colonialisme xvie–xxi siècle: De l'extermination à la repentance*, edited by M. Ferro. Paris: Robert Laffont.

Gellner, Ernst. 1983. *Nations and nationalism*. Oxford: Blackwell.

Genovese, M. A. 1993. *Women as national leaders*. Newbury Park, Calif.: Sage.

George, Sheba. 2000. "Dirty nurses" and "men who play": Gender and class in transnational migration. In *Global ethnography: Forces, connections, and imaginations in a postmodern world*, edited by Michael Burawoy and Joseph A. Blum. Los Angeles: University of California Press.

Giblin, Beatrice. 1987. Elisée Reclus and colonization. In *International geopolitical analysis*, edited by Girot Pascale and Eleonore Kofman. London: Croom Helm.

Gibson-Graham, J. K. 1994. "Stuffed if I know": Reflections on post-modern feminist social research. *Gender, Place and Culture* 1:205–24.

———. 1996. *The end of capitalism (as we knew it): A feminist critique of political economy*. Cambridge and Oxford: Blackwell.

Gilbert, Melissa. 1997. Identity, space, and politics: A critique of the poverty debates. In *Thresholds in feminist geography: Difference, methodology, representation*, edited by J. P. Jones, H. Nast, and S. Roberts. Lanham, Md.: Rowman & Littlefield.

———. 1999. Place, politics and the production of urban space: A feminist critique of the growth machine thesis. In *The urban growth machine: Critical perspectives, two decades later*, edited by Andrew E. G. Jonas and David Wilson. Albany: State University of New York Press.

Gill, L. 2000. *Teetering on the rim. Global restructuring, daily life, and the armed retreat of the Bolivia state.* New York: Columbia University.

Gilligan, Carole. 1982. *In a different voice: Psychological theory and women's development.* Cambridge, Mass.: Harvard University Press.

Gilmartin, Mary, and Eleonore Kofman. 2004. Critically feminist geopolitics. In *Mapping women, making politics: Feminist perspectives on political geography,* edited by Lynn A. Staeheli, Eleonore Kofman, and Linda Peake. New York: Routledge.

Girot, Pascal, and Eleonore Kofman, eds. and trans. 1987. *International geopolitical analysis.* London: Croom Helm.

Githens, M., et al. 1994. Introduction. In *Different roles, different voices: Women and politics in the United States and Europe,* edited by M. Githens, P. Norris, and J. Lovenuski, ix–xvi. New York: HarperCollins College Publishers.

Glassner, Ira. 1993. *Political geography.* London: Wiley.

Godlewska, Anne, and Neil Smith, eds. 1994. *Geography and empire.* Oxford: Blackwell.

Goodwin, Jeff, James Jasper, and Francesca Poletta, eds. 2001. *Passionate politics: Emotions and social movements.* Cambridge: Cambridge University Press.

Goss, Sue. 1984. Women's initiatives in local government. In *Local socialism? Labour councils and new left alternatives,* edited by Martin Boddy and Colin Fudge. London: Macmillan.

Graham, Julie. 2002. Women and the politics of place: Ruminations and responses. *World Development* 45:18–22.

Graham, Katherine A., and Susan D. Phillips (with Allan M. Maslove). 1998. *Urban governance in Canada.* Toronto: Harcourt Brace.

Graham, Stephen, and Simon Marvin. 2001. *Splintering urbanism: Networked infrastructures, technological mobilities, and the urban condition.* London: Routledge.

Gray, C. S., and G. Sloan. 1999. *Geopolitics, geography and strategy.* London and Portland, Oreg.: Frank Cass.

Greed, Clara, Linda Davies, Caroline Brown, and Stephanie Duehr. 2002. *Report on gender auditing and mainstreaming: Incorporating case studies and pilots.* London: Royal Town Planning Institute, School of Planning and Architecture, University of the West of England.

Grewal, Inderpal, and Caren Kaplan, eds. 1994. *Scattered hegemonies: Postmodernity and transnational feminist practices.* Minneapolis: University of Minnesota Press.

Günes-Ayata, A. 1995. Women's participation in politics in Turkey. In *Women in modern Turkish society: A reader,* edited by S. Tekeli, 235–49. London: Zed.

Gupta, Akhil, and James Ferguson. 1992. "Beyond culture": Space, identity and the politics of difference. *Cultural Anthropology* 7:1–23.

Habermas, Jürgen. 1985. *The theory of communicative action.* Boston: Beacon.

———. 1989. *The structural transformation of the public sphere.* Cambridge: Massachusetts Institute of Technology.

Haeri, Shahla. 1989. *Law of desire: Temporary marriage in Shi'i Iran.* Syracuse, N.Y.: Syracuse University Press.

Hague, E. 2002. The Scottish Diaspora: Tartan Day and the appropriation of Scottish identities in the United States. In *Celtic geographies: New cultures, old times,* edited by D. Harvey, R. Jones, N. McInroy, and C. Milligan. London: Routledge.

Hahnel, R. 2000. Globalization: Beyond reaction, thinking ahead. *New Politics* 8 (1).

Haif, A. 1986. Immigrant women in France. In *Migrant women claim their rights, Nairobi and after: A selection of documents for study and action.* Geneva: Migration Secretariat, World Council of Churches.

Halfacree, Keith. 1995. Household migration and the structuration of patriarchy: Evidence from the USA. *Progress in Human Geography* 19:159–82.

Halford, Susan. 1989. Spatial divisions and women's initiatives in British local government. *Geoforum* 20:161–74.

Hamel, Pierre, Henri Lustiger-Thaler, and Margit Mayer, eds. 2000. *Urban movements in a globalising world.* London: Routledge.

Hanson, Susan. 1992. Presidential address: Geography and feminism: Worlds in collision? *Annals of the Association of American Geographers* 82:569–86.

———. 1999. Is feminist geography relevant? *Scottish Geographical Journal* 115:133–41.

Hanson, Susan, and Geraldine Pratt. 1995. *Gender, work and space.* London: Routledge.

Haraway, Donna. 1988. Situated knowledges: The science question in feminism and the privilege of partial perspective. *Feminist Studies* 14:575–99.

———. 1991. Situated knowledges. In *Simians, cyborgs, and women: The reinvention of nature.* New York: Routledge.

Harcourt, Wendy, and Arturo Escobar. 2002. Women and the politics of place. *World Development* 45:7–14.

Harding, Sandra. 1991. *Whose science? Whose knowledge? Thinking from women's lives.* Ithaca, N.Y.: Cornell University Press.

Hardoy, E. George, and David Satterthwaite. 1989. *Squatter citizen: Life in the urban Third World.* London: Earthscan.

Hardt, Michael, and Antonio Negri. 2000. *Empire.* Cambridge, Mass.: Harvard University Press.

Hardy-Fanta, Carol. 1993. *Latina politics, Latino politics: Gender, culture and political participation in Boston.* Philadelphia: Temple University Press.

Hartshorne, Richard. 1954. Political geography. In *American geography: Inventory and prospect,* edited by P. James and C. Jones. Syracuse, N.Y.: Syracuse University Press.

Harvey, David. 1973. *Social justice and the city.* Oxford: Blackwell.

Hassner, P. 1997. Obstinate and obsolete: Non-territorial transnational forces versus the European territorial state. In *Geopolitics in the post-wall Europe: Security, territory, and identity,* edited by O. Tunander, P. Baev, and V. Einagel. London: Sage Ltd.

Hays-Mitchell, Maureen. 1995. Voices and visions from the streets: Gender interests and political participation among women informal traders in Latin America. *Environment and Planning D: Society and Space* 13:445–70.

Heffernan, Michael. 1994. The science of empire: The French geographical movement and the forms of French imperialism, 1870–1920. In *Geography and empire,* edited by A. Godlewska and N. Smith. Oxford: Blackwell.

———. 2000. Fin de siècle, fin du monde? On the origin of European geopolitics 1890–1920. In *Geopolitical traditions: A century of geopolitical thought,* edited by K. Dodds and D. Atkinson. London: Routledge.

Helleiner, Eric. 1994. *States and the reemergence of global finance.* Ithaca, N.Y.: Cornell University Press.

Hepple, Leslie. 2000. Géopolitiques De Gauche: Yves Lacoste, Hérodote and French radical geopolitics. In *Geopolitical traditions,* edited by K. Dodds and D. Atkinson. London: Routledge.

Herb, Guntram, and David Kaplan, eds. 1999. *Nested identities: Nationalism, territory, and scale.* Lanham, Md.: Rowman & Littlefield.

Her Majesty's Stationery Office. 2002. *Secure border, safe haven: Integration with diversity in modern Britain.* London: Author.

Herod, Andrew. 1997. Labor's spatial praxis and the geography of contract bargaining in the US East Coast longshore industry, 1953–89. *Political Geography* 16:145–69.

Holston, James. 1999. Spaces of insurgent citizenship. In *Cities and citizenship,* edited by J. Holston. Durham, N.C.: Duke University Press.

Hondagneu-Sotelo, Pierrette. 1994. *Gendered transitions: Mexican experiences of immigration.* Berkeley: University of California Press.

———. 1999. Gender and contemporary U.S. immigration. *American Behavioral Scientist* 42:565–76.

Hondagneu-Sotelo, Pierrette, and Ernestine Avila. 1997. "I'm here, but I'm there": The meanings of Latina transnational motherhood. *Gender and Society* 11:548–71.

hooks, b. 1984. *Feminist theory: From margin to center.* Boston: South End Press.

Hooper, C. 2000. Masculinities in transition: The case of globalisation. In *Gender and global restructuring: Sightings, sites and resistances,* edited by M. Marchand and A. Sisson Runyan. London: Routledge.

Hooson, David, ed. 1994. *Geography and national identity.* Oxford: Blackwell.

Huang, Shirlena, and Brenda Yeoh. 1996. Ties that bind: State policy and migrant female domestic helpers in Singapore. *Geoforum* 27:479–93.

Hudson, Brian. 1977. The new geography and the new imperialism: 1870–1918. *Antipode* 9:12–19.

Hughes, A. 2000. Retailers, knowledges and changing commodity networks: The case of the cut flower trade. *Geoforum* 31:175–90.

Hugo, Graeme. 2002. Effects of international migration on the family in Indonesia. *Asian and Pacific Migration Journal* 11:13–46.

Huntington, Samuel. 1991. *The third wave: Democratization in the late twentieth century.* Norman: University of Oklahoma Press.

———. 1993. *The clash of civilizations and the remaking of the world order.* New York: Simon and Schuster.

Hüwelmeier, Gertrud. 2001. Women's congregations as transnational communities. Working Paper Transnational Communities Program, 2K-13.

Hyndman, Jennifer. 1997. Border crossings. *Antipode* 29 (2):149–76.

———. 2000. *Managing displacement: Refugees and the politics of humanitarianism.* Minneapolis: University of Minnesota Press.

———. 2001. Towards a feminist geopolitics. *Canadian Geographer* 45:210–22.

———. 2004. The (geo)politics of mobility. In *Mapping women, making politics: Feminist perspectives on political geography,* edited by Lynn A. Staeheli, Eleonore Kofman, and Linda Peake. New York: Routledge.

Hyndman, Jennifer, and Margaret Walton-Roberts. 2000. Interrogating borders: A transnational approach to refugee research in Vancouver. *Canadian Geographer* 44:244–58.

Inglehart, R., and P. Norris. 2003. *Rising tide: Gender, equality and cultural change around the world.* Cambridge: Cambridge University Press.

Inter-Parliamentary Union (IPU). Parline Database. [accessed June 2004]. http://www.ipu.org/parline-e/parlinesearch.asp

Iredale, Robyn. Forthcoming. Gender, immigration policies and accreditation: Valuing the skills of professional women migrants. *Geoforum.*

Isin, Engin. 2002. *Being political: Genealogies of citizenship.* Minneapolis: University of Minnesota Press.

Iveson, Kurt. 2003. Justifying exclusion: The politics of public space and the dispute over access to McIvers ladies' baths, Sydney. *Gender Place and Culture* 10:215–28.

Jackson, Cecile. 1994. Gender analysis and environmentalism. In *Social theory and the global environment,* edited by M. Redclift and T. Benton. London: Routledge.

———, ed. 2000. Special issue: "Men at work"—Labour, masculinities, development. *European Journal of Development Studies* 12.

Jackson, Peter, and Jan Penrose, eds. 1993. *Constructions of race, place and nation.* London: University College Press.

Jacobs, Jane. 1996. *Edge of empire: Postcolonialism and the city.* London: Routledge.

———. 2000. Editorial: Difference and its others. *Transactions of the Institute of British Geographers* 25:403–7.

Jacquette, Jane, ed. 1991. *The women's movements in Latin America.* Boulder, Colo.: Westview Press.

———. 1994. Women's movements and the challenge of democratic politics in Latin America. *Social Politics* 1:335–40.

Jaggar, Alison. 1988. *Feminist politics and human nature.* Lanham, Md.: Rowman & Littlefield.

Jamieson, Natalie, and Michael Webber. 1991. Flexibility and part-time employment in retailing. *Labour and Industry* 4:55–70.

Janschitz, Susanne, and Andrea Kofler. 2004. Diversities and commonalities in a multicultural living space. In *Challenged borderlands: Transcending political and cultural boundaries,* edited by V. Pavlakovich, B. Morehouse, and D. Wastl-Walter. Ashgate, UK: Aldershot.

Jayawardena, Kumari. 1986. *Feminism and nationalism in the Third World.* London: Zed Books.

Jelin, Elizabeth. 1990. *Women and social change in Latin America.* London: Zed Books.

———. 1997. Engendering human rights. In *Gender politics in Latin America: Debates in theory and practice,* edited by Elizabeth Dore. New York: Monthly Review Press.

Jenkins, J. Craig. 1981. Sociopolitical moments. In *Handbook of political behavior 5,* edited by S. L. Long. New York: Plenum Press.

Jessop, Bob. 2001. Die Geschlechtsspezifische Selektivitat Des Staates (The gender selectivities of the state). In *Das Geschlecht Des Staates: Transformationen Von Staatllichkeit in Europa,* edited by Eva Kreisky, Sabine Lang, and Birgit Sauer. Opladen: Bohret. Reprint, published by the Department of Sociology, Lancaster University. Retrieved from http://www.comp.lancs.ac.uk/sociology/papers/jessop-gender-selectivities.pdf

———. 2002. Liberalism, neoliberalism, and urban governance: A state-theoretical perspective. *Antipode* 34:452–72.

Jiggins, Janice. 1994. *Changing the boundaries: Women-centered perspectives on population and the environment.* Washington, D.C. and Colvelo, Calif.: Island Press.

Joekes, Melissa, Cathy Green, and Melissa Leach. 1996. *Integrating gender into environmental research and policy.* Sussex, UK: Institute of Development Studies.

Johnson, Nuala. 1995. Cast in stone: Monuments, geography, and nationalism. *Environment and Planning D: Society and Space* 13:51–65.

Johnston, R. J. 1982. *Geography and the state: An essay in political geography.* Basingstoke: Macmillan.

———. 1991. *A question of place.* Oxford: Blackwell.

Johnston, R. J., F.M. Shelley, and P.J. Taylor, eds. 1990. *Developments in electoral geography.* New York: Routledge.

Johnston, Ron, David Knight, and Eleonore Kofman, eds. 1988. *Nationalism, self-determination and political geography.* London: Croom Helm.

Joint Committee for Migrant Workers in Korea. 2002. *Online Campaign 2002.* 19 April.

Jones, John Paul, Heidi Nast, and Susan Roberts, eds. 1997. *Thresholds in feminist geography: Difference, methodology, representation.* Lanham, Md.: Rowman & Littlefield.

Jones, K. B. 1994. Identity, action and locale: Thinking about citizenship, civic action and feminism. *Social Politics* 1:256–71.

———. 1997. Introduction to special issue: Citizenship in feminism: Identity, action and locale. *Hypatia* 12 (4): 1–5.

Joppke, Christian. 2000. *Immigration and the nation state.* Oxford: Oxford University Press.

Jordan, G., and W. Maloney. 1997. *The protest business: Mobilizing campaigns groups.* Manchester: Manchester University Press.

Joseph, S. 2000. Gendering citizenship in the Middle East. In *Gender and citizenship in the Middle East,* edited by S. Joseph, 3–32. Syracuse, N.Y.: Syracuse University Press.

Jukarainen, Pirjo. 1999. Borders change—So do spaces, identity and community. In *Curtains of iron and gold: Reconstruction borders and scales of interaction,* edited by H. Eskelinen, I. Liikanen, and J. Oksa. Aldershot, UK: Ashgate.

Kaldor, Mary. 1999. *New and old wars: Organized violence in a global era.* Stanford, Calif.: Stanford University Press.

Kandiyoti, Deniz, ed. 1991. *Women, Islam and the state.* Philadelphia: Temple University Press.

———. 1997. Beyond Beijing: Obstacles and prospects for the Middle East. In *Muslim women and the politics of participation: Implementing the Beijing platform,* edited by M. Afkhami and E. Friedl, 3–10. Syracuse, N.Y.: Syracuse University Press.

Kanjanapan, W. 1995. The immigration of Asian professionals to the United States: 1988–1990. *International Migration Review* 29:7–32.

Kaplan, Caren. 1994. The politics of location as transnational feminist practice. In *Scattered hegemonies: Postmodernity and transnational feminist practices,* edited by Inderpal Grewal and Caren Kaplan. Minneapolis: University of Minnesota Press.

Kaplan, Temma. 1997. *Crazy for democracy: Women in grassroots movements.* New York: Routledge.

Karakasidou, Anastasia. 1996. Women of the family, women of the nation. *Women's Studies International Journal* 19:99–109.

Katz, Cindi. 1994. Playing the field: Questions of fieldwork in geography. *Professional Geographer* 46:67–72.

———. 2001. On the grounds of globalization: A topography for feminist political engagement. *Signs: Journal of Women and Culture in Society* 26:1213–34.

Katz, Cindi, and Janice Monk. 1993. Making connections: Space, place and the life course. In *Full circles: Geographies of women over the life course,* edited by Cindi Katz and Janice Monk, 264–78. New York: Routledge.

Kaur Puar, J. 2002. Introduction. *Journal of Lesbian and Gay Studies* 8:1–6.

Kayatekin, Serap A., and David F. Ruccio. 1998. Global fragments: Subjectivity and class politics in discourses of globalization. *Economy and Society* 27:74–96.

Kebede, Emebet. 2002. *Ethiopia: An assessment of the international labour migration situation: The case of female labour migrants.* Geneva: International Labour Organization.

Kedourie, Elie. 1993. *Nationalism.* Oxford: Blackwell.

Keil, Roger. 1998. Globalization makes states: Perspectives of local governance in the age of the world city. *Review of International Political Economy* 5:616–46.

Kelly, R. M., Jane H. Bayes, Mary E. Hawkesworth, and Brigitte Young, eds. 2001. *Gender, globalization and democratization.* New York and Oxford: Rowman & Littlefield.

Keohane, R., ed. 1986. *Neorealism and its critics.* New York: Columbia University Press.

Keyfitz, Nathan. 1998. How do we know that there will be too many people? In *Political ecology, global and local,* edited by Roger Keil et al. London: Routledge.

King, Ynestra. 1988. Ecological feminism. *Zeta Magazine,* July/August, 124–27.

Kirby, Andrew. 1993. *Power/resistance: Local politics and the chaotic state.* Bloomington: Indiana University Press.

———. 1997. Restating what's obviously not obvious: More on why we need to think longer and harder about the state apparatus. *Political Geography* 16:33–36.

Knight, David. 1982. Identity and territory: Geographical perspectives on nationalism and regionalism. *Annals of the Association of American Geographers* 72:514–31.

Kobayashi, Audrey. 1994. Coloring the field: Gender, "race" and the politics of fieldwork. *Professional Geographer* 46:73–80.

———. 1997. The paradox of difference and diversity (or, why the thresholds keep moving). In *Thresholds in feminist geography, difference, methodology, representation*, edited by J. P. Jones, H. Nast, and S. Roberts. Lanham, Md.: Rowman & Littlefield.

Kobayashi, Audrey, and Linda Peake. 2000. Racism out of place: Thoughts on whiteness and an antiracist geography in the new millennium. *Annals of the Association of American Geographers* 90:392–403.

Kofler, Andrea Ch. 2004. Objecting political realities in border cities: Local forms of protest and their effects on life across borders. In *Rights to the city*, edited by D. Wastl-Walter, L. Staeheli, and L. Dowler. Rome: Societa Geografica Italiana.

Kofman, Eleonore. 1993. National identity and sexual and cultural differences in France. In *France: Nation and regions*, edited by M. Kelly and R. Bock. Southampton: University of Southampton Press.

———. 1996. Feminism, gender relations and geopolitics: Problematic closures and opening strategies. In *Globalization: Theory and practice*, edited by Eleonore Kofman and Gillian Youngs. London: Pinter.

———. 1997. When society was simple: The far and new right on gender and ethnic divisions in France. In *Gender, ethnicity and political ideologies*, edited by Nicky Clarles and Helen Hintjens. New York and London: Routledge.

———. 1998. Whose city? Gender, class, and immigration in globalizing European cities. In *Cities of difference*, edited by R. Fincher and Jane M. Jacobs. New York and London: Guilford.

———. 2002. Contemporary European migrations, civic stratification and citizenship. *Political Geography* 21:1035–54.

———. 2003. Political geography and globalization as we enter the 21st century. In *Globalization: Theory and practice*, edited by E. Kofman and G. Youngs. London: Continuum.

———. 2004. Family-related migration: A critical review of European studies. *Journal of Ethnic and Migration Studies* 30:243–62.

———. Forthcoming. Feminist political geographies. In *Companion to feminist geography*, edited by L. Nelson and J. Seager. Oxford: Blackwell.

Kofman, Eleonore, and Kim England. 1997. Citizenship and international migration: Taking account of gender, sexuality, and "race." *Environment and Planning A* 29:191–93.

Kofman, Eleonore, and Linda Peake. 1990. Into the 1990s: A gendered agenda for political geography. *Political Geography Quarterly* 9:313–36.

Kofman, Eleonore, Annie Phizucklea, Parvati Raghuram, and Rosemary Sales. 2000. *Gender and international migration in Europe.* New York: Routledge.

Kong, Lily. 2001. Mapping "new" geographies of religion: Politics and poetics in modernity. *Progress in Human Geography* 25:211–33.

Kost, K. 1989. The conception of politics in political geography and geopolitics in Germany until 1945. *Political Geography Quarterly* 8:369–85.

Kothari, Rajni. 1993. Masses, classes and the state. In *New social movement in the south*, edited by P. Wignaraja. New Delhi: Sage.

Kothari, U. 2001. Feminist and postcolonial challenges to development. In *Development theory and practice critical perspectives*, edited by U. Kothari and M. Minogue. Basingstoke: Palgrave.

Kovacs, Maria. 1996. Ambiguities of emancipation: Women and the ethnic question in Hungary. *Women's History Review* 5:487–95.

Krauss, Celene. 1993. Women and toxic waste protests: Race, class and gender as resources of resistance. *Qualitative Sociology* 16:247–62.

Kumar, Radha. 1995. From Chipko to Sati: The contemporary Indian women's movement. In *The challenge of local feminisms: Women's movements in global perspective*, edited by Amrita Basu. Boulder, Colo.: Westview Press.

Kuttner, S. 1997. Gender-related persecution as a basis for refugee status: The emergence of an international norm. *Refuge* 16:17–21.

Kuumba, M. Bahati. 2001. *Gender and social movements.* Walnut Creek, Calif.: Altamira Press.

Kwan, Mei-Po. 2002a. Feminist visualization: Re-visioning GIS as a method in feminist geographic research. *Annals of the Association of American Geographers* 92:645–61.

———. 2002b. Is GIS for women? Reflections on the critical discourse. *Gender, Place and Culture* 9:281–90.

———. 2002c. Qualitative methods and feminist geographic research. In *Feminist geography in practice*, edited by P. Moss. Oxford: Blackwell.

Lacoste, Yves. 1976/1985. *La géographie ça sert d'abord à faire la guerre.* Paris: La Découverte.

———. 1984. *Unité et diversité du tiers monde. Des représentations planétaires aux stratégies sur le terrain.* Paris: La Découverte.

———. 1987. The geographical and the geopolitical. In *International geopolitical analysis*, edited by and translated by P. Girot and E. Kofman. London: Croom Helm.

Landes, Joan B. 1998. The public and the private sphere: A feminist reconsideration. In *Feminism, the public and the private*, edited by Joan B. Landes. Oxford and New York: Oxford University Press.

Landless Workers Movement. [cited 2000]. *Movimentodos Trabalhadores Rurais Sem Terra.* Available from http://www.mstbrazil.org

Lang, Sabine. 2000. The NGO-ization of feminism. In *Global feminisms since 1945*, edited by Bonnie G. Smith. New York: Routledge.

Lasswell, Harold. 1936. *Politics: Who gets what, when, how.* Cambridge: Cambridge University Press.

Laurie, Nina. 1999. More than the blood of earth mothers. *Gender Place and Culture* 6:393–400.

——— (with Pamela Calla). 2004. Development, postcolonialism, and feminist political geography. In *Mapping women, making politics: Feminist perspectives on political geography*, edited by Lynn A. Staeheli, Eleonore Kofman, and Linda Peake. New York: Routledge.

———. In press. Gender/family and household in Latin America. In *A companion to gender studies*, edited by A. Kobayahsi. London: Blackwell.

Laurie, Nina, R. Andolina, and Sarah Radcliffe. 2003. Indigenous professionalization: Transnational social reproduction in the Andes. *Antipode* 35:664–91.

Laurie, Nina, Claire Dywer, Sarah Holloway, and Fiona Smith. 1999. *Geographies of new femininities.* London: Longman.

Law, John, and Kevin Hetherington. 2001. Materialities, spatialities, globalities. In *Knowledge, space, economy*, edited by John R. Bryson, Peter W. Daniels, Nick Henry, and Jane Pollard. New York: Routledge.

Laws, Glenda. 1997. Women's life course, spatial mobility, and state policy. In *Thresholds in feminist geography*, edited by J. P. Jones, H. Nast, and S. Roberts. New York: Rowman & Littlefield.

Lawson, Victoria. 1995. The politics of difference: Examining the quantitative/qualitative dualism in post-structuralist feminist research. *Professional Geographer* 47:449–57.

Leach, Melissa. 1996. *Rainforest relations: Gender and resource use among the Mende of Gola.* Sierra Leone: Edinburgh University Press.

Lederer, Laura, ed. 1980. *Take back the night: Women on pornography.* New York: William Morrow and Company, Inc.

Lenoir, N. 2001. The representation of women in politics: From quotas to parity in elections. *International and Comparative Law Quarterly* 50 (2): 217–47.

Ley, David, and Roman Cybriwsky. 1974. Urban graffiti as territorial markers. *Annals of the Association of American Geographers* 64:491–505.

Liepins, Ruth. 1998. Fields of action: Australian women's agricultural activism in the 1990s. *Rural Sociology* 63:128–56.

Lim, L. 1990. Women's work in export factories: The politics of a cause. In *Persistent inequalities: Women and world development*, edited by I. Tinker. New York: Oxford University Press.

Lim, L., and N. Oishi. 1996. International labour migration of Asian women: Distinctive characteristics and policy concerns. *Asian and Pacific Migration Journal* 5:85–115.

Ling, L. H. M. 2000. Global passions within global interests: Race, gender, and culture in our postcolonial order. In *Global political economy: Contemporary theories*, edited by Ronen Palan. New York: Routledge.

Lipset, S. M., and S. Rokkan. 1967. *Party systems and voter alignments: Cross-national perspectives.* New York: Free Press.

Lister, Ruth. 1997. *Citizenship: Feminist perspectives.* London: Macmillan.

Litoff, J. B., and D. C. Smith. 1994. Gender, war, and imagined geographies: United States women and the "far flung" fronts of World War II. In *Writing women and space: Colonial and postcolonial geographies*, edited by Alison Blunt and Gillian Rose. New York and London: Guilford.

Little, Jo. 1994. Women's initiatives in town planning in England. *Town Planning Review* 65:261–76.

Liu, T. 1998. On marginality. In *Making worlds, gender, metaphor, materiality*, edited by Susan Aiken, Anne E. Brigham, Sallie A. Marston, and Penny M. Waterstone. Tucson: University of Arizona Press.

Livingstone, David. 1992. *The geographical tradition: Episodes in the history of a contested enterprise*. Oxford: Blackwell.

Lobao, Linda. 1990. Women in revolutionary movements: Changing patterns of Latin American guerrilla struggle. In *Women and social protest*, edited by G. West and R. L. Blumberg. Oxford: Oxford University Press.

Longhurst, Robyn. 1996. Refocusing groups: Pregnant women's geographical experiences of Hamilton, New Zealand. *Area* 28:143–49.

———. 2000. Geography and gender: Masculinities, male identity and men. *Progress in Human Geography* 24:439–44.

Looss, Anneliese. 2002. *Gender and environment/sustainable development: Defining issues*. International Workshop, Gender Perspectives for the Earth Summit 2002. Retrieved from http://www.earthsummit2002.org/workshop/defining_the_issues.htm

Lovenduski, J. 1996. Sex, gender and British politics. In *Women in politics*, edited by J. Lovenuski and P. Norris, 3–18. Oxford: Oxford University Press.

Lovenduski, J., and J. Hills. 1981. *The politics of the second electorate: Women and public participation*. Boston and London: Routledge Kegan Paul.

Lutz, Catherine. 1995. Commentary on Martha C. Nussbaum: Emotions and women's capabilities. In *Women, culture and development: A study of human capabilities*, edited by Martha C. Nussbaum and Jonathan Glover. Oxford: Clarendon Press.

Mackinder, Halford. 1904. The geographical pivot of history. *Geographical Journal* 23:421–42.

MacKinnon, C. 1989. *Toward a feminist theory of the state*. Cambridge, Mass.: Harvard University Press.

MacKinnon, Mark. 2002. Girls elated as school resumes in Kandahar. *Globe and Mail* 26 January.

Magnusson, Warren. 1996. *The search for political space*. Toronto: University of Toronto Press.

Mailkki, L. 1995. *Purity and exile: Violence, memory, and national cosmology among Hutu refugees in Tanzania*. Chicago: University of Chicago Press.

Maille, Chantal. 1997. Challenges to representation: Theory and the women's movement in Quebec. In *In the presence of women: Representation in Canadian governments*, edited by Jane Arscott and Linda Trimble. Toronto: Harcourt Brace.

Malhotra, Ravi. 2001. The politics of the disability rights movement. *New Politics* 8 (3):81–101.

Mama, Amina. 2002. *Challenging subjects: Gender, power, and identity*. South Hadley, Mass.: Five College Women's Studies Research Center, Mt. Holyoke College.

Mamdani, M. 2001a. Making sense of non-revolutionary violence: Some lessons from the Rwandan genocide. Paper presented at the annual Frantz Fanon Lecture, at University of Durban, Westville.

———. 2001b. *When victims become killers: Colonialism, nativism and the genocide in Rwanda*. Kampala: Fountain Publishers.

Mansbridge, J. 1999. Should blacks represent blacks and women represent women? A contingent "yes." *Journal of Politics* 61:628–57.

Manzo, Kate. 1991. Modernist discourse and the crisis of development theory. *Comparative International Development* 26:3–36.

———. 1999. The "new" developmentalism: Political liberalism and the Washington consensus. In *The American century: Consensus and coercion in the projection of American power*, edited by David Slater and Peter J. Taylor. Cambridge, Mass.: Blackwell.

Marchand, Marianne H. 1996. Selling NAFTA: Gendered metaphors and silenced gender implications. In *Globalization: Theory and practice*, edited by Eleonore Kofman and Gillian Youngs. London: Pinter.

Marchand, Marianne H., and Anne Sisson Runyan. 2000. Feminist sightings of global restructuring: Conceptualizations and reconceptualizations. In *Gender and global restructuring: Sightings, sites and resistances*, edited by Marianne H. Marchand and Anne Sisson Runyan. New York: Routledge.

Marston, Sallie. 1990. Who are "the people"? Gender, citizenship, and the making of the American nation. *Environment and Planning D: Society and Space* 8:449–58.

———. 1995. The private goes public: Citizenship and the new spaces of civil society. *Political Geography* 14:194–98.

———. 2000. The social construction of scale. *Progress in Human Geography* 24:219–42.

Marston, Sallie, and Lynn Staeheli. 1994. Citizenship, struggle, and political and economic restructuring. *Environment and Planning A* 26:840–48.

Martin, Patricia M. 2004. Contextualizing feminist political theory. In *Mapping women, making politics: Feminist perspectives on political geography*, edited by Lynn A. Staeheli, Eleonore Kofman, and Linda Peake. New York: Routledge.

Martínez Alier, Joan. 1992. *De la economía ecológica al ecologismo popular*. Barcelona: Icaria.

Massey, Doreen. 1991. A global sense of place. *Marxism Today.*

———. 1992. A place called home. *New Formations* 17:3–15.

———. 1993. Power-geometry and a progressive sense of place. In *Mapping the futures: Local cultures, global change*, edited by J. Bird, Curtis Barry, Tim Putnam, and Lisa Tickner. London: Routledge.

———. 1994. *Space, place and gender*. Minneapolis: University of Minnesota Press.

———. 2001. Geography on the agenda. *Progress in Human Geography* 25 (1): 5–17.

———. 2002. Don't let's counterpose place and space. *World Development* 45 (1): 24–25.

Mattingly, Doreen, and Karen Falconer-Al-Hindi. 1995. Should women count? A context for the debate. *Professional Geographer* 47:427–35.

Mawdsley, Emma, Janet Townsend, Gina Porter, and Peter Oakley. 2002. *Knowledge, power and development agendas: NGOs North and South*. Oxford: INTRAC.

Mayer, Tamar, ed. 1994. *Women and the Israeli occupation: The politics of change*. London: Routledge.

———. 2000a. From zero to hero. In *Gender ironies of nationalism: Sexing the nation*, edited by Tamar Mayer, 283–307. London: Routledge.

———. 2000b. Gender ironies of nationalism: Setting the stage. In *Gender ironies of nationalism: Sexing the nation*, edited by Tamar Mayer, 1–24. London: Routledge.

———. 2004. Embodied nationalism. In *Mapping women, making politics: Feminist perspectives on political geography*, edited by Lynn A. Staeheli, Eleonore Kofman, and Linda Peake. New York: Routledge.

Mayhew, R. 2000. Halford Mackinder's "new" political geography and the geographical tradition. *Political Geography* 19:771–91.

McAdam, D., M. N. Zald, and J. D. McCarthy, eds. 1996. *Comparative perspectives on social movements: Political opportunities, mobilizing structures and cultural framings*. Cambridge: Cambridge University Press.

McClintock, Anne. 1995. *Imperial leather: Race, gender, and sexuality in the colonial conquest*. New York: Routledge.

McDowell, Linda. 1992a. Doing gender, feminism, feminists and research methods in human geography. *Transactions of the Institute of British Geographers* 17:399–416.

———. 1992b. Multiple voices: Speaking from inside and outside "the project." *Antipode* 24 (2): 56–72.

———. 1997. *Capital culture: Gender at work in the city*. Oxford: Blackwell.

———. 1999. *Gender, identity and place*. Minneapolis: University of Minnesota Press.

McEwan, Cheryl. 2000. Engendering citizenship: Gendered spaces of democracy in South Africa. *Political Geography* 19:627–51.

McKay, Deirdre. 1999. Filipinas in Canada: Transformations of identity in the transnational circuits of migration. Paper presented at the International Conference on Gendered Mobilities in Asia, Hong Kong.

McKenzie, Evan. 1994. *Privatopia: Homeowner associations and the rise of residential private government*. New Haven, Conn.: Yale University Press.

McLean, Sidney. 2002. Migrant workers and HIV/AIDS in South Africa: Historical epidemiology and the gendered geographies of blame. Honour's Thesis, Department of Geography, Simon Fraser University.

McManus, S., and C. Bullock. 1995. Electing women to local office. In *Gender in urban research*, edited by J. Garber and R. Turner. Thousand Oaks, Calif.: Sage.

McMichael, Philip. 2000. Globalisation: Trend or project? In *Global political economy: Contemporary theories*, edited by Ronen Palan. New York: Routledge.

Meadows, Donella. 1972. *The limits to growth*. New York: Universe Books.

Meinhof, Ulrike. 2002. *Living (with) borders: Identity discourse on east-west borders in Europe*. Ashgate, UK: Aldershot.

Melucci, Alberto. 1989. *Nomads of the present: Social movements and individual needs in contemporary society*. Philadelphia: Temple University Press.

Memmi, Albert. 1965. *The colonizer and the colonized*. Boston: Beacon Press.

Merchant, C. 1995. *Earthcare: Women and the environment.* New York: Routledge.

Mies, Maria, and Vandana Shiva. 1997. *Ecofeminismo. Teoría, crítica y perspectivas.* Barcelona: Icaria.

————. 1998. *La praxis del ecofeminismo. Biotecnología, consumo, reproducción.* Barcelona: Icaria.

————. 1993. *Ecofeminism.* London: Zed Books.

Milanovic, Branko. 2003. The two faces of globalization: Against globalization as we know it. *World Development* 31:667–83.

Miller, B. 2000. *Geography and social movements.* Minneapolis: University of Minnesota Press.

Millet, K. 2000. *Sexual politics.* Urbana and Chicago: University of Illinois Press.

Mink, Gwendoline. 1998. *Welfare's end.* Ithaca, N.Y.: Cornell University Press.

Miranne, Kristine. 2000. Women "embounded": Intersections of welfare reform and public policy. In *Gendering the city*, edited by Kristine B. Miranne and Alma H. Young. Lanham, Md.: Rowman & Littlefield.

Mitchell, Don. 1995. The end of public space? People's park, definitions of the public, and democracy. *Annals of the Association of American Geographers* 85:109–33.

————. 1997. The annihilation of space by law: The roots and implications of anti-homeless laws in the United States. *Antipode* 29:303–35.

————. 2003. *The right to the city: Social justice and the fight for public space.* New York: Guilford.

Mitchell, J. 1987. Women and equality. In *Feminism and equality*, edited by Anne Phillips. Oxford: Blackwell.

Mitchell, Katharyne. 1997a. Different diasporas and the hype of hybridity. *Environment and Planning D: Society and Space* 15:533–53.

————. 1997b. Transnational geography: Bringing geography back in. *Antipode* 29:101–14.

Mitchell, Katharyne, Sallie Marston, and Cindi Katz. 2003. Life's work: An introduction, review and critique. *Antipode* 35:415–42.

Mofson, P. 1999. Global geopolitics. In *Reordering the world. Geopolitical perspectives in the twenty-first century*, edited by G. Demko and W. Wood. Boulder, Colo.: Westview Press.

Moghadam, V. 2000. Transnational feminist networks: Collective action in an era of globalization. *International Sociology* 15:57–85.

Mohammad, Robina. 1999. Marginalisation, Islamism and the production of the "other's" "other." *Gender, Place and Culture* 6:221–40.

Mohanty, Chandra. 1991a. Introduction: Cartographies of struggle: Third World women and the politics of feminism. In *Third World women and the politics of feminism*, edited by Chandra Talpade Mohanty, Ann Russo, and Lourdes Torres. Bloomington: Indiana University Press.

————. 1991b. "Under Western eyes": Feminist scholarship and colonial discourse. In *Third World women and the politics of feminism*, edited by C. Mohanty, A. Russo, and L. Torres. Bloomington: Indiana University Press.

————. 2002. "Under Western eyes" revisited: Feminist solidarity through anticapitalist struggles. *Signs: Journal of Women in Culture and Society* 28 (2): 499–535.

Mohanty, Chandra Talpade, Anne Russo, and Lourdes Torres, eds. 1991. *Third World women and the politics of feminism.* Bloomington: Indiana University Press.

Momsen, Janet, and Janet Townsend. 1987. *Geography of gender in the Third World.* Albany: State University of New York Press.

Monffe, Chantal. 1993. *The return of the political.* London: Verso.

Mongia, Radhika Viyas. 1999. Race, nationality, mobility: A history of the passport. *Public Culture* 11 (3):527–56.

Morin, Karen, and Lawrence Berg. 2001. Gendering resistance: British colonial narratives of wartime New Zealand. *Journal of Historical Geography* 27:196–222.

Morokvasic, Mirjana. 1984. Birds of passage are also women. *International Migration Review* 18:886–907.

————. 2003. Transnational mobility and gender: A view from post-wall Europe. In *Crossing borders and shifting boundaries*, edited by Mirjana Morokvasic, Umut Erel, and Kyoko Shinozaki. Opladen: Leske and Budrich.

Morrill, R. L. 1976. Redistricting revisited. *Annals of the Association of American Geographers* 66:463–77.

Moser, C. 1993. Adjustment from below: Low-income women, time and the triple role in Guayaquil, Ecuador. In *Viva: Women and popular protest in Latin America*, edited by Sarah Radcliffe and Sallie Westwood. London and New York: Routledge.

Moss, P. 1995. Embeddedness in practice, numbers in context: The politics of knowing and doing. *Professional Geographer* 47:442–49.

———. 2002. Taking on, thinking about, and doing feminist research in geography. In *Feminist geography in practice*, edited by P. Moss. Oxford: Blackwell.

Moss, Pamela, and Isabel Dyck. 1996. Inquiry into environment and body: Women, work and chronic illness. *Environment and Planning D: Society and Space* 14:137–53.

Mosse, George. 1985. *Nationalism and sexuality: Respectability and abnormal sexuality in modern Europe*. New York: Howard Fetig.

Mouffe, Chantal. 1992. Feminism, citizenship and radical democratic politics. In *Feminists theorize the political*, edited by Judith Butler and Joan Scott. New York: Routledge.

Mountz, Alison. 2004. Embodying the nation-state: Canada's response to human smuggling. *Political Geography* 23:323–45.

Mrvič-Peterovič, Nataša. 2000. A brief history of the state of Bosnia-Hezegovina (from its origins to the 1995 Dayton Peace Accords). In *Women, violence and war: Wartime/victimization of refugees in the Balkans*, edited by V. Nikolič-Ristanovič, 7–20. Budapest: Central European University Press.

Mufti, Aamir/Ella Shohat. 1997. Introduction. In *Dangerous liaisons: Gender, nation and postcolonial perspectives*, edited by Anne McClintok, Aamir Mufti, and Ella Shohat, 1–12. Minneapolis: University of Minnesota Press.

Mullings, Beverley. 1999. Insider or outsider, both or neither: Some dilemmas of interviewing in a cross-cultural setting. *Geoforum* 30:337–50.

Mushakoji, Kinhide. 2001. Engendering the Japanese "double standard" patriarchal democracy: The case of the "comfort women" and military sexual slavery. In *Gender, globalization, and democratization*, edited by R. M. Kelly. Lantham, Md.: Rowman & Littlefield.

Myers, D. J. [cited 1999]. *Social activism through computer networks*. Available from www. nd.ed/~dmyers.

Nagar, Richa. 1997. Exploring methodological borderlands through oral narratives. In *Thresholds in feminist geography*, edited by J. P. Jones, H. Nast, and S. Roberts. Oxford: Rowman & Littlefield.

———. 1998. Communal discourses, marriage, and the politics of gendered social boundaries among South Asian immigrants in Tanzania. *Gender, Place and Culture* 5:117–39.

———. 2000. Mujhe Jawab Do! (answer me!): Women's grass-roots activism and social spaces in Chitrakoot (India). *Gender, Place and Culture* 7:341–62.

———. 2002. Footloose researchers, "traveling theories" and the politics of transnational feminist praxis. *Gender, Place and Culture* 9:179–86.

———. 2004. Mapping feminisms and difference. In *Mapping women, making politics: Feminist perspectives on political geography*, edited by Lynn A. Staeheli, Eleonore Kofman, and Linda Peake. New York: Routledge.

Nagar, Richa, Victoria Lawson, Linda McDowell, and Susan Hanson. 2002. Locating globalization: Feminist (re)readings of the subjects and spaces of globalization. *Economic Geography* 78:257–85.

Nagel, Caroline. 2002. Geopolitics by another name: Immigration and the politics of assimilation. *Political Geography* 21:971–87.

Naples, Nancy. 1998a. *Grassroots warriors: Activist mothering, community work and the war on poverty*. New York: Routledge Kegan Paul.

———. 1998b. Women's community activism: Exploring the dynamics of politicization and diversity. In *Community activism and feminist politics*, edited by Nancy Naples. New York: Routledge.

Nash, Catherine. 1993. Remapping and renaming: New cartographies of identity, gender and landscape in Ireland. *Feminist Review* 44:39–57.

Nast, Heidi. 1994. Opening remarks on "women in the field." *Professional Geographer* 46:54–66.

———. 1998. Unsexy geographies. *Gender, Place, and Culture* 5:191–206.

———. 2002. Queer patriarchies, queer racisms, international: Guest editor's prologue: Crosscurrents. *Antipode* 34:835–44.

Nast, Heidi, and Steve Pile, eds. 1998. *Places through the body*. London and New York: Routledge.

Natter, Wolfgang. 2003. Geopolitics in Germany, 1919–45. Karl Haushofer, and the Zeitschrift Fûr Geopolitik. In *A companion to political geography*, edited by John A Agnew, Katharyne Mitchell, and Gerard Toal. London: Blackwell.

Nelson, B. J., and N. Chowdhury. 1994. *Women and politics worldwide*. New Haven, Conn.: Yale University Press.

Nelson, Kristen. 1986. Labour demand, labour supply and the suburbanisation of low-wage office work. In *Production, work, territory*, edited by A. Scott and M. Storper. Sydney: Allen and Unwin.

Nesmith, Cathy, and Sarah Radcliffe. 1993. (Re)mapping mother earth: A geographical perspective on environmental feminism. *Environment and Planning D: Society and Space* 11:379–94.

News and Views. 1992. News and Views, 5, 1:2. New York: Women's Environment and Development Organization.

Niarchos, Catherine N. 1995. Women, war, and rape: Challenges facing the international tribunal for the former Yugoslavia. *Human Rights Quarterly* 17:640–90.

Nikolič-Ristanovič, Vesna, ed. 1999. *Women, violence and war: Wartime/victimization of refugees in the Balkans.* Budapest: Central European University Press.

Nogué, Joan, and Joan Vicente. 2001. *Geopolítica, identidad y globalización.* Barcelona: Ariel Grografía.

Nolin Hanlon, Catherine, and Finola Shankar. 2000. Gendered spaces of terror and assault: The Testimonio of Remhi and the Commission for Historical Clarification in Guatemala. *Gender Place and Culture* 7:265–86.

Norris, P. 1994. Political recruitment. In *Different roles, different voices: Women and politics in the United States and Europe,* edited by M. Githens, P. Norris, and J. Lovenuski, 85–88. New York: HarperCollins College Publishers.

———. 1996. Women politicians: Transforming Westminster? In *Women in politics,* edited by J. Lovenuski and P. Norris, 91–104. Oxford: Oxford University Press.

Nussbaum, Martha C. 1995. Emotions and women's capabilities. In *Women, culture and development: A study of human capabilities,* edited by Martha C. Nussbaum and Jonathan Glover. Oxford: Clarendon Press.

O'Brien, A. Kevin. 2001. The use of assassination as a tool of state policy: South Africa's counter-revolutionary strategy 1979–1992 (Part II). *Terrorism and Political Violence* 13 (2):107–42.

Oduol, Wilhelmina, and Wanjiku Mukabi Kabira. 1995. The mother of warriors and her daughters: The women's movement in Kenya. In *The challenge of local feminisms: Women's movements in global perspective,* edited by Amrita Basu. Boulder, Colo.: Westview Press.

Ohmae, Ken'ichi. 1995. *The end of the nation-state: The rise of regional economies.* New York: Free Press.

O'Loughlin, John, Lynn A. Staeheli, and Edward Greenberg, eds. 2004. *Globalization and its outcomes.* New York: Guilford.

Ong, A. 1994. Colonialism and modernity: Feminist re-presentations of women in non-Western societies. In *Theorizing feminism: Parallel trends in the humanities and social sciences,* edited by Anne Herrmann and Abigail Stewart. Boulder, Colo.: Westview Press.

Openshaw, S. 1996. A view on the GIS crisis in geography. In *Human geography: An essential anthology,* edited by J. Agnew, D. Livingston, and A. Rogers, 675–85. Oxford: Blackwell.

Organization for Economic Cooperation and Development. 1995. *Women in the city: Housing, services and the urban environment.* Paris: Author.

O'Sullivan, Patrick. 1986. *Geopolitics.* London: Routledge.

Ó Tuathail, Gearoid. 1996a. An anti-geopolitical eye: Maggie O'Kane in Bosnia, 1992–3. *Gender, Place and Culture* 3:171–85.

———. 1996b. *Critical geopolitics.* Minneapolis: University of Minnesota Press.

———. 1998a. Introduction to imperialist geopolitics. In *The geopolitics reader,* edited by G. Ó Tuathail, S. Dalby, and P. Routledge. New York: Routledge.

———. 1998b. Political geography III: Dealing with deterritorialization. *Progress in Human Geography* 19:82–93.

Ó Tuathail, Gearóid, and John A. Agnew. 1992. Geopolitics and discourse: Practical geopolitical reasoning in American foreign policy. *Political Geography* 11 (2): 190–204.

Ó Tuathail, Gearóid, Simon Dalby, and Paul Routledge, eds. 1998. *The geopolitics reader.* London: Routledge.

Oza, Rupal. 2001. Showcasing India: Gender, geography and globalization. *Signs* 26:1067–95.

Paasi, Anssi. 1996. *Territories, boundaries, and consciousness: The changing geographies of the Finish-Russian border.* New York: Wiley.

———. 1999. Boundaries as social processes: Territoriality in the world of flows. In *Boundaries, territory and postmodernity,* edited by D. Newman. London: Frank Cass.

———. 2003. Territory. In *A companion to political geography,* edited by J. Agnew, K. Mitchell, and G. Toal. Oxford: Blackwell.

Pain, Rachel. 1991. Space, sexual violence and social control: Integrating geographical and feminist analyses of women's fear of crime. *Progress in Human Geography* 15:415–31.

References • **295**

———. 2000. Place, social relations, and the fear of crime: A review. *Progress in Human Geography* 24:365–87.
———. 2002. Gender, race, age, and fear in the city. *Urban Studies* 38:899–913.
Painter, Joe. 1995. *Politics, geography and "political geography."* London: Arnold.
Pandurang, Mala. 2003. Conceptualizing emigrant Indian female subjectivity: Possible entry points. In *South Asian women in the diaspora*, edited by Nirmal Puwar and Parvati Raghuram. Oxford: Bert.
Pardo, Mary. 1998. *Mexican American women activists*. Philadelphia: Temple University Press.
Parker, Geoffrey. 1998. *Geopolitics: Past, present, and future*. London: Pinter.
Parr, Hester. 1977. Mental health, public space and the city: Questions of individual and collective access. *Environment and Planning D: Society and Space* 22:231–44.
———. 2001. Negotiating different ethnographic contexts and building geographical knowledges: Empirical examples from mental-health research. In *Qualitative methods for geographers*, edited by C. Dwyer and M. Limb. London: Arnold.
Pateman, Carole. 1988. *The sexual contract*. Stanford, Calif.: Stanford University Press.
———. 1989. *The disorder of women, democracy, feminism and political theory*. Stanford, Calif.: Stanford University Press.
Patton, Cindy. 1994. *Last served? Gendering the HIV pandemic*. Minneapolis: Minnesota University Press.
Paulson, S., and P. Calla. 2000. Gender and ethnicity in Bolivian politics: Transformation or paternalism. *Journal of Latin American Anthropology* 5:112–49.
Pavlakovich, Vera, Barbara Morehouse, and Doris Wastl-Walter, eds. 2004. *Challenged borderlands: Transcending political and cultural boundaries*. Ashgate, UK: Aldershot.
Peake, Linda. 1984. How Särlvik and Crewe fail to explain the conservative victory of 1979 and electoral trends in the 1970s: B. Särlvik and I. Crewe: Decade of dealignment. *Political Geography Quarterly* 3 (2): 161–67.
———. 1999a. Political. In *A feminist glossary of human geography*, edited by Linda McDowell and Joanne Sharp. London: Arnold.
———. 1999b. Politics. In *A feminist glossary of human geography*, edited by Linda McDowell and Joanne Sharp. London: Arnold.
Peake, Linda, and Brian Ray. 2001. Racializing the Canadian landscape: Whiteness, uneven geographies and social justice. *Canadian Geographer* 45:180–86.
Peake, Linda, and Alissa Trotz. 1999. *Gender, ethnicity and place: Women and identities in Guyana*. London: Routledge.
Pearson, Ruth. 1998. Nimble fingers' revisited: Reflections on women and Third World industrialisation in the late twentieth century. In *Feminist visions of development: Gender, analysis and policy*, edited by Cecile Jackson and Ruth Pearson, 171–88. New York: Routledge.
Peck, Jamie, and Adam Tickell. 2002. Neoliberalizing space. *Antipode* 34:380–404.
Penrose, Jan. 1990. Frisian nationalism: A response to cultural and political hegemony. *Environment and Planning D: Society and Space* 8:427–48.
———. 1992. Introduction: Feminism and feminists in the academy. *Antipode* 24 (3): 218–20.
———. 1994. Mmon pays ce n'est pas un pays. The concept of a nation as a challenge to the nationalist aspirations of the Parti Quebécois. *Political Geography* 13:161–81.
Perry, Peter. 1987. Editorial comment. *Political Geography Quarterly*: A content (but discontented) review. *Political Geography Quarterly* 6:5–6.
Pessar, Patricia R., and Sarah J. Mahler. 2002. Gender and transnational migration. Paper presented at the conference on Transnational Migration: Comparative Perspectives, 30 June–1 July 2001, at Princeton University.
Peters, E. 2000. "The two major living realities": Urban services needs of First Nations women in Canadian cities. In *Gendering the city*, edited by Kristine B. Miranne and Alma H. Young. Lanham, Md.: Rowman & Littlefield.
Pettman, Jan Jindy. 1997. Body politics: International sex tourism. *Third World Quarterly* 18 (1):93–108.
Phelan, Shane. 1995. The space of justice: Lesbians and democratic politics. In *Social postmodernism*, edited by Linda Nicholson and Steve Seidman. Cambridge: Cambridge University Press.
Phillips, Anne. 1991. *Engendering democracy*. University Park: Pennsylvania State University Press.
———. 1992. Universal pretensions in political thought. In *Destabilizing theory: Contemporary feminist debates*, edited by Michele Barrett and Anne Phillips. Stanford, Calif.: Stanford University Press.

————. 1996. Dealing with difference: A politics of ideas, or a politics of presence? In *Democracy and difference: Contesting the boundaries of the political*, edited by S. Benhabib, 139–52. Princeton, N.J.: Princeton University Press.

————. 1999. *Which equalities matter?* Cambridge, Mass.: Polity Press.

Phillips, Susan D. 1996. Discourse, identity, and voice: Feminist contributions to policy studies. In *Policy studies in Canada*, edited by L. Dobuzinskis, M. Howlett, and D. Laycock. Toronto: University of Toronto Press.

Pickles, John. 1995. *Ground truth: The social implications of GIS.* London: Guilford.

Pickles, Katie. 2002. *Female imperialism and national identity: Imperial order daughters of the empire.* Manchester: Manchester University Press.

Pieterse, J. N. 1992. *Emancipations, modern and postmodern.* Thousand Oaks, Calif.: Sage Publications.

Piexoto, Joao. 2001. Migration and policies in the European Union: Highly skilled mobility, free movement of labour and recognition of diplomas. *International Migration Review* 39:33–61.

Pile, Steve. 1994. Masculinism, the use of dualistic epistemologies, and third spaces. *Antipode* 26 (3): 255–77.

Pincetl, Stephanie. 1994. Challenges to citizenship: Latino immigrants and political organizing in the Los Angeles area. *Environment and Planning A* 26:895–914.

Plant, Judith, ed. 1989. *Healing the wounds: The promise of ecofeminism.* Philadelphia: New Society Publishers.

Pleck, Elizabeth. 2002. Women's suffrage. In *The American presidency*, edited by Grolier. Retrieved from http://gi.grolier.com/presidents/ea/side/wsffrg.html

Podmore, Julie. 2001. Lesbians in the crowd: Gender, sexuality and visibility along Montréal's Boul. St-Laurent. *Gender, Place and Culture* 8:333–55.

Polanyi, Karl. 1944. *The great transformation.* New York: Farrar & Rinehart.

Portes, Alejandro. 1997. Immigration theory for a new century: Some problems and opportunities. *International Migration Review* 31:799–827.

Potter, R. 2001. Geography and development: "Core and periphery"? *Area* 33:422–39.

Power, M. 2001. Geopolitics and the representation of Portugal's African colonial wars: Examining the limits of "Vietnam Syndrome." *Political Geography* 20:461–91.

Pratt, Geraldine. 1999. From registered nurse to registered nanny: Discursive geographies of Filipina domestic workers in Vancouver, B.C. *Economic Geography* 75:215–36.

————. 2004. *Working feminism.* Edinburgh: Edinburgh University Press.

Pratt, Geraldine (with the Philippine Women Centre, Vancouver, Canada). 1998. Inscribing domestic work on Filipina bodies. In *Places through the body*, edited by Steve Pile and Heidi J. Nast. London and New York: Routledge.

Pratt, Geraldine, and Brenda Yeoh. 2003. Transnational (counter) topographies. *Gender, Place and Culture* 10:159–66.

Pratt, Mary Louise. 1992. *Imperial eyes. Travel writing and transculturation.* London: Routledge.

Prescott, J. R. V. 1972. *Political geography.* London: Methuen.

————. 1987. *Political frontiers and boundaries.* London: Allen and Unwin.

Pringle, Rosemary. 1988. *Secretaries talk: Sexuality, power and work.* Sydney: Allen and Unwin.

Prügl, Elisabeth. 1999. *The global construction of gender: Home-based work in the political economy of the 20th century.* New York: Columbia University Press.

Purukayastha, B. Forthcoming. Skilled migration and cumulative disadvantage: The case of highly qualified Asian Indian immigrant women in the U.S. *Geoforum.*

Racioppi, Linda, and Katherine O'Sullivan See. 2000. Engendering nation and national identity. In *Women, states, and nationalism: At home in the nation?* edited by S. Ranchod-Nilsson and M. A. Téreault. London and New York: Routledge.

Radcliffe, Sarah. 1993. Women's place/el lugar de mujeres: Latin America and the politics of gender identity. In *Place and politics of identity*, edited by Michael Keith and Steve Pile. London and New York: Routledge.

————. 1999. Latina labour: New directions in gender and work in Latin America. *Environment and Planning A* 31 (2): 191–95.

Radcliffe, Sarah, Nina Laurie, and R. Andolina. 2004. The transnationalization of gender and re-imagining Andean indigenous development. *Signs* 29(2):387–416.

Radcliffe, Sarah, and Sallie Westwood. 1993. *Viva! Women and popular protest in Latin America.* London: Routledge.

————. 1996. *Remaking the nation: Place, identity and politics in Latin America.* London: Routledge.

Raghuram, Parvati. 2000. Gendering skilled migratory streams: Implications for conceptualising migration. *Asian and Pacific Migration Journal* 9:429–57.

———. 2004a. Crossing borders: Gender and migration. In *Mapping women, making politics: Feminist perspectives on political geography*, edited by Lynn A. Staeheli, Eleonore Kofman, and Linda Peake. New York: Routledge.

———. 2004b. The difference that skills make: Gender, family migration strategies and regulated labour markets. *Journal of Ethnic and Migration Studies* 30:303–21.

Raghuram, Parvati, and Eleonore Kofman. 2002. The state, labour markets and immigration: The case of skilled emigrants in UK's medical labour market. *Environment and Planning A* 34:2071–89.

Ralston, Helen. 1999. Canadian immigration policy in the twentieth century: Its impact on South Asian women. *Canadian Woman Studies* 19 (3):33–37.

Ramamurthy, P. 2000. Indexing alternatives, feminist development studies and global political economy. *Feminist Theory* 1:239–56.

Ranchod-Nilsson, S., and M. A. Téreault, eds. 2000. *Women, states, and nationalism: At home in the nation?* London and New York: Routledge.

Randall, V. 1987. *Women and politics: An international perspective.* Chicago: University of Chicago Press.

Rao, Nitya, and Luise Rurup, eds. 1997. *A just right: Women's ownership of natural resources and livelihood security.* New Delhi: Friedrich Ebert Stiftung.

Rathgeber, E. 1990. WID, WAD, GAD: Trends in research and practice. *Journal of Developing Area Studies* 24:489–502.

Ratzel, Freidrich. 1897. *Politische Geographie.* Munich: Oldenbourg.

Reagon, Bernice Johnson. 1983. Coalition politics: Turning the century. In *Home girls: A black feminist anthology*, edited by Barbara Smith. New York: Kitchen Table, Women of Color Press.

Reger, J. 2001. Emotions, objectivity and voice: An analysis of a "failed" participant observation. *Women's Studies International Forum* 24:605–16.

Reinelt, Claire. 1995. Moving on the terrain of the state: The battered women's movement and the politics of engagement. In *Feminist organizations*, edited by Myra Marx Ferree and Patricia Y. Martin. Philadelphia: Temple University Press.

Reingold, B. 1992. Concepts of representation among female and male state legislators. *Legislative Studies Quarterly* 17:509–37.

Reynolds, David, and David Knight. 1989. Political geography. In *Geography in America*, edited by Gary Gail and Cort Willmott. Columbus, OH: Merrill.

Rivera, S., and S. Barragán, eds. 1997. *Debates post coloniales: Una introducción a los estudios de la subalternidad.* La Paz: Sephis.

Roberts, Susan M. 1995. Global regulation and trans-state organization. In *Geographies of global change: Remapping the world in the late twentieth century*, edited by R. Johnston, Peter J. Taylor, and Michael J. Watts. Cambridge, Mass.: Blackwell.

———. 2003. Global strategic vision: Managing the world. In *Globalization and governmentality: Contested terrains and new world orders*, edited by Richard W. Perry and Bill Maurer. Minneapolis: University of Minnesota Press.

———. 2004. Gendered globalization. In *Mapping women, making politics: Feminist perspectives on political geography*, edited by Lynn A. Staeheli, Eleonore Kofman, and Linda Peake. New York: Routledge.

Roberts, Susan M., and R. Schein. 1995. Earth shattering: Global imagery and GIS. In *Ground truth: The social implications of GIS*, edited by J. Pickles. London: Guilford.

Roberts, Susan, Anna Secor, and Matthew Sparke. 2003. Neoliberal geopolitics. *Antipode* 35:886–97.

Robinson, K. 1991. Housemaids: The effects of gender and culture on the internal and international labour migration of Indonesian women. In *Intersexions: Gender/class/culture/ethnicity*, edited by G. Bottomley, M. de Laperveanche, and J. Martin. Sydney: Allen and Unwin.

Rocheleau, Dianne, Barbara Thomas-Slayter, and Ester Wangari, eds. 1996. *Feminist political ecology: Global issues and local experiences.* London: Routledge.

Rodda, Annabel. 1991. *Women and the environment.* London: Zed Books.

Rokkan, Stein, and Derek Unwin, eds. 1983. *Economy, identity, territory.* London: Sage Ltd.

Romany, Celina. 2000. Themes for a conversation on race and gender in international human rights law. In *Global critical race feminism: An international reader*, edited by Adrien Katherine Wing. New York: New York University Press.

Rose, Gillian. 1993. *Feminism and geography: The limits of geographical knowledge.* Minneapolis: University of Minnesota Press.

———. 1997. Situating knowledges: Positionality, reflexivities and other tactics. *Progress in Human Geography* 21:305–20.

Rose, Gillian, and Alison Blunt, eds. 1994. *Writing women and space: Colonial and post-colonial geographies.* New York and London: Guilford.

Rossler, Mechtild. 1996. From the ladies' programme to the feminist session. In *Géographes face au monde*, edited by Marie-Claire Robic, A. Briend, and Mechtild Rossler. Paris: L'Harmattan.

Rothenberg, Tamar. 1995. "And she told two friends": Lesbians creating urban social space. In *Mapping desire: Geographies of sexualities*, edited by D. Bell and G. Valentine. London: Routledge.

Routledge, Paul. 1993. *Terrains of resistance: Nonviolent social movements and the contestation of place in India.* London: Praeger.

———. 1997. A spatiality of resistances: Theory and practice in Nepal's revolution of 1990. In *Geographies of resistance*, edited by Steve Pile and Michael Keith, 68–86. London: Routledge.

———. 1998. Anti-geopolitics: Introduction. In *The geopolitics reader*, edited by G. Ó Tuathail, S. Dalby, and P. Routledge. London: Routledge.

———. 2003. Anti-geopolitics. In *Companion to political geography*, edited by J. Agnew, K. Mitchell, and Gerard Toal. London: Blackwell.

Rowbotham, Sheila, and Stephanie Linkogle, eds. 2001. *Women resist globalization: Mobilizing for livelihood and rights.* London: Zed Books.

Rowe, Stacey, and Jennifer Wolch. 1990. Social networks in time and space: Homeless women in skid row, Los Angeles. *Annals of the Association of American Geographers* 80:184–204.

Ruddick, Sarah. 1980. Maternal thinking. *Feminist Studies* 6:342–67.

Ruddick, Susan. 1996. Constructing difference in public spaces: Race, class and gender as interlocking systems. *Urban Geography* 17:132–51.

Rule, W. 1987. Electoral systems, contextual factors and women's opportunity for election to parliament in twenty-three democracies. *Western Political Quarterly* 40 (3): 477–98.

———. 1990. Why more women are state legislators: A research note. *Western Political Quarterly* 43:437–48.

Rumley, Dennis, and Julian Minghi, eds. 1991. *Geography of border landscapes.* London: Routledge.

Runyan, Anne Sisson. 1996. The places of women in trading places: Gendered global/regional regimes and inter-nationalized feminist resistance. In *Globalization: Theory and practice*, edited by Eleonore Kofman and Gillian Youngs, 238–52. London: Pinter.

———. 1999. Women in the neoliberal "frame." In *Gender politics in global governance*, edited by Mary K. Meyer and Elisabeth Prügl. Lanham, Md.: Rowman & Littlefield.

Ryan, Mary. 1990. *Women in public: Beyond banners and ballots, 1825–1880.* Baltimore, Md.: Johns Hopkins University Press.

———. 1998. Gender and public access: Women's politics in nineteenth-century America. In *Feminism: The public and the private*, edited by J. B. Landes. Oxford and New York: Oxford University Press.

Sachs, Carolyn E. 1996. *Gendered fields: Rural women, agriculture, and environment.* Boulder, Colo.: Westview Press.

Sack, Robert D. 1986. *Human territoriality: Its theory and history.* Cambridge: Cambridge University Press.

Said, Edward. 1978. *Orientalism.* New York: Pantheon.

———. 1994. *Culture and imperialism.* New York: Vintage Books.

Salaff, Janet. 1997. The gendered social organization of migration as work. *Asian and Pacific Migration Journal* 6:295–316.

Sassen, Saskia. 1996. Beyond sovereignty: Immigration policy making today. *Social Justice* 23:9–20.

———. 1998. *Globalization and its discontents.* New York: New Press.

———. 2000. Women's burden: Counter-geographies of globalization and the feminization of survival. *Journal of International Affairs* 53:503–24.

Savané, M. A. 1998. Dix ans de féminisme international. *ISIS: Femmes et development*, 249–52.

Savarsy, W., and Berta Siim. 1994. Gender, transitions to democracy and citizenship. *Social Politics* 1:249–55.

Schaffer, K. 1994. Colonizing gender in colonial Australia: The Eliza Fraser story. In *Writing women and space: Colonial and postcolonial geographies*, edited by Alison Blunt and G. Rose. New York and London: Guilford.

Schild, Veronica. 1994. Recasting "popular movements": Gender and the political learning in neighborhood organizations in Chile. *Latin American Perspectives: Social Movements and Political Change in Latin America* 81:59–80.

Scott, James C. 1985. *Weapons of the weak: Everyday forms of peasant resistance.* New Haven, Conn.: Yale University Press.

Scott, Joan. 1992. Experience. In *Feminists theorize the political*, edited by J. Butler and J. W. Scott. New York: Routledge.

Seager, Joni. 1993. *Earth follies: Coming to feminist terms with the global environmental crisis.* New York: Routledge.

Seccombe, I., J. Buchan, and J. Ball. 1993. Nurse mobility in Europe: Implications for the United Kingdom. *International Migration Review* 31:125–48.

Secor, Anna. 2001. Toward a feminist counter-geopolitics: Gender, space and Islamist politics in Istanbul. *Space and Polity* 5:191–211.

———. 2002. The veil and the urban space in Istanbul: Women's dress, mobility and Islamic knowledge. *Gender, Place and Culture* 9:5–22.

———. 2004. Feminizing electoral geography. In *Mapping women, making politics: Feminist perspectives on political geography*, edited by Lynn A. Staeheli, Eleonore Kofman, and Linda Peake. New York: Routledge.

Seifert, Ruth. 1994. War and rape: A preliminary analysis. In *Mass rape: The war against women in Bosnia-Herzegovina*, edited by Alexandra Stiglmayer. Lincoln and London: University of Nebraska Press.

Sen, Gita. 1994. Women, poverty and population: Issues for the concerned environmentalist. In *Population and environment: Rethinking the debate*, edited by L. Arizpe, P. Stone, and D. Major. Boulder, Colo.: Westview Press.

Sevenhuijsen, Selma. 1998. *Citizenship and the ethics of care.* London: Routledge.

Shabecoff, Paul. 1996. *A new name for peace: International environmentalism, sustainable development and democracy.* Hanover, N.H.: University Press of New England.

Sharp, Joanne. 1996. Gendering nationhood: A feminist engagement with national identity. In *BodySpace: Destabilizing geographies of gender and sexuality*, edited by N. Duncan, 97–108. London: Routledge.

———. 2000a. *Condensing the cold war: Reader's Digest and American identity.* Minneapolis: University of Minnesota Press.

———. 2000b. Refiguring geopolitics: The Reader's Digest and popular geographies of danger. In *Geopolitical traditions: A century of geopolitical thought*, edited by K. Dodds and D. Atkinson. London: Routledge.

———. 2000c. Re-masculinising geo-politics? Comments on Gearoid Ó Tuathail's critical geopolitics. *Political Geography* 19:361–64.

———. 2004. Doing feminist political geographies. In *Mapping women, making politics: Feminist perspectives on political geography*, edited by Lynn A. Staeheli, Eleonore Kofman, and Linda Peake. New York: Routledge.

Sharpe, S. 1994. *The gilded ghetto: Women and political power in Canada.* Toronto: HarperCollins.

Shelley, Fred, J. Clark Archer, Fiona Davidson, and Stanley D. Brunn. 1996. *Political geography of the United States.* New York: Guilford.

Shiva, Vandana. 1998. The greening of global reach. In *The geopolitics reader*, edited by G. Ó Tuathail and S. Dalby. London: Routledge.

———. 1993a. *Monocultures of the mind: Perspectives on biodiversity and biotechnology.* Penang: Third World Network.

———. 1993b. The greening of the global reach. In *Global ecology: A new arena of political conflict*, edited by W. Sachs. London: Zed Books.

Shklar, Judith. 1991. *American citizenship: The quest for inclusion.* Cambridge, Mass.: Harvard University Press.

Shohat, Ella. 1996. Notes on the "post-colonial." In *Contemporary postcolonial theory: A reader*, edited by Padmini Mongia. New York: Arnold.

Short, C. 1996. Women and the Labour Party. In *Women in politics*, edited by J. Lovenuski and P. Norris, 19–27. Oxford: Oxford University Press.

Sibley, David. 1995. *Geographies of exclusion: Society and difference in the West.* London: Routledge.

Siddiqui, T. 2003. An anatomy of forced and voluntary migration from Bangladesh: A gendered perspective. In *Crossing borders and shifting boundaries*, edited by Mirjana Morokvasic, Umut Erel, and Kyoko Shinozaki. Opladen: Leske and Budrich.

Silliman, Jael, and Ynestra King. 1999. *Dangerous intersections: Feminist perspectives on population, environment, and development.* Boston: South End Press.

Silvey, Rachel. 1999. Sexual geographies: Gender norms, moral codes, and political identities among Indonesian-U.S. transmigrants. Paper presented for Engendering Theories of Transnational Migration, at Yale University, Center for International and Area Studies, New Haven, Connecticut.

———. 2000a. Diasporic subjects: Gender and mobility in South Sulawesi. *Women's Studies International Forum* 23:501–15.

———. 2000b. Stigmatized spaces: Gender and mobility under crises in South Sulawesi, Indonesia. *Gender, Place and Culture* 7:143–61.

Silvey, Rachel, and Victoria Lawson. 1999. Placing the migrant. *Annals of the Association of American Geographers* 89 (1):121–32.

Singerman, D. 1995. *Avenues of participation: Family, politics and networks in urban quarters of Cairo.* Princeton, N.J.: Princeton University Press.

Singh, Ajit, and Ann Zammit. 2000. International capital flows: Identifying the gender dimension. *World Development* 28:1249–68.

Sisson Runyan, Anne. 2003. The places of women in trading places revisited: Gendered global/regional regimes and internationalized feminist resistance. In *Globalization: Theory and practice,* edited by E. Kofman and G. Youngs. London: Continuum.

Skelton, Tracey, and Gill Valentine. 2003. "It feels like being deaf is normal": An exploration into the complexities of defining D/deafness and young D/deaf people's identities. *Canadian Geographer* 47:451–66. Guest edited by Vera Chouinard and Valorie A. Crooks.

Slater, David. 1994. Introduction. *Latin American Perspectives: Social Movements and Political Change in Latin America* 81:5–10.

———. 2000. The process and prospect of political geography. *Political Geography* 19:1–3.

Smith, Anthony. 1986. *The ethnic origins of nations.* Oxford: Blackwell.

Smith, Dorothy. 1990. *The conceptual practices of power: A feminist sociology of knowledge.* Boston: Northeastern University Press.

Smith, Fiona. 2000. The neighbourhood as site for contesting German reunification. In *Entanglements of power: Geographies of domination/resistance,* edited by Joanne Sharp, P. Routledge, C. Philo, and R. Paddison, 122–47. London: Routledge.

Smith, J., C. Chatfield, and R. Pagnucco, eds. 1997. *Transnational social movements and global politics.* Syracuse: Syracuse University Press.

Smith, Neil. 1992a. Geography, difference, and the politics of scale. In *Postmodernism and the social sciences,* edited by J. Doherty, E. Graham, and M. Malek. New York: St. Martin's Press.

———. 1992b. History and philosophy of geography: Real wars, theory wars. *Progress in Human Geography* 16:257–71.

———. 1993. Homeless/global: Scaling places. In *Mapping the futures: Local cultures, global change,* edited by J. Bird, B. Curtis, T. Putnam, G. Robertson, and L. Tickner. London: Routledge.

———. 1994. Geography, empire and social theory. *Progress in Human Geography* 18:491–500.

———. 1996. *New urban frontier: Gentrification and the revanchist city.* London: Routledge.

———. 1999. Which new urbanism? New York City and the revanchist 1990s. In *The urban moment: Cosmopolitan essays on the late-20th century city,* edited by R. Beauregard and S. Body-Gendrot. Thousand Oaks, Calif.: Urban Affairs Annual Reviews, Sage.

———. 2000. Is critical geopolitics possible? Foucault, class and the vision thing. *Political Geography* 19:365–71.

———. 2001. *Global executioner: Scales of terror.* Retrieved November 2002, from http://www.ssrc.org/sept11/essays

———. 2003. *American empire: Roosevelt's geographer and the prelude to globalization.* Berkeley: University of California Press.

Smith, Neil, and Cindi Katz. 1993. Grounding metaphor: Towards a spatialized politics. In *Place and the politics of identity,* edited by Michael Keith and Steve Pile. London and New York: Routledge.

Smith, Susan. 1989. Society, space and citizenship: A human geography for the "new times"? *Transactions of the Institute of British Geographers* 14:144–56.

Smith, V. 1990. Split affinities: The case of interracial rape. In *Conflicts in feminism,* edited by Marianne Hirsch and Evelyn Fox Keller. London and New York: Routledge.

Soysal, Yasmin. 1994. *Limits of citizenship: Migrants and postnational membership in Europe.* Chicago: University of Chicago Press.

Sparke, Matthew. 1996a. Displacing the field in fieldwork: Masculinity, metaphor and space. In *BodySpace*, edited by N. Duncan. London: Routledge.

———. 1996b. Negotiating national action: Free trade, constitutional debate, and the gendered geopolitics of Canada. *Political Geography* 15:615–39.

———. 1998. Outside inside patriotism: The Oklahoma bombing and the displacement of heartland geopolitics. In *Rethinking geopolitics*, edited by G. Ó Tuathail and S. Dalby. London: Routledge.

Spivak, Gayatri Chakravorty. 1988. *In other worlds: Essays in cultural politics*. London and New York: Routledge.

———. 1996. "Woman" as theatre: United Nations Conference on Women, Beijing 1995. *Radical Philosophy* 75:2–4.

Squires, Judith. 1994. Private lives, secluded places: Privacy as political possibility. *Environment and Planning D: Society and Space* 12:387–401.

———. 1999. Rethinking the boundaries of political representation. In *New agendas for women*, edited by Sylvia Walby, 169–89. London: Macmillan.

———. 2000. *Gender in political theory*. Cambridge, Mass.: Polity Press.

Stacey, Judith. 1988. Can there be a feminist ethnography? *Women's Studies International Forum* 11:21–27.

Staeheli, Lynn. 1994. Empowering political struggle: Spaces and scales of resistance. *Political Geography* 13:387–91.

———. 1996. Publicity, privacy, and women's political action. *Environment and Planning D: Society and Space* 14:601–19.

———. 2001. Of possibilities, probabilities and political geography. *Space and Polity* 5:177–89.

———. 2003. Women and the work of community. *Environment and Planning A* 35:815–31.

Staeheli, Lynn, and Susan Clarke. 1995. Gender, place and citizenship. In *Gender in urban research*, edited by Judith Garber and Robyne Turner. Thousand Oaks, Calif.: Sage.

Staeheli, Lynn, and Meghan Cope. 1994. Empowering women's citizenship. *Political Geography* 13:443–60.

Staeheli, Lynn, and Victoria Lawson. 1994. A discussion of "women in the field": The politics of feminist fieldwork. *Professional Geographer* 46:96–102.

Staeheli, Lynn, and Patricia Martin. 2000. Spaces for feminism in geography. *Annals of the American Academy of Political and Social Sciences* 571:135–50.

Staeheli, Lynn, and Don Mitchell. 2004. Spaces of public and private. In *Spaces of democracy*, edited by Clive Barnett and Murray Low. London: Sage Ltd.

Staeheli, Lynn, Don Mitchell, and Kristina Gibson. 2002. Conflicting rights to the city in New York's community gardens. *GeoJournal* 58 (2): 197–205.

Staeheli, Lynn, and Richa Nagar. 2002. Feminists talking across worlds. *Gender, Place and Culture* 9:167–72.

Stasilius, Daiva, and Nira Yuval-Davis, eds. 1995. *Unsettling settler societies: Articulations of gender, race, ethnicity and class*. London: Sage Ltd.

Steady, Filomina Chioma. 1992. *Women and children first: Environment, poverty, and sustainable development*. London: Routledge.

Stiglitz, Joseph. 2002. *Globalization and its discontents*. New York: Norton.

Stiglmayer, Alexandra, ed. 1994a. *Mass rape: The war against women in Bosnia-Herzegovina*. Lincoln and London: University of Nebraska Press.

———. 1994b. The rapes in Bosnia-Herzegovina. In *Mass rape: The war against women in Bosnia-Herzegovina*, edited by Alexandra Stiglmayer, 82–169. Lincoln and London: University of Nebraska Press.

Stoddart, D. 1991. Do we need a feminist historiography of geography, and if we do, what should it be like? *Transactions of the Institute of British Geographers* 16:484–87.

Stoler, Anne, and Frederick Cooper. 1997. Between metropole and colony. In *Tensions of empire: Colonial cultures in a bourgeois world*, edited by F. Cooper and A. Stoler. Berkeley: University of California Press.

Storey, David. 2001. *Territory: The claiming of space*. Harlow, UK: Pearson Education Ltd.

Sudbury, K. 1998. *Other kinds of dreams: Black women's organisations and the politics of transformation*. London: Routledge.

Surin, Kenneth. 2003. Hostage to an unaccountable planetary executive. In *World Bank literature*, edited by Amitava Kumar. Minneapolis: University of Minnesota Press.

Susser, Ida. 1982. *Norman Street: Poverty and politics in an urban neighborhood*. New York: Oxford University Press.

Swarr, Amanda Lock, and Richa Nagar. 2004. Dismantling assumptions: Interrogating "lesbian" struggles for identity and survival in India and South Africa. *Signs: Journal of Women in Culture and Society* 29:491–516.

Swiss, Shana. 1993. New PHR report: Rape as a crime of war—A medical perspective. *Journal of the American Medical Association* 207 (5):612–15.

Swyngedouw, Erik. 1997. Neither global nor local: "Glocalization" and the politics of scale. In *Spaces of globalization: Reasserting the power of the local*, edited by Kevin R. Cox. London: Guilford.

———. 2000. Authoritarian governance, power, and the politics of rescaling. *Environment and Planning D: Society and Space* 18:63–76.

Sylvester, Christine. 1992. Feminists and realists view autonomy and obligation in international relations. In *Gendered states: Feminist (re)visions of international relations theory*, edited by V. Spike Peterson. Boulder, Colo.: Lynne Rienner.

———. 1998. "Handmaids" tales of Washington power: The abject and the real Kennedy White House. *Body and Society* 4:39–66.

———. 1999. Development studies and postcolonial studies: Disparate tales of the "Third World." *Third World Quarterly* 20 (4):703–21.

Tarrow, Sidney. 1998. *Power in movement: Social movements and contentious politics*. 2nd ed. Cambridge: Cambridge University Press.

Tate, J. 1993. Homework in West Yorkshire. In *Dignity and daily bread: New forms of economic organising among poor women in the Third World and the First*, edited by S. Rowbotham and S. Mitter. London: Routledge.

Taylor, Peter. 1979. *Political geography: World economy, nation-state, locality*. London: Longman.

———. 1982. Materialist framework for political geography. *Transactions of the Institute of British Geographers* 7:15–34.

———. 1990. Extending the world of electoral geography. In *Developments in electoral geography*, edited by R. J. Johnston, F. W. Shelley, and P. J. Taylor, 257–71. London: Routledge.

———. 1993a. *Political geography of the twentieth century: A global analysis*. London: Belhaven.

———. 1993b. *Political geography: World-economy, nation-state and locality*. 3rd ed. Harlow: Longman.

———. 1996. Embedded statism and the social sciences: Opening up new spaces. *Environment and Planning A* 28:1917–28.

———. 1999. Places, spaces and Macy's: Place-space tensions in the political geography of modernities. *Progress in Human Geography* 23:7–26.

———. 2000a. Geopolitics, political geography and social science. In *Geopolitical traditions: A century of geopolitical thought*, edited by Klaus Dodds and D. Atkinson, 375–79. London: Routledge.

———. 2000b. Political geography. In *Dictionary of human geography*, edited by Ron J. Johnston, Derek Gregory, Geraldine Pratt, and Michael Watts, 594–97. Oxford: Blackwell.

Taylor, Peter, and Colin Flint. 2000. *Political geography*. 2nd ed. Harlow, UK: Pearson Education Ltd.

Taylor, Peter, and Ron Johnston. 1979. *Geography of elections*. London: Penguin.

Taylor, Verta, and Leila Rupp. 1993. Women's culture and lesbian feminist activism: A reconsideration of cultural feminism. *Signs: Journal of Women in Culture and Society* 19:32–61.

Thomas, S. 1994. *How women legislate*. Oxford: Oxford University Press.

Thrift, Nigel. 2000. It's the little things. In *Geopolitical traditions: A century of geopolitical thought*, edited by K. Dodds and D. Atkinson. London: Routledge.

Tickner, J. Ann. 1992. *Gender in international relations: Feminist perspectives on achieving global security*. New York: Columbia University Press.

Till, Karen. 1999. Staging the past: Landscape designs, cultural identity, and Erinnerungspolitik at Berlin's Neue Wache. *Ecumene* 6:251–83.

Tinker, Irene. 1999. Nongovernmental organizations: An alternative power base for women? In *Gender politics in global governance*, edited by Mary K. Meyer and Elisabeth Prügl. Lanham, Md.: Rowman & Littlefield.

Title IX. 2002. *Education amendments of 1972*. Retrieved from http://www.dol.gov/oasam/regs/statutes/titleix.htm

Townsend, Janet, Emma Zapata, Jo Rowlands, Pilar Alberti, and Marta Mercado. 1999. *Women and power: Fighting patriarchies and poverty*. London and New York: Zed Books.

Truong, Thanh-Dam. 1996. Gender, international migration and social reproduction: Implications for theory, policy research and networking. *Asian and Pacific Migration Journal* 5:27–52.

Tuan, Yi-Fu. 1974. *Topophilia: A study of environmental perception, attitudes and values*. Englewood Cliffs, N.J.: Prentice Hall.

United Nations. 1999. *World survey on the role of women in development: Globalization, gender and work*. New York: UN Division for the Advancement of Women, Department of Economic and Social Affairs.

United Nations Division for the Advancement of Women. 2003. *Convention on the elimination of all forms of discrimination against women*. Retrieved from http://www.un.org/womenwatch/daw/cedaw/

Valentine, Gill. 1989. The geography of women's fear. *Area* 21:385–90.

———. 1990. Women's fear and the design of public space. *Built Environment* 16:288–303.

———. 1992. Images of danger: Women's sources of information about the spatial distribution of male violence. *Area* 24:22–29.

———. 1993. (Hetero)sexing space: Lesbian perceptions and experiences of everyday spaces. *Environment and Planning D: Society and Space* 11:395–413.

———. 2001. *Social geographies: Space and society*. Harlow, UK: Pearson Education Ltd.

Vanden Heuvel, Audrey. 1993. *When roles overlap: Workers with family responsibilities, monograph 14*. Melbourne: Australian Institute of Family Studies.

Visvanathan, Shiv. 1988. On the annals of the laboratory state. In *Science, hegemony and violence: A requiem for modernity*, edited by Ashis Nandy. Delhi: Oxford University Press.

Wainwright, Hilary. 1989. The state and society: Reflections from a Western experience. In *The new détente: Rethinking East-West relations*, edited by Mary Kaldor, Gerard Holden, and Richard Falk. London: Verso.

Walby, Sylvia. 1990. *Theorizing patriarchy*. Oxford: Blackwell.

Walker, Connor. 1994. *Ethnonationalism: The quest for understanding*. Princeton, N.J.: Princeton University Press.

Walker, N. J. 1994. What we know about women voters in Britain, France and West Germany. In *Different roles, different voices: Women and politics in the United States and Europe*, edited by M. Githens, P. Norris, and J. Lovenduski, 61–70. New York: HarperCollins College Publishers.

Wallace, Michelle. 2001. Women and workplace training: Power relations positioning "the other." *Women's Studies International Forum* 24:433–44.

Wallerstein, Immanuel. 1974. *The modern world-system*. New York: Academic Press.

Walsh, Jessica. 2002. Organising the low wage service sector: Labour, community and urban politics in the United States. Ph.D. thesis, University of Melbourne.

Walter, Bronwyn. 1995. Irishness, gender and place. *Environment and Planning D: Society and Space* 13:35–50.

Waring, Marilyn. 1990. *Counting for nothing: What men value and what women are worth*. Wellington, New Zealand: Bridget Williams.

Warkentin, Craig. 2001. *Reshaping world politics: NGOs, the Internet, and global civil society*. Lanham, Md.: Rowman & Littlefield.

Wastl-Walter, Doris, and Andrea Kofler. 1999. Dynamics of local cross-border activities between Carinthia (Austria) and Slovenia. In *Curtains of iron and gold: Reconstructing borders and scales of interaction*, edited by H. Eskelinen, I. Liikanen, and J. Oksa. Ashgate, UK: Aldershot.

Wastl-Walter, Doris, and Lynn A. Staeheli. 2004. Territory, territoriality, and boundaries. In *Mapping women, making politics: Feminist perspectives on political geography*, edited by Lynn A. Staeheli, Eleonore Kofman, and Linda Peake. New York: Routledge.

Waterman, Stanley. 1998. Political geography as a mirror of political geography. *Political Geography* 17:373–88.

Waters, Malcom. 2001. *Globalization*. London: Routledge.

Watson, Sophie, ed. 1990. *Playing the state: Australian feminist interventions*. London and New York: Verso.

Webber, Michael. 1998. Producing globalization: Apparel and the Australian state. In *An unruly world? Globalization, governance and geography*, edited by A. Herord, G. Ó Tuathail, and Susan M. Roberts. New York: Routledge.

Webber, Michael, and Sally Weller. 2001. *Refashioning the rag trade: Internationalising Australia's textiles, clothing and footwear industries*. Sydney: University of New South Wales Press.

Webster, G. R. 1997. Religion and politics in the American South. *Pennsylvania Geographer* 35:151–72.

———. 2000. Women, politics, elections and citizenship. *Journal of Geography* 99 (1): 1–10.

Wekerle, Gerda R. 1997. Gendering the local state: Women's initiatives in local government in Canada and the United States. Paper presented at the American Sociological Association Annual Meeting, Toronto.

———. 1999. Gender planning as insurgent citizenship: Stories from Toronto. *Plurimondi* 2:105–26.

————. 2000. Women's rights to the city: Gendered spaces of a pluralistic citizenship. In *Democracy, citizenship and the global city*, edited by Engin Isin. London: Routledge.

————. 2004. Framing feminist claims for urban citizenship. In *Mapping women, making politics: Feminist perspectives on political geography*, edited by Lynn A. Staeheli, Eleonore Kofman, and Linda Peake. New York: Routledge.

Wekerle, G. R., and B. Rutherford. 1988. Captive rider, captive labor: Spatial constraints and women's employment. *Urban Geography* 9:116–37.

Werbner, Pnina. 1999. Political motherhood and the feminisation of citizenship: Women's activisms and the transformation of the public sphere. In *Women, citizenship and difference*, edited by N. Yuval-Davis and P. Werbner, 221–45. London: Zed Books.

Whatmore, Sarah. 1991. *Farming women: Gender, work and family enterprise.* London: Macmillan.

Whitehead, A. 2000. Continuities and discontinuities in political constructions of the working man in rural sub-Saharan Africa: The "lazy man" in African agriculture. *European Journal of Development Studies* 12:23–52.

Wickramasinghe, Anoja. 1995. *Deforestation, women and forestry: The case of Sri Lanka.* Amsterdam: International Books.

Williams, Colin. 1986. The question of national congruence? In *A world in crisis: A geographic perspective*, edited by Ron Johnston and Peter Taylor. Oxford: Blackwell.

Williams, Colin, and Eleonore Kofman, eds. 1989. *Community, conflict, partition and nationalism.* London: Croom Helm.

Williams, Patrick, and Laura Chrisman. 1994. *Colonial discourse/postcolonial theory.* New York: Columbia University Press.

Wolch, Jennifer, and Michael Dear, eds. 1989. *The power of geography: How territory shapes social life.* Boston: Unwin Hyman.

Women's Environment and Development Organization. 1991. *World Women's Congress for a Healthy Planet: Official report.* New York: Author.

Women and Geography Study Group. 1984. *Geography and gender: An introduction to feminist geography.* London: Hutchinson.

————. 1992. Feminists and feminism in the academy. *Antipode* 24:218–37.

————. 1997. *Feminist geographies: Explorations in diversity and difference.* London: Longman.

Woodward, Rachel. 2004. *Military geographies.* Oxford: Blackwell.

World Commission on Environment and Development. 1987. *Our common future, Great Britain.* Oxford: Oxford University Press.

World Women's Congress for a Healthy Planet Official Report. 1991.

Wright, Melissa. 1997. Crossing the factory frontier: Gender, place and power in the Mexican maquiladora. *Antipode* 29:278–302.

Yeatman, Anna. 1990. *Bureaucrats, technocrats and femocrats.* Sydney: Allen and Unwin.

Yeoh, Brenda. 2000. Historical geographies of the colonised world. In *Modern historical geographies*, edited by Brian Graham and Catherine Nash. London: Longman.

Yeoh, Brenda, and E. Graham. 2002. Migrations and family relations in the Asia-Pacific region. *Asian and Pacific Migration Journal* 11:1–11.

Yeoh, Brenda, and Katie Willis. 1999. "Heart" and "wing," nation and diaspora: Gendered discourses in Singapore's regionalisation process. *Gender, Place and Culture* 6:355–72.

Young, Iris Marion. 1990. *Justice and the politics of difference.* Princeton, N.J.: Princeton University Press.

Youngs, Gillian. 1999. *International relations in a global age: A conceptual challenge.* Cambridge, Mass.: Polity Press.

————. 2000a. Breaking patriarchal bonds: Demythologizing the public/private. In *Gender and global restructuring: Sightings, sites and resistances*, edited by Marianne H. Marchand and Anne Sisson Runyan. New York: Routledge.

————, ed. 2000b. *Political economy, power and the body, global perspectives.* Basingstoke: Macmillan.

Yuval-Davis, Nira. 1997. *Gender and nation.* London: Sage Ltd.

————. 2001. Nationalism, feminism and gender relations. In *Understanding the nation*, edited by M. Guibernau and J. Hutchinson. London: Polity Press.

Yuval-Davis, Nira, and F. Anthias, eds. 1989. *Woman-nation-gender.* London: Macmillan.

Zapata, E., J. G. Townsend, J. Rowlands, P. Alberti, and M. Mercado. 2002. *Las mujeres y el poder: La lucha contra el patriarcado y la pobreza.* Mexico City: Laza & Valdez.

Zinn, Maxine Baca, and Bonnie Thornton Dill. 1996. Theorizing difference from multicultural feminism. *Feminist Studies* 22:321–31.

Contributors

Urmilla Bob is an associate professor in the Environment and Development Programme in the Department of Geography and Environmental Studies at the University of Kwazulu–Natal (Westville Campus). Her main research areas are rural development, gender issues, and natural resource management and sustainable land use.

Josepa Brú Bistuer is a professor of human geography at the University of Girona (Catalonia, Spain), where she works on gender and environment. Recent publications include "Spanish Women against Industrial Wastes: A Gender Perspective of Environmental Grassroots Mobilizations," in *Toward a Feminist Political Ecology: Global Perspectives from Local Experience*, ed. D. Rocheleau et al. (New York: Routledge, 1997); and "Globalisation, Environmental Policies and Gender Perpectives," in *Geschlechrter verhältnisse Natureverhältnisse: Feministische Auseinandersetzungen und Perspektiven der Umweltsoziologie*, ed. A. Nebelung et al. (Berlin, Leske+Budrich, 2001).

Mercè Agüera Cabo is a Ph.D. student at the Joint Research Centre of the European Commission in Ispra (Italy), where she is developing a thesis on environmental governance from a gender approach.

Pamela Calla is currently based at the University of the Cordierra in La Paz, where she works in a master's program directed by Duke University. She has worked for many years on gender, culture, and politics in Latin America, most recently examining the intersections between race and gender.

Vera Chouinard is the director of women's studies and a professor of geography at McMaster University. Her areas of specialization include the state and social policy change, struggles for social justice, and disabled women's struggles for greater inclusion in society and space.

Meghan Cope is an associate professor in the Department of Geography at the State University of New York–Buffalo. Her interests are in the social and spatial processes of marginalization in U.S. cities, broader issues of gender and race oppression, and qualitative research methods.

Joan Fairhurst is a professor emeritus at the University of Pretoria, South Africa. Her main teaching and research interests focus on social and human geography, environment and society, and geography in education. She was president of the Society of South African Geographers in 1997–1998, receiving its Gold Medal Award in 2000. She serves as a full member of the South African national committee of the International Geographical Union and is a long-standing corresponding member of the IGU Gender and Geography and Geographical Education Commissions.

Ruth Fincher is a professor of urban planning and the dean of the Faculty of Architecture, Building, and Planning at the University of Melbourne. Her research interests are in the shaping of city spaces by policies, institutions, and the politics of difference.

Mary Gilmartin is a lecturer in the Department of Geography, University College Dublin. Her recent research focuses on the relationship between education and political transformation in South Africa and Northern Ireland.

Jennifer Hyndman is an associate professor of geography at Simon Fraser University in Vancouver. Her research focuses on human displacement related to conflict and on Canadian immigration policy and refugee resettlement. She is the author of *Managing Displacement: Refugees and the Politics of Humanitarianism* (University of Minnesota Press, 2000) and coeditor (with Wenona Giles) of *Sites of Violence: Gender in Conflict Zones* (University of California Press, 2004).

Eleonore Kofman is a professor of human geography at Nottingham Trent University. Her research interests are in feminist political geography and on gender, migration, and stratification. She coauthored *Gender and International Migration in Europe* (Routledge, 2000) and coedited *Globalization: Theory and Practice* (Continuum, 2003).

Nina Laurie is a senior lecturer in the School of Geography, Politics, and Sociology at Newcastle University, United Kingdom. She has worked on issues of social development in Latin America, with specific interests in gender, neoliberalsim, indigenous development, and water politics. She works collaboratively with colleagues at San Simón University, Bolivia, and San Marcos University, Peru, through DFID/British Council Higher Education Links focused on gender and development. She is coauthor of *Geographies of New Femininity* (Longman, 1999).

Patricia M. Martin currently holds a Rockefeller Post-Doctoral Fellowship in Geography and Women's and Gender Studies at Dartmouth College. Her research interests include feminist political theory and globalization and democratization in Latin America.

Tamar Mayer is a professor of geography at Middlebury College in Middlebury, Vermont, and the editor of *Women and the Israeli Occupation: The Politics of Change* (Routledge, 1994) and *Gender Ironies of Nationalism: Sexing the Nation* (Routledge, 2000). Her research interests focus on the interplay among nation, gender, and sexuality, particularly in the Middle East, and on the relationships among nationalism, landscape, and memory.

Richa Nagar is an associate professor of women's studies at the University of Minnesota. Her research has focused on the politics of space, identity, and community among South Asians in Tanzania and, more recently, on the contradictions of empowerment in women's organizations in North India. Her new work seeks to reconceptualize transnational feminist theory and praxis through collaborations with academic and nonacademic actors across institutional, geographical, and socioeconomic borders.

Linda Peake is a professor in the Division of Social Sciences at York University, Toronto, Canada, where she also teaches in the Graduate Programmes in Geography and Women's Studies. Her research interests lie in feminist and postcolonial geographies, particularly pertaining to her work with the Red Thread Women's Development Programme in Guyana. Her latest book (with A. Trotz) in this field is *Gender, Ethnicity and Place: Women and Identities in Guyana* (Routledge, 1999).

Parvati Raghuram is a lecturer in human geography at the Nottingham Trent University. She coauthored *Gender and International Migration in Europe* (Routledge, 2000) and *Studying Culture: A Guide to the Practice and Politics of Cultural Studies* (Sage, 2004) and coedited *South Asian Women in the Diaspora* (Berg, 2003). She has published a number of articles on the experiences of migrants and minorities in the United Kingdom.

Maano Ramutsindela lectures in the Department of Environmental and Geographical Science at the University of Cape Town. His current research project examines parks and people in postcolonial societies. He is the author of *Unfrozen Ground: South Africa's Contested Spaces.*

Susan M. Roberts is an associate professor of geography and member of the Committee on Social Theory at the University of Kentucky. She does research on the international financial system and the politics of globalization.

Anna J. Secor is an assistant professor of geography at the University of Kentucky. She received her Ph.D. from the University of Colorado–Boulder in 2000. Her research interests are in gender, political participation, and urban space in Istanbul, Turkey.

Joanne Sharp is a senior lecturer in geography at the University of Glasgow, Scotland. Her research interests are in political, cultural, and feminist geography.

Lynn A. Staeheli is a professor in geography and a research associate in the Institute of Behavioral Science at the University of Colorado. Her research interests are in political, urban, and feminist geography. Recent research projects have focused on community activism, public space, and immigration.

Doris Wastl-Walter is a professor of human geography at the University of Berne, Switzerland. She is the chair of the IGU Commission on Geography and Public Policy and the director of the Interdisciplinary Centre for Women and Gender studies at the University of Berne. Her main research interests include border regions studies and gender studies.

Gerda R. Wekerle is a professor on the Faculty of Environmental Studies and Graduate Program in Women's Studies, York University. She coedited (with Patricia Evans) *Women and the Canadian Welfare State* (University of Toronto Press, 1997) and coauthored (with Carolyn Whitzman) *Safe Cities* (John Wiley, 1995). Her research focuses on women's urban movements, women and the local state, urban agriculture, community gardens and cultural landscapes, and regional movements against sprawl in exurbia.

Index

A

Aboriginal politics, 101
Abu-Khali, A., 269
Activism, 49, 52–53, 55, 71, 235
   AIDS, 207; *See also* HIV/AIDS
   black women, 79
   community, 68
   feminist, 63
   grassroots, 77, 107
   London, 77
   women's, 65, 80, 83, 85, 157, 251,
      258
Activists
   human rights, 192
   Israeli, 74
   Palestinian, 74
Actor Network Theory, 132
Afghanistan, 81, 179–180
Africa, 203
African National Congress, 204
Africans, 37–38, 47
Agency, 16, 24, 110, 130, 170
   human, 107
   political, 197
Agenda 21, 212, 214, 218–219, 222,
   224
Agents, 33
   Informal, 211
Agnew, John, 88, 118, 261
Algeria, 115
Alvarez, Sonia, 19
Anderson, Kay, 52–53
Andes, 103–104
Antagonism, 2–3
Anticolonialism, 25
   assault, 159
Antiglobalization movement, 215, 224,
   258
Apartheid, 75, 82, 120, 177, 181–183, 207,
   239
Appadurai, Arjun, 258
Asians, 36–39, 48
   men, 38, 67
Asylum, 10, 173
ATTAC (Action pour une Taxe Tobin d'aide
   aux Citoyens), 139–140

Australia, 54–56, 58, 60, 64, 66, 101,
   235–236, 253
   Australian Women in Agriculture
      movement, 64

B

Bell, David, 239
Belonging, 1, 32, 107
Beneria, Lourdes, 129, 132
Benhabib, Seyla, 17, 20
Bienman, Ursula, 145
Binaries, 13, 127–132
Bodies, 10, 22, 212
   female, 33–35, 150, 151
   sexualized, 54, 57
   women's, 157–158, 166
Body, 5, 10, 16, 122, 221
   geo, 160
   geopolitics, 125
   women's, 176, 184
Boles, Janet, 253
Bolivia, 101, 105–106
Border regions, 145, 160
   German-Polish, 145
   U.S.-Mexico, 145
Borders, 142, 151
   control of, 177, 197
   crossings, 144
   patrol, 145
   racial, 115, 120, 142, 144–146, 151
Bosnia, 95, 122, 161
Bosnia-Herzegovina, 158–160,
   176
Boundaries, 2, 15, 160–162
   blurred, 52
   heteronormative, 38
   porous, 50
   sexual, 35
   social, 67, 150
Bourdieu, Pierre, 170
Bowman, Isiah 117
Brazil, 202, 241
Britain, 113-114, 254
Brown, Michael, 3, 13, 52, 149, 240
Brownill, Sue, 9, 51, 71, 77, 254
Butler, Judith, 21

C

Camp, 162, 166, 171, 177, 183
  refugee, 238, 244; *See also* Refugees
Campani, Giovanna, 196
Canada, 34, 37, 40, 72, 170, 177–179,
  258–259
  cities, 257
  elections, 253
Capitalism, 17, 129, 132, 203, 215, 223,
  230
  global, 242, 258
Care, ethics of, 249, 257
Caring
  at a distance, 190, 193
  professions, 188
  work, 51, 53, 63–65, 84
Charnay, Jean-Pierre, 121
Chechnya, 205
Children, 160–161, 174, 197, 249
Chile, 81
China, 25
Chipko movement, 213, 216
Chouinard, Vera, 171
Chua, R.P., 109–110
Chun, Lin, 25
Citizens, 18
  urban, 245
Citizenship, 2–3, 7–8, 11, 15, 24–25, 180,
  232–236
  female, 116
  feminist geographies of, 235–236
  gendered geographies, 232–235
  global, 83
  insurgent, 248–249
  local state, 248–250
  in the North, 73
  postnational, 184–185
  rights, 228
  sexual, 249
  state power, 236–237
  universal, 1
  urban, 245, 250, 259
  women's, 248
Civil rights movement, 79
Civil society, 3, 25, 50, 62–68, 136, 202, 208,
  210, 213, 224, 239, 246
  citizenship, 248, 257
  local state, 247
Clark, Gordon, 229
Class, 35, 99, 231, 233, 248
  differences, 36
  hierarchies, 37–39, 45
  inequalities, 41
  polarization, 238
  practice, 7
  struggle, 231, 246
Clean Clothes Campaign, 83–84
Coalitions, 3
  politics of, 23, 32
Cockburn, Cynthia, 246
Collective action 200, 246, 259
Collins, Patria, 15, 23, 26
Colonialism, 11, 47, 100, 115, 177
Colonization, 114
Conflict, 96, 203
Connell, R.W., 227
Constitutive, 2–3
Consumption, 247
Containment, 169–171, 177, 187
Cooper, Davina, 235
Cope, Meghan, 58–59, 236
Corporeal geographies, 176, 241
Counterhegemonic practices, 12
Counterpublics, 53–54, 65, 68, 149
Critical geopolitics, 3–4, 94, 118, 120, 122,
  125; *See also* Geopolitics
Cultural,
  landscapes, 142
  politics, 3, 208
  strategy, 143
  turn, 3, 94, 98, 112, 234
Culture, 109
Cultures of mothering, 51
  analysis, 118

D

Daily lives, 147, 250
Dalby, Simon, 4, 94, 124
Darcy, R. 265
Dar-es-Salaam, 34, 36–37, 45–47
Dear, Michael, 13–14, 229
Decade of Women, 215–216
Decolonization, 113
Della Porta, D., 200, 204
Demangeon, André, 116
Democracy, 1, 18, 20, 24, 230, 249
  direct, 241
  local, 247
  radical, 24, 245, 258
  Western, 265
Democratization, 1, 3, 107, 125, 201–202
Deregulation, 134
Derrida, Jacques, 29, 118
De Souza, A., 204
Deterritorialization, 146–147
Development, 11, 99, 111, 136

studies, 108–110, 112, 138
sustainable, 212–213, 217–218
Diasporas, 32, 147, 193
Dietz, Mary, 20–21, 24
Difference, 8–9, 12, 20–24, 31–36, 141
   democracy, 24
   feminism, 8–9, 32–34
   locating, 31–32
   politics of, 20–23
Differencing, 232, 236, 240–241
   feminist, 235–236
   gendered geographies of, 232–235
Disability, 240
Discourse,
   analysis, 105
   androcentric, 223
   civil society, 249
   colonial, 118
   development, 104
   environmental management, 210, 212
   gender, 221–223
   global, 134
   globalization, 120, 128, 130
   hegemonic, 218
   imperial, 115
   nationalist, 144
   neoliberal, 105, 135
   policy, 229, 232, 234
   political, 94
   social movements, 199
Discrimination, 25, 267
   gendered, 73, 79, 84
   selective, 178
Discursive practices, 16
Disempowerment, 33
Displacement, 169, 170, 184
Divorce, 39
Domestic violence, 54–55, 65, 74, 76, 80,
   149
   gender identity, 80
   Guyana, 102
   violence,
Domestic work, 18
Domosh, Mona, 97
Dowler, Lynnette, 4, 95–96, 122–123, 144,
   177, 184
Dowling, Robyn, 51
Dualisms, 49–50, 221
   public-private, 52, 59

E

Eastern Europe, 201
Ecofeminism, 212–213, 220–221

Ekins, P., 202, 207
Elder, G., 239
Elections, 2, 3, 6
   geography, 261
Electoral behavior, 263
Elite, 201, 256
   actors, 4
   agents, 5
   men, 97, 230
   political, 94, 114
   women, 98
Elman, R. Amy, 55
Embedded statism, 121
Embodiment, 105
Empire, 97, 113, 116, 118, 127, 178
   American, 116
   British, 116
Empowerment, 7, 16
   feminist, 32, 97, 108, 149, 173
Enloe, Cynthia, 96, 108, 124, 144,
   155–156
Environment, 12
Environmental conflicts, 209
Environmental management, 209–212,
   221–222
Epistemology, 50
   standpoint, 91
Equality, 17, 20, 22, 24
   difference debate, 21, 24
Equal opportunities, 269
Essentialism, 21
Ethnic cleansing, 154, 159–160, 162
   genocide, 159
Ethnicity, 103–104, 208
Europe, 72, 201, 217, 238
European Union, 188, 191, 255
Everyday (the), 95
Everyday life, 82–83, 95
Everyday lives, 33, 109, 123, 146, 211, 234,
   245
   activities, 63
   Greenham Common, 78
   local state, 247
   spaces, 95
Exclusion, 1–2, 22, 25, 32, 79, 141–142, 146,
   148, 171, 239

F

Families, 5, 54–55, 137
   multiracial, 34–35
Family, 65, 149, 157
Fawcett, Charles, 116
Feldman, Roberta, 251

Femininity, 6, 10–11, 80, 105, 221
  femininities, 102
  white, 115
Feminism, 4, 13, 15
  Chinese, 25, 29
  cultural, 20
  culturalist, 221
  radical, 230
  second-wave, 17, 20, 83, 205
  state, 268
  Western, 21, 25
Feminist political geography, 98, 129
Feminist politics,
  theorists, 255
  transnational, 28, 29, 31
Feminists
  lesbian, 252
  liberal, 230–231,
  Marxist, 230
  multiracial, 32
  radical, 231
  Third World, 32, 92
  U.S., 32
Feminist theories, 7, 13, 22, 31, 199,
    233–234
  epistemologies, 26
  fieldwork, 97, 116
  imaginary, 16
  liberal, 20
  methodology, 91, 95, 97
  movements, 2, 8
  political theory, 16–17, 26, 271
  poststructuralist, 108
  state, 242–243
Feminization, 8
  of the Indian, 106
Femocrats, 66, 235, 253–254
Filipina, 196
  nannies, 238
Financial crises, 138
Fincher, Ruth, 231, 235–237, 240
Formal politics, 49, 98
Formal sphere, 95
Foucault, 16, 117
Fraser, Nancy, 18, 20–23, 33, 50, 52–53,
    149, 232, 234
Freeman, Carla 128–129

G

Gamson, William, 259
Garcia-Ramon, Dolores, 155
Garment industry, 83
Gated communities, 149

Gender
  and development, 102–103
  equality policies, 254
  mainstreaming, 102, 104, 255
  male bias, 263, 266
  and social movements, 205–208
  struggles, 246
Gendered policing, 37, 39, 47
Geographies, radical, 91–92, 114
Geography, core, 111
Geopolitical analysis, 211
Geopolitical conflicts, 209–210
  environmental, 210
Geopoliticians, 95, 116
  Anglo-Americans, 118
  critical, 122
Geopolitics, 3, 93, 97, 99–100, 145, 175,
    184; *See also* Critical geopolitics
  Anglo-American, 118
  anti, 124
  counter-critical, 123
  feminist, 169, 176–177
  gendering, 122–124
  mobility, 28, 169
  oppositional, 121–122
  popular, 122
Germany, 34, 113–114, 117, 123, 143, 170,
    255
  electoral gender gap, 269
Giblin, Beatrice, 117
Gibson-Graham, K., 130–131
Gilbert, Melissa, 251
GIS, 89–91
Global cities, 231, 238
Global economic restructuring, 17
Global economy, 102, 128–129
  gender, 131–132, 173
Global finance, 133–135
Global historical geography, 134
Globalization, 12, 15, 25, 28, 84, 105, 109,
    112, 145–146, 242, 250
  narratives, 245
  topography, 28
Global planet management, 212–215
Global political economy, 175
Global sisterhood, 83
Glocalization, 147
Governance, 245, 254
  urban, 246–247, 250
Graham, Katherine, 130–131
Green Belt Movement, 213, 215
Greenham Common, 78
Grewel, Inderpal, 131

Guatemala, 237
Guyana, 109, 111, 268

H

Habermas, Jorgen, 20
Halford, Susan, 9, 51, 71, 77, 254
Hanson, Susan, 12, 25
Haraway, Donna, 4, 11, 26, 32, 91, 174
Harding, Sandra, 12, 26
Hardt, Michael, 120, 127
Hartshorne, Richard, 2
Haushofer, Karl, 117, 143
Hegemony, 113, 118, 211
Helms, Jesse, 183
Herb, Guntram, 155
Herodote, 117, 121
Heteropatriarchy, 33–34, 47
Heterosexism, 33, 234
Hierarchies, social, 46
Hijaab, 40–41
HIV/AIDS, 177, 182, 235; *See also* AIDS
Holston, James, 248–249
Home, 2, 10, 60, 148, 162, 166
Homeland, 154–155, 167
    security, 120
Homophobia, 31, 109
Hong Kong, 191
hooks, bell, 22
Hooper, Charlotte, 105
Hooson, David, 155
Households, 5, 16, 18, 51, 65, 105, 107, 137,
    193–194, 196, 247
Hudson, Brian, 118
Human rights, 10, 81, 134–135, 175, 208,
    250
    organizations, 167
    regime, 147
    violations, 206
Hungary, 23
Hybridity, 107–108
Hyndman, Jennifer, 28, 123, 144, 197,
    238

I

Identities, 2, 206
    cultural, 3
    gender, 75, 78, 81–85, 252
    masculine, 104, 223
    political, 94, 96–97, 98, 135, 235
    sexual, 239
    social, 22
    territorial, 2

Identity, 8, 95
Ideologies,
    gender, 144
    national, 153, 155, 164
Immigrants, 178, 238
Immigration, 53, 55, 179
    policies, 186–188
    regulations, 188
Imperialism, 113–114, 119, 121, 123, 125
Inclusion, 1, 7, 17–18, 20, 76, 88, 136,
    141–142, 146, 148, 239
India, 77, 80, 115, 178, 213, 258
Indians, 178
Indonesia, 192–193
Inequalities, 35, 85, 203
    gendered politics, 47
    women's, 230
Informal politics, 107
Information technology, 201
Insecurity, 175–176
Intellectual property, 135
International conflicts, 6
International migration, 8, 249
    labor, 96
International Monetary Fund, 11, 119, 132,
    134, 137–138, 202
International political economy, 105, 138
International politics, 96–97, 116
International relations, 99, 104, 108, 138,
    174
Intersectionality, 22, 31
Iran, 45, 268, 272
Iraq, 176, 209
Islam, 34–35, 40, 43, 45, 265
Islamic fundamentalism, 40
Israel, 209

J

Jacobs, Jane, 52–53, 101
Jacquette, Jane, 251
Jaggar, Alison, 15, 17, 20
Japan, 25
Jelin, Elizabeth, 251–252
Jenkins, J. Craig, 200
Jessop, Bob, 227
Jobs, part-time, 63
Jones, Kathleen, 249, 270
Justice, 18, 23, 32, 249–250, 258, 250

K

Kandiyoti, Deniz, 265, 271
Kaplan, Cara, 131, 155

Kaplan, Temma, 249
Katz, Cindi, 12, 33, 97–98, 174
Kenya, 76, 171, 183
Kirby, Andrew, 246
Knight, David, 166
Knowledge; *See also* Situated knowledge
  building, 49
  geographical, 119
  grounded, 31
  partial, 48
  production, 1, 5, 100–101, 112
  Western, 100, 102
Kobayashi, Audrey, 12, 235, 239
Kofler, Andrea, 145
Kofman, Eleonore, 49, 157, 174, 197, 232,
  238
  boundaries, 146
  geopolitics, 131
  power, 16, 51–52
Kothari, U., 203
Kovacs, Maria, 23
Krauss, Celene, 252
Kropotkin, P., 114, 119

L

Labor market, 59–62, 197
  inequalities, 195
  unpaid, 137
Lacoste, Yves, 117, 121
Land, 202–204
Landscapes of fear, 158
Latin America, 76, 81, 105–106, 254
  cities, 251
  democratizing states, 19
  social movements, 202–203
Lawson, Vicky, 90, 95
Leadership, 206, 213
Lesbians, 34, 110
  communities, 95
Liberty, 24
Linkogle, Stephanie, 250–251
Lister, Ruth, 7, 24
Local (the), 10, 125, 129
Locality, 25, 35
Local state, 230, 245–246, 258–269

M

Mackinder, Halford, 93, 113–114, 117, 119,
  125
Macropolitics, 26
Madres, Las, 76
Mamdani, M., 208
Marginality, 12, 45

Marginalization, 1, 18, 35, 62, 75, 97
Market, 50
Marriage, 34, 36, 38–39, 82
Marston, Sallie, 10, 17, 25, 130, 148, 247, 253
Masculinism, 4–6
Masculinities, 100, 104–106, 128, 162–163,
  227
  heroic, 104
Masculinity, 6, 10–11, 58, 221, 256
  hegemonic, 105, 115, 144, 160
Masculinization, political discourse on,
  270
Massey, Doreen, 10, 26, 28, 35, 96, 129–131,
  170, 174
Maternalist thinking, 28
McClintock, Anne, 120, 155–156
McDowell, Linda, 56–57, 92
McLean, Sidney, 182
Media, 94
Men
  Chinese, 177
  African, 38–39
  Asian, 38
  Mexico, 215–217
Micropolitics, 26, 97
Middle East, 265, 268, 270–271
Migrants, 186
  Caribbean, 194
  illegal, 174
Migration, 174
  family, 190–191
  feminization, 187, 189, 195–196
  forced, 176, 180
  gender, 196–198
  labor, 187–190
  narratives of, 197
  skilled, 188
  transnational, 171
Migratory regimes, 186
Milanovic, Branko, 136
Militarization, 256
Miranne, Kirstine, 236
Mitchell, Kathryne, 27, 171, 242
Mobility, 169, 180
  geopolitics of, 180
  political economy, 170
  politics of, 170, 176–183
Mobilization, 78, 81, 149, 250, 257
Modernization, 104
Mohanty, Chandra, 26, 32, 103
Moss, Pam, 88, 96, 98
Mouffe, Chantal, 7, 21, 24, 26, 171–172,
  246, 258

Mountz, Alison, 171, 174
Movements
    disability rights, 202
    gay and lesbian, 202
    liberation, 204, 207
Muslims, 34, 36, 40, 162, 166
    Ithnasheri, 34, 36–37, 39–40, 43–46
    Shi'ites, 36, 40–41, 45
    Sunnis, 36, 46, 48
Mut'a, 34, 36, 41–47

N

Nagar, Richa, 12, 25, 59, 66–67, 69, 73, 92,
    100, 130–131
Namibia, 205
Naples, Nancy, 252
Nation, 6, 11, 154
    feminist contribution, 156–157
    feminist political geography, 156–157
    geographies, 155–156
National identity, 155
Nationalism, 2–3, 165, 167
    narrative, 155
    state, 92
    study of, 154–155
Nation building, 107, 237
    gendered, 162
Nationhood, 10, 107, 156, 178
    Serb, 161
Nation-state formation, 114
Negri, Antonio, 120, 127
Neighborhood, 3
Neocolonialism, 119–120
Neoliberalism, 102, 134–137, 245, 256
    gendered, 137–138
Neoliberal restructuring, 247–248, 259
    gender, 248
Networking, political, 108
New Zealand, 55, 72
NGOs (nongovernmental organizations), 4,
    201, 207, 215
    women's, 136
Nigeria, 73
Nogué-Font, Joan, 155
North, 78, 257–258
Northern, 111
North-South, 6
Northern-Southern, 108, 111

O

Objectivity, 87, 92, 123
O'Kane, Maggie, 95, 122

Opposition, 124
Oppression, 8–10, 12, 17–18, 22
    gender, 72, 78
    multiple, 32–33, 75, 85
    state-led, 55
    women's, 45
Orientalism, 97, 118
O'Tuathail, Gearoid, 93, 95, 118–119, 122
Out of place, 78, 143, 177

P

Palestine, 205, 209
Palestinian Liberation Organization, 204
Palestinian statehood, 35
Palestinian suicide bombers, 75, 205
Participation, 24–25, 73, 202, 206, 208, 256
    democratic, 252
    political, 252, 270–271
    women's, 213, 262, 264
Pateman, Carole, 7, 15, 18, 24, 172, 270
Patriarchal systems, 124
Patriarchy, 17, 20, 66–67, 115, 123, 148,
    170, 208, 265
    heteronormative, 158
    household, 196
Peake, Linda, 2, 12, 49, 107, 195, 239, 261
    feminist imaginary, 16
    Guyana, 101–102, 109, 111, 268
    local politics, 10
    power, 51–52
    urban politics, 269
Penrose, Jan, 49
Personal is political, 10, 95
Peru, 251
Pettman, Jan, 174
Phelan, Shane, 24
Phillips, Anne, 256, 266
Pile, Steve, 49
Political (the), 5–6, 9–10, 16–17, 32–33,
    59, 98
Political action, 52, 68, 82–85, 236
    gendered, 76
    participation, 196
Political economy, 91
Political identities, 2
Political practices, 2
    gendered, 62–63, 68
Political processes, 5, 10, 13
Political spheres, 2
Political struggles, 3, 10
Political subjects, 1, 5, 7, 10–11, 135
Political theory, 15, 108, 110, 171
    liberal, 8

Politics
  arenas, 92–98
  feminist, 16
  formal, 72–74
  gender, 39–41, 71, 73
  identities, 135
  identity, 3, 23, 79–80, 107
  institutional, 4
  Islamist, 271
  local, 92
  location of, 31
  progressive, 23
  racist, 157
  sexualized, 57
  spatialized, 31
  urban, 269
Politics of
  recognition, 23, 33
  redistribution, 23, 53
  power, 269
  support, 269
Population, 211
Positionality, 8–9, 98, 109, 116–117, 206
Postcolonial agendas, 109, 112
  studies, 173
  theory, 94, 232, 236–237
  understanding, 23
Postcolonialism, 99–102, 108, 110–111,
  120, 125
Postdevelopment, 101
Postmodernism, 3, 199, 232
  influences, 235
Poststructuralism, 118, 156
Poststructuralist
  approaches, 171, 233
  influences, 235
  theory, 21, 34, 232
  understanding, 23
Potter, Robert, 111–112
Poverty, 212–213, 250
Power, 6–7, 23, 33, 59, 143–144, 153, 201,
  207, 227
  political, 261,
  social, 141
  state, 146, 231–232
Power geometry, 28, 74, 180
Power relations, household, 104
Pratt, Geraldine, 61, 172–173
Prescott, J.R.V., 87–88
Pringle, Rosemary, 57
Privacy, 53
Private, 9, 54
  life, 2

  space, 8, 76, 148–150, 166, 179, 180
  sphere, 7–8, 53, 68, 75, 77, 159, 166
Privatization, 135, 147, 149, 256
Privilege, 8, 35, 37, 47
Production, 109–110, 246
  gendered geographies, 133
Property, 204
Protests, 39, 77–78, 80–81, 164, 199–201,
  205
Public, 9, 54
  geographies,
  life, 2
  places, 77
  sphere, 17, 20, 25, 159, 166, 196
Public-private
  dichotomies, 74, 85,
  divide, 15, 52, 71, 85, 123, 270
  spheres, 262, 270–271
  split, 17–18

Q

Quantification, 88–90

R

Race, 35, 37, 100, 115
Racial hierarchies, 38–39, 45
  inequalities, 41
Racialized practice, 3, 6
Racism, 31, 101–102, 109, 115, 124
Radcliffe, Sarah, 211, 237
Rape, 10, 108, 153, 158–159, 165
  camps, 161
  interracial, 22
Ratzel, Freidrich, 113–114, 117
Reclus, Elisée, 114–115, 117
Red Thread, 101–102, 109, 111
Refugees, 172–173, 180
  regulation, 134, 177
  settlement, 179
  women, 144
Reger, J., 95
Religion, 35
Repression, political, 206
Reproduction, 109–110, 205, 212, 227, 246,
  252
  social, 137, 247, 250
  women's, 156
Resistance, 2, 10, 75–76, 78, 96, 107, 124,
  199–201
Rights, 24–25
  discourse, 134
  indigenous, 106

political, 24, 75, 84, 172
reproductive, 80
social, 25
South African, 82
welfare, 82
women's, 200
Rose, Gillian, 4, 97, 144
Routledge, Paul, 122, 124
Rowbotham, Sheila, 250–251
Rule, W., 256
Rwanda, 158

S

Said, Edward, 97, 118
Samoa, 55
Sassen, Saskia, 196
Saudi Arabia, 180
Scale, 10, 36, 47, 85, 107, 143, 160–161, 165, 247
  binary, 127–131
  conflicts, 210
  jumped, 75, 247, 251
  jumping, 56, 173, 181, 240
  politics of, 196, 245
  social movements and, 203
  women's representation, 265
Schaffer, K., 237
Secor, Anna, 8, 33–34, 95, 123, 253
Security, 141, 143, 171, 175–176
Segmentation, 61, 181
Serbs, 159
Sevenhuijsen, Selma, 249
Sex
  trade, 108
  work, 110
  workers, 96, 110
Sexism, 115, 207
Sexual geographies, 108, 182
  harassment, 55
  victimization, 192
Sexualities, 249
Sexuality, 16, 47, 57, 102, 108, 110
  nationalism, 155
Sexualization, 239
Sharp, Joanne, 122, 174, 184
Sikhs, 179
Singapore, 53–54
  women, 189
Singaporean regionalization, 146–147
Sisterhood, 131
Situated knowledge, 1, 5, 11–12, 26, 32, 48, 91, 174, 233
Slater, David, 100, 206, 208

Slavery, 125
Smith, Fiona, 123
Smith, Neil, 117, 120, 247, 256
Smith, Susan, 24–25
Social capital, 135–136
Social movements, 2, 7, 76, 81, 108, 147, 194, 199–208, 245
  citizenship, 248
  local state, 252–253
  scale, 247
  women's, 107
Social networks, 150, 194
Social service provision, 63
Social theories, 3, 126
  critical, 232
  postmodern, 237
Social theorists, 7
Society of Women Geographers, 116
Socio-sexual regimes, 227
Somalia, 176, 180
South, 194, 211, 251, 257
South Africa, 74, 120, 177, 181–183
South Asians, 177
Southern, 10
South Korea, 190
Sovereignty, 141–143, 175–176, 179
  territorial, 210
Space, 3, 98
  economic, 247
  neoliberalizing, 135
  postnational, 185
  private, 236, 238, 241
  production of, 33, 170
  public, 75, 231, 236, 241, 256
Spatiality, 25, 154
Spatial metaphors, 26, 28
Spatial patterns of inequality, 2
Spouse, 191
Squatters, 204
Sri Lanka, 184
Staeheli, Lynn, 52, 95, 131, 149, 240
  citizenship, 25
  feminist political geography, 129
  political participation, 269
State, 2, 17, 25, 50–51, 54–55, 104, 140, 173
  feminist geography, 228–232
  formation, 3, 228, 234, 238, 242
  gender relations, 227
  institutions, 2, 5, 8
  liberal, 172
  local, 63
  migration regulations, 186–194
  neoliberal, 24, 136

State (*continued*)
  power, 121, 233, 236–239, 241
  regulations, 197, 234
  space, 75
  Third World, 34, 197
Statecraft, 97
  security, 123
  territorial, 132
Stiglitz, Joseph, 136–137
Stoddart, David, 97
Strikes, 59, 75
Structural adjustment, 11, 102, 104–105,
    107, 137–138, 195
Subaltern
  counterpublics, 20
  studies, 101
Subjectivities, 95
  gendered, 105, 112
  masculine, 32, 106, 135
  political, 100
Subjectivity, 26
  national, 15
  political, 15
  racialized, 33
Subordination, 35
  gender, 81
Susser, Ida, 251
Sustainability, 222, 225
Sweden, 263
Switzerland, 174
Swyngedouw, Eric, 173, 247
Sylvester, Christine, 123–124, 173

T

Taliban, 179–180
Tanzania, 31, 47, 54–59, 67–68
Taylor, L., 133
Taylor, Peter, 4, 93, 118, 121, 261
Territoriality, 11, 143–144, 148–151
Territory, 2
  state, 141, 166
Third World
  countries, 211
  debt, 138–139
  societies, 37
  women workers, 103
Thrift, Nigel, 122–124
Townsend, Janet, 16
Trade, 2
  liberalization, 40
Trafficking, 174–175
Transnationalism, 53, 193
Transnational networks, 257

Trotz, Alissa, 12, 101–102, 107, 109, 111,
    195, 268
Turkey, 266, 268

U

United Kingdom, 34, 37, 40, 78, 246,
    252–254
  electoral gender gap, 269
  women in politics, 268
United Nations, 137–138, 176, 180, 216,
    224, 257
United Nations Convention on the
    Elimination of all Forms of
    Discrimination against Women, 73
United States, 7, 31, 34, 72, 77, 79, 93, 113,
    170, 201, 259
  cities, 251–252, 257
  elections, 253, 264
  representation, 263–265
  voting, 269
  women in politics, 268
Universalism, 4, 8, 31, 47

V

Valentine, 33, 148, 170
Vancouver, 62
Veil; *See Hijaab*
Veiling, 33
Village, 162, 166
Violence, 148, 200, 207–208; *See also*
    Domestic violence
  sexual, 170
  sexualized, 200
  state, 76, 81
Voting, 71–73, 88, 205, 261, 270
  gender differences, 269
  gender gaps, 269
  women's, 262, 268, 270

W

Wallace, Michelle, 58
Wallerstein, Immanuel, 118
War, 3, 144, 153, 158, 160, 162–164
Water, 209
Welfare
  moms, 229, 236
  state, 254
West, 8, 15, 125, 129, 202, 236
Westernization, 40
Western theory, 4
Westwood, Sallie, 155
Whiteness, 239

Willis, Katie, 53, 58, 66, 146
Wives, 178
Wollstonecraft, Mary, 229
"Woman," 172
Women
    Aboriginal, 54, 65
    Arab, 46
    black, 74–75, 79
    Bosnian, 164
    Chinese, 177
    of color, 4, 22
    ethnic minority, 23
    Filipina, 61–62
    immigrant, 61
    Latina, 251, 253
    middle-class, 42–43, 53, 116
    migrant, 8
    Muslim, 34, 36, 159, 164–165
    Serb, 159
    Singaporean, 58, 60
    South, 22
    South African, 82
    Sunni, 46
    Third World, 103, 156
    upper-class, 11, 44, 47
    working-class, 18, 41, 53
"Women," 22
Women and Geography Study Group, 103
Women in Black, 160, 167
Women in Parliament, 264
Women representatives, 268
Women's Action Agenda 21, 210, 217, 219
Women's Environmental Network, 217
Women's initiatives, 254
Women's interests, 253, 255
Women's liberation, 17

Women's movement, 31
    Nigerian, 85–86
Women's National Coalition
    (South Africa), 82
Women's organizations, 101–102, 149,
    164–165, 210, 215–217, 252
Women's representation, 262–267, 271
Women's struggles, 229
Women's suffrage, 7, 23, 72
Women's voice, 217
Work
    childcare, 61
    formal, 103
    informal, 103
    paid, 60
    part-time, 60
    women's, 124
Workers
    domestic, 197
    male migrant, 182–183
Workplace, 3, 51, 56–59, 63, 96, 195–196,
    205
World Bank, 119, 134, 137–139, 202
World Summit on Sustainable
    Development, 218
World Systems theory, 93, 118, 229, 261
World Trade Organization, 134–135, 139,
    202
WorldWIDE Network, 217

Y

Yeoh, Brenda, 53, 58, 66, 146
Young, Iris, 23, 82, 232
Youngs, Gillian, 140, 145
Yugoslavia (former), 158, 162
Yuval-Davis, Nira, 155–156, 248